AF861760

# Small Group Communication

McGraw Hill create®
create.mheducation.com

create

Copyright 2019 by McGraw-Hill Education. All rights reserved.

Printed in the United States of America. Except as permitted under the United States Copyright Act of 1976, no part of this publication may be reproduced or distributed in any form or by any means, or stored in a database or retrieval system, without prior written permission of the publisher.

This McGraw-Hill Create text may include materials submitted to McGraw-Hill for publication by the instructor of this course.The instructor is solely responsible for the editorial content of such materials. Instructors retain copyright of these additional materials.

ISBN-13: 9781307049008

ISBN-10: 1307049001

# Contents

# Credits

*We dedicate this book to our students,*
*who teach us as much as we teach them.*

# FEATURES

## CASES



## APPLY NOW



## ETHICAL DILEMMAS

## MEDIA AND TECHNOLOGY

# PREFACE

*Coming together is a beginning; keeping together is progress; working together is success.*

**Henry Ford**

As we prepare this revision, the world seems to be falling apart—mass shootings in Orlando and San Diego; a trucker mowing down families in Nice, France; an attempted military coup in Turkey (although news is still coming in about what happened there). We humans somehow need to push the reset button on how we interact with one another and how we work together. Some of these despicable actions are the work of lone, disaffected individuals, but it is also true that many disaffected individuals are encouraged by groups working to disrupt a way of life they dislike. Much of what happens in our world—good and bad—is the result of decisions made in groups, projects conceived in and implemented by groups, and solutions developed by groups. To us, it is more important than ever that we figure out how to work with others who perhaps see the world differently from us, may not share our values, and have different approaches to work. Both of us have experienced the variety that groups have to offer, from groups that made us feel alive and productive to groups that made us want to pull our hair out. In this book, we hope to give students the tools to help them make their group experiences good ones by providing insights about how groups work and practical suggestions for applying those insights.

This book is designed for the first- or second-year student who may not have had a prior communication course and who may never take a subsequent one—but who *must* work in groups because that is the nature of corporate, educational, and civic participation in this day and age. Two overarching goals guide our writing. First, being able to work effectively in groups is not a luxury—it's a necessity. Our introductory students want to cut to the chase; they want to know what works *right now*. That is the reason for our distinctly *practical* focus in *Communicating in Groups*. Although this text uses the same research foundation as our more advanced text, *Effective Group Discussion,* we strive here to provide information in a way that is both useful and immediately usable. Second, we want students to recognize that effective group work is, to a great extent, a matter of *communication behavior,* not a matter of personality or fate. Thus, group member behaviors are what create particular group experiences. We want students to start thinking about their own communicative choices in groups and to have the tools to make wise choices so they can make the groups they belong to as rewarding and productive as possible.

To meet our goals, we use an informal writing style and provide many examples from our own and others' experiences. We also report research findings in much less detail, with more synthesis and distillation of findings, fewer footnotes, and less evaluation of competing theories than in our other text. This allows readers to focus on what is usually more important to them—the practical application of the research. Finally, we refer to ourselves, Kathy and Gloria, frequently throughout the text. We think of our readers as individuals with whom we are on a first-name basis, and we encourage you to think of us the same way, as if we were members of the same small group.

## Overview of the Text

With each revision, the hardest thing we have to do is decide what to retain and what to cut out. We try to focus on what we believe are the most important concepts, particularly those that will be most useful and practical for students to understand. General systems theory and a transactional approach to communication continue to ground our view of small group communication. We remain focused on updating the use of technologies by small groups and add material on cultural dynamics relevant to group dynamics. As before, the chapters are ordered in a way that is logical to us but that does not preclude other methods of organizing a small group course. Each chapter is self-contained and can be read in an order different from what we provide here.

**Part One** provides basic information students need to understand how groups function. Chapter 1 introduces some basic terms encountered throughout the book, shows how to classify groups according to their major purpose, and introduces the concept of ethical communication behavior of group members. Chapter 2 presents general systems theory as a framework for understanding the complexity of group communication. We provide specific illustrations of systems concepts throughout the rest of the book as well.

**Part Two** provides the foundation for understanding communication in groups. Chapter 3 discusses basic communication theory, including what constitutes transactional communication and effective listening. Chapter 4 details verbal and nonverbal messages as well as compares computer-mediated communication with face-to-face communication.

**Part Three** explores in detail how we move from being individuals to connecting as a group. Chapter 5 explains how a group develops as a team from an initial collection of individuals. Chapter 6 focuses on how groups can work effectively with multiple levels of diversity: member motivation, learning styles, personality, cognitive/informational differences, culture, gender, ethnicity, and generational.

**Part Four** focuses on the group's throughput processes. Chapter 7 discusses the creative and critical thinking skills necessary for effective group problem solving. We believe creative and critical thinking are at the heart of the group problem-solving process and that students should know something about these processes before understanding problem solving in general. Chapter 8 describes the problem-solving process and introduces the procedural model of problem solving as a helpful guideline to follow. Chapter 9 explains why group conflicts occur and how they can be managed so that the group benefits instead of suffers. Chapter 10 provides a comprehensive picture of leadership and also gives suggestions for applying leadership principles effectively and ethically.

**Part Five** presents information about oral presentations, the culmination of much group effort. In Chapter 11 students will learn about the types of oral presentations, ways to prepare effective presentations, and criteria for evaluating presentations.

Finally, the **Appendix** presents information about a number of techniques a member or outside observer can use to gather information about a problem-solving group and help it improve its performance.

## New to This Edition

- Throughout the text, we have streamlined the examples and removed redundancies.
- We have added information about surface- and deep-level diversity in Chapters 2 and 6. In addition, we have incorporated a discussion about cognitive and informational diversity to align with current research.
- We acknowledge that groups are no longer either face-to-face or virtual, but that they use a variety of technologies to help them get their work done.
- We removed the section on mind mapping as a creativity-enhancing technique and replaced it with information about appreciative inquiry.
- We have emphasized the processes of dealing with group conflict and deemphasized the identification of type of conflict.
- Leadership discussion broadened to include material on leader qualities that impact member perceptions of leadership. Add tips on leading virtual group meetings.
- The group presentation chapter now includes information about hosting pre-meetings in preparation for public meetings.
- Case studies, apply now examples, and discussion examples are updated.

## Features

***Case Studies:*** Establish the main ideas of the chapter by providing realistic scenarios for student application, and utilizing a variety of group contexts, such as business, health care, social groups, and civic organizations.

***Apply Now Boxes:*** Make concepts practical to everyday life, throughout the text.

***Ethical Dilemma Boxes:*** Encourage critical evaluation of typical ethical scenarios faced by groups, and stimulate discussion of their causes, controversies, issues, and solutions.

***Media and Technology Boxes:*** Look at how media and technology are changing the ways in which small groups can interact. Topics include online support groups, the contemporary media's effect on groupthink, and presentation technology.

The 10th edition of *Communicating in Groups: Applications and Skills* is now available online with Connect, McGraw-Hill Education's integrated assignment and assessment platform. Connect also offers SmartBook for the new edition, which is the first adaptive reading experience proven to improve grades and help students study more effectively. All of the title's website and ancillary content is also available through Connect, including:

- An Instructor's Manual that includes exercises and sample syllabi.
- A full Test Bank of multiple-choice questions that test students on central concepts and ideas in each chapter.
- Lecture Slides for instructor use in class.

## Acknowledgments

We wish to thank the reviewers, all of whom did a conscientious job of reading the manuscript and providing helpful suggestions. We appreciate their thoughtful suggestions and have incorporated many of them in this tenth edition.

Rebecca Carlton, *Indiana University Southeast*
Diana Leonard, *The University of Arizona*
Leola McClure, *MiraCosta College*
Joseph C. Moravec, *Mercy College of Health Sciences*
Bradley L. Nason, *Pennsylvania College of Technology*
Tiffany Sarkisian, *Clovis Community College*

**Katherine Adams**
**Gloria J. Galanes**

# Introducing the Small Group

PART

# ONE

# Introducing the Small Group

Part One introduces you to the study of small groups. In Chapter 1 we explain why small groups are important to understand, and we define many of the terms you will encounter in your study of small groups. We discuss the types of small groups you are likely to experience, the ethics of participating in small groups, and the participant-observer perspective we use throughout the book. Chapter 2 presents you with a popular framework, general systems theory, to help keep track of the many concepts important to understanding how groups function.

CHAPTER 1

# Small Groups as the Heart of Society

## CHAPTER OUTLINE



## CHAPTER OBJECTIVES

**After reading this chapter you should be able to:**

1. Explain why groups play a vital role in our personal and professional lives.
2. List the reasons for selecting a group or an individual to solve a problem.
3. Define a group, a small group, a team, and small group communication.
4. Describe how groups use technology to enhance their interactions.
5. Explain the major reasons why people participate in small groups.
6. Describe and give examples of primary groups.
7. Describe and give examples of secondary groups.
8. Compare and contrast the different organizational groups.
9. Explain the four ethical standards group members should exhibit.
10. Explain and give examples of a member being an effective participant-observer.

## The Best Friends Animal Society

CASE 1.1

Sinjin the cat was near death when he arrived at Best Friends Animal Sanctuary in Angel Canyon, Utah.[1] Someone had set him on fire after dousing him with gasoline, badly burning three-quarters of his body. The care at Best Friends, however, pulled him through; Sinjin the one-eyed cat became a sleek, confident creature who loved his treats! Best Friends Animal Society runs the largest animal sanctuary in the world, with over 1,700 resident animals at any one time. Best Friends has been a prime mover in the No More Homeless Pets movement, promotes spay-neuter programs and no-kill animal shelters, provides consultation services all over the world for those who want to set up no-kill shelters and spay-neuter programs in their communities, offers internships for veterinary students, runs a large volunteer program, provides wildlife rehabilitation, schedules educational programs and seminars, and, of course, takes in abandoned animals. What does this have to do with small groups? Best Friends Animal Society started out, nearly 50 years ago, as a small group of friends on a quest for spiritual fulfillment.

In the 1960s a group of friends from Great Britain traveled together to the Bahamas, Mexico, the United States, and Europe seeking a meaningful life. These diverse individuals were bound together by what members called the Universal Law and what we know as the Golden Rule: "As you give, so shall you receive. So do unto others as you would have them do unto you."[2] The "others" included animals. Although individual members ended up living in different places, they stayed in touch, with love of animals the constant that united them. In 1982 the opportunity arose to buy 3,000 acres in Angel Canyon for an animal sanctuary. A core group of 20 members pooled their personal resources to establish what would ultimately become Best Friends. The group included an architect, an artist, a real estate professional, several community organizers, and workers from another animal sanctuary run by some of the members. Over the years the group has learned (among other things) to build dwellings, raise funds, tend sick and injured animals, and communicate with the media. The sanctuary is now considered a "rock star" by animal rescue activists. Ten of the original members remain active, but new members have joined to contribute their expertise and energy.

**The true story of Best Friends illustrates vividly what Margaret Mead said: "Never doubt that a small group of thoughtful, committed citizens can change the world. Indeed, it is the only thing that ever has."[3] This group of individuals, united by a vision of a world in which animals are respected and loved, shows what a small group can accomplish that an individual could never hope to achieve alone. The group demonstrates qualities that characterize effective group behavior: Members had a vision for what they wanted to accomplish; they appreciated and used the many different talents of their members; they trusted each other to work for the good of the group (and the animals); leadership was shared among them, as different needs and challenges arose; and the group continued to learn and develop by setting new goals that would increasingly stretch the abilities of its members. We will share throughout this text what you can do to achieve success like this. The glue that holds a group together and enables it to do its work is *communication*.**

The group that formed and continues to oversee Best Friends is a voluntary group of members who choose to work together. However, many of the groups you belong to, especially where you work or study, may not be voluntary. You may be assigned to a group because you have a particular expertise needed in a group or because small groups are a part of a course you are taking. No matter what the reason, you must be able to work well in teams, task forces, committees, and all kinds of special problem-solving groups if you want to succeed in the world today. In fact, Monster.com, a popular employment website geared to college students, notes that teamwork is one of the seven "hot skills" most employers want, no matter their size or type of industry.[4] Moreover, students are reminded that they can develop this skill during college. They go on to recommend that all freshman join a club to build their group skills.[5]

Teams of all kinds are becoming more common in all areas of American life: business, industry, education, health care, the nonprofit sector, and government. The biggest companies in the United States, realize the significance of effective teamwork to their bottom line.[6] Time spent in company collaborative projects has exploded to over 50 percent. Being able to work effectively in a team is also expected in many professions. Medical schools, for instance, screen their applicants not just by grades but by their communication skills.[7] Prospective medical students are given a series of mini-interviews in which they must interact with mock patients so the evaluators can assess their social skills. Why is this important? According to the article, "medicine is evolving from an individual to a team sport," with teams coordinating patient care. The effectiveness of the teams depends as much on members' communication skills as on their expertise.

But there's a trade-off to small group work. In one study of 179 teams, only 13 percent were rated highly effective.[8] Collaboration tends to overwork those who are more than eager to help and can lead to their burnout.[9] Managers can spend one to one-and-a-half days in meetings a week.[10] One management consultant estimates that the average meeting in a large company costs approximately $15,000. Ineffectively run meetings have huge consequences not just financially but also on the health of both the company and its employees.[11]

Effective small group work—whether in meetings, on teams, on committees, and so forth—cannot be left to chance. When individuals come together, particularly individuals from differing backgrounds, perspectives, and areas of expertise, teamwork doesn't just happen. Training in *how* to be an effective team member is essential. If you want to succeed as a team member, you must learn how small groups function and what you personally can do to help ensure team success. Chapter 1 will help you start this process by asking you to consider how important groups are in your own life and by introducing you to concepts central to understanding small group processes, the variety of groups you will encounter, and the importance of being an ethical participant-observer in groups.

## Groups in Your Life

Lawrence Frey, a leading advocate for studying small groups in their natural settings, believes that the small group is *the* most important social formation: "From birth to death, small groups are interwoven into the fabric of our lives."[12] Family in many ways forms the foundation for other groups that follow. Consider how much of your identity was formed by your family group. Development and maintenance of identity remain important functions that only groups can provide for us. This is obvious when we consider groups such as fraternities or sororities, spiritually based groups (churches, synagogues, other religious organizations, and even spiritually guided activist groups like Best Friends), gangs, book clubs, and poker clubs. Groups formed at work also contribute to who we think we are. Are you a member of a union, for example? A management group? A classroom group? A neighborhood coalition trying to prevent a new business in your neighborhood? Each of these groups will affect how you see yourself in relation to other people.

Professionally, the higher you go in any organization (e.g., government, service, manufacturing, education, communications, or the military), you will need to know how to behave in ways that are appropriate and helpful to the group and to any larger organization to which the group may be attached. If you don't work well in groups, you are more likely to be laid off or frozen at a low-level job. A survey of 750 leading American companies asked businesspeople to describe characteristics of the ideal MBA (Master of Business Administration) graduate.[13] The top preference was possession of good oral and written communication skills (listed by 83.5 percent of respondents). The fourth-ranked preference, the ability to work in teams, was listed by 71.4 percent. These communication skills far surpassed even cutting-edge knowledge of the company's field (14.8 percent) and previous work experience (31.9 percent) in importance.

Students are often surprised to discover just how many groups they belong to. Humans are social beings with powerful genetic needs to belong and affiliate with others of our kind.

### GROUPS AS PROBLEM SOLVERS

You are constantly solving problems: how to find a job, where to eat lunch, how to keep your car running on a limited budget, and even how to keep your company on the cutting edge of its industry in a turbulent economic climate. Solving any problem means coming up with a plan and executing it. In times past, only high-status people—monarchs, generals, managers, and so forth—were given the privilege of planning solutions to problems, and the rest of us had to carry out the plans. But times have changed. Now we all expect to be included in planning solutions to problems that affect us, and most of this planning occurs in small groups.

## PARTICIPATING IN GROUPS

Improving group problem solving requires focusing not only on the rational side of human behavior but also knowing something about human feelings. Effective group problem solving depends on how well members understand and manage such things as informational resources, how members feel about each other and their task, how skilled they are at expressing themselves and listening to others, and how well they collectively process their information.

Group members must make sure they have the materials (information, tangible resources, time, and so forth) to complete the task, and they also must learn to manage their interpersonal relationships effectively enough to complete the task well. Thus, group communication performs two key functions: It accomplishes the group's task, and it creates "the social fabric of a group by promoting relationships between and among members."[14] This function—the group's relational communication—is just as important as the task-oriented functions of group work.

Samantha Glen's book about Best Friends describes several vivid examples of communication that convey just how much members of this group care about each other and how they express it.[15] At various times several members of the Best Friends core group encountered problems that seemed overwhelming and faced the real threat of burnout as they tried, in the early days, to keep the sanctuary running with little help, less money, and the ever-growing population of animals others had thrown away. In one encounter Faith lost it when she publicly confronted a prominent, well-respected local man who had adopted a puppy from the sanctuary but then abandoned it by the side of the road. Fellow group

### The Instinctive Need to Group Together

MEDIA AND TECHNOLOGY

Some scholars have assessed situations in which a collection of individuals begins to group together. Such effort is common in face-to-face interaction where a particular force, problem, or crisis has created the need for individuals to group. Yet little is known about how and why individuals with nothing apparently in common or with no mediating force begin to group. A good example is in a computer-mediated environment.

To examine this unique grouping process, Tom Postmes, Russell Spears, and Martin Lea collected data on students who volunteered to complete an online statistics course, which offered participants e-mail options for contacting staff. Participants also used the function to send about 1,200 e-mails to fellow students. The messages were later classified into nine categories reflecting both task and relational functions (e.g., requests, complaints, reactions, humor, emotion, personal revelations). The researchers found that 11 groups formed, in which members spent most of their time (74 percent) interacting about socio-personal topics (reactions to contributions of other group members, humorous contributions, displays of affection and emotion). Despite having little impact on the successful completion of the course, these students grouped together to fulfill their need for relational interaction with fellow classmates.

SOURCE: T. Postmes, R. Spears, and M. Lea, "The Formation of Group Norms in Computer-Mediated Communication," *Human Communication Research* 26 (2001), pp. 341–71.

member, Michael, gently but firmly made Faith face the fact that she was getting burned out and needed help. His obvious concern allowed Faith to realize how deep her exhaustion was and to accept help from the others. In another example, the group's veterinarian, Bill, brought two gifts to the sanctuary: an Airstream trailer, accepted in lieu of payment from a client, that would serve as dedicated space for an operating table, and a goat to keep Sparkle the horse company while her leg healed. Faith, expressing the whole group's gratitude, said to Bill, "We love you, you know."[16] While not typical of what you hear in most work groups, this communication conveys appreciation, gratitude, and liking and goes a long way in creating a group that is also a community, and that can be a deeply satisfying experience. The Best Friends group succeeded because members focused on *both* task *and* relationship aspects of working in teams. Work skills *and* people skills are essential.

## Groups versus Individuals as Problem Solvers

If group work can be challenging and at times complicated, why not have *individuals* plan the solutions to all problems? The benefits of having a group tackle a problem *can* (but not necessarily *will*) outweigh the costs in time and tensions.

Group solutions can be far more effective than individual ones for solving many types of problems.[17] Groups tend to do much better than individuals when several alternative solutions to the problem exist, none of which is known to be superior or "correct." They also are better at tasks where no one person has all the information needed to solve a problem, but each member has some needed information.[18] For example, which of several designs for a hybrid truck is most likely to sell well? What benefit options should be available to employees? How can the federal government give citizens a tax cut and still ensure sufficient funds for health care and homeland defense?

Many college courses require small group activities when instructors move from teacher-centered to more student-centered instruction. This forces students to become active, not passive, learners.[19] Students can improve problem solving, critical and creative thinking, and social skills in small group learning contexts. In fact, MBA programs widely use study groups to teach their students group dynamics.[20] Moreover, group activity is a preferred way to learn for some cultures (e.g., Asians, Native Americans, African Americans, and females).[21]

The Best Friends story illustrates how a group's greater resources help solve problems. Of the friends who bought Angel Canyon, one was an architect and several had rudimentary construction skills—enough to design and build places for the animals and shelter for themselves. The friends were also committed to the animals and willing to work, including feeding the growing number of animals twice daily and taking animals to public events where they might be adopted. Bill, local veterinarian, initially provided low-cost spay-neutering and other veterinary care services. Best Friends now has a veterinary internship program with much expanded animal care. Estelle, who had polio as a child and thus was unable to perform physical labor, had experience running an office and provided administrative services. Matthias, a technical whiz, used his expertise to set up a membership database and to organize the sanctuary's records. Jana used her photography skills to take pictures of the animals and increase the likelihood that they would be adopted. In recent years, Best Friends has used many different kinds of expertise to expand the reach of what it can do for animals: *National Geographic* produced a television series about Dogtown, wildlife rehabilitation specialists work with injured wild animals to return them to the wild or, if that is not possible, to use them in educational programs. Volunteer coordinators work with the many people who come to Best Friends to volunteer their efforts as dog feeders, poop scoopers, trainers, foster parents, and so forth. Others work with sanctuaries across the country to help establish no-kill shelters nationwide. The Best Friends website is remarkable and frequently updated with stories of the animals. One person working alone could never have accomplished all of this.

## WHEN A GROUP IS A GOOD CHOICE

Groups working on problems with multiple solutions typically make higher-quality decisions than do individuals for several reasons. Groups usually have a much larger number of possible solutions from which to choose. Group members can help each other correct one another's misinformation, faulty assumptions, and invalid reasoning. Several people can often think of issues to be handled in the process of solving a problem that might be overlooked by any one member. In addition, several people can conduct more thorough investigative research than one person working alone. Group members often counteract each other's tendencies to engage in self-defeating behavior.[22]

Doctors at the University of Michigan studied the value of a multidisciplinary team approach to providing breast cancer patients with a second opinion.[23] Patients who were diagnosed with breast cancer and whose doctors had recommended a course of treatment were referred for a second opinion to a team that included a variety of cancer treatment specialists: a radiologist, surgeon, pathologist, medical oncologist, and radiation oncologist. The team met, usually with the patient, to discuss options. Over half the time, the team recommended an approach different from that proposed by the original physician. Sometimes, a team member was aware of new treatment protocols or techniques the original doctor hadn't known. Other times, the original doctor had not followed national treatment guidelines. Having qualified, dedicated team members work together to address an important issue can produce better results.

A further advantage to group problem solving is that members who are involved in solving a problem or planning a procedure usually understand that procedure and work hard to implement it. In addition, people are more likely to accept a solution they had a hand in designing. Satisfaction, loyalty, commitment, and learning tend to be higher when people have a voice. This is clearly evident with the Best Friends group, who continue to expand their skills, stretch their comfort zones, and care for one another as they care for the animals. These principles have resulted in such small group techniques as self-managed work groups, and collaborative learning groups.

## WHEN A GROUP IS NOT A GOOD CHOICE

Not all problems are suitable for groups, nor is using a group always a wise or productive use of time. When a problem has a best or correct solution (such as an arithmetic or accounting task), a skilled person working alone often performs better than a group of less-knowledgeable people, even if the group includes the highly skilled person as a member. When conditions are changing rapidly (as in a weather disaster, battle, or ballgame), coordinating the work of several people may be done best by one person (a commander, chief, or coach). Likewise, if small groups have certain social, procedural, or personality-mix problems, the output may be inferior, even though members

TABLE 1.1 **Problems Appropriate for Groups versus Individuals**

| Problems Suitable for a Group | Problems Suitable for an Individual |
|---|---|
| • The problem is complex; one person is not likely to have all relevant information. | • There is a best solution, and a recognized expert is most qualified to determine that solution. |
| • There are several acceptable solutions, and one best solution does not exist. | • Conditions are changing rapidly (such as during a fire or natural disaster), and coordination is best done by one person. |
| • Acceptance of the solution by those who are affected is critical. | • Time is short and a decision must be made quickly. |
| • Sufficient time exists for a group to meet and discuss and analyze the problem. | • Group members have personality, procedural, or social problems that make it difficult or impossible for them to work as a team on the solution. |

may be bright and talented. We address how to apply small group theory—based as much as possible on scientific research—to make sure that groups work on the kinds of problems for which they are best suited, and to do so in ways likely to produce a high-quality solution (see Table 1.1).

© Kali Nine LLC/E+/Getty Images RF

**Individual or Group?**

APPLY NOW

As president of your department's Advertising Club, you are getting ready to plan your events for the upcoming year when you learn that your department, facing a serious budget crunch, has cut your expected budget from $12,000 to $7,000 for the year—a loss of $5,000. The club's budget supports the annual Ad Club competition, sends the local winners to the national conference to compete for the top prize, funds a couple of local scholarships, and hosts a "shadow day" for area high school students to spend time on campus to discover what advertising students do. As Ad Club president responsible for the budget, you can decide how to make cuts yourself or you can appoint a task force to decide where to cut.

1. How would you weigh the factors (time, energy, expertise) in deciding how to make cuts?
2. What are the advantages and disadvantages if you make the cuts yourself? What are they if you appoint a committee to decide the cuts?
3. If you appoint a committee, members will spend a lot of time together thinking through the decisions that must be made. What benefits might they gain by working on such a time-consuming project?

Your experiences in groups may have been unpleasant ones. In fact, you may dread hearing a teacher tell you that you'll be working on a group project. Unfortunately, this kind of **grouphate** is common, probably because many groups do not function as well as they should. If this is how you feel about group participation, it is especially important for you to become familiar with group processes because you won't be able to avoid group participation but you *will* be expected to perform well.

Thus far, we have seen that small groups are commonly involved in problem solving. Before introducing you to the types of small groups that engage in problem solving and the situations that create them, we will first define key terms necessary to understand group communication. We encourage you to use our definitions when you think about, discuss, and complete small group assignments as you read this book.

## Groups, Small Groups, Teams, and Small Group Communication

Before we discuss small group communication, you must first understand how we conceptualize the terms *group, team,* and *small group.*

### GROUPS

What is a group? While the answer may seem simple, scholars from disciplines such as sociology, social psychology, and communication have all tried to pinpoint the essential features of a group. Marvin Shaw, an important early small group theorist, defines

**GLOSSARY**

**Grouphate**
*Hating or dreading participation in groups*

a **group** as "persons who are interacting with one another in such a manner that each person influences and is influenced by each other person."[24] The essence of "groupness" is that members act interdependently toward a common purpose, and are aware that, together, they act as part of a unit. Just putting a bunch of people in the same place does not mean that a group has been created; it takes time for members to develop their sense of interdependence.

The following example will illustrate what we mean. At a recent communication conference, one of us stood waiting for a streetcar with three other conference attendees. We were only a collection of individuals and while we had the same individual purpose (to get back to our hotels) we just happened to be there at the same time, with no interaction, and no collective identity. As time passed, we began to talk to each and commented on the fact no streetcars had been seen. Now mutually aware of each other and our common problem, someone suggested we call Uber and share the ride to our different hotels. Mutual influence led to a common solution to our needs. While short in duration we met the criteria for a small group: mutual influence, interdependence, common purpose, and shared identity.

## SMALL GROUPS

Groups can range in size from very small (three) to very large. We define *small* not by numbers but in terms of psychological perception: A **small group** refers to a group in which individual members perceive each other and are aware of each other as individuals when they interact. This definition is precise only for a given point in time. A committee of five new members may be perceptually large until after each member has had a chance to speak repeatedly, but the initial Best Friends group of 20 seemed perceptually small because members had known each other well and had worked together on other projects over many years. At the point when they met to discuss buying Angel Canyon, members knew and could describe every other member and could also say something about what each person contributed to the discussion. We intentionally exclude the dyad (two people) because dyads function differently. They do not form networks or leadership hierarchies and if one member leaves, the dyad ceases to exist. In groups, however, members often leave, to be replaced by new members, and the group continues. Some of the original Best Friends members have left, but new members have joined and Best Friends endures.

More practically, small groups usually consist of three to seven with five being the most effective.[25] This seems to be the ideal range, so long as members possess sufficient knowledge and skills to do the job facing the group and have a diversity of perspectives and information relevant to the task. The more members, the more likely there will be inequity and communication overload for some members.

We focus on small groups in which the members meet regularly face-to-face or online to complete a task or tasks. These include work crews, task forces, sports teams, committees, classroom groups, one-meeting groups, and virtual groups whose members never meet face-to-face.

## SMALL GROUPS VERSUS TEAMS

We use the terms *small group* and *team* interchangeably. We have participated in committees, task forces, small groups, and teams and have found that, regardless

**GLOSSARY**

**Group**

*Three or more individuals who have a common purpose, interact with each other, influence each other, and are interdependent*

**Small Group**

*A group of at least three people that is small enough for individual members to perceive one another as individuals during interaction*

of what something is called, there are clear differences between *effective* groups or teams and *ineffective* ones. Our focus is to help you understand these differences and use what you know to make your groups more effective.

However, you should know that some people think there *are* differences between groups and teams. For example, Steven Beebe and John Masterson believe that teams are more highly structured, with team member responsibilities more clearly spelled out, team rules more explicitly defined, and team goals more specific.[26] An example might be a sports team that spells out the responsibilities for each position and clarifies the goal (e.g., to win the division championship). Others reserve the concept of *team* for those groups that are especially effective.[27] In our opinion, most groups could benefit from clarifying responsibilities, procedures, and goals. In addition, we have found no relationship in real life between what a group may be called and how it actually performs. Some teams we have participated in have been disasters, but some committees have had all the hallmarks of effective teams. Thus, we do not differentiate between groups and teams and freely use both terms.

## SMALL GROUP COMMUNICATION

Our definitions of *group* and *small group* have emphasized the process of members communicating with each other to become interdependent. Communication among members is *the* essential feature of a group, regardless of the group's size or purpose. Thus, to understand small group dynamics, you must tackle the complexities of communication.[28]

**Communication** is the transactional process in which people simultaneously create, interpret, and negotiate shared meaning through their interaction. In small groups, the mutually negotiated meaning allows members to coordinate their activities. **Small group communication** means that group members simultaneously send and receive verbal and nonverbal messages—words, facial expressions, and so forth—to and from one another. During this process, they develop shared meanings and are able to coordinate their activities within the group. They pay attention to one another, interpret (or misinterpret) one another, negotiate what things mean, create interdependence and accomplish something (their assigned task, we hope!). The communication itself creates the group and forges the interdependence necessary for individuals to call themselves a group.

## GROUPS AND TECHNOLOGY

Today, because technology is readily available and easy to use, most groups make use of it in some way to make their work easier. Rather than talking about face-to-face groups *or* virtual groups, it makes more sense to consider the *degree* to which groups use technology to do their work and develop their relationships.[29] Some groups may meet only face-to-face, never using any form of technology; others, such as some online support groups or geographically distributed multinational groups, always meet virtually, never face-to-face. However, many groups do something in between: combine face-to-face meetings with technological tools to complete their work.

Teleconferencing and applications such as Skype, FaceTime, and Google Hangout allow members to meet at the same time although they may be widely scattered

**GLOSSARY**

**Communication**

*The transactional process in which people simultaneously create, interpret, and negotiate shared meaning through their interaction*

**Small Group Communication**

*The verbal and nonverbal interaction among members of a small group*

geographically. Internet discussion boards and e-mail permit members to interact at different times and places that are convenient for each individual member—a real benefit when members live in different time zones or have varying work schedules. Still other applications allow members to work collaboratively on tasks whether they are in the same place or not. For instance, wikis and applications similar to Dropbox allow group members to work collaboratively on documents and to track changes made by each member. Thus, even if members live in the same city or work for the same organization, each may contribute to collaborative work from home or from their individual offices.

Gloria's work with her church's Art for Haiti committee illustrates how face-to-face groups work with technology. Tasked with planning an art exhibit and reception to benefit relief efforts for Haiti in the aftermath of the 2010 earthquake, committee members were recruited through e-mail. They planned meetings using the Doodle application and used e-mail to send out agendas. Member assignments were completed through technological tools. For instance, flyers were created and edited using Dropbox. The exhibit and reception was promoted exclusively through e-blasts, radio promotions, and e-newsletters compared to traditional print means. Facebook today is commonly used to promote events and expected attendance and applications like Twitter are used for quick, regular updates on group activities. Technology is integrally woven into the fabric of group activities.

Communication that is mediated—via computers, telephones, and so forth—is thought to lack *social presence,* or the feeling that the communication is socially and emotionally similar to face-to-face communication.[30] For instance, because computers do not convey the full complement of nonverbal communication (e.g., tone of voice, facial expressions, body movements), the person on the receiving end may feel less connected to the person sending the computer message. In particular, because social presence is an issue in computer-mediated communication (CMC) some believe CMC may impair a group's ability to form strong relationships among members. However, research calls this view into question. Walther and his associates note that human beings adapt to whatever communication environment they face.[31] Thus, when members cannot use nonverbal communication naturally, as they can with face-to-face communication, they substitute verbal communication instead. These researchers found that virtual groups, using primarily verbal communication, formed bonds of attachment that were just as strong as face-to-face groups, although the process may take longer with CMC. We elaborate on these ideas in Chapter 3, when we explore the communication process in more detail.

We will address the impact of technology on small group dynamics throughout our text. Thus, we consider many computer-mediated groups in our definition.

## Classifying Groups by Their Major Purpose

How a specific small group functions depends partly on why the group was formed in the first place. Groups form initially to address a number of human needs. We now discuss those needs and show the connection between those needs and how groups can be classified.

## WHY PEOPLE JOIN GROUPS

Listening to people talk about why they join groups, you have no doubt heard that they like hanging out with a particular group of friends or that they like working with a group of colleagues. They like getting something done that could not be done working alone, such as crafting gun regulation in the aftermath of a national tragedy or securing student fee funding for a university newspaper. People enjoy camaraderie, learning about themselves with others, and being a part of something larger than themselves. These reasons reflect psychologist Wil Schutz's long recognized motivations for human interaction: our need for inclusion, openness (formerly affection), and control.[32] Inclusion is our need to belong and be acknowledged as a member of a group. Openness is our need to tell our story and have it heard and respected by others—without this, group work is not authentic. Control is our need to feel competent and able to see our talents and abilities used to make a difference. Small groups are often classified as primary or secondary, depending on which need is the major reason for their existence.

## PRIMARY OR SECONDARY GROUPS

### Meeting Member Needs and Handling Membership Changes

APPLY NOW

The membership of Best Friends has changed over the years. Some of the people who started the group have moved on to other things while new members have found their place at Best Friends. Membership changes can present unique challenges to a group.

1. Why might a member who was initially fully committed to a group's goals and willing to work hard on behalf of a group choose to leave the group?
2. Why might a new member choose to join?
3. What challenges does member fluctuation present for group members, existing and new?
4. What can current members do to make new members feel welcomed and part of the group?

**Primary Groups.** **Primary groups** form to meet the first two types of needs, inclusion and openness. They may accomplish work, but that is not their primary objective. Loving, caring, avoiding feelings of loneliness, sharing, feeling cared about—these are the motives for which we willingly give up some freedom as individuals to be members of primary groups. We are all familiar with families, friendship groups, sororities and fraternities, drinking buddies, cliques, gangs, and those many small groups that seem to form spontaneously to meet interpersonal needs for inclusion and openness. The communication patterns you learned in your first group—your family—likely affect the way you communicate in groups now.[33]

GLOSSARY

**Primary Groups**

*Groups formed to meet primary needs for inclusion and openness*

FIGURE 1.1 Groups with Both Primary and Secondary Characteristics

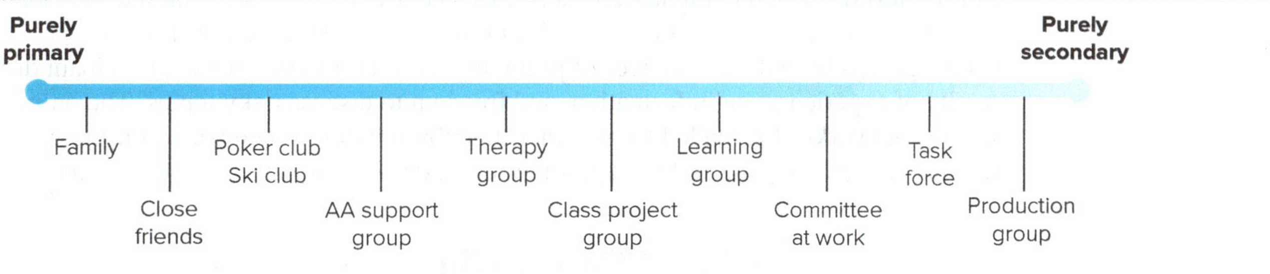


**Secondary Groups.** **Secondary groups,** or task groups, exist mainly to meet control needs: solving all sorts of problems. Control, in this sense, may include supplying physical needs, such as providing water, food, and shelter to victims of Nepal's earthquake, preventing the spread of cholera in Haiti, or combating global warming, or even more mundane matters such as fixing a flat tire or creating a budget for a struggling food shelter. This book is mostly about secondary groups. Task forces, committees, work crews, and learning groups are all secondary groups.

No group is purely primary or secondary in its functioning (see Figure 1.1). Primary groups encounter and solve problems. Secondary groups supply members with a sense of inclusion. In fact, research is clear in its findings that work on a task must be complemented with effective social skills so that members feel included, appreciated, and even loved.[34] Think of the best group you ever belonged to. Chances are, not only was this group productive, but you also formed close friendships with the other members. Most likely, a number of your psychological needs—for inclusion, openness, and control—were met. Our motives for joining groups are often mixed; we may want to participate in solving a problem, but experiencing pleasure in the interaction with others is also a main reason for our involvement.[35]

## TYPES OF SECONDARY GROUPS

Secondary groups may be formed to complete one specific job or a variety of related tasks. Examples include support groups, learning groups, organizational groups (such as committees, work teams, self-managed work teams, and quality control circles), and activity groups.

**Support Groups.** **Support groups,** or therapy, or personal growth groups, exist to help members understand and address personal issues or problems. Regardless of what they are called, their purpose is not to solve a problem *as a group* but to help individual members address personal issues in order to cope better with those problems. Groups based on the well-known 12-step process developed by Alcoholics Anonymous are examples of support groups, as are groups such as breast cancer support groups, anger management groups for abusive spouses, and so forth. A clinical psychologist recently started a grief support group for members of her church who were struggling with the 2016 mass shooting in Orlando, Florida. The premise of these groups is that individuals can better understand and cope with their own problems if they interact with others with similar problems.

**GLOSSARY**

**Secondary Groups**

*Groups formed to meet secondary needs for control and problem solving*

**Support Groups**

*Groups formed for members to help each other understand, address, and cope with personal issues or problems*

The easy availability of computers has made it possible for people to form support groups of members who never meet face-to-face, yet who experience strong support and comfort from their computer contacts. In a recent study comparing online and face-to-face support groups, Kevin Wright found that people benefited from both types.[36] Online groups have the advantages of providing 24-hour access, greater participant diversity of experience and information, and freedom to discuss risky topics. The online support networks also tended to be larger, thereby providing members with more resources. Interestingly, the online support groups did not evolve into face-to-face groups.

© Cultura Creative/Alamy Stock Photo RF

**Learning Groups.** **Learning groups** of many sorts, as we mentioned earlier, exist to help members understand or control events in their lives. Your class is a learning group (probably a large one) that may be further organized into several small learning groups. Learning groups of people from preschool to retirement age discuss all sorts of interests. Study groups are types of learning groups. Many universities group students into cohorts, whose members enter a particular program together and stay together throughout their course of study. Cohorts are encouraged to study together and to help each other learn, much like the group of young doctors in *Code Black*. In a study of adult undergraduate learning cohorts, researchers found a significant relationship between the level of group development and the individual achievement, measured by grade point average, of the members.[37] Not all groups achieved equally, which further emphasizes the importance of understanding group communication and development.

**GLOSSARY**

**Learning Groups**

*Secondary groups whose members meet to understand and learn about a particular topic*

Although our text does not specifically focus on support or learning groups, learning is a first step in many problem-solving groups, and personal affirmation and support are crucial by-products of effective group interaction in all kinds of groups.

**Organizational Groups.** Organizations such as corporations, schools, agencies, legislatures, bureaus, large departments, hospitals, and even social clubs create problem-solving groups to serve them. **Organizational groups** include any such problem-solving group formed within the context of a larger organization.

***Committees.*** Most **committees** are created by larger organizations to perform a service for the organization. The organization commits a problem or task to the small group (committee) created for that purpose. For example, at Kathy's university, a fact-finding committee was asked to investigate the possibility of establishing an honor code and report its findings to the faculty and president. Occasionally, a special committee is empowered both to select a plan and to execute it, though in most cases problem-solving committees do not go beyond making recommendations. Instead, they are usually advisory, reporting to an executive or a board that has final authority and responsibility for deciding. A different committee is created to carry out the chosen plan, or an individual may be assigned to execute the solution. Committees in organizations may be standing, ad hoc, or conference.

A *standing committee* is a permanent committee. Often, an organization's bylaws include a procedure for creating it and a description of its purpose and area of freedom to act. For example, a membership committee may be responsible for recruiting new members and for screening the applicants' qualifications. Even though a standing committee continues indefinitely, its membership is usually changed regularly by election or appointment.

*Ad hoc committees* are created to perform one special assignment and then go out of existence. The end product might be a report of findings or recommended solutions—for example, evaluations of several sites for a new plant or suggestions about how to cut costs. This report is often delivered in writing and orally to whoever created the special committee. At Gloria's university, a task force was appointed to study MOOCs (massive open online courses) and recommend the extent of her university's participation in MOOCs. Its work thus completed, the committee disbanded.

Such groups are often called *task forces,* with members selected because their knowledge and skills are thought necessary to do the group's work. Presidents have created many task forces to investigate and make recommendations on such national concerns as illegal immigration, opiate addiction, economic disparity, health care, and what was responsible for the sexual and domestic violence against women.

***Self-Managed Work Teams.*** Sometimes called autonomous work groups or modules, **self-managed work teams** are groups of peers who manage their own work schedules and procedures within certain prescribed limits. Members are highly trained and cross-trained—each is able to perform several tasks for the team. The process is similar to having a team of people building a house: "When you need more carpenters, the painters can put down their brushes and pick up hammers for a couple of hours. Or the carpenter goes and helps the plumber when he's behind."[38] These kinds of teams, used by Gore, Semco, and Proctor & Gamble, are excellent examples of how successful groups can be when members have the means to make and carry out their own decisions.[39]

**GLOSSARY**

**Organizational Groups**
*Groups created by organizations, usually to solve organizational problems*

**Committee**
*A type of secondary group that performs a specific service for an organization*

**Self-Managed Work Teams**
*Also called autonomous work groups; groups of peers who manage their own work schedules and procedures*

**What's in a Name?**

APPLY NOW

The SC Johnson Company has a meeting-intensive culture that has spawned its own vocabulary to describe various kinds of meetings. *Generals* are weekly one-on-one meetings that bosses hold with their subordinates. *Nice-to-knows* are optional informational meetings that employees often skip, and *huddles* are meetings designed to provide quick updates.

1. What kinds of group meetings do you attend?
2. What nicknames would you give to them?

A self-managed work team elects its own leader, who is a co-worker, not a supervisor or manager. The leader acts as a coordinator, not a boss. The organization establishes the work group's area of freedom, but often these groups have a great deal of latitude in how they operate. Some work groups establish their own schedules and annual budgets, prepare their own reports, develop specifications for jobs and procedures, solve technical problems that occur while completing jobs, and even prepare bids in attempting to attract new company business. For example, at one office furniture manufacturer, the custom-orders team has complete authority to bid jobs under $10,000, custom-design the furniture for the client, and schedule its manufacture. For complex jobs, the whole team goes to the client's office to listen and offer suggestions. The team's success has made the custom-order portion of the business extremely profitable.[40]

## Being an Ethical Group Member

Throughout this chapter we have emphasized how important it is for you to understand small groups so you can be a valuable participant in them. You want to be the kind of group member others can count on, thus making the small group experience a satisfactory and successful one for all members. In most small group communication classes, we have found one or two project groups plagued by slackers who want credit for the work but are unwilling to do their share of the work. Such individuals are the biggest source of animosity among group members and are responsible for derailing many projects. Other problem members include bullies, know-it-alls, and individuals who are just plain insensitive to the needs of others.

Ideally, everyone in a group wants to be a member others can count on. Members need to know what is expected of responsible, ethical members. **Ethics** are the "rules or standards for right conduct or practice,"[41] that is, what is considered appropriate behavior in certain contexts. Our professional association, the National Communication Association, has developed a credo that describes guidelines for ethical communication in all contexts (see Figure 1.2). We have used this credo as the basis for developing principles of ethical communication in small groups. In a small group, ethical behavior concerns members' willingness to communicate, treatment of fellow members, treatment of information, and commitment to the group.

**GLOSSARY**

**Ethics**

*Standards and rules for appropriate group member and leader behavior*

**FIGURE 1.2 National Communication Association Credo for Ethical Communication**

Questions of right and wrong arise whenever people communicate. Ethical communication is fundamental to responsible thinking, decision making, and the development of relationships and communities within and across contexts, cultures, channels, and media. Moreover, ethical communication enhances human worth and dignity by fostering truthfulness, fairness, responsibility, personal integrity, and respect for self and others. We believe that unethical communication threatens the quality of all communication and consequently the well-being of individuals and the society in which we live. Therefore we, the members of the National Communication Association, endorse and are committed to practicing the following principles of ethical communication:

We advocate truthfulness, accuracy, honesty, and reason as essential to the integrity of communication.

We endorse freedom of expression, diversity of perspective, and tolerance of dissent to achieve the informed and responsible decision making fundamental to a civil society.

We strive to understand and respect other communicators before evaluating and responding to their messages.

We promote access to communication resources and opportunities as necessary to fulfill human potential and contribute to the well-being of families, communities, and society.

We promote communication climates of caring and mutual understanding that respect the unique needs and characteristics of individual communicators.

We condemn communication that degrades individuals and humanity through distortion, intimidation, coercion, and violence, and through the expression of intolerance and hatred.

We are committed to the courageous expression of personal convictions in pursuit of fairness and justice.

We advocate sharing information, opinions, and feelings when facing significant choices while also respecting privacy and confidentiality.

We accept responsibility for the short- and long-term consequences for our own communication and expect the same of others.

SOURCE: Reprinted with permission from the National Communication Association. All rights reserved.

1. **Members must be willing to communicate and share ideas, information, and perspectives within the group.**

   Groups succeed because several heads are better than one. However, this advantage will not be realized if group members are unwilling to speak up or engage in group dialogue. Being silent deprives the group of your voice. Even if you are shy about talking, there are other ways to contribute, such as encouraging other members, being attentive during discussion, and volunteering for work that needs to be done outside of meetings.

2. **Group members should treat their fellow members with respect and consideration.**

   If members are to respect each other, they must operate from the belief that all group members have the same rights. Egalitarian attitudes encourage all members to contribute fully to the task at hand and value good ideas no matter who contributes them. To do otherwise undermines the potential effectiveness of the group. If members fear being scorned or belittled, they will think twice about venturing an idea or opinion. Google put all its resources together in its Project "Aristotle" to figure out the secrets of the perfect team. After wading through tons of data and research, the answer came down to one simple question: how do group members treat each other? Members who listen to each other and notice and respect each other's feelings and needs create the most effective teams. Members should not feel embarrassed, rejected, or punished for taking risks in the group.[42]

3. **Group members should use their best critical thinking skills when they evaluate information, ideas, and proposals in a group.**

   Members should evaluate information in a thorough and unbiased way. Earlier, we noted that an advantage to group processes is that members can correct each other's misinformation and faulty reasoning. In fact, it is unethical for them *not* to do so, because decisions are only as good as the information and reasoning on which they are based. Perhaps the lives of the 1986 *Columbia* space shuttle crew could have been saved had NASA officials paid attention to safety warnings more thoroughly and with less bias. Tragically, important information about the structural integrity of the shuttle was ignored. Group members must make a conscientious effort to find and present all relevant information and points of view, must not falsify data or information, and must evaluate all the information in an objective manner.

4. **Members must demonstrate a commitment to the group.**

   Some people simply are unable or unwilling to commit to a group, and they make horrible group members. For as long as they are in the group, members should place the good of the group ahead of their own individual goals. Committed, responsible members are highly involved in the activity of the group. All members are needed, and there is no room for freeloaders. A committed member supports the group's actions and decisions, even if the decision is not what the member would have chosen. If a group you belong to makes a decision you simply cannot support, it may be better for you to leave the group.

Group member communication matters because it affects other members as well as the group. Whenever you are faced with choosing how to behave in your small group, following these four principles should help you. Stand back and consider the impact of your communication on others and the group because membership in groups is not only about participation but also about observation. We turn now to the value of a participant-observer perspective.

## The Participant-Observer Perspective

Earlier, we asked you to consider all the groups to which you belong. You will continue to be a member of these groups even as you learn about small group communication from this text. This means that you will be in the role of a **participant-observer,** someone who is a regular member of the group *and,* at the same time, actively observes the group and adapts to its processes and procedures. This is especially important for the group leader or leaders. Because most group members have not been trained to be effective group participants, it is especially important for you to monitor the groups' discussions and help your groups perform as well as possible. As a skilled participant-observer, you can help a group by supplying information, procedural suggestions, and interpersonal communication skills it needs. This is an important focus of our text—to help you become a more valuable group member as you sharpen your skills in observing small group processes.

We encourage you to become a participant-observer for the groups you are in. As you read our text, try to think of examples from your own group experiences that illustrate the principles described in the text. Start paying attention in a conscious way to the processes of small group communication. In addition, use the case study and application boxes in each chapter to improve your awareness of group dynamics. As you learn more about communicating effectively in groups, you will feel more comfortable making suggestions to serve the groups to which you belong. We provide additional information about the participant-observer and other types of observers in the Appendix.

GLOSSARY

**Participant-Observer (Perspective)**

*A group member who participates but also observes the group and adapts as necessary*

### Would You Falsify Data?

ETHICAL DILEMMA

Your five-member class project group has been assigned to serve as consultants to another group. You are charged with observing this group, gathering data about it, evaluating the group's communication, and making recommendations to improve the group's functioning. The problem is that each of your project group members is very busy, and you're having a hard time agreeing on a time to observe the other group. Two of you are graduating at the end of the semester, and one of you, planning to spend the summer working in Europe, is scrambling to get all assignments finished in time to leave. Two members suggest making up data for your final project. The chances of getting caught are slim, and this "solution" would save you all several hours of observation and work. You personally strongly object to this form of cheating. For one thing, you don't want to chance having a plagiarism charge against you. But mainly you object to this form of lying, and you don't want to damage your relationship with your professor.

1. Do you speak or remain silent?
2. If you speak, what do you say?
3. What do you do if the entire group—except you—is in favor of falsifying data?
4. Do you talk to the teacher? Why or why not?

## RESOURCES FOR REVIEW AND DISCUSSION

### SUMMARY

- People in modern society need to be able to function effectively in small groups if they want to succeed and if they want to be full participants in contemporary organizational life.
- Small group members participating in decision making create and consider more issues, correct each other's misinformation, accept solutions more often, and are more loyal to the organization than members who don't participate in decisions.
- Perceptual awareness makes a group "small"; the group must be small enough for each member to participate and for each member to be conscious of and aware of the other members.
- Contemporary groups often mediate their small group communication through computers as well as use a variety of technological tools to enhance their performance.
- Groups can be classified according to their purpose. Groups can satisfy inclusion, affection, and control needs.
- Ethical group members are willing to communicate, treat others with respect, evaluate information thoroughly, and demonstrate commitment to the group.
- Participant-observers, members who know something about the small group process, can help a group succeed.

### EXERCISES

1. List all the groups to which you belong. Be sure to include family groups, friendship and other social groups, activity groups, committees, work teams, athletic teams, classroom groups, study groups, political action groups, and interest groups. Categorize them into primary or secondary groups (recognizing that no group is solely one or the other). Discuss your list with the class or in small groups.
2. Ask individuals how they have used technology (e.g., e-mail, Facebook, wikis, Twitter, and so forth) as supplements to face-to-face meetings. In what ways do these technologies help or impede group performance?
3. Break up into small groups. Devise your own list of ethical standards for group members. You can do this for a general class discussion, or you can develop a class list of standards that will be used for all future group work in the class. If the class is structured around a major group project, then individual groups can create their lists relevant to the standards of the group members.

## KEY TERMS • CONCEPTS

- Committee
- Communication
- Ethics
- Group
- Grouphate
- Learning Groups
- Organizational Groups
- Participant-Observer (Perspective)
- Primary Groups
- Secondary Groups
- Self-Managed Work Teams
- Small Group
- Small Group Communication
- Support Groups

CHAPTER 2

# Groups as Open Systems

## CHAPTER OUTLINE

What Is a Theory?

Overview of General Systems Theory

The Small Group as a System

## CHAPTER OBJECTIVES

**After reading this chapter you should be able to:**

1. Explain what a theory is and why systems theory is useful for studying small group communication.
2. Define and give examples of a system.
3. Define inputs, throughput processes, and outputs of a group system.
4. Explain why communication is the heart of a group's throughput process.
5. Describe the role of the group's environment.
6. Compare and contrast open and closed systems.
7. Describe what interdependence means for how a small group system functions.
8. Explain the role of feedback in helping a system adapt to changing circumstances.
9. Explain why all groups experience multiple causes and multiple paths.
10. Describe synergy and explain why sometimes groups exhibit positive or negative synergy.

## The 1988 Jamaican Winter Olympic Bobsled Team

CASE 2.1

A Jamaican Olympic bobsled team is about as unlikely as a Popsicle stand in the middle of the Mohave Desert—but that is the true story told in the film *Cool Runnings!* Now a part of popular culture it has inspired the reggae song, "Jamaican Bobsled," it was even mentioned in the popular television show *Futurama,* and their two-person bobsled team was a smash hit in the 2014 Sochi Olympics. In the 1988 Winter Olympics in Calgary, Alberta, Canada, with only 3 months to find equipment, secure financial backing, and qualify four of the most incompatible, untrained Jamaicans come together to compete for an Olympic gold medal. Sanka is the best pushcart driver in all Jamaica; his friend Derice is Jamaica's beloved track sprinter; Yul is a moody, angry sprinter; and Junior is a wealthy sprinter who tripped both Derice and Yul in the Olympic track qualifiers. Junior's mistake cost Derice his chance to follow his dad's legacy and compete for Olympic gold in track. Not to be denied, Derice searches for another way to try for a medal. He hears about Irving Blitzer, a disgraced Olympic bobsled medalist stripped of his medals for cheating, but who believed track sprinters would make outstanding bobsledders. Derice pleads with Irv to coach the first Jamaican bobsled team. Sanka signs on as a favor for his friend, Yul joins to get off the island, and Junior joins to get away from his domineering father.

This unlikely collection of three track sprinters, one pushcart driver, and a disgraced coach has no money, no sled, no ice and snow to practice on, no fan support, skeptical and cruel responses from fellow bobsledders, and animosity among team members. Any betting person would predict from these initial factors that they would fail. Even the Jamaican Olympic committee would not give them the money to go to Canada for the bobsled trials. Overcoming one obstacle after another, these athletes slowly emerge as a cohesive Olympic team. During the last run for gold, this team crashes before the finish line because of a loose runner on the sled. Injured but not deterred, they pick up their sled, named "Cool Runnings," and walk over the finish line to the cheers of the other bobsledders and all of Jamaica. What does "Cool Runnings" mean? It translates into "peace be the journey."[1]

GLOSSARY

**Theory**
*A "map of reality" that helps us navigate unfamiliar territory and make decisions*

**The story of *Cool Runnings* illustrates several important aspects of systems theory. We will return to the story throughout the chapter to provide examples of how various elements of systems theory apply to the Jamaican bobsled team. First, we consider what a theory is, examine an overview of general systems theory, and look at how it furnishes a useful and popular framework for examining small group communication.**

## What Is a Theory?

Most students tune out when they know a discussion about theory is looming. Many people believe theories are boring, irrelevant, and unnecessary. However, the truth is that all of us use theories every day, although we probably do not think about it. A **theory** as a "map of reality,"[2] something that helps us navigate unfamiliar terrain and make decisions. Like a map, a theory describes relationships between elements (e.g., Kansas City is 180 miles northwest of Springfield) and shows you how to get from one element to another (from Springfield, take Route 13 to Clinton, Route 7 to Harrison, and I-49 to Kansas City). This helps make a drive from Springfield to Kansas City predictable and orderly.

Good theories are practical and reliable ways to help improve your decision making. For example, assume you've agreed to meet your friends for a "Thank God It's Friday" celebration, but you're short of funds. You will have to cash Friday's paycheck before you can join the group. But you know that if you wait until 5:00 P.M. on Friday, you'll be stuck in a long line at the bank's drive-through because everybody else who got paid on Friday will be doing the same thing! So you ask your boss if you can leave at 4:00 P.M. to beat the rush. Your theory probably goes something like this: (1) Long lines at the bank are related to the number of people trying to deposit or cash paychecks; (2) in your city many people receive paychecks on Fridays; (3) the workday for most businesses ends between 4:30 and 5:00 P.M.; therefore, (4) you'll be held up at the bank if you wait until 5:00 P.M. to cash your check. Solution: Leave at 4:00 and beat the crowd. You have just theorized about the relationship between the day of the week, the time, and the likelihood of a crowd and taken appropriate action, and you've used your own implicit theory to help you.

There are many theories that have a bearing on small group communication. Some of these are broad in scope, which means they apply to all or most groups; other theories are more limited, applying in particular group situations (e.g., building good group environments) or to a few clearly defined phenomena (e.g., conflict). We will discuss a number of theories throughout this book which will be useful in helping you assess what is working well in a group and why, what isn't working and why, and what you might do about it. The theory we turn to now, general systems theory, is a comprehensive theory that applies to all living organisms, including social systems such as groups. We use this theory as a broad framework for organizing the many elements that constitute a small group.

## Overview of General Systems Theory

General systems theory was developed by a biologist, Ludwig von Bertalanffy, as a way to examine and explain complex living organisms. Because living organisms, including groups, are constantly changing, they are difficult to study. Think for a moment about your own body, one of the most complex of all organisms. Although it appears to operate as a single unit, in reality it is composed of many smaller units that work interdependently to sustain your life. For example, when you walk across the room, your muscular, skeletal, nervous, circulatory, and respiratory systems all cooperate in moving you to your destination. Even if you are sitting still, your body is involved in constant activity—your eyelids are blinking, your heart is beating, you are breathing automatically, and so forth. Your individual cells constantly change as they take in nourishment through the blood, restore themselves, and excrete waste through the cell walls. This complicated, continuous process is hard to capture. Fortunately, systems theory provides us with a way of examining and describing how a system's parts are interrelated, even while they are continuously changing. Systems theory reminds us that when we want to understand any living entity—such as a group—we not only study its parts but also how the parts operate together to understand the organism as a *whole.*

Systems theory has helped social scientists, family therapists, business professionals, and others by providing a useful framework for looking at groups. Many individual elements affect the dynamics of a group—the reason the group was formed, the personalities of group members, the information members have, the type of leadership, the way the group handles conflict, and how successful the group has been in accomplishing its assigned task, to name only a few. *But no single element functions alone;* the elements interact continuously. Systems theory concepts warn us not to oversimplify our description of group interaction. All parts interact to produce the entity called a "small group."

© Yuri_Arcurs/E+/Getty Images RF

GLOSSARY

**System**

*A set of elements that functions as a whole because of interdependent relationships*

Characterizing a group as a social system was a significant advance in small group communication theory. The assumption that *communication* connects the relevant parts of a system is fundamental to understanding a small group as a system. This moves the role of communication to the forefront of small group theory. We now take a closer look at the underlying principles of systems theory.

## The Small Group as a System

Several concepts are important to understanding a small group as a system. We will use the Jamaican bobsled case study we presented at the beginning of the chapter to illustrate these concepts.

### DEFINITION OF A SYSTEM

A **system** is composed of parts that are interdependent with each other, connected in such a manner that any change in one part ripples through the entire system. The dung beetle may have the grossest job of all, eating dung. However, by eating dung this maligned beetle breaks down dead material so that bacteria can break it up even more, thus helping recycle nutrients back into the environment. Group member interdependence, introduced in Chapter 1, is the mutual influence between members that creates a "group" from a collection of individuals; a group is interdependent as well with the environment it belongs to. Think back to the Jamaican bobsled team (see also Figure 2.1).

Several elements and their unique interaction affected the team. Consider first the members themselves, with their various abilities. A winning bobsled team needs a driver and three strong runners to push the sled—and this team had them. Sanka was loyal to Derice and was, after all, the best pushcart driver in all of Jamaica. Yul was strong and fast. Junior was also quick and sharp. And Derice was born to compete in the Olympics—both fast and driven.

A second element was the team's game plan. For example, how should the coach match these abilities with the various positions? Should the pushcart driver be the driver of the sled? The team's first conflict involved this very issue. Sanka thought he should be the driver, yet the coach pointed out that the driver had to be focused at all times and was responsible not only for the course but also for the lives of the others. So Derice was selected as the driver, and Sanka became the brakeman. The other two were the middlemen.

The third element was the leadership within the team. Derice, for instance, had to figure out how to manage the hard feelings between Yul and Junior. In addition, Yul had a personal motive that had nothing to do with the team—he wanted to use the "team" to get off the island.

The fourth element was Irv's ability to assess the team's competency, earn members' trust, and motivate them to find their own style of sledding. Notice also the interaction of the team with its surroundings. The attitudes of the Jamaicans, their families, other Olympic bobsledders and coaches, as well as the media, at first thwarted then later inspired the team. In return, the team's success influenced the entire country of Jamaica and the rest of the winter Olympic community.

FIGURE 2.1 Bobsled Team as a Small Group System

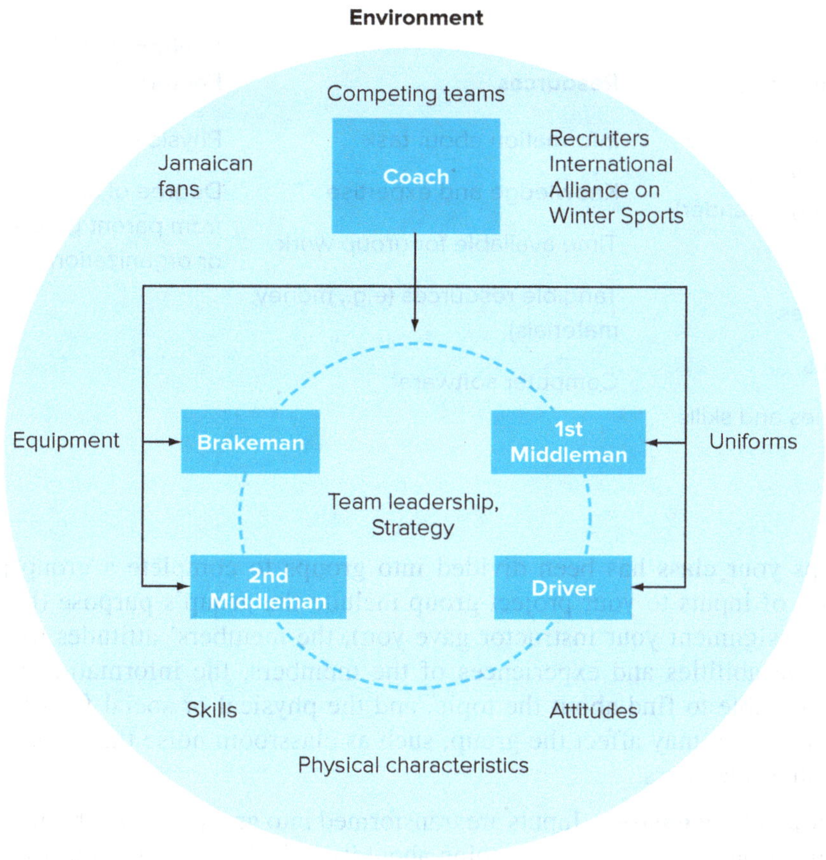


## CONCEPTS VITAL TO UNDERSTANDING SYSTEMS

To understand systems theory, you need to understand four basic concepts true of all systems: inputs, throughput processes, outputs, and environment. Our explanations of these are based on scholarly work by Daniel Katz and Robert Kahn.[3]

**Inputs.** The "raw materials" that are initially brought to the group from the outside, such as people, information, energies, and resources designed to help group problem solving, are a group's **inputs** (see Table 2.1). For example, the abilities of the bobsled players—whether they were competent or not, whether they were relatively fast or slow, how well they "read" the subtle nature of the course—were all inputs that the players brought with them to the group and that influenced how well the team performed during a run. Other inputs included the instructions on how to synchronize the movements of all four bobsledders and their sled, the continuous stream of information that Irv gathered about the strengths and weaknesses of opposing teams, the three-month time limit they had to qualify, and the attitudes of the team members toward each other, the sport, and their coach.

GLOSSARY

**Inputs**

*All the elements of a system that are present at the outset, or the initial raw materials of the system*

TABLE 2.1 **Examples of Small Group Inputs**

| Members | Resources | Environmental Factors |
|---|---|---|
| Personalities and characteristics (e.g., age, gender) | Information about task | Physical surroundings |
| Needs | Knowledge and expertise | Degree of support from parent group or organization |
| Attitudes | Time available for group work | |
| Values | Tangible resources (e.g., money, materials) | |
| Abilities and skills | Computer software | |

Perhaps your class has been divided into groups to complete a group project. Examples of inputs to your project group include the group's purpose (beginning with the assignment your instructor gave you), the members' attitudes toward the project, the abilities and experiences of the members, the information members have or are able to find about the topic, and the physical or social features of the environment that may affect the group, such as classroom noise that makes it hard to hear other members.

**Throughput Processes.** Inputs are transformed into group outputs through the activities the group engages in while going about its task. These **throughput processes** (see Table 2.2) include the group's rules, how its leadership develops, how conflict is managed by everyone, and the roles that are created and played by members. Communication is *the* central activity in this transformative process. It is through communication that a group receives information (an input), then discusses that information, argues about its credibility and what it means to the group, and finally decides to incorporate it into the final report. The discussion, debate about credibility, and process of deciding to include the information are examples of the group's throughput processes.

In our bobsled team example, the coach's placement of Derice as the driver instead of Sanka, the obvious choice, is an example of a throughput process. The informal leadership of Sanka, whose enthusiasm motivated the other members, was also part of the team's throughput processes. Significant for this team was how Yul and Junior developed a mutual respect across socioeconomic lines.

In another example, members of your classroom group may have developed a group norm of examining critically all the information they bring to meetings and arguing openly before they reach any decision. This style of handling information is an example of a throughput process. Thorough and critical evaluation of information by all group members will have a different effect on the group's decisions than if the members uncritically accept any and all information.

**GLOSSARY**

**Throughput Processes**
*Influences on the system that result from actual activities within the group as it goes about its business*

**TABLE 2.2 Examples of Small Group Throughput Processes**

| |
|---|
| **MEMBERS' BEHAVIORS** |
| Extent to which members encourage ideas |
| Extent that members show a willingness to work |
| Extent to which members are open minded |
| Extent to which members are fair and equitable in dealing with disagreements |
| Extent to which members show a sense of belonging to a unique group |
| **GROUP NORMS** |
| Support for using critical thinking skills to test ideas versus uncritical acceptance of ideas |
| Support for open disagreement versus suppression of conflict |
| Support for relative equality among members versus strict hierarchy |
| **COMMUNICATION NETWORKS** |
| Extent to which each member talks to every other member |
| Extent to which participation is distributed evenly |
| **STATUS RELATIONSHIPS** |
| Extent that leadership matches group needs |
| Extent to which power and influence are shared |
| Extent to which group roles complement each other and contribute to the group purpose |
| **PROCEDURES** |
| Communication |
| Decision making and problem solving |
| Method for implementing solutions |

Recall from Chapter 1 that all four ethical principles for group members are anchored in the National Communication Association's Credo for Ethical Communication and, in effect, describe general effective throughput processes or ways to transform initial inputs into outputs everyone can be proud of. Whether you are showing a willingness to communicate, displaying respect for others, critically assessing information, or demonstrating commitment to your group, you are engaging in a variety of *communicative* behaviors—all four standards are grounded in *what* and *how* you communicate to others. Group communication is the focus of Chapter 3 and 4.

TABLE 2.3 **Examples of Small Group Outputs**

| Tangible Outcomes | Intangible Outcomes |
|---|---|
| Reports | Feelings among members (cohesiveness, trust; disharmony, dislike) |
| Recommendations | Personal growth of members |
| Solutions and decisions | Personal satisfaction of members |
| Physical objects (e.g., table decorations, assembled cars) | Modifications in throughput procedures (e.g., alterations in the status relationships, use of different conflict resolution strategies) |

**Outputs.** **Outputs** are the continual "results" of the group's throughput processes (see Table 2.3). They include tangible outcomes, such as decisions the group has made, written reports it has completed, or Olympic races it has won. However, they also include less obvious results, such as cohesiveness, member satisfaction, personal growth of individual members, and changes in the group's structure. In our bobsled example, a clear result of the members' respect for each other was, although not a gold medal, pride in themselves and adulation from their country. Other outputs included the sledders' increased cohesiveness and new skills, Junior's independence from his father, Yul's pride in the team, and Derice's realization that a gold medal does not make one a whole person.

Although we hope that the outputs of a small group's interaction are positive and helpful, some outputs are toxic waste to both the group itself and its parent organization. Hasty decisions, dissatisfaction of group members, and shoddy products are examples of this waste, dangerous to the group as well as the organization to which it belongs.

These three elements are themselves interdependent and integral to group systems that are changing all the time. Outputs thus reenter the group system as inputs affecting throughput processes and influencing new outputs. This ripple effect can be seen when a group member enters the group unwilling to communicate to other members, this input affects the overall group communication by creating a climate of suspicion (throughput), which leads to low group satisfaction among other members (output). The members' subsequent lack of commitment to each other becomes a new input element, which continues to destroy the group's climate (throughput), leading to a group report that is never finished (output). This downward pattern will continue unless group members notice the problems and adjust their communication to change the climate of the group. We will take up the issue of group feedback after we discuss the relationship a small group has with its environment.

**Environment.** A group does not exist apart from its surroundings, or **environment,** much of which potentially affects the group. Groups are not like lead boxes that keep things from getting in or out. The "walls" between a group and its environment are porous, allowing information in and out as well as providing the opportunity for mutual

**GLOSSARY**

**Outputs**

*Those tangible and intangible products or achievements of the group system emerging from throughput processes*

**Environment**

*Systems do not exist in a vacuum but are embedded in multiple surroundings or contexts*

influence between the group and its environment. In our example, the Jamaican fans and the other bobsledders influenced the team's morale and enthusiasm. Notice also that the team affected its environment as well. When the other bobsledders discovered the courage of this Jamaican team, their disrespect turned into support, and those who had rejected the coach for his past cheating accepted him back into the bobsled fraternity.

Your classroom group's immediate environment is the classroom. Your group is affected by whether the classroom is pleasant or ugly, noisy or quiet. In addition, what your friends in other classes say or do may cause your group to change a procedure, a topic, an approach, and so forth. These friends and their classes are part of your group's environment, too.

The effect of a group's environment, or its context, is an important factor in how well a group operates.[4] To understand a small group in depth, we must consider the influence of the group's environment. Linda Putnam and Cynthia Stohl, two leading scholars of group communication, call this a **bona fide group perspective.**[5] They emphasize that real-world groups both influence and help *shape* those same environments. This interdependence occurs for several reasons. First, members of groups often belong to other groups that simultaneously influence and are influenced by them. Second, groups typically have to coordinate their actions with other groups within the same parent organization or across organizations. Third, there is frequent communication within the group as well as between the group and other larger groups over interpretation of group goals, the extent of the group's authority, and support for group actions that helps define a group's accountability for its task. Finally, members bring to their groups a variety of interests, ways of speaking, and mental models of effective group problem solving. This in turn affects how members create their sense of "group."

Consider, for instance, a student group that has decided to investigate traffic safety when a student was killed crossing a street on her way to class. Although group members had not known the victim, they wanted her death to result in positive actions to make the campus safer. The student's death—part of the group's environment—was the catalyst for motivating the group to act. The street where the student died, bordering the east side of the campus, was controlled by the city; the students did not have the authority to decide, on their own, what safety measures should be taken, but they could recommend various options. The group's written report and recommendations were summarized in an oral report given to on-campus groups that included staff from the offices of Student Affairs, Administrative Services, and the president. In addition, several off-campus groups, including the city offices of Planning and Development, Traffic Engineering, and Street Maintenance, heard the group's presentation and received the written report. These groups—also part of the student group's environment—had to be persuaded to adopt the group's recommendations before any changes could be implemented. In order to produce a compelling report, the group had to research local and state laws about changing street configurations and present their information professionally, in the format preferred by these various groups. The city ultimately accepted the students' recommendations to build a retaining wall down the center of the street and reduce the speed limit. The group's work thus brought about a lasting change to its environment.

**GLOSSARY**

**Bona Fide Group Perspective**

*The focus on the relationship between a group and its environment, which is a characteristic of real-life, naturally occurring groups*

### Bona Fide Groups: The Jamaican Bobsled Team

APPLY NOW

The Jamaican Olympic bobsled team was not an isolated group, separate from its environment. As a bona fide group, it was connected to its environment, and vice versa. Four reasons explain the interdependence between this bobsled team and its environment. Using the information from the case study at the beginning of the chapter, surmise possible answers to the following questions:

1. For each member of the team (sledders and coach), what were all the possible groups these individuals could belong to while they were members of the team (e.g., Julian was part of a controlling family)?
2. Bona fide groups are faced with coordinating their actions with other groups. Considering the list of groups for each member of the team, what actions would have had to be coordinated (e.g., Junior was supposed to leave the country and attend school to be an accountant)?
3. What kind of internal and external communication about team goals, team authority, and support existed for this team (e.g., the Jamaican Olympic committee would not financially support the team to attend Olympic trials in Canada)? With each example, discuss how the communication impacted the group.
4. How was the unique nature of *this* Olympic team shaped by the interests and past team experiences brought to it by each member?

Once you have compiled some answers to these questions, examine the complicated manner in which this bobsled team was interdependently connected with its environment.

The impact of this kind of interdependence with the environment can be seen in what real-life members report as hurting their group efforts.[6] Organizational factors in the environment beyond a group's control often have strong negative effects on the group's performance. These findings suggest that group outcomes depend on several things: input factors relating to members (e.g., motivation, interest), on throughput processes (e.g., group leadership), and on environmental factors often beyond the group's control (e.g., information and resources from the parent organization). This and other studies of actual organizational groups support the overall utility of the systems framework, which remind us to pay attention to the group's environment.[7]

Interestingly, for groups dealing with complex tasks in a very uncertain environment, how often members interact with others in the surrounding environment is more crucial to their performance than how they communicate within the group.[8] This demonstrates how important it is for groups to match their internal abilities to process information with the external informational demands of their environment.

Most of the research in small group communication has focused on groups whose members meet face-to-face with easily identifiable environments (e.g., an office space or a small group course). However, we noted in Chapter 1 that in our global world, many companies now collaborate on tasks with the help of computer technology that allows the members of multiple groups to interact with each other without being on the same site. The Boeing 767 airplane is the result of collaboration among Boeing engineers, who designed the fuel system and cockpit; Aeritalia SAI engineers, who developed the fins and rudder; and multiple Japanese firms, whose responsibility was the main body of the plane.[9]

Modern organizations are increasingly composed of employees who may not work in the same place or at the same time. Some employees belong to **virtual groups** whose members complete most or all of their work without meeting face-to-face. Virtual group members may work online at the same time or participate in telephone conference calls for their group work, or they may work at different times, as each individual's schedule permits. The group's "location" is actually an electronic network of members who may see each other infrequently or perhaps not at all. Members of these work groups may contact each other only via e-mail, text messaging, or videoconferencing.

Bona fide group theorists have begun to study such virtual groups. Because collaboration is primarily a communicative phenomenon, they ask how group members manage their roles, multiple contexts, boundaries, and tasks when they perform most of their work virtually. Traditional small group concepts are thrown into new light. For instance, traditional groups manage their knowledge internally and can more easily find out where to get needed information; in contrast, virtual groups often assume tasks that are so innovative and multidimensional as to be beyond the knowledge of any member. In addition, members may have no clue whom to contact for information. In collaborating groups, composed of members who represent other organizations, members have loyalties and responsibilities to those other groups and organizations, which can reduce their commitment to the collaborating group. Formal positions of power (e.g., chair, secretary, vice-chair) often don't exist, which means that these status positions must be continually negotiated. Decision-making procedures are often created internally in traditional groups, but, in virtual groups, such procedures are affected by the norms of parent companies, cultural changes, orders given by external agents, and even decisions made outside the group.

**GLOSSARY**

**Virtual Group**

*A group in which members do not communicate with each other in the same time and place*

## CHARACTERISTICS OF SYSTEMS

We now turn our attention to describing several important characteristics of social systems, including groups. These characteristics help explain how a system functions, internally and with its surrounding environment.

**Open and Closed Systems.** Whether a system is relatively open or closed is determined by just how porous, or leaky, the boundary is between the system and its environment. A **closed system** has little interaction with its environment, whereas an **open system** has a great deal. The model in Figure 2.2 illustrates that inputs entering an open group system are worked on and communicatively transformed during the throughput process to be sent out from the system as outputs. The model also illustrates that the environment's response becomes feedback that is recycled to the group as further inputs. The group-environment interchange should be apparent from the model. Our bobsled team had a moderate amount of interaction with

**GLOSSARY**

**Closed System**
*A system with limited flow of information between itself and its environment*

**Open System**
*A system with a free exchange of information with its environment—that is, with inputs and outputs flowing back and forth between the system and its environment*

**FIGURE 2.2** Model of a Small Group as an Open System

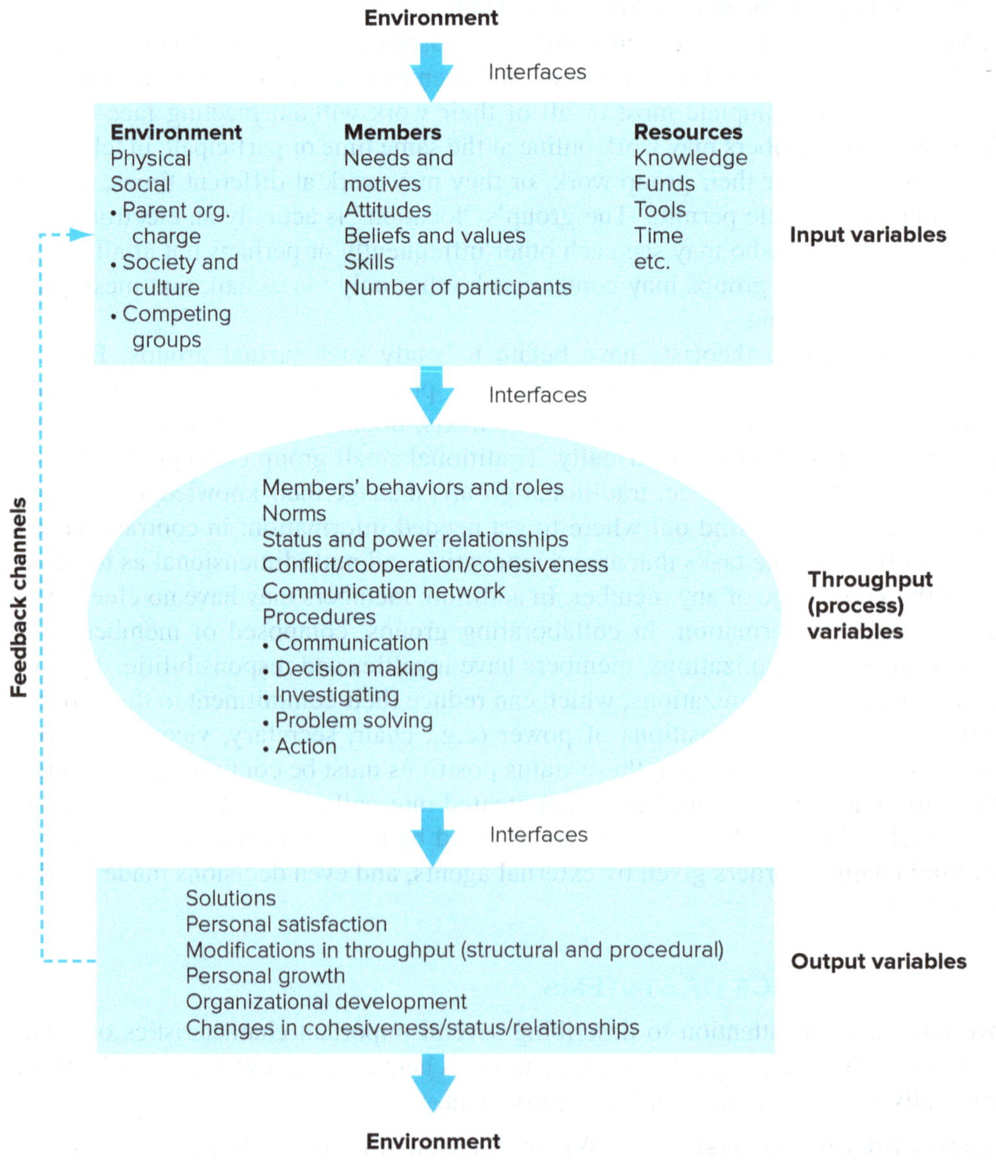

its surroundings. The team was affected by the fans' reactions, and the fans and general public were influenced by the team's successes as well. Your classroom groups also experience degrees of openness with their environments. You may not learn what another group has been doing until group presentations because its members had little interaction with other class members and the instructor. Other groups may often interact with each other in class, getting ideas from those outside groups, and may meet regularly with the instructor to clarify requirements for group projects and presentations. These groups choose more open exchanges with their environments.

Openness has advantages and disadvantages. For example, some American companies, resisting the changes brought by "outsiders," prefer to stay as closed to outside influence as possible. This enables managers to maintain more control over what happens internally, but it also cuts off the company from information that might improve its operation and profits. Courts, for instance, are finding it increasingly difficult to "close" the boundaries between a jury and its environment during trial due to the ease (openness) with which jurors can access information through social media. Court convictions have been overturned because jurors got information they should not have during trial.[10] Classroom groups that remain relatively closed in an effort to control information may miss valuable information and ideas that could have improved their critical thinking. On the other hand, groups that choose to be more open with their environments may have more information to coordinate and may run the risk of becoming overloaded; however, they can take advantage of that information in their critical thinking and in carrying out their task.

In order to help groups interact with their environments, members act as **boundary spanners,** scanning the environment and helping information flow back and forth. Boundary spanning helps bring relevant information back to the group; connects the group to useful people, resources and other groups; and protects the group from outsiders—all of which can help a group succeed.[11] For example, a nonprofit organization learned from news reports that a member of its board had pled guilty to fraud. Keeping this member on the board would have hurt the organization's reputation, but the organization did not have a provision in its bylaws for removing members. A board member used Internet resources to find examples from other nonprofit organizations of bylaws statements about when and how members can be removed. The organization's executive board examined these, consulted with an attorney (a key resource in the group's environment), and proposed that an amendment about removing members be added to its bylaws. The board approved the amendment and eventually removed the member.

Boundary spanners work in two general ways.[12] First, they look for ideas and support that can be useful to the team by *scouting* for information (the member who scouted the Internet for bylaws statements about removing members did this) and *coordinating* activities with other groups and individuals. For example, a student group wanted to bring in a popular entertainer but did not have the money to pay the fee. This group contacted several other student groups on campus and together they coordinated by pooling their resources to be able to afford the entertainer. Teams often do not have all the resources they need to succeed. Scouting and coordinating activities help extend the group's access to outside resources.

GLOSSARY

**Boundary Spanner**

*A group member who scans the group's environment to allow or prevent information from flowing into and out of the group*

Second, boundary spanners help protect the group from outside influences by *buffering* and *bringing up borders*.[13] Members who buffer help keep team resources from flowing into the environment and keep the members from being upset by external circumstances. If your classroom group has come up with a creative approach to a classroom assignment, you may want to keep your idea secret so other groups in your class don't steal it. When members bring up borders, they work to increase the cohesiveness and smooth functioning of the team. This usually establishes a stronger boundary between the team and the outside environment.

Openness and free interchange with the environment are distinct advantages for most groups and some organizations intentionally plan boundary-spanning activities. For example, Pacific Gas & Electric (PG&E), a large utility company in California, engaged in a planning and marketing process that deliberately solicited customer feedback at every step in the process.[14] Called "Voice of the Customer," the process first sought to determine how satisfied PG&E residential customers were with the company's overall service, which services customers felt were most important, and how the company might improve its services in those key areas. Among other things, customers complained about being kept on hold for a long time, experiencing unpredictable scheduling of service, and being transferred to several offices in the course of solving a problem. The company's restructuring of its service delivery processes, accomplished in teams of employees, sought and used customer feedback throughout the process. Success with the residential pilot program led to the same approach with business and commercial customers.

**Interdependence.** **Interdependence** refers to the fact that each element of a system simultaneously influences and is influenced by the other elements. Just as the system as a whole is affected by its environment, so are the system's individual components affected by each other. Geese fly farther *together* than any individual bird can fly. They can do this by taking advantage of the draft each bird's wings create together. Within small groups one element, idea, behavior, or person can change the functioning of the entire group. In our bobsled story, we saw how the sledders' abilities determined, in part, the coach's strategy, and how the personality of individual players such as Sanka, the eternal optimist, could spur a team to greater effort, which in turn increased the likelihood of team success.

That success is an interdependent goal as well. One group member, just as one bobsled member, does not reach the goal alone . . . the team wins together or loses together.

**Feedback.** One valuable feature of human systems is that they are able to adapt to changing conditions and circumstances. They can do this through the use of **feedback,** the part of the system's output that is returned to the system as input. Feedback enables the system to monitor its progress toward the goal and make corrections when needed. In our bobsled story, Irv saw that his arrangement of sledders was successful. This feedback indicated that what he was doing was working, so he didn't need to change their positions. In another example, during practice runs and after studying pictures of the course, Derice made adjustments in the team's movements for more successful runs.

**GLOSSARY**

**Interdependence**
*When the elements of a system mutually influence each other*

**Feedback**
*The return of system outputs as system inputs, which allows the system to monitor its movement toward goals and make necessary changes*

## The Influence of Computer-Mediated Communication on the System

MEDIA AND TECHNOLOGY

The integration of technology, and the potential for various modes of computer-mediated communication (CMC), has begun to influence the way we view small group systems. Technological advances have increased the potential for group members to interact more freely with the environment by opening the lines of communication between those inside and outside of the group. For instance, an input such as the time a member can allocate to the group has become less restrictive as technology has allowed interaction any time or place. The Internet also has increased group access to information about the task (i.e., search engines), increased the flow of information (i.e., e-mail and instant messaging), and allowed for telecommuting opportunities (i.e., web conferencing or face chat). What other group inputs described in this chapter may be enhanced as a result of an increased reliance on technology? What about throughputs and outputs?

Although each of these resources functions to create a more open group system, integration of technology also has a variety of drawbacks that may discourage its use. Think about how the types of inputs you bring to the group (personality, abilities, and expertise) are influenced by your physical presence. If you were relegated to working off-site for a group meeting, would it be possible for you to exert the same input? Mallia found that individuals who telecommute lose status within the group. They also reduce their prospects for upward mobility in an organizational hierarchy chain because of the lack of face-to-face interaction. Can you think of other disadvantages that may result for a group or organization fostering CMC interaction?

Open systems, as you recall, interact freely with their environments and bring change to the system. Feedback is the environment's response to a system's output. Coming in the form of information or tangible resources, it helps the system determine whether it needs to make adjustments to reach its goals. For instance, the critical response you receive from your instructor on group assignments provides your group with information on how well you are accomplishing your group task. Your project group can assess this information and decide which changes need to be made and how they should be made. The uncertainty group members experience motivates them to seek feedback and gives the feedback its value.[15] You might ask, Are we on the right track? Did we select the best service organization to work with for our project? Is our group report comprehensive enough? Are our meetings getting us anywhere?

Whether or not feedback is useful depends on the type and the source of the feedback.[16] Clear, accurate, relevant feedback helps a group more than ambiguous, inaccurate, not well reasoned, or irrelevant feedback.

Critical feedback, regardless of its clarity and accuracy, is hard to give and receive. It is best to pose it as a *group* issue, not a personal one. For example, assume that Irv noticed that the bobsled team was not bonding enough to be a championship team. Rather than tell members he was disappointed in them, he could have asked them how they could work together to be more cohesive. He might have done this by first sharing with them how much their track speed had increased, then observing that, when pressed, they seemed to fall apart, but that they had become closer than when they first met as a collection of individuals interested in going to the Olympics. The critical observation that they seemed to fall apart under pressure was sandwiched between two more favorable observations.

The source of feedback is as important as its content. Originally, Irv did not have much credibility with his bobsled team because he had left the sport in disgrace. His feedback about who should play what role on the team and how members should work toward the medal was not received well initially. He had to earn the team's respect for his feedback to have any credibility. Groups receive feedback from a variety of sources and must ascertain how trustworthy the source is, how responsive it is to the needs of the group, and what the status is of the person giving the feedback.[17]

**Multiple Causes, Multiple Paths.** One feature of all open systems, including small groups, is complexity. This complexity and the fact that group members have choices about their behaviors make it impossible to predict where a group will end up from where it starts. The concept of *equifinality* (literally, "equal ends") suggests that groups can start out at very different places but end up at the same place. For example, the Jamaican bobsled team began more inexperienced than other teams, yet ended up competing rather well with them. The concept of *multifinality* (literally, "different ends") suggests that groups starting out the same may end up in very different places. For example, given two experienced, successful sports teams, one may end up losing many of its games while the other wins a championship. Too many variables and moment-to-moment decisions can lead the groups in different directions, even if both started out in the same context with similar inputs.

It is important to remember that, with groups, many factors, not a single factor, combine to produce the final outcome, a concept we refer to as **multiple causes.** As an example of multiple causes, the Jamaican bobsled team had high morale at the end of the Olympics. This occurred for several reasons: They became medal contenders, the country supported them, they had a leader who was well liked and effective, and all the members contributed to the team's success. Too often, individuals try to pinpoint a single cause for a group outcome. For example, you may have heard someone say, "We would have come up with an excellent proposal if our chair had listened to our suggestions. As it was, everybody hated the group." The behavior of the group's chair certainly contributed to the group's low morale, but other factors had an impact as well. Perhaps members did not like each other, the task was not an interesting one, or the group did not have sufficient time or information to do its best. All these factors interact to produce the dissatisfaction.

A related principle of groups is that there is usually more than one appropriate way to reach a particular goal or endpoint. This principle is indicated by the concept of **multiple paths.** For example, there are a number of ways to plan a fun party, and a variety of ways to develop a respectable undergraduate curriculum for communication majors. Which is the "right" way? Various ways are right—the

**GLOSSARY**

**Multiple Causes**
*The idea that no single system input determines system outputs; instead, system outcomes are the result of numerous, interdependent factors*

**Multiple Paths**
*The idea that system objectives can be reached in a variety of ways*

most effective approach depends on the characteristics of all the participants. Also, the concept of multiple paths implies that two or more groups could come up with similar solutions to a problem, even though each group had members with different abilities and areas of expertise, leadership styles, and ways of resolving differences of opinion. Like multiple causes, the concept of multiple paths encourages us to recognize the complexity of small groups and avoid looking for only one way to do something and one cause to any group outcome.

**Synergy.** **Synergy,** also called *nonsummativity,* refers to the fact that when group members come together, they create an entirely unique entity that is something other than just a collection of individual parts. Sometimes a team performs better than the individual abilities of the members would lead you to expect (positive synergy) and sometimes it performs worse (negative synergy). You cannot just add up the statistics of each member and figure out how the team will perform. For example, the Golden State Warriors were favored to win the National Basketball Association's 2016 championship. They were the 2015 champions, had the best single season record in NBA history, and arguably some of the best players in the league. Yet they lost to the Cleveland Cavaliers, known as an underdog team since their 1970 beginnings with bench players and a 52-year-old curse. Even so, they fought back from a 3 to 1 deficit, a feat never seen before in an NBA championship. A small group is an entity of its own and takes on a life of its own, so it can perform better—or worse—than anyone predicts.

Groups often achieve an *assembly effect,* or a positive synergy, in which the output is superior to the averaging of the outputs of the individual members. Motivated members working interdependently as a group give rise to synergy.[18] In addition, groups with deep diversity (see Chapter 6) or a vast array of abilities are fertile ground for synergy.[19] On the other hand, groups can often experience what some have called *process loss,* or negative synergy in which the group's output is worse than expected given the abilities of the group members. For example, Gloria had a classroom group of students who had received As on their individual assignments. She predicted this group would do an outstanding job on their final project. Instead, they couldn't overcome their lack of trust in others, several members' insistence on doing things their own way, and their inability to share information. Their final project received a B- due to the negative synergy this group's ineffective communication skills allowed to develop.

Although no one knows exactly why one group experiences positive synergy and another negative synergy, it may have something to do with how much ambiguity the group faces, whether the group encounters obstacles during its problem-solving process, and how it deals with those obstacles.[20] Google's research into the secret of the perfect team revealed groups that rise above expectation, treat each other with respect, and are open and supportive of each other's contributions.[21] The Jamaican team faced numerous obstacles: a short time in which to train and qualify, little money, members with no experience, a country with no snow, a coach lacking respect, ridicule from others, ouster from the Olympics, possible loss of one member, and the list goes on. Yet the team members worked together to overcome each obstacle, finding new pride in themselves and their own style of sledding.

**GLOSSARY**

**Synergy**
*A system's ability to take on an identity separate from its individual elements*

Systems theory's contribution to small group communication research and to our understanding of the process of small group interaction is obvious. However, the theory is not without its detractors. Any theory is a human construction and therefore limited in scope—it gives *a* particular view, not *the* view. Some, for instance, have questioned whether systems theory provides merely a descriptive framework but not a useful explanatory one.[22] Others take issue with the systems theory assumption of *homeostasis,* or dynamic balance—the idea that systems are self-maintaining and work

**CNN's Reporting Disaster: What Happened?**

APPLY NOW

CNN, during its premiere of *NewsStand: CNN & Time,* a television news venture with *Time* magazine, reported in the lead story, "Valley of Death," that the United States had used lethal nerve gas in 1970 as part of a secret mission to kill American defectors in Laos. This report was broadcast June 7, 1998, on *NewsStand: CNN & Time* and reported in *Time* despite several oral and written complaints from journalists in both news organizations questioning the validity of the story. A military consultant resigned in protest. On July 3, 1998, the *Fresno* (California) Bee reported CNN's retraction of the story by Tom Johnson, CNN News Group chair, president, and CEO. Johnson admitted to serious faults with the broadcast and apologized, saying that CNN was not able to confirm the story. *Time's* managing editor admitted that he, too, could not confirm the story.

A group of television producers and print journalists conducted 200 interviews as they worked together for 8 months on the story. The group was headed by two successful producers and included an award-winning documentary producer and a Pulitzer Prize-winning journalist. An independent investigation into the validity of the story concluded that the group members had not intentionally made up the story. Instead, the reporting team drew conclusions based on questionable evidence, led sources into thinking that their suspicions could be supported by unseen evidence, and made decisions based on interview responses to a variety of hypothetical questions. The CNN investigation concluded that those involved in putting together the story so firmly believed what they were reporting that they ignored information contrary to what they were finding.

How could a team of talented individuals, after an eight-month investigation and in the face of cautionary criticism, produce a report that ended in people being fired, resigning, and facing reprimands—not to mention embarrassing two highly respected news organizations? Using the concepts of open and closed systems, interdependence, feedback, multiple causes/paths, and nonsummativity, develop your own "systems" explanation for this reporting disaster. You can do this in groups or as a class.

toward keeping on track. This emphasis on balance, some argue, draws attention to system stability rather than change. However, we have chosen systems theory as our theoretical framework because of its centrality in small group research and its focus on patterns and wholes. We hope the usefulness of the systems perspective is clear to you—it helps identify the individual components of the system, but it emphasizes that each part functions in relation to all the other parts of the system; what affects one part affects them all.

### CNN and *Time* as a System of Groups

APPLY NOW

The previous application example describes the rather complex system of groups that can make up the modern news organization. CNN, or the Cable News Network, together with *Time* produced *NewsStand: CNN & Time*. Both CNN and *Time* are owned by Time Warner. Using this information, and the information in the previous application example, construct your own diagram of the system of interlocking group subsystems. Then discuss the role of "extra-group" communication in this example. What went wrong? At which level? What could they have done differently? Is there a way to guarantee a valid, successful story all the time?

## RESOURCES FOR REVIEW AND DISCUSSION

SUMMARY

- A theory is a "map of reality" that helps us describe relationships, explain how phenomena operate, and make decisions about what to do.
- General systems theory is a useful framework for studying small groups because it reminds us that systems are complex, with all parts of the system being interdependent.
- All systems use inputs to engage in throughput processes and produce outputs. Feedback helps systems monitor their performance, which cannot be predicted by summing the individual performances of the components.
- All systems try to survive by adapting to changing conditions. Open systems freely exchange resources with their environments, but closed systems do not.
- Effective use of feedback allows systems to manage their complexity and sustain a more positive synergy than those that ignore important feedback.
- The bona fide group perspective focuses on naturally occurring groups, which are interdependent with their environments. Sometimes, a group's success is due more to what happens outside the group than within the group.

## EXERCISES

1. Bring to class a box of toothpicks and glue. Take out 12 toothpicks and use the glue to create some form out of the toothpicks. After you have finished, display your creation. Discuss all the creations and the concept of nonsummativity. Then move from discussing toothpicks to behaviors and from creations to small groups.

2. Select classmates to form one primary group: a family. Select parents, children, and any other members you want. Then select members of the class to be other individuals who may be involved in the family's life, such as a pastor, professor, and boss. With a ball of string, loosely connect all of these individuals to relevant individuals, and as you do so create a story about them. For instance, only one spouse may work and so is connected to the boss, the other spouse, and a parent. A child may be connected to only one parent, and so on. Then instruct the various individuals to role-play their parts by periodically pulling on the strings and requesting something of the individual. Use this activity to show the concept of interdependence.

3. Bring a large muffin to class. Use the muffin to discuss inputs, throughputs, and outputs. Make a list of the inputs for making the muffin. Discuss the kinds of throughputs necessary for the creation of the muffin, and then point out the output. Discuss how the environment may influence the muffin. After this discussion, compare the making of a muffin, as a relatively closed system, to the creation of a group, a relatively open system. How are they similar and how are they different?

## KEY TERMS • CONCEPTS

Bona Fide Group Perspective
Boundary Spanner
Closed System
Environment
Feedback
Inputs
Interdependence
Multiple Causes
Multiple Paths
Open System
Outputs
Synergy
System
Theory
Throughput Processes
Virtual Group

# Foundations of Small Group Communicating

PART TWO

# Foundations of Small Group Communicating

For groups to function effectively, they must create and sustain a solid foundation that supports members' efforts. Part Two focuses on this foundation, communication itself. As discussed in Chapters 1 and 2, communication is at the heart of group throughput processes, so your understanding of this process is essential. Chapter 3 presents basic communication principles you should understand to be an effective group member, whether communicating face-to-face or through an electronic medium. Chapter 4 focuses on the verbal and nonverbal behaviors that are key to conveying and interpreting messages in a small group.

CHAPTER 3

# Communication Principles for Group Members

## CHAPTER OUTLINE



## CHAPTER OBJECTIVES

**After reading this chapter you should be able to:**

1. Define *communication*.
2. List and explain the five major characteristics of communication.
3. Describe the difference between listening and hearing.
4. Describe the four listening preferences and explain their implications for small groups.
5. Describe paraphrasing as a technique for active listening.
6. Discuss the ways technologies are used in groups.

## Public Relations Club's Confusion

CASE 3.1

The Public Relations Club, an organization of communication and business students, meets monthly to network and to participate in seminars, open to all students that are addressed by local PR practitioners about current, interesting topics. PR Club has a small budget to cover all its activities, including giving token gifts (such as T-shirts) to the speakers who volunteer their time. The group's executive committee schedules and publicizes each month's speakers.

At one meeting Rhea suggested that they invite Robert Grimes, owner of a local PR firm and author of a new book about using social media in public relations work. Mr. Grimes was a nationally known speaker who commanded large fees for his seminars, so Rhea suggested paying him a $250 honorarium as a gesture of appreciation. Members agreed that Mr. Grimes's seminar would be worth the money but paying him would set a precedent for future speakers, which the group could not afford. Wade, chair of the executive committee, said, "I don't know how we would be able to afford that, although I agree that he's certainly worth the money." Rhea then said, "OK, that sounds good to me." The group went on to discuss other matters. At the next executive committee meeting, Sonya reported that publicity for Mr. Grimes's seminar was proceeding well, and the upcoming Sunday paper was planning a feature story on him and the seminar. Rhea thanked the group for agreeing to pay Mr. Grimes for his time. At that point, the meeting exploded into cries of "What? What do you mean, pay him? We didn't agree to do that!" Members had misunderstood each other and as a result, Rhea had obligated them to a $250 gift that would nearly wipe out their budget. The members felt they couldn't back out at this point, but it took them several meetings to get over their anger and start to trust each other again.

**Scenes like this occur every day in small groups and illustrate what can happen when people fail to understand each other. To function effectively as a team, members must work together to create mutual meaning and understanding. However, glitches can (and often do) occur as members attempt to do this. In our example Wade said, "He's certainly worth the money." He meant, "It would be great to pay him and all of our speakers—they do such a wonderful job—but there's no way our budget can handle it, so let's stick to T-shirts." Rhea heard his actual words: ". . . I agree that he's certainly worth the money," yet interpreted them to mean, "He is certainly worth the expense, so we'll figure out some way to pay him." She said, "OK," meaning, "Great, I'll tell him we'll make an exception in his case." Wade heard her, yet he *interpreted* her meaning as, "I see what you mean about the expense, and I agree with you." These collective failures in message interpretation and failure to check understanding between group members cost the group time, money, and energy. Unfortunately, this is not unusual within a small group. We know you can think of plenty of instances you have experienced in your own groups!**

Whether you have had a previous course in communication or not, this chapter will serve as a brief review of communication principles most relevant to small groups and help you improve your own contribution to your group's communication. Chapter 4 expands on these ideas to focus on verbal and nonverbal aspects of communication.

## Communication: What's That?

We use **communication** to refer to the transactional process in which people simultaneously create, interpret, and negotiate shared meaning through their interaction. There are five major characteristics to this seemingly simple definition.

### COMMUNICATION IS SYMBOLIC

Communication involves verbal and nonverbal messages that include words and messages, including gestures, sounds, and actions. All of these are symbolic.[1] A **symbol** is anything people use arbitrarily to represent something else: things, ideas, people, experiences, and so forth. There is no inherent or direct relationships between any symbol—such as a word—and what it represents. For instance, there's no natural reason we call something we sit in a *chair* instead of *pig* or *une chaise*. Even within a single language, the same food might be called *dinner, supper,* or *the evening meal* by different people. In addition, most of our symbols stand for concepts that have no tangible form, such as a *relationship, cohesiveness, love,* and *democracy*. Even the concept of *communication* holds no tangible form.

Symbols allow people to talk about ideas, things, and other people without those being present. In Case 3.1 the members can talk meaningfully about Robert Grimes, even though only Rhea had met him. Moreover, symbols can take a variety of forms. Words are the most common, but we also use numbers, pictographs (such as the international signs for pedestrian crossings and restrooms), Morse code, emoticons such as those used in e-mail to convey feelings or objects, and gestures like those we use for *OK*.

**GLOSSARY**

**Communication**
*The transactional process of simultaneously creating, interpreting, and negotiating shared meaning through interaction*

**Symbol**
*Anything that arbitrarily stands for something else*

Because symbols are arbitrary, *their meaning must be interpreted.* Two people can use a symbol to represent different concepts and therefore misinterpret each other without knowing it, as Rhea and Wade did. In addition, symbols are ambiguous and can mean many different things to people. Ninety-nine people died in a 1972 Eastern Airline crash due to the ambiguity of messages between air traffic controllers and the pilots.[2] The controllers were concerned about the plane's loss of altitude and asked the pilots, "How are things comin' along up there?" The pilots thought "things" referred to the landing gear and responded "okay" not realizing they were referring to the loss of altitude due to an inactive autopilot . . . seconds later they crashed. Misunderstandings and multiple interpretations are especially likely in small group communication, which makes it necessary to monitor the communication processes in our groups more thoughtfully than we normally do in our everyday conversations.

## COMMUNICATION IS PERSONAL

The symbolic nature of human communication renders meaning very personal. For example, when you say "I love you," do you mean the same thing as your boyfriend or girlfriend does? Even when two people agree on the dictionary definition of a word, they may disagree vehemently about what that word means to them. For instance, to your group an *excellent* group report may mean one that is free of typographical errors and turned in on time. To your teacher *excellent* may be reserved for a group report that not only is grammatically perfect but also shows considerable insight and creativity. You both are using the same word, but not meaning the same thing. This fact leads directly to the next principle of communication.

## COMMUNICATION IS A TRANSACTIONAL PROCESS

*Transactional* has two major meanings relevant to communication among members of a small group. First, communicating is a simultaneous, multidirectional process. That is, regardless of who is speaking at any given moment, *every* member is simultaneously sending verbal and nonverbal messages that every other member (including the speaker) could potentially receive and interpret. Older models of communication depicted it as a linear, back-and-forth process, like two people playing tennis. But this overly simplistic view fails to capture the fact that two people interacting are *simultaneously* engaged in sending, receiving, and interpreting verbal and nonverbal creating shared meaning. We attempt to contrast these views of the communication process in Figure 3.1. Moreover, adding additional people to the mix—as in small group communication—complicates the process even more! The implication is clear: To be most effective as a group member, you must be aware of actions from all members, even when you are speaking. For example, a speaker may notice from facial expressions that group members are reacting negatively to her suggestions and thus modify her ideas as she speaks.

Second, *transactional* implies that members *together* create mutual understanding for what words and concepts mean and nicely complements the interdependence between members. Individual meanings exist alongside meanings that are the result of mutually crafted understandings. Members participate together in

**FIGURE 3.1** Picturing communication as a transactional process

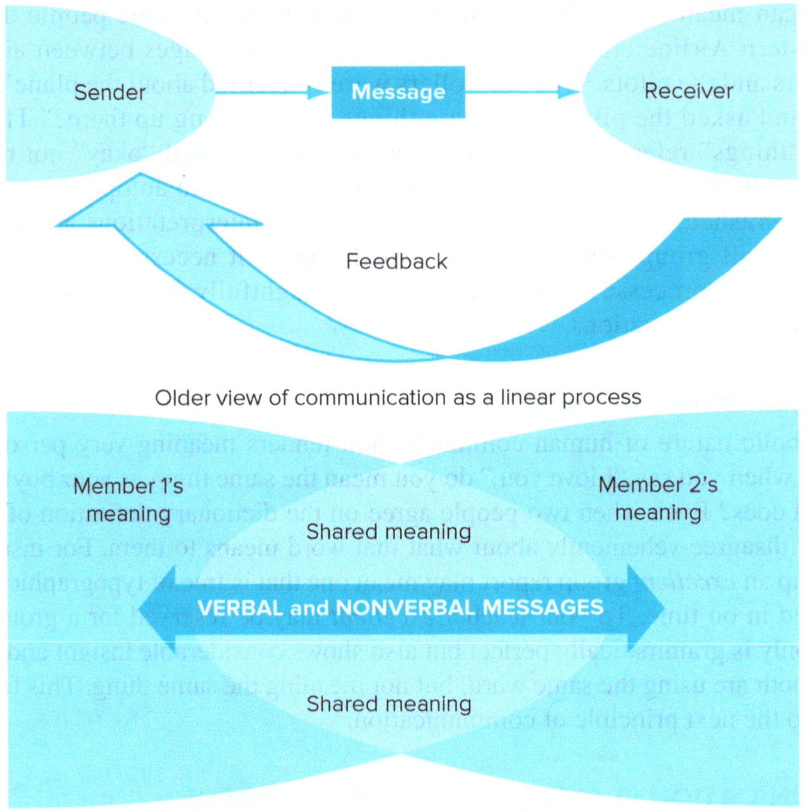


Communication as a transactional process

these creations and are also able to consciously observe these processes and help each other out.

For example, consider the following exchange between Rhea, Wade, and Sonya, another member of the PR Club group. Notice how Sonya, an alert member, helped prevent the misunderstanding from happening any further.

**Wade:** I don't know how we'll be able to afford something like that, though I agree that he's certainly worth the money.

**Rhea:** OK, that sounds good to me.

**Sonya:** Whoa, I'm confused! Rhea, *what* sounds good to you? That we *will* pay Mr. Grimes or that we *will not* because we can't afford it? I'm not sure you're both on the same page here. Which part of what Wade said are you responding to?

**Rhea:** Wade, I thought you said that you thought he was worth it, and we would make an exception in his case. Did I hear you wrong?

**Wade:** You heard me that I think he's worth it, and if we ever made an exception we'd do it for him, but I didn't mean that we *would* make an exception here—we just can't afford it.

**Rhea:** Oh, okay. I completely misunderstood what you mean. I'll tell him we can't pay him.

This didn't happen, but if it had, it would have ensured Rhea's, Wade's, and the rest of the group's mutual understanding of how they would handle Mr. Grimes's visit. Notice how well Sonya played both participant and observer to this group process. She carefully listened and participated in a transaction that helped everyone clarify Wade's meaning. Meanings are not so much *re*ceived intact from each person, but instead *con*ceived or created in context between persons.

## SHARED MEANING IS THE RESPONSIBILITY OF ALL MEMBERS

As can be seen in the previous exchange, shared meaning is the responsibility of *all* group members. In the case of the PR Club, Wade could have been clearer in his statement about Mr. Grimes being worth the money and Rhea could have tested her understanding of his message more directly. In their exchange, Sonya demonstrated her listening skills to keep everyone on the same page—shared meaning. Clarity and checking understanding are the responsibility of all members.

In fact, the last principle of the National Communication Association's Credo for Ethical Communication, discussed in Chapter 1 and displayed in Figure 1.2, speaks to this. All communicators need to accept responsibility for the short- and long-term consequences of their communication. The communication problems between Wade and Rhea in Case 3.1 resulted partly from how the messages were sent but were also never clarified by other group members.

Even though we have stressed the responsibility of all group members to help create shared meaning and mutual understanding, you must know one thing: Perfect understanding among group members is impossible. Because of all the communication characteristics we discussed earlier—that it is symbolic, personal, and transactional, perfect understanding cannot occur. Some degree of difference in meaning will always exist between two or more people interacting. Perfect understanding is unrealistic. In a group you need only communicate well enough to coordinate your behavior toward a common goal. When you can do this, you are communicating well enough for group success, even though you haven't achieved perfect understanding.

## COMMUNICATION INVOLVES CONTENT AND RELATIONSHIP DIMENSIONS

The **content dimension** of a message involves the message's ideas or the *what* of the message. When you listen to a teacher's lecture, the content of her or his messages is what you record in your notes. When you listen to a research report from a group member, you often attend to the ideas the member is summarizing for the group. The **relational dimension** of a message is *how* the message is expressed and what that implies about the relationship between the speaker and listener. Both dimensions help determine meaning.[3] For instance, the teacher's lecture can be given in a variety of ways. Does the teacher talk down to you as if you are a child who must be told

### GLOSSARY

**Content Dimension**

*The ideas or "what" of a message*

**Relational Dimension**

*The "how" of a message expressing the perceived relationship between communicators*

**Communication and the Public Relations Club**

APPLY NOW

Public Relations Club members share a common interest in understanding PR techniques and principles. However, as we saw, even groups composed of members with a common interest can encounter communication problems. Reflecting on the five characteristics of communication in small groups, consider the following:

1. Which symbols do you think were the most problematic for the group? Why?
2. What different forms did the symbols take in this case study?
3. Explain how there is no definite beginning and ending to their story.
4. How was the communication among the members transactional?
5. How did the group members work together to create the misunderstanding?
6. Change the script of the meeting, and show how the members together could have produced a better outcome.
7. List what you think are the content issues and then list what you believe are the relational issues expressed in how the messages may have been expressed.
8. How can the conflict between Wade and Rhea be seen transactionally, or as one with no clear cause but as mutually created by both of them?

what to think, or does the teacher share the information with you as if you are someone with your own valid experiences and knowledge? You usually do not write this dimension in your notes, yet you may talk about it to your friends during and after a lecture: "I really like how Professor Jones treats us like we have something to say, too," or "I am insulted by the way Professor Jones treats us like we are children with no opinions worth listening to!" These same messages are processed in small groups as members offer how it is they see themselves in relation to each other through their messages. We often focus more explicitly on the content of messages; however, the relational aspects of messages are always present and just as integral to the communication dynamics of groups. Both verbal and nonverbal behaviors convey relational messages, as we will discuss in Chapter 4.

We cannot stress enough how important it is to pay attention to the relational elements of messages. As we noted in previous chapters, Google found this out in their search for the ingredients to a perfect team.[4] Ethical communicators, according to the NCA's credo, strive to understand and respect other communicators before evaluating and responding to their messages and also work to promote a climate of caring and understanding. In small groups they avoid condemning or belittling others because that creates a toxic atmosphere preventing all members from doing their best work on behalf of the group. As group members you have a responsibility to consider *how* you talk to each other.

Coordinating the efforts of group members in a functioning system is more dependent on good listening than on good speaking skills, although we often concentrate on speaking. We turn now to a discussion of listening and its importance in small group communication.

## Listening: Receiving, Interpreting, and Responding to Messages from Other Group Members

If a small group is to operate effectively, members must understand each other. Listening well helps this process. A survey reported in Monster.com noted that 73 percent of business leaders rated listening as an extremely important skill businesses look for in new hires.[5] Both members and leaders of small groups must be good listeners. Members perceived as poor listeners won't be chosen as group leaders, and leaders usually are perceived as good listeners.[6]

### LISTENING DEFINED

**Listening** is a four-step process that begins with perceiving a message, then interpreting it, deciding what it means, and finally responding to it.[7] *Listening* is not the same thing as *hearing*. Hearing is the physical process of receiving sound waves, but listening is an active process that also includes paying attention to and interpreting what is heard.

Most people do not listen well. The same survey reported in Monster.com noted that those same business people thought only 19 percent of high school graduates have good listening skills.[8]

Effective listening requires that the listener hear what the speaker said, interpret it accurately, and respond appropriately. Usually, hearing what the speaker said presents little problem. Group members are accustomed to asking a member to repeat a statement they weren't able to hear. However, the interpretation and response steps can be tricky because of the symbolic nature of communication. Different people mean different things with the same words and actions. Major factors that influence what words and actions mean to us include our culture, gender, age, sexual orientation, learning style, and personalities. We take a closer look at such diversity in small group interaction in Chapter 6. In addition, the relational dimension of group messages helps members understand how they see themselves in relationship to each other. This requires that members listen "between the lines" for this information, because it often is not directly stated but found in *how* (e.g., tone) the message is expressed. When members of the PR Club expressed their displeasure with Rhea, they did so with raised voices and harsh tones, something that would have been hard for Rhea to misinterpret.

You can become a more competent listener in small groups. In the next sections we describe four listening preferences, list several bad listening habits, and provide suggestions to improve your listening behavior.

**GLOSSARY**

**Listening**

*A complex process involving perceiving, interpreting, and responding to messages*

## LISTENING PREFERENCES

Over time and in a multitude of conversations, we all develop listening preferences. When do you enjoy listening? When is listening difficult for you? There are four general listening preferences: people-, action-, content-, and time-oriented.[9]

Each preference has its advantages and disadvantages. Being an effective group member means identifying your own preference and those of the other members. It may mean shifting your preference to meet the needs of the group.

**People-oriented listeners** focus on how their listening behaviors affect relationships. These are the members others go to when they want someone to listen. They are attentive and nonjudgmental. Their listening behaviors may include the use of *we* more often than *I*, and they incorporate emotional appeals into their discussions. For instance, they might be heard telling a human-interest story to calm members who are upset. Showing concern for others is important, but people-oriented listeners can attend too much to others' moods and get distracted from the group's task.

The **action-oriented listener** focuses on the job at hand. Such listeners help the group stay on task by paying attention to the details and giving feedback about the goal and how the group may achieve it. They enjoy listening if material is presented in an

**GLOSSARY**

**People-Oriented Listener**
*A listener who is concerned about how her or his listening behaviors affect relationships*

**Action-Oriented Listener**
*A listener who is concerned about how her or his listening behaviors contribute to the task at hand*

### The Public Relations Club and Listening

APPLY NOW

Earlier you met two members of the Public Relations Club's executive committee: Wade and Rhea. Now let's meet three other members: Sonya, Bob, and Eric. Each of these members has his or her own listening preferences, some of which may be seen in the case study. Rhea is a people-oriented listener, and Wade is an action- and content-oriented listener. Sonya is a content-oriented listener, Bob is a time-oriented listener, and Eric avoids listening situations but is required to show up and vote. Wade and Rhea do not get along at most meetings, often arguing over who should be supported by the group. Wade thinks that Rhea gets too upset when others are upset, and Rhea thinks that Wade is overly critical. Sonya is close friends with Eric, who often votes with Sonya. Bob contributes to the group only when he has something worthwhile to say and does so in a very precise fashion. He gets along well with Rhea and Sonya.

Imagine you are a community member who is interested in bringing Dr. Jessica McGehee, a leading authority on organizational branding, to the attention of the group. You would really like the group to sponsor a seminar with Dr. McGehee. You also know the group is low on funds due to the most recent expenditures, but Dr. McGehee will be in town and will be available. You know a generic presentation to the group will not work, so you decide to tailor your presentation to the listening preferences of the group.

1. Whom would you select as the target of your presentation, and why?
2. What specific strategies would you use in your presentation to appeal to those you believe you need to convince most?

organized fashion. However, sometimes these listeners may appear overly critical, tune out when the discussion seems aimless, and interrupt if the discussion gets off track.

The **content-oriented listener** appreciates highly credible sources and enjoys analyzing what she or he hears. These listeners dissect information and can show a group the many sides to an issue. However, they can seem overly critical and intimidating. In addition, their listening preference slows the group's problem solving because they like to spend considerable time analyzing information. They also minimize nontechnical information such as anecdotes and devalue information from unknown sources.

The **time-oriented listener** values time, sets meeting times, reminds members of their time constraints, and frowns on wordy discussions. Such members discourage discussion as the time nears for the meeting to end and grow impatient with the more creative, spontaneous activities in groups.

No preference is the best. Each one has positive and negative tendencies, summarized in Table 3.1. Use them productively and curtail the negative characteristics of each one. Do this by knowing your own and the others' preferences and encouraging the productive use of each preference.

Regardless of your listening preferences, there are several habits of poor listeners that we all have to guard against. These are listed and briefly described in Table 3.2. The more you work to overcome these bad habits, the better a listener you will be, no matter your listening preference.

## LISTENING ACTIVELY

One way to overcome poor listening habits is to listen actively. Listening is active, not passive, behavior. When you pay close attention in an effort to understand what a speaker means, your heart speeds up as your metabolic rate rises, because your whole self is paying attention.

A good test for **active listening** is to paraphrase (put in your own words) what you think the other person meant. Merely repeating another's words, like a parrot, does not demonstrate that you understood, because paraphrasing requires the listener to process the information cognitively. When you paraphrase what you thought the speaker said or the relational message you inferred from how it was expressed, you give the speaker a basis for deciding whether you understood the original message adequately or whether you missed or distorted parts of it. The original speaker, after hearing the paraphrase, should accept it if it is accurate or correct the parts that were distorted or omitted, then ask you to try paraphrasing again. Only when the original speaker is completely satisfied that you have understood adequately should you proceed to agree, disagree, elaborate, or change topics. Here is a bit of dialogue that illustrates active listening between two group members discussing medical insurance:

**Karla:** Medical costs are incredibly high. On average it costs about $4,400 per day in the hospital. No wonder 20 percent of nonelderly citizens lack hospital insurance! Too many people are making too much money off the illnesses of others. We've gotta stop that!

**Jeannie:** You're saying that the reason so many people lack hospital insurance is that hospital costs are high, and they are so high because a lot of people are paid too much in the health care business. Is that right?

### GLOSSARY

**Content-Oriented Listener**

*A listener who prefers information from perceived credible sources and is drawn to analyzing the information she or he hears*

**Time-Oriented Listener**

*A listener who values time and is focused on efficient discussion*

**Active Listening**

*Listening first to understand another's message before critically judging the message*

**TABLE 3.1 Listing Preferences**

| | |
|---|---|
| **PEOPLE-ORIENTED LISTENERS** | |
| Advantages: | Focus on relationships.<br>Show concern for others.<br>Are inclusive and nonjudgmental. |
| Disadvantage: | Can become distracted by others' moods. |
| Example: | "How would you feel if we went ahead with that option?" |
| **ACTION-ORIENTED LISTENERS** | |
| Advantages: | Focus on the job.<br>Help the group stay on task.<br>Help the group stay organized. |
| Disadvantage: | May sacrifice relationships in favor of task. |
| Example: | "I know you're upset, but we have a lot of work to do so we'd better get down to business." |
| **CONTENT-ORIENTED LISTENERS** | |
| Advantages: | Help the group analyze information.<br>Look at issues from many sides. |
| Disadvantages: | Seem overly critical.<br>Dismiss anecdotal or nonexpert information. |
| Example: | "We aren't ready to decide yet because we haven't really heard every side of the issue." |
| **TIME-ORIENTED LISTENERS** | |
| Advantages: | Help the group stick to schedule.<br>Discourage rambling discussions. |
| Disadvantage: | May stifle creativity by expressing impatience with spontaneous discussion. |
| Example: | "Let's make up a schedule so we know we can get done by our deadline." |

[Jeannie attempts to check whether she understands what Karla said by paraphrasing so as to clarify Karla's reasoning.]

**Karla:** Well, basically, but I really don't mean people don't have insurance because the hospital costs so much, but because they can't afford it. That may be partly because it costs a lot for the insurance—like $600 a month for a young couple with no kids—and partly because the insurance companies have to pay such high hospital and other

**TABLE 3.2 Habits of Poor Listeners**

| |
|---|
| **PSEUDOLISTENING**<br>Pretending to listen while thinking about something else or while daydreaming. |
| **SILENT ARGUING**<br>Mentally rehearsing objections to the speaker's idea without first understanding what the speaker meant. |
| **ASSUMING MEANING**<br>Interpreting the speaker's behavior by using the cultural rules appropriate for the listener. |
| **FOCUSING ON IRRELEVANCIES**<br>Becoming distracted from a speaker's message by unimportant details such as dress, accent, physical appearance, or things in the environment. |
| **SIDETRACKING**<br>Changing the topic because they weren't paying attention to the speaker; not connecting remarks to statements of the previous speaker. |
| **DEFENSIVE RESPONDING**<br>Failing to listen or failing to try to understand what a speaker is saying because they feel psychologically threatened by something the speaker said or did; responding with "chips on their shoulders." |

medical bills. [Karla corrects the paraphrase and clarifies her own reasoning.]

**Jeannie:** Now let's see if I understand your thinking: 20 percent of nonelderly citizens lack hospital insurance because they feel they can't afford it. Part of the reason they can't afford it is that high medical costs have made premiums very high, like $600 a month for a young couple. And a lot of people are making more money than you think they should out of the illnesses of others. [Jeannie's second attempt at paraphrasing Karla's statements.]

**Karla:** Right. [Karla confirms the second paraphrase as accurate.]

**Jeannie:** I partly agree and partly disagree. I think . . . [The paraphrase accepted, Jeannie now begins to explain her position on the issue about why so many people lack hospital insurance.]

Active listeners confirm their understanding *before* they state evaluations. Then, confident of what the speaker meant, active listeners evaluate what they have understood.

One effect of active listening is that the discussion slows down. Most of us are our own best listeners—we like to talk and, given half a chance, we will. We may become impatient, not taking time to paraphrase even when we should. You should listen

© Tetra Images/Getty Images RF

actively all the time but paraphrase only part of the time—when a controversial issue is being discussed, when you can see some possibility that the speaker has a different meaning from what you think, when you are confused by what the speaker has said, and when there has been a lot of topic switching or misunderstanding.

### Poor Listening Habits and Misunderstandings

**APPLY NOW**

Reconstruct the PR Club meeting. Your agenda item is the discussion of whether to sponsor a seminar featuring Mr. Grimes, a prominent local leader. Get together with six other members of the class to role-play group members. Before your discussion, hand out envelopes to each member. Four of the envelopes will contain a description of one poor listening habit (pseudolistening, silent arguing, assuming meaning, focusing on irrelevancies, or sidetracking). The other three envelopes will instruct the member to practice active, focused listening. Allow yourselves to role-play the meeting for about 25 minutes. Ask your classmates to watch the meeting and take notes on the listening behaviors. After the meeting, discuss how the poor habits were displayed and what their impact was on the discussion.

1. Were any behaviors particularly destructive? How so?
2. How well were the members practicing active, focused listening, and did they reduce the effects of the poor habits? How typical are some of these poor habits?
3. How was the role-play of the meeting different from a real meeting?

## Communication Principles and Technology

Up to this point, we have been talking about communication principles as if groups meet face-to-face, with all members in the same room. However, as we said in Chapters 1 and 2, most groups use various technologies to help them get their work done, and some groups may meet only virtually. With technology, members can exchange messages during meetings or be in different places but still "talk" to each other simultaneously or when it's convenient. Such exchanges, involving computers to interact with fellow group members during or between group meetings, are called **computer-mediated communication (CMC)**. CMC takes many forms: e-mail, chat room discussions, electronic bulletin boards, listservs, net conferencing (audio-, video-, or computer conferencing), texting, and tweeting to name a few. Used appropriately, CMC enhances a group's work, saves an organization time and money, and can replace some routine meetings. Groups communicating via technology can be just as effective and have just as strong a belief in their ability to succeed as face-to-face groups, particularly after they become comfortable with the technology.[10]

### HOW GROUPS USE TECHNOLOGY

Chapter 1 described the Art for Haiti planning committee that organized an art show to benefit survivors of the earthquake in Haiti. Initially, the group formed when the minister of the church called several people to see if they would be interested in planning the art show. Then she e-mailed everyone to confirm their interest and invited them to participate in a Doodle poll to find the best date and time to meet. One member was late to that first meeting, so another member texted her to find out if she was coming. After the meeting, when members had formulated their plan for the art show and had assigned themselves tasks, they kept in touch via e-mail to let everyone know what progress they had made and to ask for advice. For example, the artist designing the posters sent out a preliminary design and asked for feedback before she had the posters printed. All the technologies used in this example—*telephone, e-mail, texting*—are readily available and easy to use.

Our students use these and more sophisticated technologies to work on group assignments. One such group created virtual space using Dropbox to store their group paper. As individuals completed sections and uploaded them into the Dropbox space, the group's strongest writer edited the paper, made sure the writing style was grammatically correct and consistent throughout, and that transitions between sections were smooth. All members were able to see what she had changed and made sure her edits didn't misstate something. Another group set up a **wiki** through Blackboard, the university's online course management system, to accomplish the same thing. Like Dropbox, wiki software allows multiple users to work on a single document and tracks the changes each one makes. Group members can work on a single document or project from their individual locations at times that are convenient, which makes group work more efficient.

These days, many students and business professionals carry laptops or tablets to meetings. Often, one member may want to check a fact, locate an address, or verify a reference. With ready wifi access to the Internet, this is easy to do, in the moment. Student groups in a photojournalism course planned the showcase of their work making sure it did not clash with any university event. They had easy Internet access through their university portals to the university calendar to check on those dates.

Increasingly, groups use video- and audioconferencing technology to help save time and money. Audioconferences, which allow members to talk with one another by telephone,

GLOSSARY

**Computer-Mediated Communication (CMC)**

*Any interaction between group members via computer technology*

**Wiki**

*Software that allows multiple users to access and work on a single document from their individual computers*

have been used for years. During a summer search for a new department administrative assistant, Kathy's committee was trained by human resources and held its meetings using Google Hangouts because committee members were in different cities at the time. Faculty and staff search committees routinely interview applicants via Skype, which saves considerable money and allows search committee members to interact with a job applicant in a more realistic way than just by telephone. All that is needed for a Skype interview is a computer or tablet and a camera—and most computers and tablets now have these built in.

Whether group communication is face-to-face or mediated, it is still symbolic, personal, transactional, involves content and relationship dimensions, and relies on all group members for accuracy and effectiveness. For instance, international virtual group member report complicated language challenges with each other unique to these kinds of groups.[11] An American's polite message of "Thank you in advance," can come across as rather trite to a group member in Tel Aviv.[12] In addition, face-to-face communication rules about listening, treating one another with respect, and behaving ethically apply equally to CMC. Being polite is particularly important. San Bolkan and Jennifer Homgren found that instructors who received e-mail messages from students liked them more, and were more motivated to help them, when the students were polite.[13] Using polite, appropriate computer etiquette and being ethical will likely get you higher cooperation from fellow group members.

In the next chapter, we expand on some of the specific differences between CMC and face-to-face communication as we explore how verbal and nonverbal factors affect group communication.

### Helping a Group with Schedule Challenges

APPLY NOW

Your class project group is facing serious schedule challenges. You have one month to complete a group report and present it to your class, but there is literally no way all five of you can meet at the same time. Wally commutes; he lives 90 miles away and comes to campus only on Tuesdays and Thursdays, when your class meets. Sandy and Raj work afternoons and evenings, but are free on weekends. As soon as your class ends at 3 P.M., they each rush off to their jobs, from 4 to midnight. Esther can meet during the week, but as an observant Orthodox Jew, she cannot leave home or do class work from sundown Friday to sundown Saturday. You are free during the week, but have a weekend job at a juvenile shelter where you have to stay all weekend. The only way you can get your project finished is by using technology. All of you have Facebook pages; four of you have computer access at home and one of you accesses the Internet from the library; your class has a Blackboard site where your teacher can set up a wiki for you, or you can set up Dropbox to work on documents collaboratively; all of you have cell phones.

1. How are you going to use what you have to get to know one another and get your task completed?
2. What, exactly, will you suggest to your fellow group members about how you can proceed?

## RESOURCES FOR REVIEW AND DISCUSSION

### SUMMARY

- Communication is the transactional process in which people simultaneously create, interpret, and negotiate shared meaning through their interaction.
- Symbols, including words, are arbitrary, which makes perfect understanding impossible and means that effective communication among members is the responsibility of every member.
- Listening and hearing are not the same. Each of the four listening preferences—people, content, action, and time—have strengths, weaknesses, and implications for small groups.
- Active listening by paraphrasing helps members understand one another more clearly.
- Most groups use various technologies to help them get their work done. These range from simple ones (telephones, texting, and e-mail) to more sophisticated ones that allow multiple members to work on the same document from different locations or to participate in audio and video conferencing.
- Face-to-face communication rules about listening, treating one another with respect, and behaving ethically apply equally to computer-mediated communication, particularly rules for politeness.

### EXERCISES

1. Recall three recent conversations you have had. (If you are taking part in a major project, think about three recent conversations in your group meetings.) For each conversation, write down who participated, what you talked about, how well you listened (on a scale of 1 [not well at all] to 10 [very well]) and what some of the reasons were for your good or poor listening (e.g., boring topic, time of day, monotone delivery, preoccupation with something else). During a class discussion, look for factors common to good and poor listening.
2. This exercise is designed to help you apply and practice active listening. Divide into groups of five or six members. Select a controversial topic and practice active listening as you discuss the topic. Remember that paraphrasing is not simply restating the previous speaker's words. Each group should use the following rules:

   *a.* A discussant may not have the floor or add anything to the conversation until she or he paraphrases what the previous speaker said to that speaker's satisfaction.

   *b.* If the paraphrase is not accepted, the discussant may try again until the speaker accepts the paraphrase.

   *c.* One member of the group should keep track of the number of times paraphrases were accepted or rejected. Each attempt should be recorded.

   After the activity, discuss the difficulties encountered in active listening. Look for the benefits of paraphrasing and the problems that may be encountered. Discuss why it may be so hard for group members to understand others before contributing to the discussion.

### KEY TERMS • CONCEPTS

Action-Oriented Listener
Active Listening
Communication
Computer-Mediated Communication (CMC)
Content Dimension
Content-Oriented Listener
Listening
People-Oriented Listener
Relational Dimension
Symbol
Time-Oriented Listener
Wiki

CHAPTER

4

# Using Verbal and Nonverbal Messages in a Group

## CHAPTER OUTLINE



## CHAPTER OBJECTIVES

**After reading this chapter you should be able to:**

1. Define *message* and explain how verbal and nonverbal actions are interpreted holistically by group members.
2. Explain four ways to use language for maximum effectiveness in small groups.
3. Describe the principles and functions of nonverbal communication.
4. Discuss the significance of the major categories of nonverbal communication to small groups.
5. Discuss how computer-mediated communication compares to face-to-face communication in groups.

### The Convocation Speaker Committee

CASE 4.1

The Convocation Speaker Committee, with members Emma, Maria, Marshall, Jayden, and Jamal, is responsible for selecting a speaker for their university's Freshman Convocation Welcome to kick off the school year in August. Members must select a speaker who represents the university's mission, plan for several events surrounding the talk (e.g., meeting with students, community members, and administrators, and participating in a press conference with media), and stay within their budget. This prestigious, hand-picked committee is appointed each September to plan the following August's convocation events. Committee members have worked all fall to identify their top choices, and Emma has been an active, valued member of the committee—but she will spend spring semester in a study away program to Barcelona, Spain, to enhance her Spanish minor. The entire committee wanted to keep Emma on board. Committee members had a face-to-face meeting to brainstorm plans before Emma left. They also kept in touch regularly via e-mail (for longer messages), text (for short messages), and Skyped every couple of weeks for issues they needed to talk through. Meeting minutes and other written plans were posted in the group's Dropbox.

At one Skype meeting, when the group was discussing how to arrange for the press conference and contact local media, Emma said, "I'm not going to be a lot of help with that from Spain because I don't have the contacts, and my Internet is not always reliable." Marshall responded with, "Yeah, sure, great excuse! You're just a lazy butt!" All committee members—including Emma—laughed and went on to talk about the press conference.

**At first glance, "You're just a lazy butt" sounds like an insult, but clearly, none of the members took it that way. How did they know that Marshall was teasing, and that the *last* thing he meant was that Emma wasn't pulling her weight? Something else is going on here, and that something else involves all the elements that come together in communication to determine what something means: not just the words, but the context, the relationships, and most of all, the nonverbal behavior that accompanies the words. Emma and the others got the *intended* message: we like you, Emma, and we are glad you're part of our group.**

GLOSSARY

**Message**

*Sounds, words, and actions that are interpreted as a whole by group members*

**Bypassing**

*Occurs when group members think they have the same meaning for a word or phrase but in actuality do not*

A **message** is any sound, word, or action that is interpreted *as a whole* by someone else.[1] In human communication—including small groups—verbal and nonverbal behaviors are indivisible. They operate *together* to create a message and help us interpret what that message means. All communicative acts are expressed via multiple verbal and nonverbal channels, which together create meaning. Think of an orchestra.[2] No single note conveyed by one instrument constitutes a symphony. Notes played together via a multitude of instruments create a symphony. Meaning in the music is found both in the combination of notes and the way they are played. When you document and analyze your group's communication (symphony), you are in fact scoring *both* the notes (words) *and* how they are played (nonverbals).

In this chapter, we extend the discussion about communication principles we introduced in Chapter 3. We focus on how both words and nonverbal behaviors contribute to what something means, and we conclude with a discussion of how verbal and nonverbal elements differ in face-to-face and computer-mediated contexts.

## Verbal Communication in Small Groups

We have noted several times that verbal and nonverbal messages work together to create meaning among people. However, studying verbal and nonverbal messages together can get complicated. To make them easier for you to understand, we discuss them separately. We start with verbal communication by focusing on the key characteristics of language and providing suggestions so you can use language appropriately in your groups. These suggestions are summarized in Table 4.1.

### ADJUST TO THE SYMBOLIC NATURE OF LANGUAGE

You know that words are symbols, but this fact carries important implications for communicating effectively in groups. Because words are symbols, they do not have meanings in and of themselves. Thus, good listeners ask, "What does the speaker mean?" rather than, "What do those words mean?" or "What would I mean if I said that?" Be on guard against **bypassing,** in which two or more people have different meanings for a word but do not realize it. Bypassing can lead either to a false agreement or to the perception that a disagreement exists when it really doesn't. For example, the meaning of *patriotism* has become complicated for many Americans. Imagine yourself in a small group class trying to figure out what your group's community service task is going to be for the semester. Members begin to brainstorm ideas about how they can show their patriotism in their local community. Everyone appears eager to show their patriotism, so they decide that *patriotism* will be their theme. During a subsequent meeting, while the group begins to figure out what to do specifically, Lucinda suggests they organize a peace rally. Other members immediately challenge the idea by claiming it is not right to oppose our country's military actions while we still are sending troops abroad. In addition, they become angry with Lucinda because they thought they had all decided to do a patriotic-theme project. This group bypassed on the meaning of *patriotic,* which led to a false agreement that affected a future meeting.

**TABLE 4.1 Use Language Appropriately to Help Your Group**

**ADJUST TO THE SYMBOLIC NATURE OF LANGUAGE**
- Guard against bypassing.
- Be as concrete and precise as possible.
- Give specific examples of what you mean when you have to use an abstract term.
- Quantify when possible.

**ORGANIZE YOUR REMARKS AND THE GROUP'S DISCUSSION**
- Relate your statement to the preceding statement.
- Make one point at a time.
- State your case directly and concisely.
- Keep yourself and other members on topic.

**BE SENSITIVE TO THE EMOTIONS OF OTHERS**
- Recognize trigger words that may trigger strong emotional reactions in others.
- Substitute neutral words for potential trigger words.
- Never name-call.

**FOLLOW THE RULES OF THE GROUP**
- Code-switch appropriately: Use the language, terminology, jargon, and rules of the group.
- In a professional, business, or educational group, use standard sentence structure, vocabulary, and correct grammar.

### When to Code Switch and When Not To?

ETHICAL DILEMMA

We have suggested that group members adapt to the different rules for communication, or code switch, when the context of the social system changes. Competent communicators are aware that different groups use different rules of communicating and are able to change to meet the expectations and obligations of those different groups. However, the various ways we use language to communicate is highly personal and often resistant to change.

1. When you move from group to group, how easily do you adopt the rules of communicating in that group?
2. Are there times when your personal way of communicating should not be given up?
3. Are there appropriate ways of blending both your own personal style and that of the group?
4. Is adapting to the rules of communicating in a particular group a violation of personal language use?

Many words, especially abstract ones, will be interpreted differently by different people. The most concrete words refer to one and only one thing: *Dr. Galanes' desk, star Beyonce,* or *golden retriever number PD736251.* However, abstract words and phrases such as *successful, productive, spiritual, democracy,* and *love* are highly ambiguous and likely to be understood quite differently by different group members.

Using abstract words is OK; in fact, having a meaningful discussion without them would be impossible. Many of the ideas we discuss in groups include fairly abstract words such as *consensus, criteria, leadership, trust, success,* and *climate.* Even so, you can make your remarks more specific and thus clearer. First, speak as concretely as possible to express what you mean. Don't use jargon to show off. For example, in a group of members with mixed computer literacy and experience, not everyone may know that *shoot-ém-up* refers to control of a character or vehicle to shoot enemies and that *reblog* is used on Tumblr to refer to reposting someone else's post.

Second, whenever you use a highly abstract term that may be problematic, give concrete examples of what you mean—for instance, "He was a really controlling chair [abstract concept]. He decided, by himself, when the group would meet, what would and would not be on the agenda, who could and could not speak at the meetings, and what the committee should recommend to the president of the fraternity [concrete examples of the abstract idea of *controlling*]."

Third, define highly abstract terms by using synonyms or descriptive terms or by explaining an operation the term refers to. Thus, you might define *drunk driving* as "having a level of .08 percent alcohol in the blood as measured immediately after driving by a Breathalyzer," which is the Driving While Intoxicated (DWI) definition used in many states. This definition combines both a procedure (i.e., measured by a Breathalyzer) and precise quantification for the term (i.e., .08 percent alcohol in the blood).

Fourth, quantify when possible. Frequently, groups use relative terms for comparisons when precise quantification is possible. For instance, instead of saying, "The chances of developing melanoma are *higher* [a relative term] if you visit a tanning bed once a month than if you don't," you can state quite precisely that you increase your chances of developing melanoma 45 to 55 percent if you visit a tanning bed once a month.

Up to this point, we have focused on what the speaker can do to make communication clear, but remember from the previous chapter that communication is transactional and all members are responsible for their communication. As a listener, ask speakers who use highly abstract language to quantify, give examples, or define their terms with less abstract language: "Sam, when you say that you want us to pick an 'interesting' topic for our debate, I'm not sure what you mean by 'interesting.' Could you give me an example or two of what would be interesting to you?" This will help you interpret the speaker's meaning more accurately.

### ORGANIZE REMARKS

Frequently, group discussions jump almost aimlessly from topic to topic, with no one responding to prior comments. This makes it hard to tell exactly what issue or question a speaker is addressing, or even what the point is of some remarks. Good organization can do a lot to overcome these communication challenges.

Consider the following discussion by a group of students planning publicity for an upcoming career day seminar:

**Lori:** OK, the seminar is planned, so any ideas on where to go from here?

**Deidre:** We forgot to include a session on portfolios.

**Tony:** One of the things we could do is send a memo to all the people in the dorms. That worked well last time.

**Chris:** I know someone who would do a great job with portfolios, and I'll be glad to call her.

**Kevin:** I think a memo is a really tacky idea, and we ought to do something more professional.

**Lori:** I don't like memos either. I'd be happy if we didn't do one.

It's hard to tell from that discussion whether Lori's initial question is being addressed, what each member means by their comments, and how they are specifically playing off of each other's ideas. Let's help the individuals organize their remarks so the discussion is more organized as a *group* process:

**Lori:** OK, the seminar has been planned, so now it's time to start working on publicity. What ideas do you have for how we could promote the career day seminar? [Lori's question to the group is more focused than before. We discuss the importance of forming appropriate focusing questions later in the chapter.]

**Deidre:** Lori, could we postpone our discussion of publicity? I'd like to talk first about something we overlooked in the planning. We forgot to schedule a portfolio session. [First, Deidre responds directly to Lori and Lori's question before suggesting a different initial topic.]

**Lori:** That's a good idea, Deidre. OK, everyone, let's spend time making sure the plans are finalized before we talk about publicity. What did you mean by a portfolio session? [Direct response to Deidre, acknowledgment of the legitimacy of her request to postpone discussion of publicity and request for clarification.]

**Deidre:** That was the session where someone showed us how to put together a public relations portfolio so that when we apply for jobs we'll be able to show people what kinds of assignments we've completed. It's like a résumé with specific examples of your work. [Direct clarification response from Deidre.]

**Lori:** You're right; we need that. Big oversight. Glad you thought of it. [Affirming Deidre's good thinking on behalf of the group's project.]

**Tony:** One thing we could do is send a memo to all the people who live in the dorms to let them know about the seminar. [This remark seems

**GLOSSARY**

**Emotive Words**
*Words that trigger strong emotional responses*

to be about publicity and does not appear to respond directly to the portfolio topic.]

**Chris:** That might be a good idea, Tony, but I'm not sure we're ready to go on to that yet. Were we finished with the portfolio session planning? [Chris doesn't ignore Tony or put him down, but he does help the group keep focused on the topic, and he makes it a group issue by using *we*.]

**Tony:** Sorry! I thought we were ready to move on. What do we need to do yet with portfolios? [Apology and direct acknowledgment of the topic under discussion.]

**Chris:** Well, for one thing, we need to figure out who would be a good person to handle that session. [Direct response to Tony, moves the discussion forward.]

**Kevin:** I know someone at Walker, Beard, and Korma Public Relations. I'll call and see if she's available, and, if she isn't, maybe she can suggest somebody else. [Direct response to Chris.]

**Lori:** OK, Kevin, do I understand you right? You'll take care of getting someone to handle the portfolio session and let us know who that is by next week? [Lori has detected an ambiguity in Kevin's earlier remark ("maybe she can suggest somebody else"), so she helps him clarify.]

**Kevin:** Yes. [Direct answer clears up the ambiguity.]

**Lori:** OK, Kevin will find someone to handle the portfolio sessions. Now, are we ready to turn to publicity? [Group members nod.] That's great. What ideas do we have for publicizing career day?

In the second version each comment begins with acknowledgment of the prior speaker, often using the other member's name. No one switches topics abruptly. Statements are right to the point. In almost all cases, the speaker stays with one point. Notice, too, that this discussion takes longer—members do not assume they understand but work to make the connections between speakers and topics explicit. Specific suggestions are included in Table 4.1.

## BE SENSITIVE TO THE FEELINGS OF OTHERS

**Emotive words** are terms that ignite strong feelings, trigger words that spark almost instantaneous emotional responses that interfere with good listening. The example in the Ethical Dilemma box illustrates such a trigger word. Among the worst trigger words are sexist terms and racial epithets (such as *raghead, feminazi,* or *faggot*). Your linguistic choices matter to your group because what you say to each other and how you convey those messages create your group's climate. Are you creating the kind of climate you want? The most significant element of a successful team, you will remember, is whether or not members feel they can take interpersonal risks.[3] Members can destroy this kind of safety with the thoughtless use of emotive words.

© Image Source RF

### What Do You Do When Emotive Words Are Offensive?

ETHICAL DILEMMA

Two African American members of your group refer to each other as "nigga" when they greet each other at the beginning of group meetings.[4] You and one other member find the use of the term highly offensive and do not believe any person, no matter her or his color, should use the term. One other member really does not care and does not see the point in making a big deal out of it.

This racial epithet is a highly emotive trigger word in the American culture, and people weigh in with all sorts of opinions on its use.

1. As a group what do you do? How would you discuss this issue?
2. When do the references in personal member greetings become an issue for a group?
3. What new rules might this group create to allow for emotive words yet avoid the consequences of their use?

Suppose someone said to you, "He's just a failed politician, not a scientist, and he's grandstanding as he looks for a new platform. What could he know about global warming?" You could paraphrase as follows: "So, in other words, you think that the opinions of a nonscientist are not valid on scientific issues such as global warming, and you mistrust his motives?" This helps defuse the trigger words (*failed politician, grandstanding*) so the group can focus on the merits of the message itself. It also provides the speaker an opportunity to clarify if you have misunderstood.

### How Do You Know When Someone's Teasing?

APPLY NOW

In reply to Emma's comment about not being able to help much from Spain with the press contacts for the convocation, Marshall said, "Yeah, sure, great excuse! You're just a lazy butt!" Everyone, including Emma, recognized this as teasing and knew that Marshall meant the opposite of what the words seemed to mean. Holistically, the meaning of the statement was, "We like you, we think you're doing a good job, and we know you can't plan a press conference from Spain."

1. What are all the factors that contributed to helping the members interpret the accurate meaning of Marshall's remarks? How did they know he was teasing?
2. If Emma had not been sure that Marshall had been teasing, how could she have clarified what he meant? Do you think this would have been difficult for her? Would it have been difficult for you to clarify if someone really thought you were a "lazy butt"?
3. Under what conditions do you think it is OK to use a term like "lazy butt"? When would you, and when would you *not,* use language like that?

Defusing the trigger words helps the group begin a more objective, less emotional evaluation of the person's qualifications.

## FOLLOWING THE RULES OF THE GROUP

Because different groups and cultures have different rules for communicating, you will increase your chances of being accepted and understood if you follow the rules for the particular group you are in. For example, some groups are formal: Members address each other by title (e.g., Dr. Adams or Ms. Galanes) and use many abstract words with a complex sentence structure. However, these rules would be inappropriate in a self-managed work team in an auto factory, where concrete language with a clear and concise sentence structure is more effective. Virtual groups facing the challenge of less frequent and direct communication with each other will create their own Communication Charters which lay out their rules of communication, like when to reply by e-mail or phone.[5] They will also post in a shared workspace, how to interpret a "no" response or "yes" response. Be aware of and adapt to appropriate standards of behavior *for the particular group*. This kind of code-switch happens all the time, often without your conscious thought. You would not speak to your grandparents' card club the same way you speak within a group of your friends, would you?

Even as we advise this, however, we note that many of the secondary groups you participate in will take place in the mainstream of the U.S. business, professional, and educational communities. In such cases you should conform to the vocabulary and grammar rules of standard English. This will help other people understand you and increase your influence because numerous studies have shown that nonstandard dialects and usage lower the credibility of speakers with a variety of listeners. Rick Ayers, a former Berkeley High School teacher, is famously known for helping his students create their own slang dictionary, giving them a creative opportunity to use their own rich language.[6] As he recognized, "I want to make them [his students] aware of their brilliance, that the way they speak is not wrong, it's just another form of discourse. . . . The trick is teaching them how to translate it into standard English when they need to."[7]

Now that we have considered the implications of group verbal communication, we turn our attention to nonverbal group communication. We will explore its principles, functions, and categories of nonverbal behavior relevant to group communication.

GLOSSARY

**Nonverbal Behavior**

*Anything in a message that is not the word itself*

## Nonverbal Communication in Small Groups

**Nonverbal behavior** is anything in a message except the words themselves. We pointed out early in this chapter that meaning is created when we consider verbal and nonverbal communication *together*. Two communication scholars, John Stewart and Carol Logan, believe we make sense of this complexity by using a continuum.[8] At one extreme are primarily verbal behaviors such as written words; in the middle are mixed behaviors such as spoken words, vocalics (e.g., pitch, rate, volume), pauses, and silences; and at the other extreme are primarily nonverbal behaviors that can occur without words such as eye gaze, touch, and facial expressions. Verbal and nonverbal behavior are inseparable, just as two sides of a paper are inseparable.[9]

### PRINCIPLES OF NONVERBAL COMMUNICATION

Most of the time in a small group, only one person is speaking, but *all* members are sending nonverbal signals *all* the time. Understanding something about nonverbal behaviors is crucial to understanding what is happening in your groups. However, interpreting nonverbal behaviors can be trickier than interpreting verbal signals.

1. **Nonverbal behaviors are ambiguous.**

   The "thumbs up" gesture you give to a friend for a job well done translates into "up yours" in Greece or the Middle East! Do you think that someone who has her arms folded across her chest is uninterested in hearing what you say? Maybe. But maybe she is merely trying to keep warm. Many factors influence the meaning of nonverbal behaviors, including cultural differences. Nonverbal behaviors should be interpreted in context and in conjunction with the words group members are using.

2. **People cannot stop sending nonverbal behaviors, even when they are not talking.**

   Usually, only one person in a group speaks at a time, but all members continuously process nonverbal behaviors. Even if you choose to be quiet in a group meeting, other people will interpret your silence. For example, a church board member unhappy with the way the church secretary was handling office business chose not to say anything when personnel matters were discussed. However, after the meeting the board chair asked him why he had seemed uninterested at the meeting. This example highlights two features of nonverbal behavior. First, even though the member chose not to say anything, he certainly was communicating *something* nonverbally. Second, nonverbal behaviors are easy to misinterpret. The emotion the board member was feeling was anger at the church secretary, but the board chair thought he was uninterested in the meeting. Thus, we shouldn't jump to conclusions without first checking them out.

3. **When verbal and nonverbal behaviors clash, most people believe the nonverbal behaviors.**

   In fact, when a person is trying to interpret what someone else means in a face-to-face interaction, the nonverbal part of the message counts almost twice as much as the verbal.[10] Many nonverbal behaviors, such as sweating, blushing, and shaking, are controlled by primitive structures of the brain over which we have little or no conscious control. You can choose your words, but your nonverbal behavior often gives you away. When you clench your fists, turn red, and scream at another group member, "No, I'm NOT mad!" no one will believe you.

## FUNCTIONS OF NONVERBAL BEHAVIORS

Nonverbal behaviors perform what a friend of ours would call the "heavy lifting" in communication, particularly regarding relationships. Without them we would not know how to "take" the words that people say. "Right," says member Sarah. *How* she says it—a nonverbal behavior—can make that "Right" a statement of agreement ("Yes, you are right and I agree") or one of disagreement (if said sarcastically, as in "Yeah, sure you're right" but meaning exactly the opposite). One of the most important functions of nonverbal behavior is to express *how we feel.* We convey emotions, such as anger, sadness, and happiness, through our nonverbal behaviors. We laugh when we are happy, frown and glare when we are angry, and so forth. Emma knew Marshall didn't mean she was a "lazy butt" because he smiled and winked at her when he said that.

Nonverbal behaviors also perform the important function of indicating *how we perceive our relationships to other people*; like status and liking. When asked what nonverbal behaviors are exhibited by people who have social power (status), those with high social power were perceived to hold themselves more erect, gesture more, invade others' space and be more successful at interrupting others, be more open and expressive, and have speech that was smoother and more confident.[11] Whether someone likes another person seems to be strongly associated with that person's nonverbal—but not verbal—behavior.[12] In one study teachers liked students who were nonverbally responsive, such as sitting upright (not slouching), making direct eye contact, having positive facial expressions, and taking notes in class. Interestingly, teachers were also more willing to comply with students' requests (e.g., extending a due date on an assignment) if the students had been nonverbally responsive to the teacher. This applies directly to small group behavior. Showing you like someone helps them like you in return. Kory Floyd and George Ray found that people interacting with someone who showed them signs of liking (e.g., eye contact, smiling, leaning forward) continued to increase their own liking behavior.[13]

Another function of nonverbal communication is to *supplement* words by emphasizing them or, in effect, repeating them, just as <u>underlined</u> or **boldfaced** words in a text are emphasized. For instance, a person may say, "Look at the rise in air pollution in the Valley during peak traffic hours" while pointing at a bar graph. Thus, nonverbals can call special attention to the words they accompany.

Nonverbal behaviors can *substitute* for spoken or written words. In this case a gesture becomes a symbol, substituting for the more conventional words. For instance, a circled thumb and index finger can express "OK," or a beckoning finger can indicate that you want someone to lean closer to you. Kathy and some of her graduate students bring their two forefingers together to indicate a "shared moment," a gesture they picked up from the 1997 romantic comedy *Chasing Amy*. Much of the communication among members can be with unspoken substitutes for spoken words. If you aren't conscious of these behaviors and don't look for them, you will be only half-listening and may miss important information.

### What If . . . ?

APPLY NOW

Earlier you met a group of students planning publicity for their Freshman Convocation Welcome. In their meeting they discussed the logistics of their press conference and how to connect with local media. Recollect the following dialogue:

**Emma:** You're right; we need that. Big oversight. Glad you thought of it.

**Jayden:** One thing we could do is contact people in the local media who know about this event.

**Jamal:** That might be a good idea, but I'm not sure we're ready to go on to that yet. Were we finished with writing our press release and organizing the press conference?

**Jayden:** Sorry! I thought we were ready to move on. What do we need to do yet with press conference?

**Jamal:** Well, for one thing, we need to figure out who would be a good moderator and to design the press kit.

The goal of this application is to show you how much the context and nonverbal behavior influence the meaning of what we say. Select four trios. Each trio is to role-play the dialogue but from a different relational context. The first trio is composed of close friends who have worked together on several committees. Members of the second trio have never met before, and one member is not sure he or she even wants to be on this committee. The third trio has a highly aggressive member who believes he or she knows how to run this group. The fourth trio is composed of individuals who really dislike each other but are trying to be civil.

During the role-plays, have audience members take notes. Ask them to observe the nonverbal behavior and how it changes the meaning of the conversation. When the trios are through, discuss the principles and the functions of nonverbal behavior. You can even discuss how the trios used such things as gestures, facial expressions, movements, and spacing to create the relational context.

**GLOSSARY**

**Proxemics**
*The study of how people use space*

Another major function of nonverbal behaviors is to *regulate* the flow of verbal interaction among members. For example, nods, eye contact, and hand signals indicate who should speak next. Direct gaze from listeners means, "Continue," whereas looking away is a nonverbal way of saying, "Shut up!" People who want to speak lean forward, slightly open their mouths, extend a hand or finger, and even utter a sound such as "um." Speakers who ignore such cues are judged inconsiderate and rude. One of us observed a group that contained a blind person who obviously could not see such regulating cues. Other members began to judge this member as arrogant and self-centered for "talking out of turn." Some discussion of visible regulatory cues increased the members' sensitivity to the communicative problem experienced by their blind member and helped the group pull together.

Finally, as noted earlier, nonverbal behaviors can *contradict* words we utter. A person who says, "I agree," hesitatingly, with a rising pitch at the end of the words, may be perceived as having reservations, or even as disagreeing. When you observe nonverbal behaviors that seem to contradict what a person has just said, and it matters to you what the person really thinks, try saying, "I heard you say . . . , but the way you said it confuses me." Then explain the apparent contradiction you perceived, and ask the person to clarify it for you.

## CATEGORIES OF NONVERBAL BEHAVIORS

Several categories of nonverbal behavior are especially important to your understanding of small group communication. Personal appearance, space and seating, facial expressions and eye contact, gestures and body movements, voice, and time cues are among the major types of nonverbal behaviors most relevant to small groups.

**Appearance.** Members of a group form impressions of each other, accurate or not, long before anyone says anything. Sex, race, height, build, dress, grooming, and other visible cues have been shown to influence responses. Cues such as sex, body shape, and ethnicity particularly affect how group members interact with each other initially.[14] Such personal characteristics as status and wisdom may be associated with a member's age and sex. Members also create impressions of each other's physical characteristics based on clothing, makeup, and other body "artifacts." These impressions may very well determine whether a group member interacts with another member and, if so, what type of interaction they have. For instance, violating societal norms about dress, grooming, makeup, and accessories can arouse suspicion or even mistrust. Dressing noticeably differently from other members will almost certainly be interpreted as a sign that you do not identify with them. You may have to prove yourself in other ways to be accepted. To date, no research has examined the impact of the relative physical attractiveness of group members on group throughput and outcome variables.[15] This is surprising given how much attention is placed on physical attractiveness in American culture at large and in interpersonal communication research specifically.

**Space and Seating.** **Proxemics** is the study of how people use space to communicate. The amount of space people prefer between them depends on a variety of factors, including culture and gender. For example, in the United States most business transactions are conducted at what Edward Hall calls *social distance,* which is between four and eight feet.[16] We are comfortable allowing only our intimate friends within a foot or two. However, four feet is much too far for someone from the Arab world or from Latin America. In these countries people transact business at what we consider close personal distance, which often makes Americans very uneasy. In the dominant culture of the United States, females tend to sit closer together than males, as do people of the same age and social status and those who know each other well.

The seating arrangements in groups and even the way furniture is arranged is called **group ecology.**[17] In a group, sitting close together, especially if the room is large enough for members to spread out, indicates that members like each other and share a sense of cohesiveness. A member who sits apart from the others may be signaling that he or she does not feel a part of the group.

Group ecology and group processes such as status, leadership, power, and member participation are linked to each other. Dominant people often claim more than their fair share of space, and a group's leader usually is given more space by the other members than they claim. In addition, group leaders generally sit in a central position, such as at the head of a rectangular table, where they can see as many other members as possible. Quite simply, the most central place in a group's ecology allows members who occupy that space more influence, participation, domination, and opportunity to foster attributions of leadership.[18] People who sit across from each other respond to each other more than people sitting side by side or on the edges of each other's vision. The ideal table for most small group discussions is a round table, where members have easy eye contact with each other. If that is not possible, group members are advised to position themselves around the table, whatever shape it happens to be, in something close to a circle or oval.

Violating space norms is risky, unless you are a high-status member.[19] High-status members have a kind of extra credit within their groups and can get away with moving both closer to others and farther away. These violations in expectation actually increase their status. Low-status members are not so fortunate because their deviations are interpreted within the context of their low status. Thus, if they move closer to others they can be seen as pushy, and if they move farther away they can be seen as aloof; in both cases their attractiveness and persuasiveness diminishes.

Altering seating arrangements may also appear nonconsequential; however, the seating choices you and your group members make indicate how socially accessible you have made yourselves to each other. Social accessibility is important if members are to promote social contact and enhance the more relational group outcomes, such as respect and cohesiveness.[20] For example, a student executive committee one of us once advised, conducted their meetings sitting—at a long head table, with all six members on the same side of the table. Members showed signs of frustration, anger, confusion, and so forth, until they took the suggestion to use a round table instead of the head table for the executive meeting. Both the content of the meetings and the relationships among members improved dramatically with that simple space change.

**Facial Expressions and Eye Contact.** Eye contact and facial expressions are among the most important nonverbal behaviors for group members, as you can see in the cartoon on the next page. For Americans, making eye contact signals that the channel for communication is open. This is why many students look down at their

**GLOSSARY**

**Group Ecology**

*A group's space as created by seating choices and furniture arrangements*

notebooks when a teacher asks a question—they avoid eye contact so they won't be called on to answer. Prolonged eye contact can signal cooperativeness or competitiveness, depending on the circumstances. Most Americans establish eye contact before speaking and continue it intermittently when talking to someone they like. However, people from other cultures are sometimes offended by Americans' direct gazes, while others prefer to maintain an intense, unbroken stare when conversing, which is uncomfortable for Americans. As with other nonverbal behavior, numerous cultural factors influence what a person considers to be appropriate eye contact. In unified and cohesive groups, members tend to look continuously at each other during a discussion. In hostile or tense groups, members avoid eye contact.

People can accurately determine the type of emotion someone in a photograph is experiencing from looking just at the face and eyes. Anger, sadness, happiness, support, disagreement, interest, liking—all are indicated by facial expressions.[21] In addition, the emotion does not need to be displayed for a long time. People can recognize microexpressions that last as little as one-fifteenth of a second, and they can be trained to improve their ability to detect microexpressions.[22] Some people have "poker" faces; their facial expressions change very little. They tend to be trusted less than those whose faces express their feelings more openly. Most of us monitor the facial expressions of others because they provide clues about what is going on in the group.

**Movements.** Movements of the hands, arms, and body signal many feelings and attitudes. For example, people turn directly toward others they like and away from

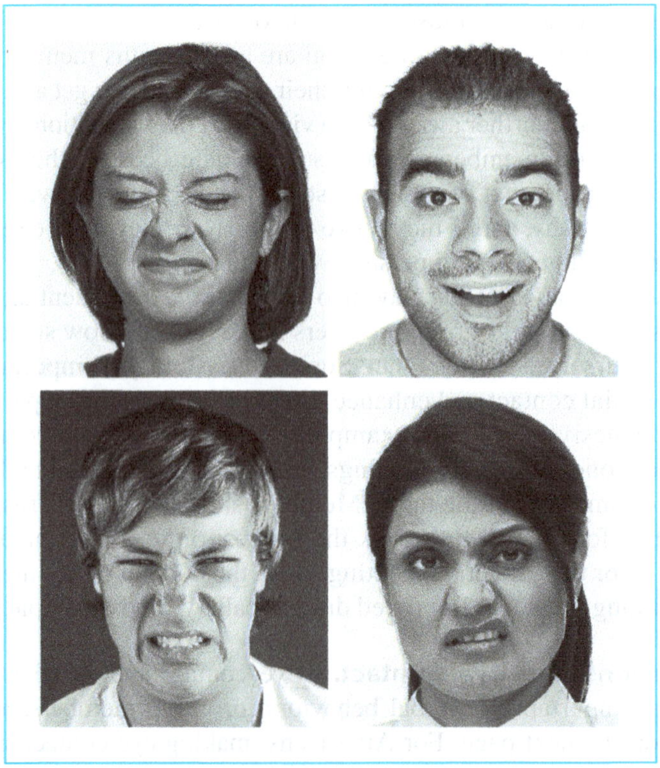

(Top left): © Image Source/Getty Images RF; (Top right): © Ingram Publishing RF; (Bottom left): © themacx/Getty Images RF; (Bottom right): © SIBSA Digital Pvt. Ltd./ Alamy Stock Photo RF

those they dislike. Leaning toward each other indicates a sense of mutual inclusiveness, whereas leaning away signals rejection.[23] When group members feel a sense of unity with each other, they tend to imitate each other's posture and body movements. This takes place automatically, without conscious awareness. Edward Mabry found that body orientation can change significantly from one meeting to another.[24] As group members get to know, like, and trust one another more, they tend to increase their eye contact and angle their bodies more directly toward each other.

Both tension and status can be revealed with movements. Members who are swinging a foot, twisting a lock of hair, or tapping a pencil may be indicating tension. It may be hard for the other members to know whether the movements indicate frustration, impatience, or annoyance with the group's progress. Movement can also indicate who has high status in the group. High-status members tend to be the most relaxed, so they lean back and look around.[25] Members are more likely to imitate the movements of high-status members than those of low-status members.[26]

**Voice.** Vocal cues include such factors as pitch, speed, fluency, loudness, and pauses. We rely on tone of voice to interpret someone's mood. Someone who says, "Yeah, I could live with that" softly in a questioning tone of voice is not likely to be believed. In addition, listeners tend to judge the status, educational level, ethnicity, and attitudes of speakers on the basis of vocal cues.[27] In the United States people who speak in a monotone have less credibility and are less persuasive than those who speak in a more animated tone of voice. However, those who are extremely animated may appear to be irrational or hysterical.

Nonverbal voice signals that regulate interaction express group member involvement, dominance, competition, and cooperativeness.[28] For instance, people make nonverbal backchannel sounds, such as "mm-hmmm" and "uh-huh," to indicate involvement and understanding when listening. Interestingly, cultures vary in the use of the backchannel. Most people from western European backgrounds use the backchannel less frequently than African Americans, Hispanics, or people with southern European backgrounds. If conversational partners do not share the same backchannel norms, they can begin to stereotype each other and develop negative perceptions.[29] In addition, when people from the same culture converse, the fact that they use the backchannel similarly helps increase their recall of the conversation later.[30] However, when people with different backchannel norms converse, they seem to give each other misleading feedback that reduces their later recall. We discuss backchannel differences between African Americans and European Americans in more detail in Chapter 6. Backchannel sounds may be interpreted as showing either interest or agreement. These differences can cause misunderstandings if group members are not aware of them and thus influence how smoothly members can agree on issues. If, for example, you believe group members agree with your ideas based on their "uh-huhs," only to discover later that they were just trying to show that they were paying attention to you, you'll probably be upset!

*Dialect* refers to regional and social variations in pronunciation, vocabulary, and grammar. The different dialects you hear in your groups can influence perceptions of intelligence, competence, and credibility.[31] Countries such as the United States, Great Britain, and Japan have regional and social class language deviations from the "standard" dialect. Group members who use nonstandard dialects—saying *ain't* instead of *isn't,* for example—are often given lower status and credibility ratings. General American dialect is rated higher on pleasantness and socio-intellectual status than the dialect of South Boston or the Bronx. Be very cautious about stereotyping group members with dialects different from your own.

**Timing.** Time cues are both culture-related and relational. Most rural people tackle business at a slower pace than their urban counterparts. In the fast-paced U.S. business world, people who come late to meetings are judged inconsiderate and undisciplined. North Americans will allow only about a five-minute leeway before they expect an apology from someone who is late.[32] In the predominant culture of this country, coming late and leaving early indicates to fellow group members that your time is precious but it's OK to waste theirs. In dozens of case studies of student groups, one consistently late member was the subject of bitter complaints by the others.

Time is a vital commodity during meetings. Excessive talkers are considered rude and selfish. Although they did not protest at the time, many students have complained about fellow project group members who waste time by chattering at length about social matters or other topics irrelevant to the group's purpose. On the other hand, those who talk just somewhat more than the average are judged favorably on leadership characteristics.[33] In fact, talkativeness, or speaking time, is considered a strong factor in determining how much power a group member is perceived to have.[34] Likewise, people who structure the group's time so that every item on an agenda can be discussed are appreciated.

No type of nonverbal behavior can be overlooked if you want to understand what is going on in a group. However, much remains to be discovered about how nonverbal communication operates in small groups. Relatively little, for instance, is understood about the influence on group behavior of member touch behavior, artifacts such as clothing, emotion, and different kinds of group contexts (e.g., groups in submarines).[35] Remember also that you cannot state with confidence exactly what someone else is thinking or feeling from nonverbal cues alone. We hope the list of nonverbal behaviors presented here encourages you to increase your awareness and sensitivity, but you should not consider this list exhaustive. We summarize this list, in tongue-in-cheek fashion, in Table 4.2, which reminds you how to behave in a group if you want the others to dislike you.

**TABLE 4.2** **Nonverbal Behaviors Guaranteed to Get Other Members to Dislike You**

Nonverbal behavior plays an especially important role in creating and maintaining group relationships. Here are several suggestions for getting your fellow group members to dislike you:

1. Show the others that you don't like them:
   - Don't smile.
   - Don't lean forward.
   - Don't make eye contact.

TABLE 4.2 ***Continued***

**2.** Be unresponsive to the others:
- Slouch.
- Don't pay attention.
- Scowl.
- Text message on your cell phone when someone else is talking.

**3.** Keep a poker face to make the others guess what you're thinking.

**4.** Violate an important group appearance norm:
- If your group dresses casually, wear formal attire.
- If business casual is the norm, wear torn sweats. This is especially important if your group is giving a presentation; that's when you should wear your grungiest clothes.

**5.** Violate your group's space norms:
- If group members sit far apart, move in close to another member (and watch him or her squirm).
- If members sit close to each other, you sit farther apart. It might be especially helpful to turn your body so that you seem to have your back to the group.

**6.** Indicate rejection by leaning away from the group.

**7.** Violate your group's movement norms:
- Gesture wildly.
- Don't gesture at all.
- Get up and leave the room without explanation; when you return, don't tell them where you've been.

**8.** Violate your group's vocal cues:
- Talk r-e-a-l-l-y s-l-o-w-l-y.
- Talkasfastasyoucan.
- SHOUT.
- Whisper so others have to ask you to repeat.
- Use jargon the others won't understand.
- Refuse to use the jargon or special vocabulary of the group.
- Overuse the backchannel when others are speaking.
- Don't do anything to indicate that you're paying attention.

**9.** Violate your group's norms about timing:
- Come late to meetings (especially without explanation).
- Leave meetings early (don't explain this, either).
- Hog the group's time by talking constantly.
- Don't say anything at all.

**GLOSSARY**

**Social Presence**

*The degree to which a person feels that another is actually present during an interaction*

## Comparing Face-to-Face and Computer-Mediated Group Communication

We noted earlier that groups fall along a continuum from purely face-to-face to purely virtual and everything in between. While the same characteristics of communication (e.g., that it is symbolic, transactional, etc.) and principles (e.g., treating others with respect) apply, there are differences between face-to-face and computer-mediated communication.

One major similarity is that verbal communication—words—provides the foundation for both FtF and CMC. Research by Amy Gonzales, Jeffrey Hancock, and James Pennebaker on linguistic style confirms this.[36] These researchers analyzed the language style of 41 FtF and 34 CMC groups and found that similarity of verbal style among group members predicted the degree of cohesiveness in both types of groups. This was true regardless of the sex of the members or the number of people in the group. Members of cohesive groups tend to mimic one another's verbal style, suggesting that such members have developed similar mental models of how to work and interact. This is true both for face-to-face and online groups.

Nonverbal communication operates differently in CMC. For example, if members cannot see one another, they will miss important facial expressions, gestures, and body language, although if they can *hear* one another, they can still pick up vocal cues. Timing may be off. The inability to read nonverbal cues is reported by virtual team members as their number one virtual challenge.[37] If group members must achieve consensus about an important issue, CMC can impair a group's sense of sharing, involvement, and team spirit.[38]

Compared to FtF communication, CMC has less **social presence,** which is the extent to which group members perceive the CMC (e.g., a telephone, a video conference, computer e-mail) to be like FtF interaction socially and emotionally. Members'

### Interpreting the "Lazy Butt" Comment

APPLY NOW

Let's go back to the "lazy butt" conversation between Emma and Marshall and assume that, instead of using Skype (which allowed them to see and hear one another), the members were communicating by computers and could see only the typed words being sent back and forth.

1. Describe at least three ways in which Marshall could have reduced the risk that Emma would get insulted or hurt by his comment.
2. Describe at least three things that Emma could have done if she was hurt or offended, or if she wasn't sure whether or not Marshall was kidding.
3. What if the members in the United States had never met Emma before, but she had expressed an interest in serving on their committee once she returned to the university after her semester abroad. How could members have gotten to know her and to have figured out ways to include her in their group—not just in the task of the group, but in the relationship fabric of the group?

perception depends on the degree to which they perceive that other members are actually *there* during the interaction.[39] Virtual team members, for example, can go days without interacting face-to-face (if they ever do so) and team leaders have been found to use InstantMessaging as a way to increase social contact among members.[40]

However, group members have found ways to compensate for the reduced nonverbal cues in CMC—they use verbal communication to fill the gap. We noted in Chapter 1 that humans have a need to affiliate and to be included and in Chapter 4 that nonverbal communication carries the heavy lifting in relationship development. Joseph Walther and his associates, who have studied CMC extensively, have found that when group members' "normal" ways of affiliating are not available, they will use what *is* available.[41] In CMC, words take over the job that nonverbal communication does in face-to-face interaction. For example, group members may be able to sandwich face-to-face meetings in between CMC meetings to enhance their "groupness." They may increase the social presence of CMC by using **emoticons,** the typographic symbols that convey a variety of emotions (e.g., ☺ for happiness or ☹ for sadness). Or, they may state what they are feeling. For example, if a member makes a sarcastic statement that may be misinterpreted, that member may state "I'm just kidding" to reduce the chance of miscommunication. Walther has found that groups communicating virtually can form relationships that are just as strong and just as high quality as face-to-face partners do. Social presence is important, and if nonverbal avenues are restricted, humans become textually inventive in creating social presence.

**GLOSSARY**

**Emoticons**

*The typographic symbols used in CMC to convey a variety of emotions*

## RESOURCES FOR REVIEW AND DISCUSSION

### SUMMARY

- Group members communicate via messages, verbal and nonverbal signals they send and interpret.
- Verbal communication flows more smoothly when members clarify abstract concepts, keep discussion organized, are sensitive to others' feelings, and follow the language rules of the group.
- Nonverbal behaviors, more believable because they are harder to control, are especially hard to interpret accurately; they supplement or substitute for verbal communication, regulate the flow, and express feelings.
- Nonverbal categories especially relevant to understanding small group communication include appearance, use of space, facial expressions, eye contact, movements, vocal cues, and timing.
- Group members increasingly use computers to communicate, and computer use dramatically influences the nature of a group's nonverbal messages in particular.

### EXERCISES

1. Browse through several magazines for interesting advertisements. Cut out a variety of advertisements and bring them to class. Discuss with your group or your class each of the advertisements. Identify what the audience for each ad is and how the language of the ad is designed to appeal to its audience.
2. Tape-record a group meeting. Watch the tape, and note the group's seating arrangements and the space between members. Examine the facial expressions and eye contact, and note voice qualities and timing. When you are finished, discuss your observations. How do you think these nonverbal behaviors contributed to the overall communicative character of this group?

## KEY TERMS • CONCEPTS

- Bypassing
- Emoticons
- Emotive Words
- Group Ecology
- Message
- Nonverbal Behavior
- Proxemics
- Social Presence

# From Individuals to Group

PART THREE

# From Individuals to Group

Part Three focuses on the interaction among group members as they begin to merge their own individual personalities, cultures, behaviors, and so forth into a functioning group. Chapter 5 looks at how a group develops from an initial collection of individuals into a team, with roles, norms, and a unique group climate. Chapter 6 continues this discussion of group formation by examining various aspects of diversity among members and exploring how to manage this diversity so the group can perform at its best.

CHAPTER 5

# Becoming a Group

## CHAPTER OUTLINE

How Communication Structures the Small Group

Challenges in Group Development

Group Socialization of Members

Group Roles

Rules and Norms

Development of a Group's Climate

Ethical Behavior during Group Formation

## CHAPTER OBJECTIVES

**After reading this chapter you should be able to:**

1. Explain how communication creates and maintains a group through the process of structuration.
2. Describe the two major tasks groups must manage and how these create an equilibrium problem for a group.
3. Define primary, secondary, and tertiary tension, and give examples of each.
4. Describe Tuckman's model of group development and Gersick's two-phase model and explain how each describes the process many groups experience.
5. Describe the communicative dynamics of each stage of group socialization.
6. Describe each of the three main categories of roles in groups.
7. Differentiate between formal and behavioral roles, and describe how behavioral roles emerge during group interaction.
8. Differentiate between rules and norms, and describe the four ways norms develop.
9. Explain what you would say and do if you wanted to change a group norm.
10. Describe each of the three main components that contribute to a group's climate.

## The *Man of La Mancha* Cast and Crew

CASE 5.1

Noel, his church's choir director, broke his back in an airplane crash. To make his hospital time pass more quickly, he imagined the choir performing one of his favorite plays, *Man of La Mancha*. When he got out of the hospital, Noel decided to realize his dream by directing the play; he cast all the roles with choir members and performed the lead role of Don Quixote himself. Geoff, an experienced actor, was sidekick Sancho. Geoff couldn't carry a tune, but his acting experience and his unfailing good humor helped the cast mesh into a cohesive team. Gena, in the role of Aldonza, was also an experienced actress but had never before sung solo; however, she had a good sense of rhythm and was able to coach the dancers. Very few of the choir members could sing well, but they had an amazing array of other talents. Davida, who was both shy and clumsy, nevertheless was an outstanding artist and created two fabulous horse heads out of papier-mâché. She also created a minimal but effective set that could be positioned and removed quickly from the sanctuary. There were not enough men for all the roles, so Noel cast women in several parts, including the Barber and the horses. Delores had no sense of rhythm and could sing only whatever part the person next to her was singing, but she was a whiz at creating costumes out of Salvation Army thrift shop treasures.

The cast had only three weeks to rehearse, from the play's first read-through to opening night. Given the lack of singing and acting talent, lack of experience, lack of money for costumes and set materials, and time constraints, this play should have been a disaster. Instead, it was a great success. Several experienced theater patrons said that, although they had seen more professionally mounted productions of *Man of La Mancha,* this performance had touched them emotionally more than other performances.

The cast and crew had grown into a cohesive team whose output far exceeded reasonable expectations. Members contributed all their talents (singing and otherwise) to make the performance a success. Why did this small group work when all "objective" assessments suggested it would fail?

**GLOSSARY**

**Structuration**

*The idea that group communication creates, maintains, and continually re-creates a group's norms and the way it operates*

**The heart of any group's throughput process is the mutual influence that occurs when group members communicate with each other. This chapter explores more fully some of the throughput processes of an emerging group and how groups, such as the *Man of La Mancha* cast and crew, become effective. Groups whose individual members mesh into a productive team consistently figure out how to manage their tensions to create and maintain constructive roles, norms, and a supportive group climate. These groups must also develop and support a stable leadership structure. Leadership is so central to group dynamics that it will be covered more completely in Chapter 10.**

## How Communication Structures the Small Group

**Structuration** refers to the way members create and maintain a group, including establishing a group's roles, norms, rules, and climate. Developed by Marshall Scott Poole, David Siebold, and Robert McPhee, the main idea of this theory is this: Verbal and nonverbal communication among members creates the group norms, operating procedures, and climate *and* maintains them once they are established.[1] Communication among members, *the* essential throughput process, influences what members talk about, how they relate to one another, and how they structure their group (e.g., roles, leadership).

The theory contains three important assumptions. First, group members do not come to a group with a clean slate about how to behave. They have been taught what is appropriate by their general culture, by their participation in other groups, and by the organizations they belong to. For example, Gena and Geoff, from their community theater experience, knew how to behave professionally, with their lines learned, and how to help the others feel comfortable on stage. They brought theater values and expectations into this *particular* group. Notice their communication behavior involved both the group's task (putting on the play) and the group's relationships (being helpful and supportive to other cast members). They modeled supportive, welcoming behavior to the cast. The more members continued to behave supportively, the more "supportive" the standard of behavior became entrenched: "This is how we operate in our group."

Second, although people pick up rules and standards for behavior from the general culture, no law forces them to follow those rules. Goeff and Gena could have taken the attitude, "We're experienced community theater actors, we know more about theater than the rest of you, so you have to do what we say." Individuals may choose to ignore norms and rules for supportive behavior. If Gena and Geoff had been arrogant instead of helpful, do you think Davida would have felt comfortable creating her papier-mâché horse heads, or Dolores constructing inventive costumes from scraps? More likely, they would have hesitated to volunteer and the production would have missed out on several creative ideas and suggestions.

Third, a group is never finally created; instead, it constantly re-creates itself through communication so that it is always in a state of becoming. Thus, change usually happens incrementally. Once having established a climate of supportiveness, the momentum within the *Man of La Mancha* cast continued along this path. That's what structuration is all about—how communication creates and maintains the group over time.

How members talk to one another directly affects team success.[2] Communication that focuses on analyzing the problem, providing ideas about how to proceed, clarifying members' comments, prioritizing tasks, taking personal responsibility and action planning help a group succeed. In contrast, complaining, criticizing, and losing one's train of thought in the details of a story or a sidetrack hurt group performance. Structuration reminds us to focus on members' communication as a major contributor to a group's outcomes.

## Challenges in Group Development

All groups must resolve certain issues while becoming fully functioning groups and teams. Among those are handling the two key issues all groups face: managing social tensions and moving smoothly from one stage of development to another.

### A GROUP'S MAJOR FUNCTIONS

The first key issue, managing social tensions, involves both the group's task and the relationships among members. These two functions, task and socioemotional, must be handled simultaneously, thus producing what group members may experience as a tug-of-war between group task and social demands. When members spend emotional and mental energy on the interpersonal issues, they take away from the energy needed to attend to their work. On the other hand, when members attend to the task at hand, they pay less attention to each other's human needs. Robert F. Bales calls this the equilibrium problem.[3] A group's attention must shift between concentrating on its task and concentrating on the relationships between members. First, the group must develop dependable, harmonious relationships that will give it stability—the *socioemotional* concern. Second, the group must focus on its assignment, or *task* concern. Both need to be attended to, in some degree, throughout the life of the group.

Task and socioemotional concerns surface at predictable periods in a group's life cycle. Initially, before members have gotten to know each other well and developed smooth working relationships, the group must necessarily spend more time on socioemotional issues. Members work out their relationships with each other in a structuration process during which norms, rules, roles (including leadership), and the group's climate emerge. In Case 5.1, for instance, Geoff could not sing well but had valuable acting experience. Gena had not sung solo but had the dancing skills necessary to help coach the dancers. Both were encouraged to put their talents—whatever they were—to use for the group. The *Man of La Mancha* cast and crew did a particularly good job of working out their relationships effectively and finding a valuable role for everyone.

Notice that, while the individual relationships were being worked out, the group was engaged in rehearsing and preparing for its performances. In other words, it

GLOSSARY

**Primary Tension**

*Anxiety arising early in a group's formation, as members work out their relationships and roles*

**Secondary Tension**

*Task-related tension that stems from differing opinions about the substantive work of the group*

**Tertiary Tension**

*Tension that stems from power and status struggles in a group*

could not ignore its task while members got to know each other. In fact, the group relationships developed *in the process of* working on the group's task. Rarely does a group have the luxury of members getting to know each other well before they have to start working—they usually have to get to work right away! Thus, instead of a group's task and socioemotional functions occurring separately and sequentially, the group works on both at the same time (i.e., the equilibrium problem), but at any given time one may be more important than the other.

One final note: Groups never stop dealing with both main functions. Task concerns are always present, and relationships among members must be monitored, with problems addressed as they arise. One function may be in the foreground at any given moment, but the other hasn't disappeared from view. Both task and socioemotional concerns remain key functions groups must manage.

## SOCIAL TENSIONS IN GROUPS

There are three typical tensions most groups experience. **Primary tension** occurs early on, as members are getting to know each other. During periods of primary tension, interaction is overly polite, with long, uncomfortable pauses in the conversation.[4] This kind of social tension is similar to *stage fright*.[5] Recall how you typically feel the first time you meet with a new group. Like most people you probably worry whether the others will like you and whether you will belong. This makes most members careful not to say or do something that might offend the other members; behavior is tentative, stiff, and cautious. That is why newly formed groups often seem overly formal and excessively polite.

**Secondary tension** usually occurs later in a group's life cycle.[6] This work related tension stems from differing opinions about substantive issues. It is inevitable in task groups because members bring different perspectives to their group's task concerns. If secondary tension is not managed well, it can continue to resurface.[7] Poor management of secondary tension can evolve into a destructive group climate.

Much of the tension we have observed in groups is not strictly primary or secondary. Instead, groups often become bogged down in arguments that seem to recycle over and over. This inability or even unwillingness to manage issues often represents a power or status struggle between members. This is a modified form of primary tension that can appear on the surface to be secondary tension over content issues. Below the surface, however, it is a power struggle over who is in charge. These power struggles produce **tertiary tension** among members. Members struggle over who will decide the rules and procedures for the group. Conflict may occur over how to make decisions, how to resolve conflicts, who has the authority to determine what will happen in the group, who can make assignments, who is an expert at what, what are the rights and privileges of group membership, and so forth.

One of us observed a classroom group experiencing tertiary tension. The group's assignment was to observe a task group and gather data about it. Mike insisted that the group use *his* questionnaire as one method of gathering data. Michelle demanded instead that the group use *her* questionnaire. This endless argument was a thinly masked power struggle. If this really had been only secondary tension, Mike and

© Rawpixel Ltd/Getty Images RF

Michelle could easily have combined their questionnaires. Instead, each demanded to be in charge of deciding the group's procedures while the others frustrated themselves trying to come up with a compromise that neither would accept. This destructive power struggle is an example of tertiary tension that appears secondary but goes deeper than disagreement over the task.

For a group to perform at its best, social tension must be managed appropriately.

1. **Group members can move through the primary tension stage more quickly if they know each other.**

   The choir described in Case 5.1 had an advantage in that members already knew each other fairly well when they began play rehearsals. A get-acquainted period helps members do this—even when members *do* know each other. Don't hesitate to suggest this, even if your group's designated leader doesn't. The members can accomplish their task much more effectively and quickly if they know where the other members are coming from, what they do on the job, and even what hobbies and outside interests they have. Joking, laughing, storytelling, sharing a meal, and having fun together before getting down to work help as well.

2. **Members can reduce both primary and secondary tension by sharing what they know about the problem at hand.**

   For instance, if a committee is charged with recommending solutions to a campus parking problem, each member's perception of the scope and seriousness of the problem can be shared so that all will have some common understanding of the problem. This mapping process will be described in Chapter 8.

3. **Secondary and tertiary tensions can be managed if group members demonstrate tolerance for disagreement.**

   When group members believe that their opinions and ideas are appreciated, even if these opinions are contrary to the ideas of others, they feel valued by the group. They also are less likely to demand high status if they already believe the group appreciates them. Showing that you appreciate someone else's thoughtful analysis, even if you don't fully agree, can help. For example, saying, "I see what you mean about the hidden costs of that option, Tom, and that's something I hadn't considered" shows Tom that you were listening and that you appreciate the careful thought he gave to the issue. Statements that acknowledge confidence in the group (e.g., "We'll be able to find an answer—we've done a good job so far") help develop solidarity in the group system.

4. **Humor is also an effective way to handle group secondary and tertiary tension.**

   A well-timed, lighthearted comment can move a group past an obstacle that seems insurmountable. Joking and laughing together increase the members' good feelings toward each other. This in turn helps members become more open toward each other, which can lead to resolution of their substantive and status differences. However, *never* joke to change the topic or to put someone in his or her place because this can destroy the cohesiveness the group has developed.

Tertiary tension is always tricky to handle; indirect methods often don't work. Group members may have to address the problem directly by saying something to the offending members. Either a group's designated leader or one of the other members can politely but firmly confront the members involved in the status struggle by pointing out the negative effects the power struggle is having on the rest of the group.

The process of managing task and socioemotional demands and their accompanying social tensions can be further complicated if a group uses electronic technology as a tool. Some people believe that computer-mediated technology increases a group's task communication and makes its socioemotional communication more challenging: This occurs because electronic tools keep groups focused on such task-related processes as keeping records, listing ideas, and structuring the problem-solving process. In addition, tools such as e-mail, which provide limited ways to express nonverbal cues, may encourage members not to think of each other as individuals. However, as we noted in Chapters 3 and 4, groups using CMC have discovered ways to communicate socioemotional information but in different ways from how it is exchanged in face-to-face groups.[8]

## PHASES IN GROUP DEVELOPMENT

Small group scholars have observed that many groups experience predictable phases as they develop. We will discuss two such models: Tuckman's model of group development and Gersick's two-phase model.

## Managing Tertiary Tensions

APPLY NOW

A situation that arose between Gena and Geoff on the set of *Man of La Mancha* illustrates the type of situation that often leads to tertiary tension. Gena had been in several plays and had studied acting informally. She loved the process of uncovering a character from the inside out and discovering the meaning of a scene or a line through the rehearsal period. Geoff was a more experienced actor with some directing experience as well. He had strong ideas about how certain lines should be read and certain scenes played. When he took it upon himself to advise Gena about how to read certain lines, she was both irritated and confused. She liked Geoff and respected his experience, but she had her own preferred way of developing a character. She knew she had several choices about how to handle the emerging conflict with Geoff, with some choices likely to be more effective than others for the entire enterprise. Consider Gena's situation:

1. What were several options Gena had for handling this situation? For example, she could do nothing or she could quit the cast. (List at least five in addition to these two.)
2. How was Geoff likely to react to each of these choices?
3. What were the likely outcomes for the group as a whole of each of these choices?
4. If you were faced with this choice, what would be more important to you—keeping control of "your" character or maintaining harmony among the cast? Are there other things that would be more important to you in this situation than harmony or control? If so, what would those be?
5. What choice would you be likely to make, and why? How effective do you think this choice would be?

Ask two class members to select one of Gena's options and to role-play this situation. After discussion about what worked and what didn't, ask two different class members to role-play a different option. Which communication strategies seem to be more effective? Why?

**Tuckman's Model of Group Development.** Bruce Tuckman's model of group development is a popular model for describing typical stages in how groups develop.[9] This model assumes that groups move through five stages in order. *Forming* occurs when group members first meet. Members form initial impressions of one another, start to get a handle on the group's task, and focus on getting along. The group avoids conflict and controversy as it deals with primary tension. Next, *storming* occurs when members start to tackle the group's important issues and strong feelings start to surface. In this stage, members argue to defend their points of view.

In the *norming* stage, the group has worked through its initial conflicts to establish its rules and norms about how it will operate. Members have gotten to know and appreciate one another's skills and abilities and feel like they are part of a group. During the *performing* stage, group members are able to work smoothly and effectively together. Not every group reaches this stage of development, but for groups that do, members are interdependent, responsibilities shift appropriately, and group identification is high. The fifth stage, *adjourning,* was added to the model later. As the group completes its task, members prepare for the group to disband. They may agree to keep in touch, and, in fact, some relationships are likely to continue after the group's life has ended.

Many small group scholars consider linear phase models too simplistic. There are multiple factors that can affect whether a group progresses through stages in an orderly way, what stages a group experiences, what order those stages occur in, and how long a stage may last. However, phases such as those in Tuckman's model seem to describe what many people have experienced. Thus, even though these stages are not universal, they do seem to capture the common experiences of many of us.

**Gersick's Two-Phase Model.** Connie Gersick's model contrasts somewhat to linear models such as Tuckman's.[10] In her examination of real-time work teams, Gersick discovered that no matter how long the group had to complete its task, a major change in focus occurred at the group's midpoint. For example, if the group had six months to complete its task, a significant transition point likely occurred at the three-month point. If the group was given three months, the transition occurred at one and a half months. During the first half, members oriented themselves to the task, gathered information, and planned their work. During the second half, they executed those plans. Each of these time periods represented fairly stable sustained work.

Before the midpoint, team members figured out what their charge was and how they would approach the task; they then worked steadily within that framework. At the halfway point, however, the groups suddenly seemed to realize that their time was beginning to run out. Members broke from their routine work to assess their progress toward the group's task; successful teams made adjustments in their work procedures, timelines, and so forth. If constructive changes were not made at this midpoint, they likely wouldn't be made at all because, during the second half of their time frame, teams moved into another long period of stability in how they went about their work. Then, as teams approached the end of their time period, they rushed to meet the expectations of outsiders, such as the boss, the teacher, or the parent organization. If the initial work procedures were appropriate, or the team made the right adjustments at midpoint, the team succeeded. Otherwise, the team failed to achieve its goals.

We see this pattern all the time in small group communication courses with semester-long assignments. At first, members make their plans and chug along the path they have set. Many groups get set in their ways early in their life cycle and tend to resist change. At midterm, reality hits and members get serious about completing their assignment. The midpoint seems to be a natural time when members are most open to assessing their progress and they often make changes at that point. They may scale back the scope of their project or tweak their timelines. Some groups effectively adjust their plans, but others do not make the necessary adjustments and may fail in their task.

Group members can assess how well they are proceeding by paying attention to important factors that affect the group's development. One such factor is the change brought on by the addition of a new member to the group, as is common. We now turn our attention to how both individuals and groups deal with socialization of members.

GLOSSARY

**Group Socialization**

*The process by which new and/or established members learn to fit together through communication*

## Group Socialization of Members

*Socialization* generally refers to someone learning to become part of something, such as a group. Just as children are socialized into families and school, group members are also socialized into newly formed and established groups. Carolyn Anderson, Bruce Riddle, and Matthew Martin, recognizing the central role of communication in group processes, define **group socialization** as a

> *reciprocal process of social influence and change in which both newcomers and/or established members and the group adjust and adapt to one another through verbal and nonverbal communication as they create and re-create a unique culture and group structures, engage in relevant processes and activities, and pursue individual and group goals.*[11]

### Integrating a New Member

APPLY NOW

One week before a community theater's opening night of *Hotel Paradiso,* leading man Richard, who had been complaining of shortness of breath, was told by his doctor that he needed heart bypass surgery—immediately! The cast was devastated. Members were concerned about Richard, of course, but they also were concerned about watching their six weeks of rehearsals go down the drain. The cast and crew had become a tight, cohesive group. Rehearsals had been going well, with the play promising to be the season's top moneymaker. The director debated canceling the run but prevailed on his talented friend Ted to assume Richard's part. Opening night was delayed for a week to give Ted time to learn the lines and the cast time to integrate a new cast member.

1. If you were the director, what would you do to help the reformulated cast get through its formation phase so members could focus on the play? Is there anything that can speed up the cast's formation phase?
2. If you were Ted, what would you do to help the other cast members feel comfortable with you?
3. If you were the cast members, how would you help Ted feel at ease?

There are three implications worth noting in this definition. First, the adapting and adjusting that happens when new members enter an established group occur through *communication* among group members. For group socialization to be effective, everyone involved—new and old members—must practice open communication, be accepting of one another, and welcome the positive change new members can bring.

Second, the definition recognizes that effective socialization requires a balance between individual member and group goals. In the Apply Now box, for Ted to become integrated into the cast, both his needs to do a good job *and* the other cast members' needs to have a good performance had to be met for the socialization experience to be a positive one.

Finally, the definition acknowledges socialization as an ongoing process that is not only about the new member but also about the group. The process is a mutual one: Both the newcomer *and* the group members initiate and engage in socialization activities, and although the newcomer must adjust to the group, so must the group adjust to the new member. We now consider, specifically, the phases typical of this socialization process.

## STAGES OF GROUP SOCIALIZATION

Anderson, Riddle, and Martin describe five stages of group socialization: antecedent, anticipatory, encounter, assimilation, and exit.[12] Each stage has its own unique communication demands, and behaviors in one stage have a ripple effect on subsequent stages. The stages are summarized in Table 5.1.

**TABLE 5.1 Stages of Group Socialization**

| Socialization Stage | Description |
|---|---|
| Antecedent | Before new members join the group, new and old members have attitudes, beliefs, motives, and behavior patterns that affect how they will function in the group. |
| Anticipatory | New and old members have expectations about one another; the new members have expectations about the group. Welcoming activities that introduce old and new members (informal dinners, getting-to-know-you meetings) help members overcome primary tension. |
| Encounter | New and old members begin to work together and adjust to one another; the new member's role is negotiated in the group, and old members' roles may change. |
| Assimilation | The new members are fully integrated into the group; role relationships have been worked out. |
| Exit | Members must cope with the loss of a member or the termination of the group. Discussion and formal disbanding activities help members say goodbye. |

Individual characteristics play a key role in the **antecedent stage** of group socialization, before the member has joined—or perhaps even thought about joining—the group. All members bring their own attitudes, motives, and communication behaviors to a group. This profoundly affects how ready and able they will be to engage in the socialization process and how willingly they approach group work and building relationships. For example, an individual who is friendly and open will create a different socialization experience than someone who is shy or resentful.

In the **anticipatory stage,** the potential member has begun to see him- or herself as becoming part of the group and has formed initial expectations of what group membership will be like. Group members, too, have formed expectations of how the new member will fit in. These mutual expectations lay the groundwork for the new member's eventual entry. This is what the sorority and fraternity rush process does, for example. Potential members meet current members and both decide who is and is not a good fit.

Generally, group socialization is enhanced when groups have systematic ways in place to integrate new members.[13] Examples include the orientation programs many clubs and organizations use. In the case of the community theater cast, this might have included a meeting with Ted in whom members introduced each other and talked about their expectations, an informal dinner with Ted, and a tour of the theater, stage and dressing rooms. These activities are *audition practices*; they help both the new member and the group draw a realistic picture of what the relationship will be between the new member and the group.[14]

The third stage of group socialization is the **encounter stage,** where the member actually joins the group. This is the stage where the expectations of the prior stages meet the reality of the group, and lasts for an indefinite period.[15] In this stage, the member and the group mutually adjust to one another as the member negotiates his or her role. Even when that role is given—such as a "pledge" in a fraternity or sorority—the new member's personality, attitudes, expectations, and so forth, will affect how the role is performed. Newcomers who seek information proactively about role expectations are socialized more effectively than those who do not seek this type of information.[16] We talk more about roles and norms later in the chapter.

The **assimilation stage** is characterized by full integration into the group and its structures.[17] In full integration new members have become comfortable with the group culture and show an active interest in the group's task and relationships. In turn, the existing members demonstrate acceptance of the new member. Members show a productive and supportive blending, enacting communication necessary to sustain the group's culture. If this integration does not occur smoothly, as is often the case, secondary tension can throw the group back into the anticipatory and encounter stages. Do not be surprised if these regressions occur because, over a group's life span, members will often have to negotiate a good fit between themselves and the rest of the group.

The fifth stage of group socialization is the **exit stage.** The process of socialization is experienced at both the individual and the group level and actually ends when a member leaves or when the group ceases to exist. Exiting a group, whether because an individual leaves or a group breaks up, can be a difficult transition and is one that group members often minimize.[18] If a member leaves, such as Richard in the community theater example, the group must deal with why he left, how he left, how his

**GLOSSARY**

**Antecedent Stage**
*The stage in group socialization during which members bring previous group experiences, attitudes, beliefs, motives, and communication traits to the process*

**Anticipatory Stage**
*The stage in group socialization describing individual and group initial expectations of each other*

**Encounter Stage**
*The stage in group socialization in which members' expectations meet with reality as members adjust and fit with each other*

**Assimilation Stage**
*The stage in group socialization in which group members show full integration*

**Exit Stage**
*The stage in group socialization in which individuals leave a group or the group disbands*

departure changes their communication, and what comes next. When an entire group disbands, members deal with variations of the same issues.

In some cases, the member may have left psychologically earlier than she or he left physically. One of your authors watched as a colleague and good friend retired. Almost a year before he actually left the department, he mentally pulled out. His interest in department issues faded, which affected what issues he fought for and how he voted in faculty meetings. Should you or anyone else leave a group voluntarily, it is a good idea to let others know you are leaving, help the group adjust to your departure, and try to remain in some sort of contact after you leave.

Group turnover is common. Your group can effectively manage turnover by developing a positive group attitude toward turnover—seeing it as a way to redefine who you are. When an entire group ends, do not treat it lightly—how you disband affects the kind of experiences you take into the next group. Joann Keyton recommends that groups give themselves an opportunity to say good-bye and to process their experience.[19]

CMC groups also experience bidirectional socialization—newcomers do not wait for the group to begin the socialization process but are proactive in initiating and managing that process.[20] For example, newcomers to online groups often lurk to get to know the group before they start participating. They do such things as emphasizing their identity with the other members by describing their similarity to the group's social category and they ask for help from group members. How newcomers manage their end of the socialization process can have lasting effects on their satisfaction and acceptance by the other members. This emerging area of research underscores, again, that online groups—despite the so-called limitations of nonverbal communication with technology—form and manage relationships, just as face-to-face groups do.

Group socialization is a complex process spanning the entire life of a group as groups adjust to members coming and going. We turn now to a discussion of group member roles and their importance to group dynamics.

## Group Roles

Your **role** is the part you play in a group. It emerges as a function of your personality, your behavior, your expectations, the expectations of other members, and any formal titles or instructions you may have been given regarding that group. Just as an actor has a role in a play, so do we all have a part to play in each group we belong to. And just as an actor has different parts in different plays, so do we have a unique position in each group we join.

> **GLOSSARY**
>
> **Role**
> *The part a member plays in a group*

### TYPES OF ROLES

Member roles are formal or informal. Formal roles are assigned on the basis of a member's official position or title and are sometimes called *positional* roles. For example, *secretary* is a formal role that carries with it certain requirements and expectations, which the group's rules will state: "The secretary shall write and distribute minutes of all meetings and provide a written summary of the group's work to the president of the student senate."

Informal roles, sometimes called *behavioral* roles, are the parts people play that reflect their personality traits, habits, and behaviors in the group. Through trial and error, every member of a group begins to specialize in certain behaviors within the group. For example, one work group included a member who knew how to use databases to find pertinent research reports. She became the group's researcher, as well as its prodder by constantly encouraging everyone to finish assignments when promised. Specific roles result from an interplay between the individual's characteristics and other members of the group; they emerge from group interaction.

## ROLE FUNCTIONS IN A SMALL GROUP

Members' roles in small groups are categorized according to what they do for the group: How does this behavior help or hinder the group in achieving its goal? Small group roles are typically classified into three main behavior categories: task, maintenance, and individual. The first two are helpful to the group; the third is not.

**Task Roles.** A **task role** contributes directly to the accomplishment of the group's task. You probably can think of many task-related behaviors you have seen performed in groups. Recently, one of us served on a church building committee trying to find a new place to meet. One member said, "Let's make a list of all the possibilities in our price range." After the committee completed the list, the member said, "Now, let's split up the list and each visit one or two before our next meeting. Who will volunteer to look at the two buildings on Glenstone Avenue?" These remarks, which *suggested procedure* and also helped *coordinate* the work of the group, are examples of task behavior and, as we noted earlier, help groups succeed. Other examples of helpful task roles are provided below. You can no doubt think of others:

- **Initiating and orienting:** proposing goals, activities, or plans of action; defining the group's position in relation to the goal. ("Let's get started by assigning ourselves tasks to complete before the next meeting.")
- **Clarifying:** making ambiguous statements clearer or interpreting issues. ("When you say the cost shouldn't be outrageous, do you mean it should be less than $10,000?")
- **Summarizing:** reviewing what has been said previously; reminding the group of items previously mentioned or discussed. ("So by next week, Delores will have the costumes made and Noel will have cast members committed to the play.")
- **Suggesting procedure:** suggesting a method or procedure to follow. ("Why don't we try brainstorming to help us come up with something new and different?")

**Maintenance Roles.** **Maintenance roles** help the group maintain harmonious relationships and a cohesive interpersonal climate. One member of the church building committee welcomed another member back from a three-week trip by saying, "It's great to have you back! Here's a summary of everything we did while you were gone. We held off making a decision until you got back because we really wanted to know what you thought." These remarks demonstrate a *gatekeeping* function by allowing the absent member to contribute to the discussion, and they *show solidarity* and *support*. Helpful maintenance behaviors include

- **Supporting:** expressing support for another's idea or belief; agreeing; following another's lead. ("I agree with Carla. We lose our focus when we meet until midnight.")

### GLOSSARY

**Task Roles**

*Roles that encompass behaviors that contribute directly to accomplishment of a group's task*

**Maintenance Roles**

*Roles that encompass behaviors that help a group maintain harmonious relationships and contribute to a cohesive interpersonal climate*

© Chris Ryan/age fotostock RF

- **Harmonizing:** reducing tension by reconciling disagreement; suggesting a compromise or new alternative acceptable to all; combining proposals into a compromise alternative; calming an angry member. ("Gena and Geoff, I think there are areas where you are in agreement. Let me suggest a compromise.")
- **Relieving tension:** joking and otherwise relieving tension; making strangers feel at ease; reducing status differences; encouraging informality. ("We're starting to get on each other's nerves, let's take a break.")
- **Showing solidarity:** indicating positive feelings toward one another; reinforcing a sense of group unity; promoting teamwork. ("We've done a great job pulling together. I have no doubt our performance will win rave reviews.")

**GLOSSARY**

**Individual Roles**

*Roles that encompass self-centered behaviors that place the individual's need ahead of the group's needs*

**Individual Roles.** **Individual roles** consist of self-centered behaviors. A self-centered member places his or her needs ahead of the group's. These roles do not help the group in any way and may be extremely harmful. Self-centered members generally are less well liked and have less influence within the group. And as we noted earlier, behaviors such as complaining and criticizing hurt group performance. Members prefer colleagues whose communication is other- rather than self-centered.[21] Unhelpful individual roles are:

- **Withdrawing:** giving no response to others; avoiding important differences; refusing to cope with conflicts; refusing to take a stand. ("Do whatever you want; I don't care.")

- **Blocking:** preventing progress toward group goals by constantly raising objections, repeatedly bringing up the same topic or issue after the group has considered it and rejected it. ("I know we already voted, but I want to talk about this again.")
- **Playing:** refusing to help the group with the task; excessive joking, dramatizing, and horsing around; making fun of others who are serious about the work. ("Don't be such a stick-in-the-mud; we've still got lots of time to finish. One time I remember . . .")
- **Acting helpless:** trying to elicit sympathy by constantly needing help to complete tasks; showing inability for independent thought or action; forcing others to complete or redo work turned in. ("I don't know what you want me to do here. I have never done research online and I don't think I can do it.")

The task, maintenance, and individual roles category system has held up well over time.[22] In addition, different types of behaviors and ways of approaching issues are needed at different points during a group's life cycle; having individuals who provide a balance of roles and whose roles complement one another enhances a team's performance.[23]

## THE EMERGENCE OF ROLES IN A GROUP

Through communication with each other, members gradually structure their unique contributions and roles. Think for a moment about the groups you belong to. Do you act exactly the same way in each one of them? Probably not. There are variations in your behavior because each group brings out different combinations of your skills, abilities, and personality characteristics. Normal people want to contribute their unique talents and abilities so they will be valued by the group. When the other group members appreciate and reward those behaviors, they perform them more often. In that way roles and a division of labor develop in the group.

Let's look at an example of how this occurs. Xion had a gift for storytelling. Because Xion felt uncomfortable whenever there was a lull in her seminar's discussion, she generally filled the silences with a story. Stories about her extensive travels easily captured the other members' attention and relieved the uneasiness that silence sometimes caused. The rest of the group encouraged her to relate her stories. Because of both Xion's ability to entertain and the other members' desire to listen, she carved out an informal (behavioral) role as the group's storyteller.

The other members of the group must reinforce a member's behavior if a role is to become stable and strong. If the other members had not been eager to set aside their work momentarily to listen to Xion, they would not have encouraged the development of her storyteller role. Instead, they would have discouraged her by paying little attention or reminding her that she was deflecting the group from its task. In that case Xion might have downplayed her storytelling and searched for another way to contribute. For example, she also was an active listener who clarified and summarized what others said. If she had not won esteem as the group's storyteller, she might have become the group's recorder or historian. From this example you can see how a member's role in a group depends not only on that member's characteristics, but also on how the other members respond.

The advent of new communication technologies such as net conferences and electronic group support systems can affect the process of role emergence.[24] Members skilled with technology may assume leadership roles they might not otherwise be open to.

### Creating a Space for Yourself in the Group

APPLY NOW

Everyone needs to feel valued and appreciated by his or her fellow group members. Sometimes, it isn't clear what your contribution—your role—should be. It was especially hard for members of the *Man of La Mancha* extras to know what their contributions should be. Most of them were not actors or dancers; quite a few were not even very good singers! Assume you are Davida, one of the people cast as extras, with limited performing talent. However, you like the idea of the project, you like your fellow cast members, and you really want the project to succeed. What can you personally do to make this project your own?

1. As Davida, do a brainwriting assignment: List your assets and talents. (In addition to the artistic talent we know you have, list at least five other assets.)
2. How could those assets and talents be used for this project?
3. Of the talents/assets listed in step 1, which one or ones would you prefer to use to help this project?
4. What strategies could you use to help ensure that you get to contribute in this way?

Just as roles emerge from members' trial-and-error interaction, groups create their rules and norms through interaction. We now focus on how rules and norms form and change over a group's life cycle, as well as how they affect group dynamics.

## Rules and Norms

Our premise throughout this text is that communication is *the* essential throughput process within a small group. Structuration theory, introduced earlier, helps explain how a group's communicative patterns create and sustain the group's norms and operating procedures. Recall from this earlier discussion that group members do not come to a group with a clean slate about how to behave. Instead, they bring ideas about how to behave from past group experience. These past experiences do not force members to act in a certain way but act as guides for behavior. Group member behavior can maintain these standards, modify them, or even ignore them and create new ones.

The whole process of communication among group members is rule-governed.[25] **Rules** and **norms** are the standards of behavior and procedures by which group members operate. Norms (informal standards) are not written down. In contrast, rules are more formal and usually are written in minutes or bylaws. Norms and rules tell members what they are allowed to do (e.g., "Members may call for a soda break after an hour"), what they are not allowed to do (e.g., "The seat at the head of the table is reserved for the group's chair, and no one else may occupy it"), and what they should do (e.g., "The designated leader is responsible for reserving the meeting place"). Rules and norms differ from each other only in their degree of formality. Norms are enforced by peer pressures, whereas rules are usually enforced by the designated leader. Rules

**GLOSSARY**

**Rules**

*Formal, explicit standards of behavior and procedures by which a group operates*

**Norms**

*Informal, implicit standards of behavior and procedures by which members operate*

...ay agree to change norms after an informal

...al functions for the group. By letting group members ...acceptable behavior, rules and norms reduce the uncertainty ... how to act. They establish procedures for working as a coordinated ...long run, productive rules and norms help the group achieve a high level ...ciency and quality control so that it can accomplish its assigned task well. Can you imagine how hard it would be if, every time you had a meeting, you had to negotiate the procedures by which the group should operate? You would be wasting all your valuable time deciding *how* you should work instead of getting your job done.

Formal rules are constructed in a couple of ways. Sometimes committees and other small groups establish their own formal rules for how they want to operate. Other times the parent organization that created the group also gives it rules by which to operate. For example, many large organizations use the committee procedures in *Robert's Rules of Order Revised* to govern meetings.

Norms usually are not discussed openly, but they still have a strong effect on the behavior of the group members. A friend of ours served on the city council of a small town. The council had developed a norm of meeting until all old business had been cleared, which meant that they sometimes met until midnight. Carla, a new member appointed to fill a vacancy for a council member who had been transferred, started to pack up her materials to leave at 9 o'clock. She explained that she assumed the group would end the meeting by 9 whether members had finished or not, and she had not made child care arrangements past that time. The other members looked at her in surprise. Some were sympathetic, but all continued to meet after she had left. At subsequent meetings Carla, who realized her mistaken assumption about meeting norms, changed her child care arrangements so she could stay until the meeting's end.

## DEVELOPMENT OF GROUP NORMS

How do you suppose the council members established their norm of working until the old business was cleared business? There are four ways norms are set in a small group.[26]

1. **Behaviors that occur early in the group's history often establish norms through primacy.**

   When group members first meet, they feel uncertain and uncomfortable. Anything that reduces the uncertainty is welcomed. Thus, what first occurs in a group can easily become habit because it helps reduce the feeling of uncertainty. For example, suppose you serve on a committee that includes faculty and students. Initially, you aren't sure whether to address the faculty members by their first names; if you hear a fellow student member addressing them by titles, chances are you will follow that lead.

2. **Sometimes norms are established by explicit statements that a leader or another member makes.**

   For example, one member might tell a new member, "The boss likes to have proposals in writing. If you want to make a suggestion about work procedures at the staff meeting, you should bring a handout for everyone to use." This statement relays information about the group leader's preferences and also subtly lets the

### Norm Enforcement in Internet Groups

MEDIA AND TECHNOLOGY

Social network users sometimes experience bullying (i.e., insults, sarcasm, intense language) through postings on their profile pages. Bullying has become a distinct characteristic of CMC and has been interpreted by many providers to be unsuitably hostile. These behaviors range from personal attacks to a mild form of teasing, and a number of researchers have found that they can serve an unintended purpose online. In his examination of Internet mailing lists, Hongiie Wang found that bullying was one of the only tools users had to enforce the informal rules they believed to exist. It was used as a form of policing or a method to "educate the ignorant" about the rules and norms of the online community. Despite the unintended consequences that bullying has to facilitate the norms and rules for Internet groups, most social networks attempt to hinder this practice by establishing their own explicit norms for the behavior of members.

SOURCE: H. Wang, "Flaming: More Than a Necessary Evil for Academic Mailing Lists," *Electronic Journal of Communication* 6 (1996).

new member know that suggestions are supposed to be well thought out before being presented to the group.

3. **Some norms are established through critical events that occur in a group.** For example, one of us once taught a graduate seminar of nine people who came to trust each other, often revealing personal information in class. Two of the students told nonmembers some of what occurred in the class. When the other members discovered this, they felt angry. At the next class meeting, members expressed their feelings of betrayal. Before the critical incident, some members thought it was all right to reveal in-class information to selected outsiders, but after the meeting it was clear to all members that such behavior was a serious violation of a group confidentiality norm.

4. **Many norms are taken from the general culture in which the group members live.** For example, you know a lot about how to behave as a student, no matter what the class. True, some professors are more formal than others, but certain standards of behavior (such as raising your hand when you have a question or a comment and not calling the professor or other students rude names) carry over from one class to another. Thus, many carryover behaviors in a group are ones we have learned as members of a particular culture.

This particular origin of small group norms may become troublesome when we interact with members from different cultures. For example, we have observed students from Asian cultures behave very submissively in groups of American students. These international students were following the norms of their native cultures, just as were the American students. Likewise, African Americans and Hispanics tend to use the vocal backchannel (saying things like "mm-hmm" and "OK" while another is speaking) more frequently than European Americans. Lack of understanding of another's cultural norms can cause problems in a group.

## ENFORCEMENT OF GROUP NORMS

If norms are not written down, how do group members learn them? To infer what the norms are, pay attention to two types of behaviors: those that occur regularly and those that incur disapproval.

Behaviors that occur consistently from one meeting to the next probably reflect a group norm. For example, if at every meeting each group member sits in the same seat and waits for the leader to start the discussion, you are seeing evidence of two norms.

Behaviors that are punished by peer pressure also indicate norms. The strongest evidence of a group norm is members' negative reaction to a particular behavior. Most peer pressure comes in the form of nonverbal signals, as group members roll their eyes at each other, glare, shake their heads, or turn away from the violator. Sometimes they pointedly ignore the offending member's contributions. Carla, the new council member who left early, received only mild expressions of surprise and even some verbal expressions of sympathy, but there was no doubt that she had violated a norm, and she quickly came into compliance with that norm at the next meeting.

Members who consistently violate important group norms are called **deviants,** and they make the other group members very uncomfortable—even angry. To conscientious group members, deviants seem to thumb their noses at the group by implying that their own needs and wishes are more important than those of the group. The other members try to force the deviants to fall in line by applying increasing pressure to conform (see Table 5.2).[27] This is what the rest of the city council might have done had the new member not corrected her behavior right away.

Just because groups usually pressure a deviant to conform does not mean the deviant should automatically cave in to such pressure. Sometimes groups consider people deviant if they disagree or won't go along with the group's plans. However, such people can actually be helpful to a group if they cause the other members to examine information and ideas more carefully. Even so, the other members may not recognize that such disagreement, or idea deviance, can be helpful, so they try to force agreement. This pressure can be hard to resist, even when the deviant has a good case. We present more information about the effect of idea-deviant disagreement in Chapter 9.

**GLOSSARY**

**Deviants**

*Members who consistently violate group norms*

## CHANGING A GROUP NORM

We noted earlier that behaviors occurring at the first few meetings may become norms that can cause problems later. For example, recall that when members first meet, they experience primary tension, which makes them so polite and stiff that they do not confront or disagree with each other. This can easily develop into a norm of "no conflict," which stops members from expressing disagreements or doubts. This "no conflict" norm can be detrimental to the group's later decision-making abilities.

Although it isn't always easy, groups recognizing and using their own structuration process can change unproductive norms. One effective approach is to focus the group's attention on the norm and the harm it is creating rather than on the person violating the norm. In addition, do not try to force other members to accept your suggestions for changing the norm. They are likely to become defensive, refuse to change, and

**TABLE 5.2 How Groups Deal with Deviant Members**

**FIRST, MEMBERS TRY TO PERSUADE THE DEVIANT MEMBER TO CONFORM TO THE GROUP NORMS:**

- They try reasoning with the deviant: "When you aren't here, Carla, we miss your important input."
- They try to persuade the deviant, first with teasing and then more insistently: "Your husband can survive one evening without you, can't he, Carla?" and "Look, Carla, it really messes up the rest of our schedules when you leave early. Why don't you get a babysitter for one night a week—that wouldn't be so bad, would it?"
- They may attempt to punish or even coerce the deviant: "If you really want to be a part of this council, Carla, you're going to have to put in the same amount of effort as the rest of us. Otherwise, we can't support that ordinance you've been promoting."

**SECOND, SOLIDARITY BUILDS AMONG THE OTHER MEMBERS AGAINST THE DEVIANT:**

- "I don't see why we should go out of our way to help Carla pass that ordinance—she doesn't seem to care about any of our schedules!"

**THIRD, MEMBERS IGNORE AND WILL EVENTUALLY ISOLATE THE DEVIANT:**

- "Carla, we've all agreed that it would be better if you resigned from the council. We need a full-time member."

## When Is It OK to Be Deviant?

ETHICAL DILEMMA

In the 1980s Beechnut, the second-largest producer of baby food in the United States, was found knowingly to have sold adulterated apple juice it advertised as 100 percent pure.[28] The company had been losing money, and using concentrate with artificial ingredients saved millions of dollars. Beechnut officials argued that other companies were also selling fake juice and that it was perfectly safe.

Assume you are a Beechnut executive who strongly disagrees with the action the rest of the Beechnut officials seem determined to take. You've mentioned your disagreement a couple of times and have been getting both subtle and not-so-subtle pressure to keep quiet. Members have said things to you like, "We've been over this and over this. You keep bringing this up after we've decided." You're marketing the juice as "100 percent pure," which isn't accurate. But on the other hand, no one is claiming that

***Concluded***

ETHICAL DILEMMA

the impure juice is unsafe. Is that really so bad, when it's saving money and jobs for the company?

Groups can be vicious to members who are deviant, and you are definitely a deviant in this group.

1. What do you say to the other members?
2. How can you withstand the pressure the others are placing on you? Should you withstand it?
3. For what reasons would you go along with the other members?
4. For what reasons would you resist?
5. What would you do?

resent your attempt to control them. Instead, you want the group to think of ways to change the norm so that all the members participate in establishing a more productive group norm, for only the group can make a lasting change in a norm. The guidelines in Table 5.3 will help you.

**TABLE 5.3** **Changing a Group Norm**

**PREPARATION**

1. Make sure you are seen as a responsible, loyal member of the group; others won't appreciate your comments if you have been unreliable or act "holier than thou."
2. Ask yourself, "What harm is the norm causing?" Observe the effects of the group norm on the members and the group as a whole; count the offending behaviors and make notes of your observations.

**CONSTRUCTIVE CONFRONTATION**

1. Select an appropriate time to share your information with other members.
2. Share your observations about the effects of the unproductive norm on the group; explain the unproductive norm you have observed and what problems it causes.
3. Ask whether others also have observed these effects or share your concerns.
4. Express yourself supportively, not defensively:
   *a.* Defensive comment: "I'm sick and tired of always being on time while the rest of you wander in any time you please!"
   *b.* Supportive comment: "For the past four meetings we have started between 15 and 25 minutes late. We seem to have developed a norm that scheduled starting times do not need to be observed. Two of us have had to leave these meetings before they were finished in order to go to class. As a result we have missed several key decisions, and the rest of you have had to bring us up to date on what happened. Does anyone else see this as a problem?"

**GLOSSARY**

**Group Climate**

*The atmosphere or environment within a group*

The elements we have discussed thus far—how group members manage their tensions, how they work through important tasks in their development and formation, and what roles, rules, and norms they establish—all help create the group's climate. We now examine how the group's climate contributes to the formation of an effective team.

## Development of a Group's Climate

Maintaining a pleasant interpersonal climate was the most frequently mentioned communication skill needed, as reported by managers of work groups.[29] Joseph Folger and Marshall Poole, experts in group conflict, define **group climate** as "the relatively enduring quality of the group situation that (*a*) is experienced in common by group members, and (*b*) arises from and influences their interaction and behavior."[30] This general environment, atmosphere, emotional tone, or "air" of a group is pervasive; emerges from and impacts the group's communication; and is experienced by all members of the group. Climates, whether positive or negative, are the ongoing consequences of member communication and relationships, just as structuration theory suggests.

### Changing a Norm You Believe Is Harmful

APPLY NOW

Carla, our city councilwoman, chose to accept the group norm of meeting as long as it took to complete the group's work. However, there are pros and cons to that norm. Yes, the work was not permitted to pile up, and the group achieved closure at each meeting. But members were visibly fatigued at midnight, and there was a noticeable loss of concentration and productivity after 10 P.M. Assume Carla's position for a moment and address the following questions:

As Carla you genuinely believe the group would be more productive and make better decisions if they had more, but shorter, meetings. List at least three choices you have for dealing with this norm.

1. What are the consequences, both to you and to the group, of each choice?
2. What strategy do you think would be most likely to succeed? Why?
3. If you decide to try to change this group norm, how would you go about doing it? In your answer include any planning you might do for bringing this up to the group. Also, describe exactly what you would say to bring this up.

Select five people, including one to play Carla, to role-play a city council meeting where Carla brings up the question of the meeting length norm. After the role-play, discuss as a class what worked and what did not. Make sure to let the participants in the "meeting" express any feelings they might have experienced during the role-play.

Members who could disagree without being disagreeable, who could admit mistakes, and who could keep emotions on an even keel were particularly valued by the work group managers mentioned earlier.[31] You probably have attended group meetings in which you felt the warmth and affection of the members for each other. The climate was empowering, flexible, and participatory. Conversely, you probably also have observed meetings in which you felt tension and distrust. The climate was defensive, rigid, thwarting, hostile, and authoritarian. These are but two examples of types of group climates or atmospheres. There are many dimensions of a group's climate. We explain three we consider most important: trust, cohesiveness, and supportiveness.

GLOSSARY

**Trust**

*The general belief that members can rely on each other*

## TRUST

**Trust** refers to the general belief that members can rely on each other. When group members trust each other, they do not have to worry that others might be lying to them or may have secret reasons for their behavior. Instead of being suspicious and secretive, members who trust one another are more likely to create an open climate in which people share freely. Two kinds of trust are particularly important to groups: task-related and interpersonal.

### Can You Be Trusted?

ETHICAL DILEMMA

Imagine that this is a particularly busy semester for you, and you feel as if you barely have time to breathe. You will graduate at the end of the semester, and you don't know how you'll manage all your coursework, to say nothing of job hunting. One of your courses entails a group project; you have just met with your team members for the first time in class. The others are enthused about the project and have already started to make a schedule of meeting times for the semester. You think they are planning far too many meetings—many more than the project will need. Privately, you think you can get your own work on the project finished and attend perhaps half of the meetings the others have scheduled. But if you say that to your fellow group members, you're afraid that they'll think you don't care about the project. And if you just skip meetings without saying anything now, you're afraid they'll think you're a slacker. But then again, you'll probably never see these people again. Either way, though, it seems like you can't win.

1. What other choices do you think you have besides saying no to the meetings now and just not showing up later?
2. Do you stay silent and make a private decision to make the meetings you can and not worry about the rest?
3. Do you say something to the group? If so, what?
4. For each of the options you came up with, what are the consequences to the group of that action?
5. What action is least likely to undermine the group's trust in you?

A member who is trustworthy regarding the task can be counted on to complete assignments and produce top-notch work for the group. The higher the quality of the individual work that members do for the group, the higher will be the quality of the group's outputs. Failure to complete assignments for the group quickly destroys trust. A member who does not come through for the group forces the other members to pick up the slack. This is one of the most common sources of conflict and can poison a group's climate.

*Interpersonal trust* refers to the belief that the members of the group are operating in the group's best interests and that they value their fellow members. Suppose a member you trust says to you, "I think there are lots of problems with your idea." You are likely to ask that member for reasons and to pay careful attention to the reasons given. On the other hand, if the same statement comes from someone you don't trust, you may wonder what's behind the statement, ignore it, get into a shouting match, or try to find subtle ways of sabotaging that member's suggestions. Members who appear to operate from **hidden agenda** motives, or personal and private motives, are seen as untrustworthy by others. So are "politicians" who always seem to have a personal angle for their behavior that has nothing to do with the group. In fact, politicians can be so destructive to a group that Carl Larson and Frank LaFasto, who studied excellent groups, recommend that the group leader get rid of them as soon as possible.[32]

Recent research on trust suggests that the two components of interpersonal and task-related trust emerge at different times over the life of the group.[33] Early on, trust among members is one-dimensional and is especially influenced by how familiar members are with one another's strengths and weaknesses. However, once members begin to work together, they base their judgments of trust on the other members' actual behavior. Interpersonal trust develops when members are willing to help one another and take a personal interest in one another and the team. Task-related trust develops when members prove themselves to be reliable performers at the task. Although these two trust factors develop separately after members have had time to work together, interpersonal trust actually has a stronger relationship with team performance and lasts longer. Ideally, group members are trustworthy on both counts.

**GLOSSARY**

**Hidden Agenda** *An unstated private goal a member wants to achieve through a group*

**Cohesiveness** *The bonds of attachment members have for each other*

## COHESIVENESS

**Cohesiveness** refers to the attachment members feel toward each other, the group, and the task—the bonds that hold the group together. In a highly cohesive group, members feel a strong sense of belonging, speak favorably about the group and the other members, and conform to the norms of the group. In a group that is not cohesive, members do not feel much sense of belonging. They may not attend faithfully or may even leave the group because they find other groups more rewarding.

As with trust, there are two types of cohesiveness: task cohesiveness and social (or interpersonal) cohesiveness.[34] In a group that has high task cohesiveness, members understand and accept the task, are committed to completing it, may be excited about working on it, and experience what has been called *group drive*, or motivation to accomplish the task.[35] This describes the *Man of La Mancha* cast very well. Interpersonal, or social, cohesiveness means that members like and are attracted to each other. They like to spend time together and enjoy each other's company. These two forms of cohesiveness affect group productivity and decision-making quality in different ways.[36] When a group's cohesiveness is due to interpersonal attraction, the task may take a back seat, which can lower the quality of a group's decisions. In addition, sometimes groups high in interpersonal cohesiveness develop norms that keep productivity low or find themselves getting off track easily. A friend of ours sorted letters for the Postal Service. His co-workers let him know that he was working too fast and that if he wanted to stay in their good graces he would not exceed the informal production norm they had developed. In contrast, groups with high task cohesiveness generally are more productive, and decision making is enhanced. Thus, the presence of task-focused norms in a group moderates the effect of cohesiveness—groups with strong task norms and high cohesiveness outperform cohesive groups without strong task norms.[37] The relationship between cohesiveness and performance is a complex one, but is generally positive.[38] The strength of that relationship, though, depends on the type of task and the extent to which members must communicate interdependently to complete the task.

Although highly cohesive groups are satisfying to their members, such groups need to be particularly careful to guard against **groupthink,** the tendency not to examine critically all aspects of a decision or problem.[39] The term was coined by Irving Janis, who conducted an exhaustive study of the disastrous 1961 decision made by President Kennedy and his advisers to invade Cuba at the Bay of Pigs. This now-classic study concluded that although the advisers were well-informed experts, the group's cohesiveness contributed to their poor decision making. Members made it difficult for those who disagreed to speak up by implying, both subtly and overtly, that disagreement was tantamount to disloyalty to the group. This is similar to the situation Beechnut faced, as described in the Ethical Dilemma box on page 109. We discuss groupthink in detail in Chapter 7.

Trust and cohesiveness are related to the personality characteristic of agreeableness, which refers to how cooperative and sympathetic people are to others.[40] Bradley and his associates found that face-to-face groups with more agreeable members performed better than groups with less agreeable members. They suggest that when members are agreeable, they tend to be interested in and want to communicate with one another. This communication encourages social interaction that promotes cohesiveness. In addition, members high in agreeableness seek to maintain good relationships with their fellow group members, which increases trust.[41] Table 5.4 provides suggestions you can use to increase the cohesiveness of a group.

**GLOSSARY**

**Groupthink**

*The tendency of highly cohesive groups not to evaluate thoroughly and critically all aspects of a decision or problem*

## SUPPORTIVENESS

In a supportive climate members encourage each other, care about each other, and treat each other with respect. Supportive members uphold ethical principles about how to treat each other. Because members feel safe from psychological assault, they are free to direct most of their energy toward helping the group accomplish its task. On the other hand, a defensive climate emerges when members try to control, manipulate, and criticize each other.[42] If members are afraid they will be attacked by other members, they hesitate to offer their opinions. They spend so much time defending themselves or being on the alert for psychological assault that they do not pay much attention to

**TABLE 5.4 Increasing Cohesiveness in a Group**

1. Develop a strong group identity.
2. Encourage group traditions, such as annual parties, special greetings and handshakes, and rituals.
3. Develop in-group insignias, such as T-shirts and sweatshirts, pins, or hats.
4. Refer to the group members as *we* and *us*.
5. Give credit to the group as a whole when representing the group to outsiders or other groups.
6. Give credit to individuals within the group for contributions they make toward the group's goal achievement.
7. Support both disagreement and agreement by encouraging openness and freedom of expression.
8. Create a climate of supportiveness in which every individual feels appreciated and believes his or her ideas are valued.
9. Set clear and attainable goals for the group.
   a. Goals should be difficult enough to provide a challenge and produce group pride when they are met.
   b. Goals should not be so hard that they are nearly impossible to attain, because failure will lower cohesiveness.

the task of the group. Table 5.5 provides a list of supportive and contrasting defensive behaviors with sample statements for each.

All the defensive behaviors include an element of negative judgment that hurts interpersonal relationships within a group. Instead of critically evaluating ideas, members are critical of each other as persons. Notice, also, the relationship between cohesiveness and supportiveness. It is hard to feel strongly attached to a group if you don't know from one moment to the next when you are going to be attacked. Can you begin to see how each element of the group system is related to all the other elements?

All the factors we have discussed in this chapter contribute to the structure that creates a team out of individual members. The way members develop over time and manage their tensions, the roles and norms that develop, and the climate members create—all work together to construct each team's unique culture.

## Ethical Behavior during Group Formation

Members need to pay attention to the ethics of their behavior particularly as a group's roles and norms develop. Patterns that form early in a group's life guide their future interaction and can be hard to break. That is why it is critical for those

**TABLE 5.5** **Defensive and Supportive Communication Behaviors and Statements**

| Defensive Behaviors | Supportive Behaviors |
|---|---|
| **Evaluation** Judging the other person; indicating by words or tone of voice that you disapprove of a person: "That's a pretty dumb idea!" | **Description** Desiring to understand the other's point of view without making the other person wrong: "Tell me more about how your idea would work." |
| **Control** Trying to dominate or change the other person; insisting on having things your way: "I want to do it this way, so that's what we're going to do." | **Problem orientation** Trying to search honestly for the best solution without having a predetermined idea of what the solution should be: "What ideas do you all have about how we might solve this?" |
| **Strategy** Trying to manipulate the other person; using deceit to achieve your own goals: "Don't you really think that it would be better if we did it this way?" | **Spontaneity** Reacting honestly, openly, and freely: "I really like that, and here's something else we could do. . . ." |
| **Neutrality** Not caring about how the other group members feel: "We don't have time to hear about your car accident right now; we have work to do." | **Empathy** Showing by your words and actions that you care about the other group members: "You had a car accident on the way here? Are you OK? Is there anything we can do to help?" |
| **Superiority** Maximizing status differences; pulling rank on other members with title, wealth, expertise, and so on: "Well, I'm chair of the committee, and I believe I make the final decision about how we do this." | **Equality** Minimizing status differences; treating every member of the group as an equally valued contributor: "I know I'm the chair, but the solution belongs to the whole committee, so don't give my ideas any more weight than anyone else's." |
| **Certainty** Being a know-it-all; acting positive that your way or belief is the only correct one: "I know exactly what we ought to do here, so I'll take care of it." | **Provisionalism** Being tentative in expressing your opinions; being open to considering others' suggestions fairly: "I have an idea I think might work. . . ." |

patterns to be productive and to adhere to the highest standards of ethical behavior. The following ethical guidelines emerge from the National Communication Association Credo for Ethical Communication that we introduced in Chapter 1. They speak to those issues, such as the development of norms and group culture, that have been the focus of this chapter.

1. **Group members should communicate in ways that help establish a supportive climate.**

   Members will not do their best thinking if they feel they have to hold back for fear of being ridiculed or attacked. Ironically, honest disagreement is more likely to occur in a supportive climate of trust. Members must monitor their own and one another's behavior to ensure that their communication encourages others to share freely. Each member is responsible for working actively to create a supportive climate.

2. **Communication that degrades other members must not be tolerated.**

   This principle represents the flip side of the previous principle. Behaviors that degrade, ridicule, attempt to intimidate, or bully others must be stopped immediately. Such behaviors violate the mutual respect that should be present among group members and contributes to poor decision making.

3. **Freedom of expression, diversity of perspective, and tolerance of disagreement must be encouraged.**

   If every member of a group has exactly the same perspective (unlikely in any case) and believes exactly the same thing, why bother to assemble the group? The best group work emerges when members share their diverse perspectives and points of view. This means that disagreement will surely occur—and should be welcomed! We discuss group conflict fully in Chapter 9.

4. **Members must be willing to express their genuine personal convictions, even if this requires courage to disagree with other members.**

   Ultimately, members are responsible for their own behavior. Ideally, a group's climate encourages free expression and tolerates disagreement, but even when it does not, individual members must be willing to speak their minds. To say that you agree with something the group plans to do when you privately disagree is unethical. Be willing to hear what the other members have to say and to be persuaded, but in the end, if you think the group is about to make a big mistake or do something unethical, you must be willing to speak out. You may prevent a disaster down the road.

## RESOURCES FOR REVIEW AND DISCUSSION

### SUMMARY

- Communication among group members creates, maintains, and changes a group through a process of structuration.
- As groups form, members must handle both task and socioemotional issues simultaneously, as well as deal with primary, secondary (task-related), and tertiary tension over power struggles.
- Many groups experience predictable phases in their development. Tuckman's model describes five phases of forming, storming, norming, performing, and adjourning; Gersick's two-phase model describes a make-or-break transition occurring at the midpoint of a group's time frame.
- Group socialization of new and/or established members and the group is a complex process of learning how to fit together. Effective communication between all parties is crucial to successful and positive socialization, which in turn influences other group processes such as leadership, roles, norms, and climate. The process can be described in five phases: antecedent, anticipatory, encounter, assimilation, and exit. Group socialization continues throughout the life of the group until the new member leaves or the entire group disbands.
- Task, maintenance, and individual roles are three main categories of roles members perform in the group.

- Rules and norms, the standards of behavior for members of the group, differ only in their degree of formality. Group norms, or informal rules, are established through primacy, explicit statements members make, critical events in the group's history, and carryover behaviors from the culture at large.
- The group's climate is the atmosphere in which members work. Three important aspects of a group's climate are trust, cohesiveness, and supportiveness.
- Four ethical principles are particularly important during group formation: creating a supportive climate, stopping behaviors that degrade others, encouraging freedom of expression, and being willing to speak honestly.

EXERCISES

1. Watch a film that shows group formation (classic examples include *The Breakfast Club, The Commitments*, and *Lord of the Flies*), and discuss the following questions:
   - *a.* How did the group manage important issues in its formation phase? Were there any unresolved issues that later hurt the group?
   - *b.* What instances of primary, secondary, or tertiary tensions did you observe?
   - *c.* Who became the emergent leader of the group? Why did this person emerge? What were the sources of this person's power as a leader?
2. Observe an actual group or watch a video of a task-oriented group. (Two videos produced especially for this textbook contain suitable segments for this exercise.) Make a chart based on the task, maintenance, and individual behaviors described in the chapter. List the people's names at the top and the task, maintenance, and individual behaviors along the left side. Whenever each person speaks, categorize his or her remarks by making a note in the appropriate category. For each person in the group you observe:
   - *a.* What sort of role profile would you draw for that person?
   - *b.* How would you label that person's informal role?
   - *c.* Do you think the person's behaviors were helpful or not? Why?
   - *d.* How would you change the category system to be more useful for you?
3. Look at the partial list of task, maintenance, and individual roles described in this chapter. What additions would you make to this list? What other helpful, and unhelpful, behaviors have you observed, and how would you label those behaviors?
4. Think of the most (or least) cohesive group you have ever belonged to, and explain why this group was so cohesive (or uncohesive). Which supportive (or defensive) behaviors were most prevalent in the group? What forms of trust did you observe (or not observe) that made the biggest difference in the group's climate?

KEY TERMS • CONCEPTS

Antecedent Stage
Anticipatory Stage
Assimilation Stage
Cohesiveness
Deviants
Encounter Stage
Exit Stage
Group Climate
Group Socialization
Groupthink
Hidden Agenda
Individual Roles
Maintenance Roles
Norms
Primary Tension
Role
Rules
Secondary Tension
Structuration
Task Roles
Tertiary Tension
Trust

CHAPTER 6

# Working with Diversity in the Small Group

## CHAPTER OUTLINE



## CHAPTER OBJECTIVES

**After reading this chapter you should be able to:**

1. Define *diversity* and give several examples of diversity within a group.
2. Describe and explain the differences between surface-and deep-level diversity.
3. Explain how diversity benefits a group.
4. Describe the four learning styles identified by Kolb and explain how each can benefit a group.
5. Describe the four dimensions of the Myers-Briggs Type Indicator® personality inventory.
6. Define cognitive/informational diversity and explain how it can affect group outcomes.
7. Define *culture,* describe three dimensions on which cultures differ, and explain how each can affect group interaction.
8. Explain how racial or ethnic, gender, and generational differences can be considered cultural.
9. Explain why symbolic convergence and fantasy can help group members bridge differences by contributing to a group identity.
10. Explain the principles that will help group members make the most of their differences.

## The Misfit

CASE 6.1

Judy, a gregarious and sociable class member, had the gift of making everyone laugh. When the class formed task groups that would stay together for the entire semester to complete a major project, several groups wanted Judy to join them. She chose to join a group with two other women and two men who, from their participation in class discussions, seemed bright and conscientious students. This group had a good mix of talent—members who could organize a task, members who could write well, members who had many contacts throughout the university to help them find the resources they needed, and members, like Judy, who could make the task enjoyable. All the elements existed to make this a productive and fun experience.

Several weeks later, group animosity ran dangerously high. Three members wanted to fire Judy from the group. The fourth member, Misty, liked Judy well enough but was also frustrated by her constantly pulling the group off-task. Her incessant joking, socializing, and attempts to ensure that everyone was having a good time had backfired. Instead, the others concluded that Judy was an airhead; they were frustrated by her inability to stay on task and what they perceived as her lack of seriousness. The members wanted an A+ for this major project. They had decided to give the finished project to their instructor a week early for feedback about how to revise and polish it, but Judy's constant socializing had slowed them down. The others blamed her for missing their original, self-imposed deadline. By the end of the semester, Misty was the only member who would speak directly to Judy and thus served as the only link between Judy and the others, who ignored Judy whenever they could. The project was turned in on time but not early enough to receive instructor feedback; it received a B, for which everyone (but Judy) blamed Judy.

These students' journals revealed that none of them had much insight into their own or other members' behavior. Misty and the others held Judy responsible for everything that went wrong. But Judy was the most puzzled and frustrated member of all. She never understood why the others were so "cold." She had looked forward to making some new friends during the project, but her group members didn't seem to be interested in her. The harder she tried to take an interest in them, the more she felt rebuffed.

Judy's sociability and humor could have added quite a bit to the process—if she had only recognized that the others' priorities were not social. But the others, with their extreme task-orientation, were unable to see how Judy's personality could potentially have benefited their group. Instead, group members were locked into a struggle for control over their priorities, and no one won!

**This situation is all too typical. Many groups self-destruct because they mishandle members' diverse perspectives and personalities. Most of us think others should share our goals, priorities, communication patterns, and working styles. When they don't, we often blame them for being wrong. Few of us appreciate others who are quite different from us. Ironically, it is our very differences that contribute to making a group potentially more effective than an individual. After all, if you and I think alike, act alike, and process information alike, one of us is unnecessary to the process! Diversity itself is central to effective group problem solving, but unproductive views about diversity and poor management of diversity cause the difficulties so many groups experience.**

**This chapter will show you how you can accept and capitalize on diversity to produce a better group outcome. We discuss several types of diversity, including differences in motives for joining a group, in personality, and in cultural backgrounds. We conclude by discussing symbolic convergence and fantasy as a way members can bridge their differences.**

## What Is Diversity?

Small groups provide a valuable means for solving the variety of problems we face daily. To be effective, groups must process all kinds of resources—including each other—and this requires coordinating differences. This chapter addresses a fundamental feature of effective group work: diversity.

**Diversity** in a group refers to differences among members. There are endless ways in which members can differ, from how members learn, to personality differences, to differences of opinion. Misty wanted to get right down to business; for her, chitchat was a waste of time. Judy, on the other hand, couldn't focus on the task until she had connected informally with others.

A main reason to assemble a small group is to capture diverse views. Working with diversity means finding the "good mix" of member and group characteristics that promotes

GLOSSARY

**Diversity**

*Differences among group members, from personality and learning style differences to differences of opinion*

© Digital Archive Japan/Alamy RF

but does not impair effective group outcomes. From the outset we want to emphasize that simply recognizing that differences are essential to group problem solving and then "mixing up" group member characteristics are not enough. Finding the different pieces and then throwing them together is a recipe for disaster, as our classroom group found out. Successful groups realize that diversity is not simply a matter of "managing" but valuing and capitalizing on differences. That means remembering that group members are human beings who value their identities and their individual stories.[1] Group members want to be known and acknowledged by their teammates; this sense of being known within the group increases trust, individual learning, and satisfaction in both virtual and face-to-face teams.[2]

The diversity of group member composition has understandably intrigued small group researchers for years. **Homogeneity** (similarity) and **heterogeneity** (difference) are terms typically used to capture the degree of variance in group composition. Marvin Shaw, an early pioneer in small group research, said, "The general assumption is that most group activities require a variety of skills and knowledge; hence the more heterogeneous the group, the more likely the necessary abilities and information will be available and the more effective the group is likely to be."[3] Sounds simple enough, but getting that "good mix" is not easy. Group members can differ in any number of ways, yet coordinating those differences is no easy task. Scholars differentiate between

GLOSSARY

**Homogeneity**

*Groups composed of members who are similar or alike in member characteristics*

**Heterogeneity**

*Groups composed of members who are different on one or more dimensions*

**GLOSSARY**

**Surface Diversity**

*Diversity based on immediately observable characteristics such as age, sex, race, and ethnicity.*

**Deep-Level Diversity**

*Diversity based on attitudes, believes, values, and personality characteristics that are revealed over time through members' communication.*

**surface diversity**, which is based on immediately observable characteristics such as age, sex, race, and ethnicity, and **deep-level diversity**, based on attitudes, beliefs, values, and personality characteristics that are revealed over time through members' communication.[4] Much of the diversity research has focused on surface characteristics, which has produced inconsistent results, sometimes showing that such characteristics matter and other times showing they do not. A closer look at the research suggests that surface diversity may be initially important but that importance diminishes over time, with deep-level diversity having much more influence on such things as group cohesiveness and performance. A recent review of field studies found that deep-level factors (particularly member agreeableness, conscientiousness, openness to experience, collectivism (contrasted with individualism), and preference for teamwork) all affected team performance.[5] When similarity dominates a group, members can take more for granted about their values, perceptions, perspectives, and so forth. Communication is easier, in the beginning, with more overlap and shared meaning. In contrast, when members are more heterogeneous, there is less initial overlap or shared meaning, so they have to do more explaining and pay more conscious attention to their communication, at least at first. This is depicted in Figure 6.1.

Today the issue of group diversity and its effect on group processes and outcomes is more relevant than ever. William Johnston and Arnold Packer tell us that the workplace in the twenty-first century will be characterized by unprecedented diversity in terms of gender, age, ability, and minority and immigrant status.[6] Creativity and the development of new knowledge depend on embracing diversity and open discussion.[7] Failure to do so increases the chances that group members will see far sharper differences between themselves and others in the group. When this occurs members have a harder time attaching themselves to a group identity and run the risk of increased conflict between members.[8] A negative climate can serve to undermine any attempt to coordinate group differences. Groups have to find ways to safely identify member differences that can best serve the task at hand. Be careful though because deep-level differences are not readily obvious. The surface-level ones, such as race, age, and sex, are often not as central to the task as the more subtle ones such as members' values and how they go about solving problems.[9]

**FIGURE 6.1** Homogeneous versus heterogeneous interaction

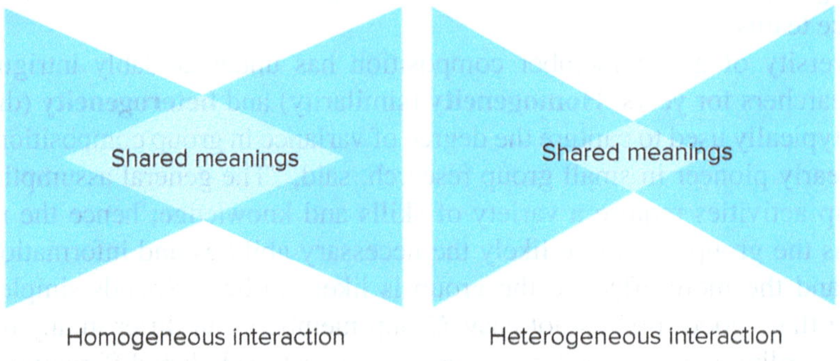

The best teams have a balance of member abilities, with individual approaches and skills complementing one another.[10] Avoid assuming that you are doing things right and that others need to conform to your preferences. Working effectively with diversity in your groups is a matter of understanding how diversity influences group processes and also being willing to listen to and value others' explanations for their ideas and behaviors. Understanding, sensitivity, and positive beliefs about diversity are more likely to produce a safe group climate where there is a willingness on everyone's part to adjust behavior so differences can enhance, not detract from, a group's relationships and its work.[11]

As we have noted, there are many diverse characteristics on which group members can differ. We have organized our discussion into two broad categories of diversity: those that are associated with deep-level individual personal differences (motives, learning styles, and personality) and those that are linked with more surface-level characteristics of culture (ethnicity, gender, and age).

# Diverse Member Characteristics

## DIFFERENCES IN MOTIVES FOR JOINING A GROUP

One of the most obvious differences to face group members is realizing they haven't all joined a group for the same reasons; a lesson we addressed in Chapter 1 when we discussed three broad needs fulfilled by group membership. Members who join primarily to meet control or achievement needs will be task-oriented, whereas members whose needs for openness and belonging predominate will focus on the interpersonal relationships in the group. These needs, and their corresponding approaches to the group's work, can often compete with each other in a group, as you saw in Case 6.1.

Task-oriented individuals, with their focus on control needs, believe the group's task is the reason for the group's existence. They perceive any digression from the task as a waste of members' time, like Misty in the opening case, so they keep chitchat to a minimum. They become frustrated when the group digresses. They value accomplishment and feel a tremendous sense of achievement and relief when the group's task is completed.

Relationally oriented individuals, like Judy, value human relationships more than they do task accomplishment. These individuals want to get to know the others in the group and want to experience each member as a friend. Their needs for openness and inclusion take precedence over their needs for control. These members will willingly sacrifice the group's task accomplishment to help a member with a personal problem.

Carolyn Anderson and Matthew Martin suggest that some motives, particularly the needs for control and affection (recently renamed openness), are actually consistent traits.[12] This poses particular challenges for members with control needs, who tend to focus solely on the task and may downplay the importance of camaraderie and chitchat. These authors note that cohesiveness and satisfaction increase when group members help each other meet their needs.[13] Relationship-oriented members may actually do a better job of accomplishing their tasks when their personal needs for openness are met. Both kinds of members are valuable to the group.[14] Most of us do participate in groups for several reasons, of which accomplishing the task is only one. We want to experience the pleasure of each other's company and the fun of interaction.[15]

### Handling Different Motives and Orientations toward Work

APPLY NOW

Judy and her fellow group members were highly frustrated by each other, in part because their needs and corresponding orientations toward the group's work were so different. However, instead of recognizing this as a potential plus, they responded by blaming each other for not doing things "right."

Assume you are Judy, and you're having a hard time understanding why your group members consistently rebuff your attempts at friendship.

1. What is your perception of the group's situation? If you were to describe the situation to a friend, what would you say about it?
2. What effect is your perception of the situation having on your behavior in (and outside) the group?
3. What could you do to make the situation better, from your perspective? List at least five possible things you could do.
4. Which of those actions do you think is most likely to improve the situation, and why?

Assume you are one of the other members of the group, and you don't understand why Judy isn't getting the message.

5. What is your perception of the group's situation? If you were telling a friend about it, what would you say the problem was?
6. What effect is your perception of the situation having on your behavior in (and outside) the group?
7. What could you do to make the situation better, from your perspective? List at least five possible things you could do.
8. Which of those actions do you think is most likely to improve the situation, and why?

John Oetzel, in his studies of effective group decision making, reminds us, that most members can and do care about both needs at the same time.[16] Their differences become apparent in how they get to the goal. Task-focused members use work to facilitate good relationships, and socially focused members use relationships to facilitate work dynamics. Judy's group failed to see the interrelatedness of these behaviors and failed to understand each others' social realities. Each expected the other to change or to switch focus instead of realizing that they needed both functions in their group. Appreciation and open discussion, rather than harping in private journals, could have helped them work with these two relevant dimensions of group dynamics.

## DIVERSITY OF LEARNING STYLES

Group members bring different learning styles to their group experience, and we believe learning styles are relevant to group problem solving. Working on a problem as a group requires members to learn new information, integrate this information into commonly shared information, and then coordinate the informational resources of the group and its members.[17] Our learning preferences reflect our different cognitive styles and affect how and what we talk about, whether we understand one another, and what aspects of a group's task we feel most comfortable taking on. Our learning style differences can set us up for misunderstandings if we aren't careful. For example, Gloria is a visual learner. In one group meeting a member tried to explain something to her in several different ways, none of which got through. Then a third group member drew a simple diagram and Gloria instantly "saw" what they were talking about. Had the third member not observed that she needed a different type of explanation and been flexible enough to provide it, both Gloria and the rest of the group would have stayed stuck on one point.

David Kolb has developed a model that demonstrates several key differences in learning styles that can affect how group members work together.[18] He suggests that people have one of four basic preferences for learning new information, and they enter the learning cycle by way of their preferred style (see Figure 6.2). This information can heighten your awareness of the learning style differences among your group members and help you identify the advantages of each style for your group.

The **concrete experience learning style** describes those individuals who learn well from events they actually observe or activities in which they actually participate.

**GLOSSARY**

**Concrete Experience Learning Style**
*A preference for learning by participating and doing*

**FIGURE 6.2 The Kolb Learning Cycle**

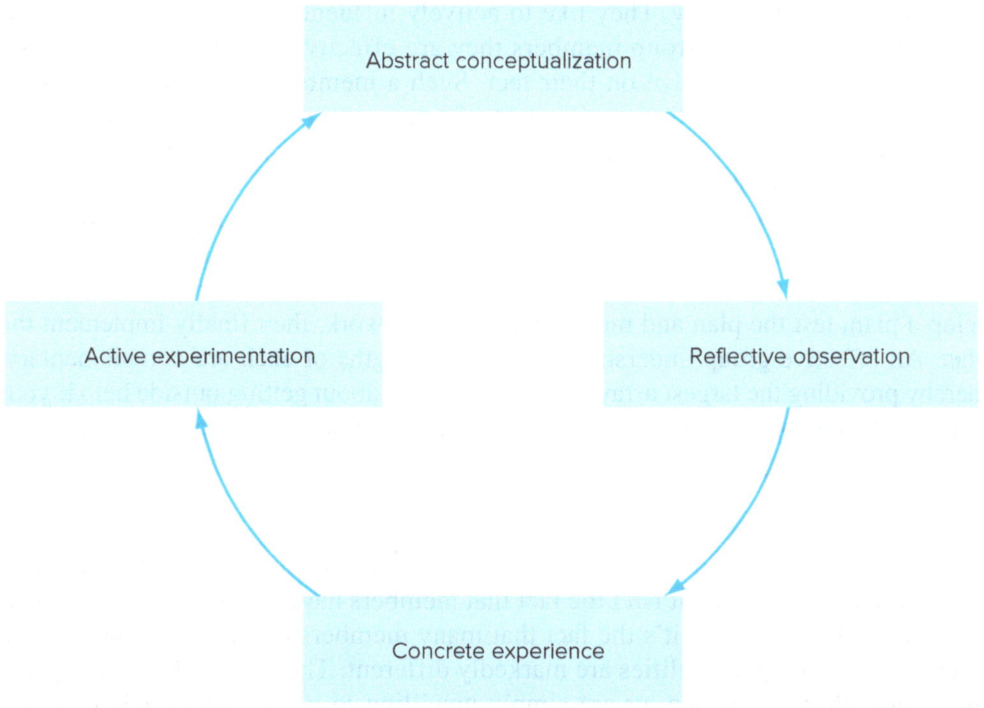

They are concerned with unique, particular experiences rather than theories and generalizations. They are "doers" and may become impatient with theoretical discussions or research on background information. For example, if your group is charged with investigating a parking problem on campus, a concrete experience learner may volunteer to count cars illegally parked or observe how many cars leave a lot without finding a parking place. But such a person may be uncomfortable if asked to synthesize three theoretical articles about traffic flow and facility usage.

The **reflective observation learning style** describes the "thinkers" in the group who prefer to get perspective on their direct experience by standing back, gaining psychological distance from it, and thinking about it reflectively. They mull information over in their minds, may talk to others about it, and learn particularly well by writing about the experience. They are likely to enjoy discussing the parking issues on campus helping the group think through the problem and less helpful jumping in to implement a group's decision.

The **abstract conceptualization learning style** describes the "synthesizers" who process a considerable amount of information by reading and solitary study. They are comfortable working alone, can perceive broad patterns, readily understand theoretical material, and can pull together information from a variety of sources in a way that makes sense. They are logical and emphasize thinking as opposed to feeling. In a group they enjoy pulling together available research on traffic flow and facility usage; however, they too may be less enthused about conducting observations or implementing the project.

The **active experimentation learning style** describes the "inventors" who learn by trying different things until they find one that works. Such people are comfortable trying something new. They like to actively influence others and prefer to *do* rather than observe. As group members they are effective in a crisis because they can think and problem-solve on their feet. Such a member might like to be given responsibility for conducting a pilot test of your group's recommended solution to the parking problem but is likely to have less patience for solitary thinking and writing about the problem.

Generally, our preferences lead us to develop strengths in some styles more than others. In a balanced group, though, all styles are represented; the group has members who can research a problem, extract the important information from the research, develop a plan, test the plan and modify what doesn't work, then finally implement the plan. An effective group understands that the strengths of each are complementary, thereby providing the largest array of benefits. Think about getting outside help if your group is missing one of the styles, and talk openly about how you can capitalize on the variety of styles in your group.

## PERSONALITY DIFFERENCES

Mishandled personality differences create as much havoc in groups as any other factor. As mentioned earlier, it isn't the fact that members have different personal styles that causes the problem—it's the fact that many members don't know how to work with others whose personalities are markedly different. They waste their energy trying to get others to change, or are simply unwilling to work with people different from themselves.

**GLOSSARY**

**Reflective Observation Learning Style**

*A preference for gaining perspective about one's experience by thinking reflectively about it*

**Abstract Conceptualization Learning Style**

*A preference for reading and solitary study*

**Active Experimentation Learning Style**

*A preference for trying different things to see what works*

Hundreds of personality characteristics have been investigated by social scientists. Instead of making an inventory of characteristics that affect group interaction, we have chosen to look in depth at one popular classification system, the **Myers-Briggs Type Indicator® (MBTI).** The MBTI, based on the work of psychologist Carl Jung, is a personality measure developed by Isabel Briggs Myers and Katherine Briggs.[19] The system looks at four dimensions that relate to how individuals interact with the world. Each dimension is a continuum with opposite characteristics at either pole. Each of us leans, a little or a lot, toward one or the other of the poles. Thus, MBTI assesses our preferences, describes the characteristics we display and the behaviors with which we are most comfortable. However, no one is a "pure" type—we all display some characteristics of all the personality types. In this next section, we will describe the four dimensions that underpin the MBTI (see Table 6.1) as they may relate to group dynamics.

The **extraversion/introversion dimension** concerns how your energy is directed, whether it is toward the outer, observable world or your inner, mental landscape. *Extraverts* look a lot like Judy in Case 6.1; tuned in to the outer world, are outgoing, and get along well with other members. While open to other's ideas, they can be seen, as in Judy's case, as "not very serious." Extraverts also tend to use group discussion to figure out what they think rather than come to a meeting with their minds made up. You may want to turn to an extravert when you want someone to interview sources for information or moderate group presentations. *Introverts* may not like working in groups at all; however, they enjoy working on ideas and can contribute effectively to group problem solving. They may prefer, for example, to work independently and then bring their work to the group rather than working on a task together during a meeting. Introverts tend to come to meetings having thought carefully about how they stand on group task issues and can lose patience with the extraverts who are "thinking out loud." If these two types do not appreciate one another's styles, their approaches can appear so different that misunderstandings can easily occur.

The **sensing/intuiting dimension** captures the type of information you naturally tune in to, whether that be the immediate facts or imagined possibilities. The *sensing* group member is careful and factual and may lose patience with abstract theories. Sensing members can provide a group with specific and concrete examples to complement abstract discussions in group reports. During group presentations these members can report on the background of the project as well as the details of the solution the group is proposing. The *intuitive* group member can be very creative and imaginative, losing patience with detail but very interested in the novel. Whereas the sensor may be focused on the details of a complicated issue, the intuitive member is focused on the bigger picture that contextualizes the problem. Intuiting members can be invaluable when brainstorming possible solutions to problems; they are very good at arriving at innovative plans or novel ways to present a project for class presentations.

The **thinking/feeling dimension** concerns how individuals make decisions, whether by analysis and objective evidence or through empathy for others and subjective feelings. The *thinkers* in groups are those who enjoy evaluating information critically, spotting flaws in arguments, and producing logical plans. They do not jump to conclusions;

GLOSSARY

**Myers-Briggs Type Indicator®**

*A personality measure, based on Jung's work, that classifies people into 16 basic personality types according to their scores on four dimensions*

**Extraversion/Introversion Dimension**

*The Myers-Briggs® dimension that describes whether someone's energy is directed outward toward observable events or toward an inner, mental landscape*

**Sensing/Intuiting Dimension**

*The Myers-Briggs® dimension that describes whether someone focuses on present facts or future possibilities*

**Thinking/Feeling Dimension**

*The Myers-Briggs® dimension that describes how people make decisions, by analysis of objective evidence or empathy and subjective feelings*

TABLE 6.1 **Strengths and Weaknesses of the Myers-Briggs® Dimensions**

| | **Introvert** | **Extravert** |
|---|---|---|
| STRENGTHS | • Can work independently<br>• Likes working with ideas<br>• Is careful before acting | • Interacts well with others<br>• Can be great at generating ideas<br>• Is an active doer |
| WEAKNESSES | • Dislikes being interrupted<br>• Misses opportunities to act<br>• Can be secretive or appear unsociable | • Is impulsive and impatient<br>• Needs change and variety<br>• Needs others to work best |
| | **Sensor** | **Intuitor** |
| STRENGTHS | • Pays attention to details and facts<br>• Is patient and systematic<br>• Is practical | • Sees possibilities<br>• Likes complicated issues/problems<br>• Likes working on novel problems |
| WEAKNESSES | • Can't see the forest for the trees<br>• Cannot see possibilities or imagine the future<br>• Is frustrated by complexity | • Lacks patience with tedious work<br>• Is inattentive to detail or practical considerations<br>• Jumps to conclusions |
| | **Thinker** | **Feeler** |
| STRENGTHS | • Is logical, analytical, organized<br>• Has good critical ability<br>• Is fair but firm | • Is considerate of others' feelings<br>• Understands others' needs/feelings<br>• Is interested in maintaining harmony |
| WEAKNESSES | • Doesn't notice others' feelings<br>• Is uninterested in harmony; shows less mercy<br>• Misunderstands others' values | • Can be disorganized<br>• Is overly accepting (of others, of information)<br>• Is not logical or objective |
| | **Perceiver** | **Judger** |
| STRENGTHS | • Sees all sides of an issue<br>• Is flexible, spontaneous<br>• Is nonjudgmental, accepting | • Is decisive<br>• Persists in staying with a task<br>• Makes plans and sticks to them |
| WEAKNESSES | • Is indecisive<br>• Is easily distracted; does not finish tasks<br>• Does not plan | • Is stubborn and inflexible<br>• Is controlled by the plan/tasks rather than in charge of the plan<br>• Decides with insufficient data |

SOURCE: Adapted from John N. Gardner and A. Jerome Jewler, *Your College Experience: Strategies for Success*, 2nd ed. (Belmont, CA: Wadsworth, 1995), pp. 83–89.

rather, they use evidence and careful analysis, essential to critical thinking in a group. The *feelers* in a group use empathy for others as their standard for making decisions and are more willing to adjust standards to meet individual circumstances, with a focus on group harmony. You will see feelers making efforts to take members' feelings into account and helping to ensure that a decision is acceptable to those most affected by the decision.

The **perceiving/judging dimension** refers to the way people organize the world around them, whether they are spontaneous and flexible or planned and orderly. The *perceivers* in your group are like sponges, gathering as much information as they can and putting off a decision for as long as they can. They are open to new perspectives and multiple sides to issues. Perceivers roll with the circumstances and are not freaked out if the group's work plan is disrupted. These members can have difficulty reaching closure, and when the task is finished, they can second-guess by wondering aloud whether there was a different or better way to have solved the problem. Group members who are *judgers* set plans and stick to them. They finish tasks and are ready to move on, much like Misty in Case 6.1. They are less willing to roll with changing circumstances.

GLOSSARY

**Perceiving/Judging Dimension**

*The Myers-Briggs® dimension that describes whether someone is spontaneous and flexible or planned and orderly*

### Balancing the Church Board

APPLY NOW

A friend of ours served on the board of directors of a Unity church. The board and congregation were having problems getting things done. The board made decisions and set policies, but no action resulted. For example, the board noticed that, although many new members had joined the church, they often drifted away after a few months. Board members decided to create a program that would help new members integrate themselves quickly into the church community so that they would feel part of the congregation and be motivated to stay. They instituted a volunteer program to help members, especially new ones, identify their talents and find places where they could make their talents available to the church. However, this program never got off the ground, and although new members continued to join, they also continued to leave.

About this time, a representative from the Association of Unity Churches came to conduct a board/congregation seminar based on the Myers-Briggs® classifications. Of the seven board members, six were identified as intuitive feelers and one as an intuitive thinker.

1. What relationship do you see between the classification of board members and the kinds of problems the church was experiencing?
2. What classifications do you think would be most helpful in supplying balance to this board?
3. If you were the board president, what would you do with this information? For instance, would you ask potential board members to construct their profile before endorsing them to run for the board? What ethical problems might this create?

These group members can help the group get their work done by establishing a work plan and encouraging members to follow the plan. Perceivers and judgers can drive each other crazy, yet group dynamics requires both stability and change, not one or the other process.

## Cognitive/Informational Diversity

One additional form of diversity important to good group decision making can also cause misunderstandings in a group. **Cognitive/informational diversity** refers to differences members have in their knowledge, skills, experiences, and the way they process information. Often, this diversity comes from the specific education, training, and past experience a member has had. For example, if you are trained as a surgeon, as a medical team member you may be tempted to look to surgery as a first option to address a patient's symptoms. Groups are called to solve complex problems in large part because the diversity of knowledge, perspectives, and information can produce better solutions. However, it can be challenging for a group to ensure that all informational perspectives are shared and considered within the group. We talk about this in more detail in Chapter 8, but we introduce it here so you are aware that cognitive/informational diversity is an important diversity issue groups must attend to.

Abby Mello and Joan Rentsch, in their recent review of studies about cognitive diversity, note cognitive/informational diversity is defined in many different ways, which has somewhat complicated our understanding of how groups are affected and has sometimes produced inconsistent findings.[20] What they did conclude, though, is that cognitive diversity seems to help a group perform more effectively, but may negatively affect group members' feelings about one another. You can imagine that, when group members have diverse information, perspectives, and approaches, communication and conflict management skills are important to helping members bridge their differences. When members directly address and actively manage conflict, they can overcome the potential harm to cohesion that cognitive diversity tends to produce.[21] A recent study found that informational diversity encourages members to communicate with one another.[22] For example, if you notice that another member has information and an understanding of a problem that is different from yours, you may be motivated to ask that member questions so you can better comprehend the information. Thus, you have formed a stronger communication tie with that member than if his or her information was the same as yours. Such communication ties can enhance a group's task and creative performance.

If you noticed some common themes between individual motives, learning styles, and personality types, you have been paying attention! For example, introversion and reflective observation exhibit similarities, as do extraversion and active experimentation. Concrete experience preferences are related to sensing; abstract preferences are related to intuiting. Thinkers and judgers may exhibit strong task motives. Likewise, feelers and extraverts may be motivated by social needs. As group members we need to be sensitive to the benefits and drawbacks of each characteristic and recognize that we are often a mix of these apparently contradictory preferences, which do not have to

**GLOSSARY**

**Cognitive/Informational Diversity**

*Differences in knowledge, skills, experience, and the way information is processed, acquired by experience and disciplinary training*

be mutually exclusive. Each group member and the group together needs to find their balance. In the next section we will discuss differences that have come to be most associated with diversity: cultural differences.

## Cultural Diversity

Cultural differences represent a major form of diversity in a group, and as we indicated previously, groups in the twenty-first century will be increasingly diverse. Researchers who explore why culturally heterogeneous groups sometimes have problems note that the positive impact of diversity is due to the interplay among several interrelated factors, including cultural, individual, and group factors (e.g., group composition, nature of the task, and the group's emotional climate).[23] Cultural factors encompass both surface- and deep-level characteristics we presented earlier.

### DIMENSIONS OF CULTURE

**Culture** is the system of beliefs, values, symbols, and rules that underlie communication patterns within a discernible grouping of people. It doesn't necessarily refer to people from another country. A co-culture is a smaller identifiable group contained within a larger cultural grouping and has its own norms and patterns of communication. For example, you belong to the co-culture of "college students." We use the word *culture* to refer also to race, gender, and generational differences, which we'll discuss later.

Unless someone calls our attention to a feature of our culture, we don't think too much about the significant role it plays in shaping our behavior. In addition, we tend to assume that individuals from other cultures share our values, behaviors, and communication patterns, but they don't necessarily! Cultures differ along a number of dimensions that affect communication rules and preferences; we discuss three of them here (see Table 6.2).[24] Knowing something about them will help you communicate better in groups made up of individuals from diverse cultures so that you can capitalize on the strengths of these cultures. Moreover, because American business is increasingly becoming global in scope, at some point you likely will belong to a group composed of members from more than one country. In that case it will be especially important for you to be sensitive to cultural differences, not only so you don't offend others but also so you can participate profitably in a global economy.

The first important dimension along which cultures vary is the individualist/collectivist dimension. An **individualistic culture**, such as the predominant culture of the United States, values individual goals more than collective, or group, goals. In a **collectivist culture** the needs of the group take precedence over the needs of the individual, and conformity to the group is valued. So, for example, a group member from a collectivist culture will willingly abandon personal plans to attend a group meeting, but a member from an individualistic culture will say something like, "I've already got plans, so you'll either have to meet without me or reschedule the meeting at a time that I can make." The underlying value—what's most important—differs. Group members who value collectivism can become easily frustrated with a highly individualistic member, whom they will perceive as selfish and uncaring. However, it is also easy for individualistic members to perceive collectivist ones as caring too much about what others think.

**GLOSSARY**

**Culture**
*The system of beliefs, values, and symbols shared by an identifiable group of people*

**Individualistic Culture**
*A culture that values individual needs and goals more than group needs and goals*

**Collectivist Culture**
*A culture that values group needs and goals more than individual needs and goals*

**TABLE 6.2** **Three Important Dimensions of Culture**

| | |
|---|---|
| | **Individualism/Collectivism** |
| HIGH INDIVIDUALISM | Values independence, autonomy, and privacy; encourages dissent; encourages people to "do their own thing."<br>• "I won't be at the meeting tomorrow. I've got a chance to go skiing with a friend and I really need some time off from school."<br>• "I know you all agree, but I don't, and I won't support that decision." |
| HIGH COLLECTIVISM | Values harmony, conformity, and loyalty to the group; discourages dissent.<br>• "I'm taking my mother to the hospital for surgery in the morning, but I'll be at our meeting for sure at noon. I can call from there to see how she's doing."<br>• "I'll go along with whatever you all want to do." |
| | **Power Distance** |
| HIGH POWER DISTANCE | Maximizes status differences between members; values hierarchical structure and strong authoritarian leadership.<br>• Leader says, "I've decided that we're going to do it this way." |
| LOW POWER DISTANCE | Minimizes status differences between members; values sharing power, participatory decision making, and democratic leadership.<br>• Leader says, "We've all got to live with the decision we make, so we should all have a say in it. Tell me what you think?" |
| | **Context** |
| LOW CONTEXT | Lets the words themselves carry most of the meaning; values direct, unambiguous communication.<br>• "Your idea is intriguing. Maybe we should explore it in more detail" (said with a smile) means, "I'm interested and I want to explore it in more detail."<br>• "I love that idea" means "I love that idea." |
| HIGH CONTEXT | Lets the situation, or context, carry most of the meaning; communication is indirect; nonverbal signals are crucial to understanding a message.<br>• "Your idea is intriguing. Maybe we should explore it in more detail" (said with a smile) may mean, "I hate it" or "I really like it" or "It might have some possibilities but I can't commit yet." |

Asian, Native American, and Latin American cultures (including the Latino American co-culture within the United States) tend to be more collectivist than the cultures of the United States or Western Europe.[25] For instance, in Asian cultures relationships are crucial. If your company sends you to negotiate a contract with a group of executives in Taiwan, you must plan on a perhaps lengthy social engagement before business can be discussed. Americans who rush the process have inadvertently insulted their Taiwanese hosts. Individualistic Americans also tend to be competitive and argumentative, particularly in comparison with collectivist cultures, where allowing group members to "save face" is necessary to preserving group harmony. In conflict situations they are comfortable forcing their opponents to capitulate, but this can backfire in groups with collectivist members.

Individuals from collectivist and individualistic cultures have developed different communication preferences. For instance, individualistic members value clear and direct communication that is unambiguous.[26] In contrast, members from collectivist cultures prefer ambiguous communication that is more subtle and tentative and can preserve harmony. For example, suppose both Nguyen and Sam disagree with something contained in a group report being prepared. Nguyen, the collectivist member, says, "I wonder if we should look more closely at Part 2 of the report? Was anyone else confused in that section?" But Sam, the individualist member, says, "I think Part 2 is terrible and has to be done over." Nguyen likely thinks Sam is selfish and rude, whereas Sam sees Nguyen as wishy-washy and spineless.

Each way of stating the same opinion has advantages and disadvantages. Nguyen's way is polite and allows the writer of Part 2 to save face; however, we can't tell how strongly Nguyen feels about it, so Part 2's writer can easily misinterpret Nguyen. In contrast, there's no mistaking how Sam feels, but his statement may so insult the author that nothing in Part 2 gets changed.

The second dimension of culture we discuss is **power distance,** or the extent to which a culture maximizes or minimizes status and power differences among individuals. In a low-power-distance culture (the United States has relatively low power distance), status and power differences among individuals are downplayed. Individuals believe that power should be distributed evenly, that just because someone has a title or money does not entitle them to privileges under the law that others don't have, and so forth. In a group, members from a low-power-distance culture believe that they have as much right to speak up and participate in decisions as the group's leader. In high-power-distance cultures such as Mexico and the Philippines, status differences are magnified and a rigid hierarchy exists. Members of such cultures believe that each person has a preassigned place in the society and should not seek to step out of that niche. In a group, members from high-power-distance cultures expect the leader to control and direct the group and may become frustrated with participatory leadership.

Members from low-power-distance cultures expect to participate in decision making, prefer a democratic leadership style, and assume that everyone else wants to participate in decision making as well. For instance, group leader Sarah says to her group, "What ideas do you all have for solving the parking problem?" Members from high-power-distance cultures value authoritarian leadership and may see a democratic leader as weak and incompetent. They expect low-status members to conform to high-status members. They assume others will accept the leader's control and direction. For example, group leader José says to his group, "I believe the parking problem is due to bad class scheduling. Here's what I want you to do. . . ." You can see the possibility for misunderstanding and hurt feelings here!

**GLOSSARY**

**Power Distance**

*Whether a culture maximizes or minimizes status and power differences*

GLOSSARY

**Low-Context Culture**

*A culture in which the words used convey more meaning than the situation or context*

**High-Context Culture**

*A culture in which features of the situation or context convey more meaning than the words people use*

The third dimension is that of context. In a **low-context culture,** such as that of the United States and New Zealand, the verbal part of the message carries the meaning—what you say is exactly what you mean. If you say that you like my proposal, I can trust the fact that you really *do* like it. In a **high-context culture,** such as most Asian and Native American cultures, features of a situation or context are more important than the words themselves. So if you tell me you like my proposal, I'd have to take into account the setting, the people, the purpose of our conversation, and other factors to know for sure whether you *really* liked it or you were just being polite to avoid hurting my feelings. High-context cultures tend to be collectivist, with group harmony an important value. Ambiguity and indirectness may help preserve this harmony by allowing disagreement to happen gently, in a way that doesn't upset the balance of the group.

Group members from low-context cultures sometimes try to force others to be direct and clear. They may perceive members who are not straightforward as manipulative or

## Euro-Disney Stumbles

APPLY NOW

According to Carl Hiaasen in *Team Rodent: How Disney Devours the World,** Disney's venture in France, Euro-Disney, got off to a slow start when it opened in 1992. Disney executives decided to import the Disney concept intact when they created their European theme park. The Disney parks in the United States have a clean-cut image—at least, as Americans define *clean-cut.* Those who work in the park, mostly young people, abide by strict rules of dress and demeanor. For example, they must not wear bright nail polish, heavy makeup, or facial hair. In addition, the parks do not serve wine or other alcoholic beverages, which contributes to the clean-cut image in the United States.

However, these rules seemed offensive and ridiculous to Europeans, particularly the French. Not serve wine in France? Unthinkable! These factors contributed to Euro-Disney's dismal early performance. However, Disney rethought its rules and relaxed several, in particular the makeup, facial hair, and wine rules. Euro-Disney is beginning to catch on in Europe, the way it has in the United States.

1. Are there any other "rules" or communication patterns observed by North Americans that Europeans might consider silly?
2. Are there any "rules" or communication patterns observed by Europeans that North Americans might consider silly?
3. What does the above story suggest to you about cultural practices, particularly applying in one culture practices that are normal in another?
4. Disney executives are intelligent and experienced. What factors do you think might have contributed to this not-well-thought-out decision by Disney?

*Carl Hiaasen, *Team Rodent: How Disney Devours the World* (New York: Ballantine Books, 1998).

insincere. On the other hand, members from high-context cultures perceive members who are verbally blunt as rude and aggressive. As the earlier example demonstrates, the advantage of being clear, like Sam, is that your meaning is unmistakable. However, the advantage of being tentative, like Nguyen, is that you allow discussion to occur without polarizing members' opinions or making them lose face.

Appreciation of cultural differences in a group is very important. The United States is a pluralistic culture to which many different cultures have contributed and continue to contribute. This means that little can be assumed or taken for granted, including assuming that a person's cultural identity predicts everything said and done in a group. Small group researchers like John Oetzel remind us, that individuals *within* a culture vary.[27] As Oetzel points out, we are *individuals* acting within cultures; thus, we must not oversimplify the situation by using *only* culture to predict individual behavior.

Oetzel argues that whether we define ourselves as independent or interdependent has a significant bearing on our social behavior. Those group members who have an independent image of themselves see themselves as unique, with their thoughts and feelings as their own. They are goal-driven, seek clarity, and attend less to nuances of context. Those who hold interdependent images of themselves define themselves in connection to others. They value helping others meet their goals. They value fitting in, work to uphold the self-image of the other, and also try to avoid negative assessments of themselves. These two types of self-image are found in everyone, regardless of their cultural identity. What is important to note is that Oetzel has found that *both* cultural inputs *and* personal self-images influence the contributions of members.

## RACIAL AND ETHNIC DIFFERENCES

We began our discussion of cultural diversity with a global emphasis, talking broadly about differences group members from different countries may bring to a group. In this section we focus more on those same cultural and co-cultural dimensions within the boundaries of the United States. Discussions of racial and ethnic differences are complicated and are often very difficult as demonstrated by the events of the summer of 2016 in the United States. We seem to shout at each other, producing more heat than light, or pretend there are no differences or problems anymore. However, if we do not find ways to effectively negotiate one another's relevant ethnic and racial differences within a climate of mutual respect while solving problems impacting all of us, we will not find the benefits in cultural diversity. In the twenty-first century multiracial and multiethnic groups are the norm, so we have to do better than we have in the past.

Major ethnic and racial groups in our country include African Americans, Asian Americans, European Americans, and Hispanic Americans. In this section we provide information about some of the major differences in communication styles and patterns in these groups, but we focus on differences between African Americans and European Americans because relationships between these two groups are among the most discussed and debated in this country. We offer an important caution. Although we discuss each culture as if members from that culture display a single consistent pattern of communication, this is not the case. There are as many communication style differences *within* these co-cultures as there are between them. We know we are overgeneralizing, but if you aren't aware of differing cultural practices, your lack of knowledge may interfere with effective group discussion. If you find yourself uncomfortable in an encounter with someone whose race or ethnicity is different from your own, and your impulse is to blame the other person for your discomfort, stop! Your discomfort may be due to unexamined differences between two cultures; the other person may be just as uncomfortable as you are.

The relationship between African Americans and European Americans can be particularly complicated. These two cultural groups have traditionally misunderstood each other, often with serious consequences to both. American polls taken in the summer of 2016 showed at least 70 percent polled believed there were deep racial challenges facing America. We hope the information we provide about communication differences between these groups will prevent you from saying or doing something insensitive that contributes to group self-destruction.

The African American culture values sharing, emotionality, verbal expression, and interactivity.[28] These values express themselves in a variety of ways. African Americans appreciate verbal inventiveness and expression. Verbal play as a type of performance is particularly valued. However, what African Americans intend as a playful display is often interpreted by European Americans as bragging or strutting. African Americans are generally more expressive and interactive. Open expression of feelings is encouraged as an important way to share and connect. However, this too can be misinterpreted. African Americans think European Americans are cold and underreactive because they don't share feelings as readily and are not as expressive. Similarly, European Americans think African Americans are overly emotional and overreactive.

Each group perceives the other negatively.[29] A number of communication patterns may contribute to this. For instance, African Americans stand closer to each other than European Americans, who may interpret that nonverbal behavior as threatening. European Americans make more direct eye contact when they listen than when they talk. For African Americans the pattern is reversed; they make more direct eye contact when they talk than when they listen. This can seriously affect perceptions of trust, interest, and acceptance.

The African American communication style is much more interactive than the typical European American style. For instance, traditional African American church services often display the call-response style, whereby congregation members shout "Amen!" and "Tell it like it is, brother!" while the preacher is talking. They also use the backchannel more than European Americans. This means that they say things like "Uh-huh" and "Mm-hmm" in everyday conversation to signify interest and attention. However, European Americans can easily interpret someone talking while another is speaking as rudeness. On the other hand, African Americans, who are used to getting such verbal signs of attention, may interpret that lack of backchannel responses from European Americans as lack of interest. African American conversational style is a narrative, storytelling style. European Americans may interpret it as disorganized, rambling, or off-task. To European American teachers a paper written in traditional African American narrative style can appear disorganized and rambling.

Most African Americans have had more practice in understanding European American culture than vice versa because they have been forced to.[30] Many African Americans consider themselves bicultural because they can negotiate "typical" African American conversational contexts as well as the European American contexts that currently predominate in the business and education arenas. However, it is difficult for minority group members to express themselves fully in groups composed primarily of individuals from other cultures.[31] Unfortunately, this suggests that multicultural groups are not realizing their full potential as groups because they aren't incorporating fully the ideas of the minority group members.

## GENDER DIFFERENCES

You will never be able to escape one of the most important influences of culture: the effect of gender roles in a group. The masculine-feminine continuum is often listed as another dimension of culture, along with individualism/collectivism, high or low context, and power distance.[32] Broadly speaking, more feminine cultures (e.g., Norway, Costa Rica, Sweden) prefer an overlap of roles such that both males and females are expected to be modest, nurturing, and generally other-oriented. In more masculine cultures (e.g., Australia, Mexico, the United States, Japan), gender roles that complement each other are reinforced, with men acting assertive and women acting modest. The gendered communication rules we all use have been taught and reinforced by our cultures. Culture, and our own construction of gender, influences how we experience behaviors in groups and what choices we make. Nina Reich and Julia Wood examined research studies about male-female behavior in small groups. Four areas emerged in which women and men show different tendencies; these are not absolute differences but rather are matters of degree.[33]

The first area of difference is between *expressive* and *instrumental* behaviors. Expressive behaviors focus on feelings and relationships. For instance, before the meeting gets under way, Susan may ask Allen how he did on the calculus test he was worried about. Instrumental behaviors focus on accomplishing the group's tasks. Allen may tell Susan he'll talk to her about it after the meeting, but first they have to assess where they are on their group project.

### Different Voices for Making Ethical Decisions

ETHICAL DILEMMA

Assume you are on a student judicial committee charged with deciding the punishment of students who have violated your institution's rules and policies. Rob, the student before you, is charged with plagiarism. He submitted a paper very similar to one that another student had turned in the previous semester to another teacher for the same course. Sections of Rob's paper are identical to the earlier paper, but some parts of the paper contain new research and appear to be Rob's own work. Rob has admitted that he plagiarized portions of the paper but pleads extenuating circumstances and asks for your committee's mercy. Soon after he started his research for the paper, he learned that his younger sister, still in high school, had been diagnosed with leukemia. She is being treated, so far successfully, but for the last few weeks Rob has driven home on weekends to be with her. He and his sister are close; she relies on him for emotional support, which he has been happy to provide. But helping her has drained him of the ability

*(continued)*

***Concluded***

ETHICAL DILEMMA

to concentrate and consumed all his time. He took the easy way out but made sure that he incorporated his original research into the paper he "borrowed." Rob asks you to let him drop the course with no penalty so he can take it again the next semester. However, your institution has an honor code all students sign as freshmen; the code specifies a *minimum* of one semester's suspension for all honor violations, including plagiarism. In practice, though, the student judicial committee's recommendations are accepted. Here are your choices:

- Let him drop the course with no penalty.
- Give him an F in the course.
- Give him an F in the course with a notation that the F is due to plagiarism; this remains on his permanent record.
- Give him an F in the course and suspend him for one semester.
- Give him an F in the course and expel him from school permanently.

1. Before you form groups of five or six, what would you personally recommend for Rob? What is your reasoning for your recommendation?
2. Get together in groups, as if you were the student judicial committee, and come to consensus about what you would recommend. Then discuss what your reasons were for your ultimate recommendation. What considerations were most important to you?
3. How did you balance being fair to Rob, being fair to other students, and upholding your honor code?

This example allows for a number of individual differences in ethical reasoning to emerge. Educator Carol Gilligan, in her book *In a Different Voice,** suggests that men and women use different ethical logic systems when making decisions like this. Men are believed to make ethical decisions from so-called objective positions that focus on abstract concepts such as justice, freedom, and truth. Women, Gilligan believes, make ethical decisions based on concerns for people, taking compassion, desire to alleviate suffering, and loyalty into account.

4. Did you observe either of these ethical systems during your discussion? Did any other ethical systems emerge during your discussion?
5. To what extent do you agree with Gilligan's assessment of men's and women's reasoning during ethical dilemmas like this?
6. What implications might the conflict of different ethical systems have for small groups?

*Carol Gilligan, *In a Different Voice: Psychological Theory and Women's Development* (Cambridge, MA: Harvard University Press, 1982).

A second, related difference is *task* versus *relationship* focus. Women generally place more emphasis on relationships and are more likely to show that they care and want to help. One woman we know, a particularly effective leader, touches base with members between meetings, especially if there has been a disagreement, to make sure everyone is OK and no one's feelings are hurt. She believes that things go better when relationships are harmonious. As with expressive and instrumental behavior, men and women both communicate caring as well as interest in the group's task.

Third, there are differences in *forcefulness,* which involves how much someone talks, interrupts others, claims personal space, or otherwise calls attention to him- or herself in the conversation. It also refers to how directly and assertively someone communicates. Men tend to be more forceful than women. They talk more than women, interrupt more, engage in more self-promotion, claim more space, and are more assertive. A man is more likely to say, "OK, here's what I think we should do," but a woman is more likely to say, "This seems like a good idea, but what do the rest of you think?" The first statement is more direct and powerful, but the second is more polite and inviting.

Finally, male-female differences have been observed between *individual* and *group* orientation. Men exhibit more individualistic behavior that calls attention to their own personal status. They tend to seek the spotlight more often and to highlight their own individual accomplishments: "I think I did a great job of researching our topic." In contrast, women show more collectivist behavior that emphasizes the group as a whole: "We have done a wonderful job of gathering all the information we need." They stress building the team rather than increasing their own individual status.

Interestingly, sex itself seems to function as a status characteristic in small groups, with men having higher status. In one study in which group members interacted anonymously via computer-mediated communication, men were more likely than women to reveal that they were men.[34] Women hid identifying information or even represented themselves as men. Women believed that their contributions were more readily accepted when they were anonymous than when they engaged in face-to-face interaction and could clearly be identified as women. They preferred to remain anonymous during computer-mediated interactions because they believed they had more influence that way.

Generalizing about male and female behavior is misleading for all sorts of reasons. Multiple factors—such as the nature of the task, group composition, member roles, the behaviors used to show status, and individual identity preferences—can mediate the influence of gender. As with any cultural variable, we should stay away from either-or thinking—that is, thinking that men are only *this* way and women are only *that* way, and one way is better. Lindsey Grob and colleagues, in studying gender differences in small group communication contexts, make the case that too much scholarship in this area focuses on the differences between men and women and not the similarities.[35] When men and women are treated as being socialized in two different cultures, we tend to stereotype men as instrumental/powerful and women as affiliative/powerless. You see this dichotomy in the previous expressive/instrumental, task/relationship, forcefulness, and individual/group tendencies.

Typically, powerful speech has been defined as speech heavy in interruptions (seen as assertive) with minimal use of speech that can be seen to soften discourse, such as disclaimers (e.g., "*This could be wrong,* but don't we need more cash?") and tag questions (e.g., "Increasing tuition will lead to higher dropout rates, *won't it*?"). Women are stereotyped as using more disclaimers and tag questions, and men are stereotyped as using more interruption and being interrupted less. When we change our theoretical approach to one of emphasizing the similarities between men and women, we are not as apt to dichotomize male and female behavior. Grob and colleagues found that males and females interrupted others with similar frequency and used disclaimers and tag questions similarly. In fact, they found that it was the *males* in the groups who were interrupted more. However, they also found that when males interrupt others, they are more successful than females. Moreover, men seem to be penalized less than women when they do interrupt, in part because conversational dominance—of which interruption is an example—is expected of men.[36]

### Diminishing Implicit Assumptions of Group Diversity

MEDIA AND TECHNOLOGY

Diversity in experience, expertise, and perspective is encouraged in group interaction because of the potential it adds to the quality of group decisions. However, a number of implicit assumptions about diversity (personality, culture, gender, etc.) can sometimes diminish the rewards that would otherwise be gained by having a group with a mixture of personalities and experiences. Think how your group interactions might differ if you had no preconceived assumptions about the members you were about to work with. How would that change the way your group started its meetings? What things would you talk about to develop relationships?

One feature of group support systems is anonymity, a feature that can be used to help circumvent many assumptions members bring to the group (e.g., males are better at working on task, or younger group members know more about technology). Consider some of the stereotypes you have about male and female group members. Do you have different expectations for male group members compared to females? Are there tasks that you feel certain genders are better at? In her examination of gender masking on the Internet, Brenda Danet found that, when given the opportunity, individuals (both male and female) enjoyed experimenting with altering their identity because of the freedom that came from gender-free interaction. The anonymous interaction of a CMC environment gives people a chance to understand how social and cultural information about others is used to guide interaction.

SOURCE: Based on Brenda Danet, "Text as Mask: Gender, Play, and Performance on the Internet," in *Cybersociety 2.0* ed. S. Jones (Thousand Oaks, CA: Sage, 1998).

In addition, the gender composition of a group seems to make a difference in actual behavior and perceptions of behavior. When individuals are dissimilar to other team members on the basis of sex (e.g., the lone male in a group of females or *vice versa*), and when they have a strong sense of identification with their own sex, they perceive a higher level of relational conflict within their groups.[37] As the lone member of your sex in a group, you are likely to place more importance on sex than if the group were mixed. In addition, it seems that group composition affects how men's and women's contributions are evaluated. Rajhubir and Valenzuela examined episodes of the television program *The Weakest Link* and conducted simulations modeled on the show.[38] Women voted males off when there were fewer women in the group, when the women overall performed well, and when there was greater variation in the performance of the men (even if the top performer was a male). Likewise, men voted women off when there were fewer men in the group, when men overall performed well, and when there was greater variation in the performance of women (even if a woman was the top performer). These two studies found a complex relationship among sex, sex composition, and performance that suggests men and women use sex strategically, with both sex composition and performance explaining the strategy.

What are we to make of all this? Once again, it's important not to lose sight of the fact that there are many similarities between cultures, and cultural groups have a lot more differences *within* groups than *between* them. Also, when we approach difference from an either-or perspective, we tend to draw destructive value judgments about behaviors—we have to behave *this* way or *that* way, but not both ways. Chapters 3 and 4 on communication fundamentals emphasizes that our communicative choices are not limited or mutually exclusive. In addition, any communicative choice can serve multiple functions rather than just one, no matter who the messenger may be. For instance, interruptions can show support for another individual's arguments, disclaimers can be used to help the other person save face or maintain positive face, and tag questions may be important as group members begin to converge on issues. Finally, remember that we are studying male and female behavior in groups, not dyads. In mixed groups we see less stereotypical behavior, with members showing different patterns of mutual influence as groups develop over time.[39]

## GENERATIONAL DIFFERENCES

A few years ago, one of us served on the board of directors at a church. As a baby boomer and the youngest member of the board, she believes all people—women included—have the right to express opinions; she also values frank and open discussion in the course of making decisions. It simply never would occur to her that she *shouldn't* say what she thought. Most of the other members of the seven-member board were a generation older. During their board meetings they signaled—primarily through their nonverbal behavior—that they were uncomfortable with her high level of participation. It seemed to her that she was violating an unspoken rule of "be seen and not heard until you've paid your dues." Her values and beliefs seemed to clash with the others' values, and she interpreted the clash as stemming

## GLOSSARY

**Builders**

*Individuals born from 1901 to 1945; influenced by the Great Depression and World War II*

**Boomers**

*Individuals born from 1946 to 1964; influenced by TV and the social upheaval of 1960s*

**Gen-Xers**

*Individuals born from 1965 to 1976; influenced by Watergate and general mistrust*

from generational differences. These kinds of generational differences can negatively influence feelings of trust, for instance, among group members of different generations. When age differences are not apparent, such as in virtual work teams in which members interact via computer, the impact of age on trust is not as readily apparent.[40] Understanding the potential effect of generational differences on group processes at school or at work may not seem important to you now but it is important.

A number of writers have characterized major generational differences that appear in the U.S. workplace today. Much of this information has been synthesized by Rick and Kathy Hicks and others.[41] Although the Hickses do not use the term *co-culture,* that is in fact what they describe. Each generation forms a particular co-culture, with similar values, goals, and outlook on life based on the major events, people, and activities prominent during their formative years, particularly when they were about 10 years old. At 10 years old, forces outside the family—friends, teachers, the media—begin to assume increased and lasting importance in our lives. To really understand the core values of a particular generational co-culture, it is necessary to take a look at those influential events.

The Hickses describe four broad generations that are found in today's workplace: builders, boomers, generation X, and the Millennials (the Hickses call this generation the net generation, but Millennials is the more common usage). Table 6.3 summarizes this information. As we describe these generations, we remind you that we are again overgeneralizing and oversimplifying. However, you are bound to experience generational clashes in every arena of life—including in small groups you join. Appreciating some of the differences—and perhaps the reasons for them—will help you draw from the strengths of these generational differences instead of being mired in resentment. Please note that different sources provide different ending years for Gen-X; we have chosen 1981 as the most common.

The **builders,** born between 1901 and 1945, lived through two world wars and the bust of the Great Depression. Many are retired yet remain active in their communities and in political circles. The values of personal discipline and self-sacrifice may seem old fashioned, but builders can provide loyalty and stability to groups. Although they can resist change and may act very reserved during conflict, their perseverance in seeing a job through is tremendously beneficial to a group.

The **boomers,** born between 1946 and 1964, are the children of the builders who, because they tried to make the world easier for their kids, created a generation of people who believe in their own importance! They can appear idealistic and self-centered, but they do bring valuable resources to the group. Boomers are responsible for the team concept in business and the continuing focus on service. Their confidence and ease with alternative views that may be contrary to those of the establishment can help in projects. Boomers value being noticed for their contributions and can help group members show gratitude to other members. Boomers are still in many leadership positions in industry, education, and government—holding those places the gen-Xers and Millennials would like to have!

**Gen-Xers** were born between 1965 and 1981 and became our latchkey generation. Living through Watergate and President Nixon's resignation, they do not so much resist authority as mistrust it. They are not willing to sacrifice their

TABLE 6.3 **Characteristics, Strengths, and Weaknesses of Four Dominant Generations**

| | Characteristics | Strengths | Weaknesses |
|---|---|---|---|
| **BUILDERS (1901–1945)** | • Major influences: Depression and WWII<br>• Are cautious about spending money<br>• Will work hard at single task until completed<br>• Put own interests aside for common good | • Are careful with resources (e.g., money)<br>• Plan ahead<br>• Are reliable, dependable<br>• Are disciplined | • Are too cautious with resources<br>• May lack spontaneity and flexibility |
| **BOOMERS (1946–1964)** | • Major influences: TV, Vietnam War, the Pill, assassinations, civil rights movement, size of generation<br>• Major consumers; value "good life"<br>• Are self-absorbed; believe they're special<br>• Work as end in itself; expect to be fulfilled at work<br>• Value education | • Are confident<br>• Will put in whatever time task takes<br>• Will challenge "old ways" of doing things<br>• Will take on big causes | • Think they're right all the time<br>• Expect others to hold similar beliefs/values<br>• May break rules of ethics if they think it's best for them |
| **GEN-XERS (1965–1981)** | • Major influences: rising divorce rate, Watergate, Pentagon Papers, MTV<br>• Distrust institutions, particularly government<br>• Are comfortable with diversity<br>• Work as means to an end<br>• Value family (broadly defined)<br>• Are comfortable with technology<br>• Endure education | • Are independent thinkers<br>• Are sensitive to people; value relationships<br>• Are tolerant; accept competing points of view<br>• Are comfortable with change<br>• Are highly computer literate | • Appear pessimistic and negative<br>• Are unwilling to put personal life/concerns aside to complete task<br>• May seem alienated and unmotivated |

(continued)

TABLE 6.3 **Continued**

| | Characteristics | Strengths | Weaknesses |
|---|---|---|---|
| MILLENNIALS (1982–1997) | • Major influences: AIDS, technology and Internet, death of Princess Diana<br>• Were the most wanted generation in history; raised by overinvolved (helicopter) parents<br>• Value diversity; highly tolerant<br>• Are major consumers<br>• Are nonlinear thinkers<br>• Value family | • Are open-minded and tolerant; welcome different viewpoints<br>• Are completely technology and media savvy<br>• Are optimistic<br>• Are innovative<br>• Are comfortable with and like collaborative work, networking | • Seem to lack initiative; seem unmotivated<br>• Are unlikely to conform to bureaucracy, hierarchy, organizational "rules"<br>• Seem to need constant praise and do not take criticism well<br>• Do not link rewards (grades, promotions) to performance |

personal relationships for work and thus bring multitasking to group work. This generation has grown very adaptable; gen-Xers build careers not in one place or with one company but around themselves. Although they may not appear to be team players or interested in long-term commitments, they are flexible and are much more at ease with diversity than previous generations. They speak their minds more than boomers or traditionalists might and are motivated best when they perceive that they have control over their tasks and can still value aspects of their personal lives.

The **Millennials** were born after 1981. They are sometimes referred to as the *echo boom,* net *generation,* and *generation Y*. This group is particularly large and the first truly wired generation; this generation uses computers for *everything*. In fact, they are the most receptive to the use of emoticons in e-mail correspondence (the builders are the most uncomfortable with emoticons and prefer instead more personal correspondence, such as handwritten letters).[42] More hopeful than the Xers, Millennials are even more comfortable with diversity and more confident in their skills (especially computer skills), and they have better relationships with their parents. Many of their parents waited a long time to have them and wanted to be the best parents they could be, so they became heavily caught up in every aspect of their children's lives. Consequently, this generation expects to get a gold star or a trophy just for participation, not for actual accomplishment. Millennials are accustomed to collaborative work in school and via the net, which makes them value peer relationships rather than hierarchical relationships. In groups they value others based

**GLOSSARY**

**Millennials**
*Individuals born from 1982 to 1997; influenced by computers and the information/digital revolution*

© KidStock/Blend Images RF

on their contributions not their ascribed status. They have a strong live-and-let-live philosophy tempered by the stress of relying on their day planners. They look to mentors to provide guidance and are multitaskers who can be in more than one place at one time, accomplishing several different things at once.

The previous discussion, as we mentioned earlier, represents overgeneralization and oversimplification. We all can see characteristics of each generation in ourselves. We also know people who display few or none of the characteristics that are supposed to exemplify their generation. However, the point to remember is this: Our early influences from family, friends, and institutions such as the media affect the way we perceive the world around us and the way we communicate, which in turn affects our behavior in small groups. Understanding something about generations different from yours—what their hopes and fears are, what pressures operate on them, what the formative events were in their lives—will help you make the most of your differences in small groups instead of bogging you down.

We have not intended to teach you everything there is to know about cultural differences. Rather, we have tried to alert you to some common causes of misinterpretations in the listening process and factors that make creating a common social reality challenging. Remember that cultural rules are not automatic; they are taught and constantly evolving. Remember also that cultural differences are not a matter of right or wrong and that you have absorbed the rules of your culture so completely that they are invisible to you until you start to examine them or to interact with people from a very different culture.

### Mom's in My Group!

APPLY NOW

In the early 1990s one of us observed a classroom group of five members who included two men and two women in their early 20s and one woman in her mid-40s. This group had made some progress on its assignment, but tensions were beginning to build between one of the young women, Mindy, and the older woman, Sarah. A single mother with teenagers at home, Sarah had a very full schedule. She tried hard to keep the group task-focused so the project could be completed early, in time for feedback from the instructor. The more she made suggestions about the content of the project, about meeting more often, or about establishing deadlines for the members' individual assignments, the more Mindy resisted: "I can't meet then, I've paid for tickets to a concert and I'm not going to give them up," and "Chill, Sarah, it'll get done" were typical remarks. Mindy, exasperated with Sarah's task focus, complained to one of the other members that Sarah reminded her of her mom—"Always hassling me about something!" This conflict threatened to derail the group's progress.

1. What generations do Mindy and Sarah represent?
2. In what ways does each seem typical of her generation? What communication behaviors seem rooted in generational differences?
3. With whom do you personally have more sympathy? Why?
4. Assume that you are one of the other students in the group. How might you use what you know about generational differences to help the group resolve this problem?

## Working with Diversity/Bridging Differences

So far we have stressed the value of diversity and provided information and examples to illustrate how member and cultural diversity can make small group communication more complex. We emphasized that the value of diversity does not just happen by mixing together people with differences. Those differences have to be recognized, valued, and matched to the social and task needs of the group. This takes work, and the National Communication Association Credo for Ethical Communication reminds us that ethical communication transcends cultures and enhances human worth and dignity (see Figure 1.2). The credo guides a group's best practices: listening actively to understand before passing judgment, building communicative climates that foster respect for the unique needs of members, and avoiding communication that is harmful to the humanity of another.

Stella Ting-Toomey, a respected scholar of intercultural communication, has written extensively on the complexities of difference in our communicative lives. Working with diversity does not happen without **mindful communication.**[43] We have

**GLOSSARY**

**Mindful Communication**

*Communication that is open to multiple perspectives, shows a willingness to see the world from another's standpoint, and shifts perspective if necessary*

to be alert, open, willing, and reflective if we are to bridge differences. No practice or helpful tips will work unless group members are reflective participant-observers and believe in the value of diversity. You simply cannot stay stuck in your routine ways of doing things, unwilling to experiment, listen, learn about and from others, or be open to new possibilities. Our goal is to help group members blend into a well-functioning team that respects and uses member diversity to best advantage. The key to mindful communication is obtaining knowledge of the values behind those differences and being flexible enough to create new possibilities. Symbolic convergence is one way groups merge into a cohesive, productive team through fantasy chains (see below) that promote a team identity out of individual cultural and personal identities.

## CREATING A GROUP IDENTITY THROUGH FANTASY

Diversity is potentially useful, and somehow group members must find common ground if they are to transcend their diverse styles, talents, and perspectives and operate as a team. Developing a symbolic life meaningful to all members can help accomplish this.

Even in the most hardworking, task-oriented groups, members do not stick to business all the time. They often get sidetracked, as if they have made a tacit agreement to "take a work break." Whenever a group is not talking about the here and now of the group, it is engaged in **fantasy.** This technical definition of fantasy does not mean "unreal" or "untrue." It simply means that group members are not discussing the present task of the group but are discussing an apparently unrelated topic.

Fantasy is based on the theory of **symbolic convergence,**[44] which recognizes that human beings create and share meaning through their talk. This was a central element of our definition of the communication process: Members simultaneously create, interpret, and negotiate shared meaning. *Convergence* signifies that members have "come together" on what certain events, ideas, words, and so forth will mean. Members have developed similar feelings and beliefs about certain things (e.g., "We hate the boss's pep talks because she has no clue whatsoever about our work"). They may have in-jokes, a shared identity, or special meanings for words that only they understand (e.g., "We use 'fish face' as a term of affection because everybody in our group loves to go trout fishing"). They may also have developed rituals that are meaningful to them (e.g., "We always go out for a pizza on Friday afternoon before everybody goes their separate ways on the weekends"). These shared symbols help establish common ground and common bonds and help groups overcome differences among members.

Fantasy helps such shared symbols become a reality to a group. The process works like this. One member introduces a fantasy, and other members pick up on it and add to it. This group storytelling, called a *fantasy chain,* is similar to a party game most of us played as children. One person starts a story, the person to the left adds something, and this continues around the room until each person has contributed to the final story. Group fantasy chains are created in a similar way, and like the party game they have a central idea, or *fantasy theme,* that suggests what the fantasy is about.

**GLOSSARY**

**Fantasy**

*Group discussion not focused on the present task of the group*

**Symbolic Convergence**

*The idea that humans create shared meaning through their talk; the basis of group fantasy*

The following is an example of a fantasy theme that occurred at a student government association executive committee meeting, in which members were bemoaning the lack of a day care facility on campus and were trying to figure out what to do about it. This group includes three men and two women, one of whom (Nan) was a nontraditional student with children.

**Char:** I'm not surprised that we don't have a center! We have such a retro-administration. [Char introduces the fantasy, which contains the retro idea.]

**Rob:** I know; they're stuck in the 1970s. Next they'll probably let their sideburns grow! [Rob picks up the fantasy and starts the chain.]

**Bill:** Can't you just see President Kramer coming to school in a tie-dyed suit? [Bill adds his part in a vivid, colorful way.]

**Nan:** Better yet—a tie-dyed leisure suit! That would be about his speed.

**Joel:** I can just see a big, tie-dyed sunspot on his chest and peace-sign earrings in his ears! And they ought to change the sign on the administration building to Retro-Administration Building! [Joel joins in, embellishing Nan's and Bill's comments.]

**Rob:** I feel like we're trying to drag all of them into the twenty-first century. [Rob's comment hints at what this fantasy might mean to this group.]

**Char:** I know they're really behind the times, but we really need to get back to the day care center. How can we get our retro-administration to listen to our ideas about that? [Char ends the fantasy and gets the group back on track.]

What do you think this fantasy is about? Fantasies actually have two themes—the manifest, or obvious, theme and the latent, or underlying, theme. The *manifest theme* is what the fantasy chain is about at the surface level. The student government committee members were imagining the 70s attire of their retro-administration. The manifest theme was "Wouldn't that kind of clothing be funny?" The *latent theme,* which was actually not very far below the surface, was hinted at by Rob: "I feel like we're trying to drag all of them into the twenty-first century." In other words, "We, the students, are very forward thinking, but our retro-administration has to be forced to move forward, and we're the ones who have to drag them forward." It's an "Aren't we wonderful, but aren't they a mess" type of self-identity. The operative word here is *we*—these students, different though they may be, have defined themselves as "we" and the retro-administration as "they."

Fantasies—digressions apparently unrelated to the group's task—are introduced by members all the time, but not all fantasies are picked up on by the rest of the members or are meaningful to the group. When a fantasy captures the group's imagination, it usually means that it has some deeper relevance to the members. Thus, although it may appear during a fantasy chain that a group is goofing off, the group may be accomplishing something quite important. Fantasies can help the group define itself by creating symbols that are meaningful and that help determine its values.[45] For example, the student government committee members who sidetracked into a discussion of tie-dyed clothing were actually using fantasy to help define themselves as forward-thinking representatives of the student body.

## PRINCIPLES FOR BRIDGING DIFFERENCES

In this chapter, we have described a number of personal and cultural factors that make members different from one another, thereby increasing the challenges of communicating effectively in groups. Valuing diversity and taking advantage of it in a group is challenging because we tend to place ourselves into social groupings of similar people; dealing with difference is hard.[46] Working with groups that appear similar to us makes it easier to develop shared meaning and relate to a group identity. We can experience smoother conversations and easier problem solving with less conflict. Negative diversity beliefs, poor group climate that does not promote interpersonal risk taking, and tasks that arouse group member sensitivities can create divisive fault lines that seem impossible to cross.[47] However, a major strength of group work is that members do provide different perspectives, information, approaches to problem solving, and expertise. The good news is we are quite capable of facilitating a productive, more humane recognition of our differences without destroying the common areas that connect us. In this section we provide several principles for helping group members overcome the challenges of diversity and capitalize on their differences to improve group outcomes. Specific tips based on these principles are suggested in Table 6.4.

1. **Appreciate the value of diversity.** Enjoying the benefits of diversity requires you to value it, not simply "manage" it. Remember we prefer working with others like ourselves—we do not have to work as hard to communicate! But there is ample evidence that diversity improves group outcomes. And although cultural diversity makes things more difficult and less cohesive initially, groups can overcome problems associated with diversity to outperform homogeneous groups in the range of perspectives considered and the number of alternatives generated.[48] Working in a diverse group requires members to pay greater attention to their beliefs about diversity and their communication behaviors, but the payoff can be significant! Remembering that diversity can be a strength is an important first step to bridging differences.
2. **Openly acknowledge the differences.** Although pointing out differences runs the risk of creating seemingly insurmountable faultlines between members, difference can be valued in a way that cuts across the lines we believe separate us.[49] One thing you can do is actively promote the value of diversity. We have found that finding a common vocabulary to talk about our differences can help us appreciate them and also can be fun. For example, our students appreciate personality or work style inventories and self-tests, such as the Myers-Briggs instrument, that identify our individual styles. When we offer such inventories in our classes early in the semester and spend a class period talking about the specific strengths and blind spots of various characteristics, we find that our student groups go smoother! The inventories give group members a vocabulary to talk and even joke about their differences: "Mary, that's your *perceiver* side coming out! But we really need to decide something, not gather more information," or "Sam, we know that you want to get this project over with—your *judging* nature screams for it—but we haven't finished getting all the information we need yet." Openness to such diversity facilitates collaboration and open discussion.[50]

**TABLE 6.4 Tips for Appreciating Diversity and Bridging Differences**

1. Decide that you want to appreciate the differences among you. Making understanding and appreciating your diverse talents, approaches, and styles a priority for your group is the single best thing you can do.
2. Schedule plenty of "get to know you" time. This can be a purely social gathering with no business conducted, or you can set aside a brief "check-in" time before you get started on your business. However, don't rush this process. You will need time to learn about each other.
3. Be willing to talk about and praise the differences among you. When people believe their unique approaches or contributions are valued, they relax and are willing to contribute more to the group process.
4. Be open to new ways of doing things. Nothing dampens the positive potential of diversity more than rigid adherence to doing things the same way they've always been done. Be willing to listen and to try new ideas.
5. Avoid seeing difference as a zero-sum game. Think of ways to integrate differences. For example, consider how you can both work on the task and build relationships.
6. Find ways you can create common experiences for group members. For instance, you may want to schedule a retreat, an outdoor activity, or a baseball game—anything that gets all members participating in the same experience.
7. Create rituals for the group. Meaningful rituals can go a long way toward reminding members that their purpose in coming together is greater than any individual differences they may possess. For example, one church board always begins its routine meetings with a prayer and its annual retreat with a communion service. However, rituals don't have to be serious. Some work groups pass out cookies or bagels at the beginning of the meeting, with members taking turns bringing the snacks.
8. Encourage members to create symbols that represent the group. Many groups have T-shirts with a meaningful saying or symbol. Sometimes members participate in creating symbols or logos for the group.

3. **Find ways you are similar.** Although this chapter has emphasized ways in which members are diverse, the truth is that there are usually many similarities among group members: all want to do a good job on their project, they may be in some of the same classes, may share hobbies or other interests, attend the same worship services, or like the same music! Tessa West and her associates found, for example, that racially diverse dyads and groups where members perceived one another to be similar performed better and had less anxiety than when members perceived dissimilarities.[51] Take some time to get to know one another and learn how you are alike.

4. **Talk openly about how you will integrate your differences.** In one recent study of groups that included diverse experts, groups improved their performance when the members explicitly discussed how they would coordinate and integrate the individual members' work.[52] Diversity of expertise, by itself, does not necessarily improve team performance unless members are able to incorporate those diverse perspectives into the problem-solving process. The teams that received intervention about how to collaborate were better able to integrate information, capitalize on members' strengths, and utilize all the information available in an appropriate way. If members do not feel safe sharing, then those unique perspectives and skills will not be shared let alone integrated into a group decision. Safe climates promote member contributions, but a word of caution is in order. Safe climates also encourage those who are not experts to contribute; respect their contributions while moderating their influence. You should consider bringing in a process expert to help you or spend time, yourselves, understanding one another's strengths and discussing how, specifically, you each can contribute to the group's project.
5. **Form a group identity around your differences.** Rink and Ellemers constructed dyads that were similar in work goals and information, or different in one or both of these characteristics.[53] The dyads that were different on both qualities actually came to use that difference to define their dyads in positive ways. The social identities they created revolved around those differences, in a constructive way. Perceiving difference does tend to get in the way of group member attachment to a group identity. However, it has been found that a positive emotional climate and belief about diversity will mediate this.[54] Common identity among members affects how well a group functions. You can also use your differences to create a common identity and set your group apart: "We are really different in how we approach things, and that has helped us think through our solutions much more thoroughly."
6. **Use communication practices that build collective competence.** We hope that, throughout our text, you have been learning about competent communication practices. Jessica Thompson recently completed a study of interdisciplinary research teams.[55] In such teams, members are experts in certain areas—a form of cognitive diversity we alluded to earlier—but may have a hard time negotiating mutual understanding and meaning because of their different approaches and knowledge bases. Two communication practices that set effective groups apart were listening with genuine interest and using reflexive talk—in other words, talking about the team's processes and their social behavior (e.g., "I think, at the last meeting, we did a particularly good job of hearing each other out and trying to understand where we were each coming from."). Reflexive communication builds mutual trust and promotes shared learning. Another practice of effective teams was backstage communication—communication exchanges that take place outside the formal meetings—that provides members with opportunities to get to know one another and bond. When members get to know one another on a personal

basis, the team's work performance is enhanced. The final practice was using humor and shared laughter to relieve stress, defuse potential problems before they became overwhelming, and strengthen group bonds.

7. **Don't use practices that detract from competence.** Thompson also identified practices that interfered with members appreciating one another's diversity.[56] Specifically, using negative humor and sarcasm, getting into chest-beating contests about one another's expertise, jockeying for power, and acting bored with the group, its discussion topic or process prevented diverse teams from working together well. Being disagreeable hurts group effectiveness, but being agreeable improves team performance and cohesiveness.[57] Small groups that deliberate public policy are often racially and ethnically mixed. When rules of respect and openness are followed those members of color are especially appreciative of the opportunities to contribute, be heard, and learn from others.[58]

Group members can easily make negative attributions about others whose communication styles and practices differ from ours. We have to learn to avoid interpreting others' actions through the lens of our own culture but to appreciate what other cultures have to offer. We have presented several ways in which group members can bridge their differences and capitalize on their diversity. But the most important thing that members can do to transcend their differences is to *want* to do so. Assuming you want to work together productively and mindfully, the suggestions we have provided will help you find the potential in your diversity.

## RESOURCES FOR REVIEW AND DISCUSSION

### SUMMARY

- Diversity is the essence of group problem solving. The differences by themselves are not a problem, but members often don't know how to or don't want to manage their diversity so the group can benefit.
- Diversity comes in many forms. Members may have different motives for joining a group; they may differ in their learning and personality styles as well as their information bases and expertise.
- Another major way group members differ is in their culture or co-culture. Three main dimensions along which cultures differ are collectivist/individualistic, power distance, and context.
- Gender and racial or ethnic differences are, at heart, cultural differences. Men and women consistently differ in four ways; similarly, African, Asian, European, and Hispanic American cultures have developed different communication patterns that can be misunderstood by outsiders.
- Diversity is valuable, and group members can bridge their differences through fantasy and intentionally addressing their differences.

EXERCISES

1. Look at the descriptions of four different work styles below:

- Task-oriented people, who believe a group's main job is to get down to business as soon as possible
- Relational people, who believe that group work can be fun and that getting to know each other is part of the fun
- Systematic decision makers, who believe in gathering all the facts and weighing them before deciding
- Intuitive decision makers, who assess a situation instantly and leap to a conclusion

*a.* Each of the four work styles should be assigned to a different corner of the room. Then, without thinking about it too long or too hard, go to the corner of the room that represents the work style most like yours.

*b.* Elect a reporter to record your group's responses and report to the class at the end of the session.

*c.* In five to six minutes, write down all the advantages people like you have to offer a group.

*d.* In five to six minutes, write down all the disadvantages people like you bring to a group.

*e.* Reconvene the class as a whole, and have each group report, first the advantages and then the disadvantages, while a class member or your teacher writes each one on the board for all to see.

*f.* After each group has presented its list, the other groups may add advantages or disadvantages to the list.

*g.* Talk as a class about what you learned from this exercise and what you perceive can be the advantages such diversity of approach represented in the group.

2. Your family represents one example of a co-cultural grouping. Form into groups of four to six, and ask each person to assume that he or she has invited the rest of your group members home for Thanksgiving dinner with the family. Each person should describe what the "rules" are for Thanksgiving dinner. For example, where does everyone sit? When do you know you may start to eat? Does the food get passed around, or does someone put food on each person's plate and pass the plate down? What are acceptable topics of conversation? Is conversation lively or muted? How did the "rules" become established in the family, and so forth?

When everyone has finished, discuss the differences you discovered among each other's "cultures." What dimensions of culture seem to be most important in each family grouping? Were there any surprises? What does each family do when it encounters a violation of the rules? Are the rules ever discussed openly among family members? Are there rules that prohibit what you can talk about?

3. Class members should divide themselves into groups of four to six along gender, race/ethnicity, or age lines. For example, the class might form several single-sex groups. Each group should first appoint a recorder/spokesperson to take notes. Then each group should discuss the following two questions:

*a.* How do you see yourselves as group members? What characteristics do you believe you have?

*b.* How do you see the other group as group members? What characteristics do you believe they have?

Finally, when each group is finished, all should share their results with the class and the class should take this opportunity to talk about the stereotypes they hold and how accurate those stereotypes are (or are not).

## KEY TERMS • CONCEPTS

Abstract Conceptualization Learning Style
Active Experimentation Learning Style
Boomers
Builders
Cognitive/Informational Diversity
Collectivist Culture
Concrete Experience Learning Style
Culture
Deep-Level Diversity
Diversity
Extraversion/Introversion Dimension
Fantasy
Gen-Xers
Heterogeneity
High-Context Culture
Homogeneity
Individualistic Culture
Low-Context Culture
Millennials
Mindful Communication
Myers-Briggs Type Indicator®
Perceiving/Judging Dimension
Power Distance
Reflective Observation Learning Style
Sensing/Intuiting Dimension
Surface Diversity
Symbolic Convergence
Thinking/Feeling Dimension

# Understanding and Improving Group Throughput Processes

PART FOUR

# Understanding and Improving Group Throughput Processes

In Part Four we continue the discussion of throughput processes we began in Part Three. As members form into a productive team and learn to manage their differences, they are simultaneously engaging in several important throughput processes. Chapter 7 explains why both creative and critical thinking are important and shows how group members can enhance both processes. Chapter 8 discusses group problem-solving procedures and describes what members can do to help ensure effective problem solving. Chapter 9 describes the dynamics of group conflict and how it can be managed to improve the group's problem solving. Finally, Chapter 10 explores important leadership principles and their successful application.

CHAPTER

# 7 Creative and Critical Thinking in the Small Group

## CHAPTER OUTLINE



## CHAPTER OBJECTIVES

**After reading this chapter you should be able to:**

1. Define creative thinking and explain why it is important to small group problem solving.
2. Describe brainstorming, synectics, and appreciative inquiry, and explain how they can be used to help enhance group creativity.
3. Define critical thinking and explain why it is important to small group problem solving.
4. List and describe the attitudes most conducive to critical thinking in a group.
5. Explain how group members should use critical thinking during the information-gathering stage of problem solving.
6. Describe and give examples of each of the five steps crucial to evaluating information.
7. Define and give examples of each of the five reasoning errors: overgeneralizations, attacks on a person instead of the argument, confusing causal relationships, either-or thinking, and incomplete comparisons.

## Ozarks Greenways, Inc.

CASE 7.1

The "Rails to Trails" movement in the United States is committed to converting unused railroad tracks to biking and hiking trails and establishing usable greenways for citizens to enjoy. Today this conservancy has helped create over 20,000 miles of trails that span communities, regions, and even states (see www.railstotrails.org). Several years ago, a group of committed citizens in Springfield, Missouri, formed Ozarks Greenways, Inc. (OGI), whose mission was to preserve green space through the creation of linear parks. This long-term project required members to raise funds to buy and acquire access rights for the greenway. One proposed spur of the Ozarks greenway system would connect a park near the center of Springfield to Wilson's Creek Battlefield, a national Civil War battlefield 10 miles to the southwest.

Bikers and hikers prefer trails that allow them to proceed at a steady pace without worrying about traffic and traffic lights. That presented a major challenge for OGI because to connect the park and the battlefield, the greenway would have to cross Kansas Expressway, a busy highway dangerous for bikers and hikers. The most obvious solution was to reroute the greenway to have it cross Kansas Expressway at a traffic light. But this would have meant rerouting the trail to run parallel to two major highways—a major hazard for bikers, who travel not on sidewalks but on highways next to speeding cars. In addition, rerouting the greenway would have forced OGI to acquire additional access rights along commercially developed areas. Even if that could have been done, it would have been prohibitively expensive and would have delayed completion of the greenway for years. OGI's goal was to establish a route that was both safe and allowed steady biker and hiker movement by avoiding stoplights and travel on major highways. The OGI committee decided to stick with the original route.

The problem OGI faced could be stated thus: How can the greenway path cross Kansas Expressway safely and without forcing long waits at traffic lights? OGI needed (and eventually found) a creative solution that met all its main criteria: safety, cost, and ease of use. Read the chapter to find out what OGI did.

**This chapter examines two processes essential for problem solving in small groups: creative and critical thinking. Both kinds of thinking are necessary for effective discussion groups; neither one alone is sufficient to ensure effective solutions. In addition, they cannot be done simultaneously; that would be like trying to drive a car with one foot on the accelerator and one foot on the brake! Group members must learn when to be creative, when to be critical, and what kinds of procedures help the group do both.**

## What Is Creative Thinking?

Typically, when we think about the dynamics of problem solving in groups, we focus only on work that is rational, logical, and critical to the process and neglect creativity. In Chapter 6 we showed that creativity is an important component of working with diversity. Creativity "involves the generation, application, combination, and extension of new ideas."[1] **Creative thinking** is fostered in small groups when members use imagination, intuition, hunches, insight, and fantasy to devise unusual or innovative solutions that probably would not emerge from ordinary group discussion. Contrary to the popular myth of the solitary genius working alone, groups produce many of today's creative ideas and innovations.[2]

American business and industry, in particular, recognize how important creativity and innovation are to their success and have focused on how to enhance creative processes. An investigation of more than 2,000 senior managers from around the world found four factors related to an organization's ability to innovate: how much support there is for risk taking, how much tolerance there is for making mistakes, how effectively members can work together as a team, and how quickly decisions can be implemented.[3] A team's climate is especially important, particularly support for innovation, or the ability to get things done.[4] Creative thinking in groups is the cornerstone of innovation and helps us invent better, less expensive products or services that improve our lives. How to enhance that creativity is important for you to understand.

Group creativity involves both *divergent* and *convergent* thinking, each requiring slightly different communication behaviors to succeed.[5] During divergent thinking, ideas should vary—members must think as differently as possible from one another so the team will have a wide array of options from which to choose. Quantity of ideas and breadth of thinking are important. A climate of safety is essential for divergent thinking because members must be willing to share new and perhaps crazy ideas. Being overly critical at this point stifles creativity. For example, in one study of an electronic problem-solving group, the group's leader gave members feedback privately via computer; even this feedback, designed to motivate, was interpreted as critical and choked group creativity.[6] However, at some point members must select the best ideas or converge them in ways that will actually work. During this phase "constructive debate" among members helps them identify the best ideas and eliminate the less useful ones.[7] Successful creative project teams appropriately balance their shorter cycles of discovery and divergence with longer cycles of correction and convergence.[8] Too much playing around prevents critical assessment of ideas and too much correction prevents discovery of unique ideas.

**GLOSSARY**

**Creative Thinking**
*Encouraging use of hunch, intuition, insight, and fantasy to promote creativity*

For a group to be creative, both *individual* and *group* creativity are needed. Creative individuals tolerate ambiguity, have low levels of communication apprehension, and aren't afraid to violate societal norms and rules (think of the student whose hair is dyed purple).[9] They don't fear rejection by others, are open to new ideas, and like to play and have fun. This sort of individual openness to experience contributes to group creative processes but in a measured way. Too many members open to experience and your group can get lost in all the divergent ideas. You need to seek a mix of openness for that balance of divergence and convergence in your group.[10] Group creativity fostered by individual characteristics is also facilitated by group norms. That is why a friend of ours structures her group meetings so that they will feel like parties—she reasons that people are more creative when they are relaxed and having a good time. She makes sure food is served, people are introduced, and no one feels left out. Ironically, she works hard to help others have fun so that members' potential for creativity isn't derailed by the group's own norms and processes.

Bernard Nijstad and Paul Paulus synthesized considerable research on group creativity and grouped the factors influencing group creativity into four areas: diversity, discussion rules, climate, and environment.[11] First, creative groups are diverse. Members bring a variety of skills, knowledge, problem-solving approaches, and perspectives to the table. Group diversity doesn't guarantee creative thinking—some groups cannot overcome the challenges that diversity brings (we discuss some of these in Chapter 6). Second, creative groups structure their discussions to enhance, not lose, their creative potential. Be mindful, however, because both individuals and

© Caiaimage/Glow Images RF

groups prefer closure, or completing discussion, because they fear being judged, grow tired during and after intense discussions, or feel pushed to make a decision.[12] Stay alert to premature closure tendencies by avoiding early consensus and refraining from pressuring others to conform. Alert, mindful groups must do two things: encourage diverse ideas *and* help each other mutually understand what connects all these diverse ideas. A multitude of different ideas is worthless to a group unless members can help each other see the similarities connecting those ideas.[13] This ability for a team to combine diverse knowledge is called "integrative capacity" and although it can be challenging to achieve, it is necessary if a team is to create novel solutions.[14] Third, the importance of a group's climate cannot be overemphasized. Human communication, we learned in Chapter 3, is about both content and relationship messages. Both in what they do and how they do it, members can facilitate a climate of openness to new ideas, high levels of trust, and a willingness to disagree with respect. Forgetting the balance between playing with ideas and evaluating them respectively can lead to groupthink, discussed later. Finally, a group's creativity is affected by the larger environment in which it operates. If a group's parent organization doesn't value creativity or won't allow the group to operate with some autonomy, group creativity will be hurt. Table 7.1 summarizes the individual, group, and environmental characteristics that promote both individual and group creativity.

**TABLE 7.1 Individual, Group, and Environmental Factors That Promote Creative Thinking**

| |
|---|
| **MEMBERS** |
| Are willing to communicate |
| Are willing to be unconventional and violate societal norms |
| Tolerate ambiguity |
| Are not afraid of rejection |
| Are open to new ideas |
| Are playful and like to have fun |
| **GROUPS** |
| Have diverse knowledge, skills, perspectives, approaches |
| Work to overcome norms that interfere with creativity (premature consensus, pressures to conform, groupthink) and promote norms that foster creativity (take time to learn each other's unique contributions, encourage sharing of diverse ideas) |
| Develop an appropriate group climate (foster trust, encourage constructive debate) |
| **ENVIRONMENT** |
| Place high value on creativity |
| Give the group autonomy and room to breathe |

Creative thinking is always appropriate, yet it is especially useful at the beginning of a group's problem-solving process. An ideal time to use creativity-enhancing procedures is after members have learned something about a problem but before they delve into the details. Members can create a number of creative ideas that they later can examine carefully and critically. Creative processes can take time, so reserve this kind of thinking for important decisions.

## Enhancing Group Creativity

At some point groups will be faced with the task of discovering an innovative solution to a problem—an idea for a new product, an eye-catching print advertising campaign, a way to bridge two very different perspectives on the problem, a novel group presentation that will earn an A, or an innovative way to build a safe greenway across a busy expressway. Group creativity has to be facilitated and your group may need to be shocked out of its habitual ways of thinking and behaving to find those creative ideas that can be implemented into an innovative solution. You can use brainstorming, synectics, or appreciative inquiry to tap into a group's creative potential.

### Creative Fund-Raising for the College

APPLY NOW

Members of the Advisory Council of the College of Arts and Letters where one of us works met one year to discuss creative fund-raising ideas to enhance the college's endowment for student scholarships. One council member mentioned a combination lecture/dinner fund-raiser a museum in New York City had initiated, which had become a highly successful event. Members began to talk about ways that event could be modified to work in their town. They decided to have faculty give presentations or performances based on their expertise, combined with a dinner at one of the council member's homes. For instance, a film professor followed his lecture about a particular film director with a special showing of one of the director's lesser-known films, followed by dinner. Another professor gave a brief piano concert followed by an elaborate dessert. These events, known as the A La Carte Series, succeeded. In addition, the events sold out quickly, sometimes the first day that tickets became available, and enough money was raised to support a college lecture series. This is an example of how a group can modify an existing idea to arrive at something unique. Before you read further in this chapter, address the following questions:

1. What communication behaviors and skills would group members have to demonstrate to encourage the kind of creativity demonstrated by the advisory council?
2. What member behaviors would interfere with this kind of creativity?
3. What group rules, norms, and procedures would support this type of creativity?
4. What group norms would interfere?

**FIGURE 7.1 Guidelines for Brainstorming**

| | | | | |
|---|---|---|---|---|
| 1. Group previews the rules for brainstorming. → | 2. Group is presented with a problem to solve. → | 3. Members generate as many solutions as possible, without any criticism. → | 4. All suggestions are recorded for group to see. → | 5. Ideas are evaluated at another session. |

## BRAINSTORMING

Many groups use **brainstorming**, a popular procedure designed especially to release a group's creativity, especially when they are generating ideas.[15] Brainstorming consciously separates idea creation from idea evaluation by not allowing any criticism to occur while the group is generating ideas. Years of research into the practice has helped us understand how to use it effectively to help groups generate ideas and avoid group tendencies to close off discussion prematurely. Two measures help ensure quantity and quality of ideas: If you have the time, allow members to generate ideas initially alone and then to the group and follow tested rules for getting the most out of this technique.[16] Later, often at a separate meeting, the group evaluates the ideas, combines or modifies them, and selects the best ones. The basic procedure is described below. Figure 7.1 summarizes these brainstorming guidelines.

1. Any technique used to promote creative thinking does not just happen. You need to preview the spirit of the procedure before beginning the process so you can avoid both individual and group tendencies toward premature closure. The best way to do this is to set the scene by calling for alert, conscious participation and reviewing the stages of brainstorming and the rules members will be expected to follow and monitor.
2. The group now is ready to turn its focus on a problem to solve. The problem can range from something specific and concrete ("How can we raise more money for student scholarships?") to something abstract and intangible ("How can we improve the quality of work life for employees?").
3. Members are encouraged to come up with as many solutions as possible to the problem. Quantity is the goal here, and several rules must be followed. Most importantly no evaluation is permitted during brainstorming. With judgment temporarily suspended, members are encouraged to turn their imaginations loose, to let wild and crazy ideas surface, to build on each other's ideas, to combine ideas, and to strive for more and more suggestions. Second, do not stop generating ideas too soon. Often, the best ideas—the ones a group eventually selects—are listed during the latter part of the brainstorming session.[17] Third, groups must stay focused on the task of generating ideas. The best brainstorming occurs when the fewest words are spoken. This means avoid storytelling tangents and explanations of ideas—the gist of the idea is what you are after. Fourth, during lulls in discussion, keep generating ideas by encouraging more or reviewing the

**GLOSSARY**

**Brainstorming**

*A procedure designed to tap members' creativity by asking them to generate as many ideas as possible without evaluation* categories developed earlier in the discussion. Good brainstorming occurs when members follow its rules in an effort to stay focused and minimize evaluation.[18]

4. All ideas are recorded so that the whole group can see them. Usually, the group's recorder will write ideas on a large pad of paper. How the ideas are recorded, on paper or electronically, is not as important as all group members being able to see the ideas. Seeing ideas often triggers other ideas and prevents premature closure of the creative process.[19] Extraverts are particularly effective idea generators in computer-mediated groups during brainstorming sessions if they are exposed to the ideas generated by others.[20]
5. The ideas are evaluated at another session. Just because brainstorming requires temporarily suspending critical evaluation does not mean critical thinking is unimportant. Also, incubation is an important feature of creative thinking allowing for the diverse ideas to find their connection. Olga Goldenberg and her associates found that brainstorming worked better if members were encouraged to freely create ideas first, without constraints, and were later (perhaps at a separate meeting) encouraged to combine or build on one another's ideas.[21] After brainstorming has generated a lot of ideas and the group has had a chance to let the ideas sit for a while, members can modify or combine ideas into workable solutions to the problem.

The basic brainstorming technique has several variations. Often groups have one or two vocal people who are highly creative, share many innovative ideas, and intimidate others into not participating. In this case it may be more productive for each person to brainstorm silently rather than openly in a group. In this form of brainstorming, called *brainwriting,* each person quietly records as many new and different solutions as possible. Then each person shares one new idea, round-robin fashion, as the facilitator posts it for all to see. The sharing continues until all ideas have been posted. Members are encouraged to add to the list as new ideas occur to them.

Another variation that works well with a quiet or introverted group is *brainwaving*, where each person has a piece of paper with the focus question and writes down an idea. The person then passes the paper to the right. The group keeps going in this way until the paper returns to the original member. The ideas are then consolidated into one master list.[22]

Brainstorming in its various forms is work, and members can become tired. When this happens their ideas decrease and they tend to get stuck on similar ideas and idea categories.[23] Hamit Coskun suggests that when your group begins to show signs of fatigue or premature convergence, take a break from the task and complete a divergent thinking activity unrelated to the problem at hand. This can be as simple as throwing out a list of fun terms and asking members to generate opposite terms. The key is to take a mental break so members can get back to divergent thinking mode. After the activity is completed, move back into the brainstorming or brainwriting task.

*Electronic brainstorming,* another variation, has proven useful in addressing the factors that can lead face-to-face groups into early convergence or premature closure. The anonymity can help prevent individuals from censoring themselves. In this variation each group member sits at an individual computer terminal (all of which may be in the same room) and types out her or his ideas. The ideas are posted onto a large screen

FIGURE 7.2 Guidelines for Synectics

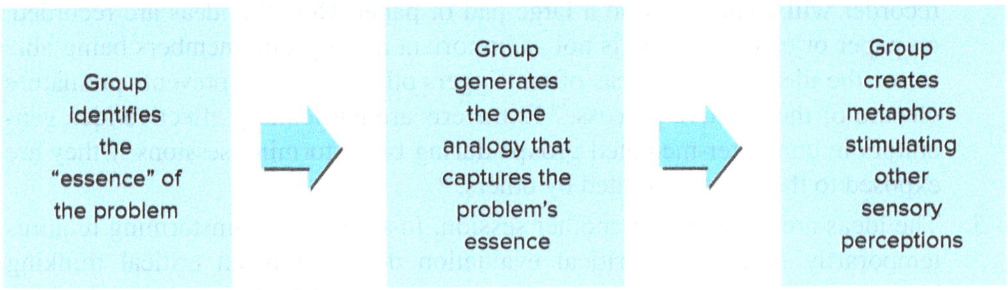


visible to everyone, so the group can keep track of previous remarks. In addition, members who may tend to remain quiet in face-to-face group interaction find it easier to contribute online, and members do not have to deal with the fatigue or frustrations that can come from people talking all at once.[24] Because no one knows who contributed what, electronic brainstorming, especially with 8- to 10-member groups, often generates more and better ideas than traditional brainstorming.[25] One disadvantage of brainstorming variations that do not allow for face-to-face group freewheeling is that cohesiveness among members can be reduced.[26]

## SYNECTICS

**Synectics** is a technique that stimulates thinking in metaphors and analogies.[27] Why is that important to creativity? Consider the example of how Velcro was created. One day after a walk, Swiss engineer George de Mestral noticed cockleburs stuck to his jacket.[28] Examining one under a microscope, he observed how the hooks latched onto the fabric, and saw its potential as a hook-and-loop fastener. It took him eight years to develop and perfect, but today Velcro turns up everywhere, from shoes to children's clothing to camping equipment. The cockleburs served as the nature-based analogy, or metaphor, for the manufactured fastener.

A chance encounter with burrs led de Mestral helped to create this new kind of manufactured fastener. The synectics technique (shown in Figure 7.2) tries to stimulate such chance connections between apparently unrelated elements. First, the group identifies the essence of the problem. For instance, "sticking together" could have been the metaphor that led to Velcro: "How can I create a fastener that sticks together like burrs do to clothing?" Second, the group is asked to create analogies that capture that essence. For instance, group members might ask, "Where in everyday life do we find things that stick together?" Answers could include things like burrs, gooey stuff from plants, white glue, and zippers. Finally, group members look for metaphors or analogies that use a different sensory perception than the one being observed. For example, if the analogy relates to touch, such as the cocklebur example, members might be asked to think of a visual or hearing metaphor. A visual metaphor could include a fishhook; an auditory metaphor might include the sound of a zipper closing and opening. A different kind of metaphor could be just the thing producing the "aha"

**GLOSSARY**

**Synectics**
*A procedure designed to stimulate creative thinking by using metaphors and looking for similarities in different things*

insight that leads to a solution. Asking the group to consider the following questions helps trigger such insights.

1. Change your perspective. Sometimes, changing the angle from which you view a problem gives you a different insight. For example, if you are an Ozarks Greenways member, imagine that you are Superman and can view the city's streets from above.
2. Look for a direct comparison, something from another field that is similar to your problem. This is exactly what happened in the Velcro example—the physical attachment of the burrs provided the idea for this new type of fastener.
3. Temporarily suspend reality to use fantasy and imagination. Ignore objective reality for a moment to learn what you can discover. Imagine that your bicycle has wings and can fly over the Kansas Expressway to solve the greenway problem.

Synectics may seem strange at first because it forces group members to jump out of their self-imposed conceptual boxes and stimulate rather than reduce ambiguity,

### Creating Suggestions for Crossing Kansas Expressway

APPLY NOW

Ozarks Greenways, Inc. had to come up with a solution to the following problem. Land had been acquired on either side of the busy Kansas Expressway for a greenway, a bicycle and hiking path to link Springfield with Wilson's Creek Battlefield. However, there was no traffic light where the land reached the expressway, and the city had no plans to put a light there. Your task is to come up with a solution for the greenway that will keep bikers and hikers moving and that will be safe and inexpensive.

Divide the class into groups of five or six. Appoint a facilitator to record suggestions and make sure the group follows the "no criticism" rule. Ask each group to brainstorm a list of suggestions for the greenway problem. The groups should brainstorm for 10 minutes and think of as many suggestions as possible. At the end of the period, all the suggestions should be posted at the front of the class so that all can see. The class should then address the following questions:

1. Was it easy or difficult to follow the brainstorming rules? What was the hardest to do?
2. How did members feel during the process?
3. What do members remember thinking during the process?
4. Did anything stand in the way of being imaginative and having fun? If so, how might the process be modified to encourage more imagination and fun?

As an alternative to this exercise, some groups can brainstorm in the traditional way while others use brainwriting. If this is done, class members can compare the efficacy of each technique. Groups can also use a facilitator to help members stick to the brainstorming rules.

**FIGURE 7.3** Steps in Appreciative Inquiry

| | | | |
|---|---|---|---|
| Discover: What is working well now? Share stories to illustrate what works. | Dream: Imagine what could be. Team creates shared vision. | Design: How can we translate the dream into reality? | Destiny (Deliver): How do we create and implement the design? |

but that's exactly why it works. Some corporations deliberately send groups of employees away from their normal work settings to jolt them out of possible ruts so they can come up with new ideas.[29]

## APPRECIATIVE INQUIRY

**Appreciative inquiry** was developed by David Cooperrider and his associates in response to what they perceived as an overemphasis on problems and deficiencies by organizations and teams.[30] Typically, teams approach problems from a deficiency standpoint: What is wrong and how can it be fixed? Cooperrider believes that focusing on strengths can lead to creative insights and solutions that a problem focus might miss. For example, if an organization is trying to improve customer service, instead of starting with problems reported in customer service, the appreciative inquiry approach would start with stories about exemplary customer service—what is already working well—and build on those. Appreciative inquiry seeks to "expand the realm of the possible" by discovering "new ideas that are compelling to people," which means people are motivated and enthused about putting those new ideas into practice.[31] There are four phases to appreciative inquiry, each providing a specific focus. Figure 7.3 depicts this process.

1. Discover: What is working well? In this phase, group participants are asked to share stories about what currently works well. What are the strengths of the team or organization as it currently exists? What is the best of "what is?" For example, if a university seeks to strengthen its academic advising program, a group of faculty, students, and administrators might share stories about advisers who have gone above and beyond the call of duty to help students. Sharing stories creates common vision and strong relationships, both of which are important to the transformative change process appreciative inquiry can bring about.
2. Dream: Imagine what could be. After hearing and discussing the stories revealed during the Discover phase, team members are asked to dream about a future in which the best of what they have discovered could exist routinely. If our organization operates at its best, what would it look like? For example, after hearing about exemplary advising stories, the group may conclude that advising works best when students know their advisers, are willing to share their dreams with them, and advisers have time to get to know their students as individuals and have access to a variety of helpful resources. This might result in a vision

**GLOSSARY**

**Appreciative Inquiry**

*A technique that focuses on an organization's or situation's strengths and seeks to build on those strengths.*

statement like the following: Our vision is that each student, when entering the university, forms a relationship with an academic adviser who represents someone who cares deeply about the student's success and will work to help that student succeed.

3. Design: How can we translate the dream into a reality? In this phase, the team moves from the dream to the ultimate reality. What relationships, structures, and human networks would need to exist for our organization to function the way we know it sometimes functions? In the advising sessions that work well, what are the common features? How did the adviser get to know the student so well? How did the adviser know what resources to use to help the student? What can we, as an organization, do to foster strong student–adviser relationships? In answering these and similar questions, the team may create more effective orientation programs, work at creating better matches between students and advisers, and provide ample social opportunities to foster the student–adviser relationship.
4. Destiny (formerly Deliver): How will we create what we want to achieve? How will we implement our vision? What relationships do we need to create or strengthen? What resources do we need or need to redistribute? Who in the team has the passion for working on which parts of the vision? In this phase, the team gets down to business. For example, interested team members may work together to redesign the new student orientation program to give new students better opportunities to get to know and work with their advisers.

Appreciative inquiry capitalizes on the fact that positive feelings among team members enhance creativity.[32] It is likely that focusing on positive emotions and team accomplishments relaxes members and frees up their thinking.

Creative thinking plays a significant role in group problem solving. Groups trained in creative thinking have been found to show more humor and to have higher rates of participation than those not trained to think creatively. Members of such groups support more ideas and criticize less, both of which are important to creative thinking.[33]

Creativity in group members and group processes is essential to productivity and effective problem solving, and it must work alongside critical thinking. Critical thinking, like creative thinking, is found both within individuals and in a group's norms. Critical thinking involves careful and systematic examination of the information used by the group. Surprisingly, groups have more problems being critical than being creative, which can have dire consequences. Failure to be critical is more dangerous than failure to be creative, because it can lead to groupthink, introduced in Chapter 5. Group problem solving can be effective because several heads are potentially better than one. However, simply placing divergent talents and perspectives in a group does not make critical thinking happen! Groups are notorious for not being vigilant or critical in their discussions because members tend to avoid challenging each other.[34]

We now turn our discussion to how groups can help ensure good decision making and problem solving to complement their creativity. We will use a case study (Case 7.2) to help show the implications and consequences of poor critical thinking.

GLOSSARY

**Evidence**

*Facts, data, opinions, and other information that back a claim or conclusion*

**Arguments**

*Claims supported by evidence and reasoning*

**Critical Thinking**

*Systematic thinking using evidence, reasoning, and logic to promote soundness*

## What Makes Thinking "Critical"?

We have seen that creative thinking is intuitive, unsystematic, and spontaneous. In contrast, two principles differentiate critical from creative thinking: (1) the use of **evidence** (facts, data, opinions, and other information backing a claim or conclusion) and (2) the logical **arguments** speakers and writers make with that evidence to support what they believe are valid reasons to accept their claims and assertions. **Critical thinking** occurs when a problem is analyzed thoroughly, using as much relevant information as possible. Then the solution is developed on the basis of all that information and the best reasoning and logic you can use.

### Problems at NASA

CASE 7.2

On February 1, 2003, many watched in horror as the space shuttle *Columbia* disintegrated upon reentry after what had been a successful mission in space. The National Aeronautics and Space Administration's (NASA) investigation into the causes zeroed in on pieces of foam insulation that detached at liftoff, damaging or knocking off some insulation tiles designed to protect the shuttle from the extreme heat of reentry.[35] No longer shielded from the heat, the fuel tank exploded. NASA records disclosed that foam insulation had caused damage to the tiles since the very first shuttle launch! One NASA official lamented, "How were the signals missed?" In early 2004, NASA released the results of an internal survey of its employees, which showed that the culture of NASA contributed to why these signals were missed.[36] The survey, completed by only 45 percent of employees, revealed that many employees are afraid to speak out about safety concerns and are reluctant to "express dissenting views in a large group." One NASA administrator pointed out that in NASA's culture, both managers and peers pressure dissenters to conform, even when they have safety concerns: "We don't have time to listen to everybody moan and groan about every issue out there." NASA concluded that this mind-set contributed to the *Columbia* disaster.

This isn't the first time NASA's culture has been implicated in a disaster. The 1986 explosion of the shuttle *Challenger* shortly after takeoff was caused by malfunctions of the O-ring seals on one of the solid rocket boosters—a particularly distressing event because, like the problems with the foam insulation, NASA knew about potential problems with the O-rings failing to seal in cold weather. In other words, the *Challenger* disaster was predictable. The decision-making procedures *should* have revealed the O-ring safety concern—but did not.

So even a group of highly trained experts can arrive at a fatally flawed decision that ignores relevant information—in other words, the group doesn't think critically.

Critical thinking, like creative thinking, is both necessary and time consuming. Sometimes, it is okay to make a decision that is just "good enough" without analyzing all your choices. For example, suppose your committee is charged with deciding whether to give coffee mugs or comparably priced pens with your organization's logo as souvenirs at your annual banquet. Does it really matter which favor is selected? Will anyone be hurt by your choice? Such a decision probably does not warrant taking the time to agonize over every aspect of the choice. However, for consequential decisions where human lives are at stake, critical thinking is essential.

## Enhancing Critical Thinking in a Group

Enhancing critical thinking in groups is a central principle of ethical communication. Treated as an important skill, it is often placed front and center in models of ethical decision making in organizations.[37] No matter the setting of your group—work, school, church, community—critical thinking is so important that it is the first principle in the National Communication Association's Credo for Ethical Communication, introduced in Chapter 1: "We advocate truthfulness, accuracy, honesty, and reason as essential to the integrity of communication."

Critical thinking in groups involves five key factors: how members view information, gather information, carefully evaluate the pooled information, make reasoned judgments on the basis of that information, and how alert they are to facilitating group processes that foster critical thinking.

### HAVING THE RIGHT ATTITUDE

The most important "technique" to help groups do a good job of critical thinking is not a technique at all—it is the attitude of the members, specifically the desire to make the best possible decision. You have to *want* to make a good decision, because doing so takes a great deal of time and effort. Critical thinkers are **open-minded,** or willing and eager to consider new information and ideas, even if that information contradicts what they previously believed. They go out of their way to look for relevant information and tap a wide variety of sources in their attempt to gather information that supports all sides of an issue. Finally, they pride themselves on being objective and fair about evaluating information. Being open-minded and fostering a climate of openness helps to counter the group tendency to "seize and freeze" onto early positions, especially ones that appear to be shared by others.[38] Communication scholars who have studied NASA's flawed decision making (Case 7.2) made several observations about their process.[39] Those officials involved in making the original *Challenger* launch decision showed prejudice in favor of the launch in part because of several previous postponements. Any prelaunch information was uncritically accepted while antilaunch data were treated hypercritically.

A second important attitude is a "show me" skepticism that indicates members want to think for themselves rather than being told what to think by others. Critical thinkers do not assume that anything they read or hear is true or accept something as true just because a parent, friend, or teacher "said so." They challenge any information, even when it comes from experts, high-status individuals, or the group's majority,

**GLOSSARY**

**Open-Minded**
*Willing to consider new information and ideas, even if they contradict previous beliefs*

**TABLE 7.2 Probing Questions to Evaluate Evidence and Reasoning**

- What evidence do you have to suggest that the statement is true?
- Where did that evidence come from?
- Does anyone have any evidence to contradict the statement we just heard?
- If we make that decision, what will it lead to?
- What might the consequences be if we are wrong?
- How much danger is there that we have reached the wrong conclusion?
- How did you arrive at that conclusion?

by raising questions about it.[40] This also means they are willing to hold off making a decision until the facts are in, which suggests they can tolerate ambiguity, at least for a while. They don't latch onto a premature conclusion just to get a tough decision-making process over with. They know that better decisions result from applying the same skeptical approach to all claims, including their own. At NASA, employees who had safety concerns did not speak out because at NASA "We don't have time to listen to everybody moan and groan about every issue out there" (Case 7.2).

Skeptical decision makers try to test information and opinions as well as their sources rather than discount information like NASA officials did. They do not accept information just because it sounds good, supports what they already believe, upholds the majority stance in the group, comes from someone in authority, or is presented in an entertaining way. A significant way members can test the adequacy and quality of information, reasoning, and sources is by asking each other **probing questions** like the ones in Table 7.2.

According to Dennis Gouran and colleagues, failures to ask probing questions at several stages of the decision-making process were prime contributions to the *Challenger* disaster.[41] The problem with the O-ring seals in cold temperatures had been observed for years before the launch, but no one asked the tough questions about what was being done to correct the flaw. One engineer who opposed the launch assumed that his objections had been passed on to superiors, without asking whether this was actually the case. When representatives from North American Rockwell, the manufacturer of the shuttle, relayed their concerns about the launch in vague terms, no one asked whether they were trying to tell NASA to postpone the launch. All these isolated incidents, in which no one asked probing questions, contributed to the disaster that followed.

The "show me" skepticism of a good critical thinker needs to be expressed by group members and supported as a group norm. Probing questions reflect a willingness to inquire into the accuracy of the information and the appropriateness of the reasoning group members are being asked to accept either by outside sources or by each other. This is tough work, because if this kind of skeptism is not communicated with respect for other group members, it can be seen as threatening and could backfire—by shutting down critical thinking. Questions, like any of our messages, have both content and relationship dimensions (see Chapter 4).[42] We often focus only on their content and forget that *how* they are asked can mean the difference between respectful critical thinking and harmful badgering of group members. One way members can do this is

**GLOSSARY**

**Probing Questions**

*Questions designed to help critical thinking by examining information and reasoning in more depth*

**TABLE 7.3** **Attitudes and Behaviors Counterproductive to Critical Thinking**

- Oversimplification of the thinking process; evaluation of information and ideas in either-or, black-and-white terms
- Impulsiveness; jumping to premature conclusions
- Overdependence on authority figures; waiting for someone else to tell you how to think, what to conclude, or what to do
- Lack of confidence; withdrawing if someone challenges your ideas
- Dogmatic, inflexible behavior; closing your mind and being afraid of change
- Unwillingness to make the effort to think critically; taking the easy way out

to explain the purpose of the question—for example, "I am asking this because I want to make sure that I completely understand what your main point is about this issue." In addition, remember that your questions can be thrown out to the entire group. Sometimes directing a probing question to the group deflects it from any one member and reinforces the notion that the group itself engages in critical thinking.

Finally, critical thinking is an active (rather than passive) process of testing information. It demands hard work to find the information necessary to understand the problem and subject solutions to the most rigorous tests possible. Mentally lazy group members object to this hard work, but critical thinkers look forward to it.

The information just presented describes attitudes essential to critical thinking in a small group. Several attitudes and behaviors make it difficult for group members to engage in critical thinking, and these are worth looking at briefly. It is just as important for you to know what *not* to do as to know what to do, so Table 7.3 summarizes these counterproductive behaviors.

## GATHERING INFORMATION

One skill essential to critical thinking is the ability to organize ideas.[43] Groups create complicated informational environments; members not only process the information brought into the group but also must assess information from multiple sources outside of the group.[44] The first step to organizing your ideas is to assess the information you already have, identify gaps in that information, and only then establish and carry through with a plan for filling those gaps. At this stage you cannot tell what is important and what is not, so you should act like sponges—absorbing as much information as you can about your topic or issue and watching for that "seize and freeze" habit of groups mentioned earlier.[45] Information gathering activities are just as essential to critical thinking in groups as evaluation of that information in later stages.

**Assessing Information Needs.** Before you begin your research, you need to take stock of the information you have initially (see Table 7.4). The quality of your output, such as a plan or policy, matches the quality of the information you gather and assess. Make an outline or list of all the information you have so you can see the gaps in what you need. For example, a university committee was charged with revising the curriculum for communication majors. Members first pooled all the information they had, such as

**TABLE 7.4** **Gathering Information in the Critical Thinking Process: Assessing Information**

1. Take stock of existing information.
2. Identify holes and weaknesses.
3. Make a master list of what information is needed and where it can be found.
4. Collect needed resources by assigning members specific responsibilities for items in the master list.
5. Use all appropriate information gathering techniques:
    - Direct observation
    - Reading
    - Interviews (individual or group)
    - Other sources (radio, television, casual conversation)

the current major requirements, the problems and issues they had observed, and information about what nearby colleges and universities required of communication majors. Committee members soon realized that they needed to fill several important information gaps before they could begin any adequate discussion of the problem. For instance, they hadn't assessed the perceptions of current students and alumni about the strengths and weaknesses of the existing program—a major oversight! In addition, prospective employers could provide information about the skills and deficiencies of recent graduates and current student interns. Finally, they knew they must have information about current practices in the field of communication, including what communication professionals were saying about the direction of the field.

Information lists help determine not only what information is missing but also where it can be found. The next step in the critical thinking process is the careful gathering of information to fill the gaps.

**Collecting Needed Resources.** You know what you are missing and now you want to organize the procedures you will use to gather needed information. First, from the master list, list all the information you still need. Then assign research responsibilities on the basis of member preferences, strengths, and time schedules. Play to group member strengths, which you should know if you have mindfully worked with the diversity in your group and become familiar with member learning styles, motivations, personality characteristics, cultural preferences, and cognitive styles (see Chapter 6). Finally, as you proceed with your research, you will discover additional information you need that should be added to the list and assigned to the appropriate group members.

The information a group needs is rarely found in one location. Usually, a variety of information is needed and will have to be gathered in various ways. Some of these are described briefly.

***Direct Observation.*** Sometimes information you need will come from firsthand observation. At California State University, Fresno, the demolition and renovation of the library meant that student study areas had to be created across campus. Members of a group from a senior small group communication course took it upon themselves to advocate for a study area in their Speech Arts building. Their primary means of information gathering was to visit the different areas of campus and note the study area architecture. From those field notes they designed a study area for their own building. One campus administrator, who had been sent the proposal, remarked at how impressed he was that these students had visited each site and then used that information as the basis for their proposal.

***Reading.*** A wealth of information can be found in many kinds of printed sources, such as newspapers, books, magazines, scholarly and professional journals, technical and trade publications, and government documents. The sheer number of sources available can be intimidating. A reference librarian can help save hours of wasted effort by pointing you in helpful directions and steering you away from likely dead ends. Reference librarians are most appreciative of students who come to the library prepared with their topics and assignment instructions. This kind of preparedness will also increase your chance of a successful trip to the library!

In addition, a number of publications can save you time and effort in locating printed information. Specialized indexes and abstracts frequently can help you save time in locating relevant information. For example, the *Business Periodicals Index* summarizes articles from numerous business and trade journals.

***The Internet.*** An easy and convenient way to access information is through the Internet. Top-rated browsers such as Google Chrome, Mozilla FireFox, Internet Explorer, Opera, and Safari are known for their quickness, security, and simplicity of use. Advanced searches embedded in these browsers, like Google Scholar, lead you to other sources of information as well as the ability to search formats like PowerPoint. No single search engine covers the entire Internet so use more than one. Use keywords for your search, following the rules of the particular search engine you're using. Although you may have thousands of hits, most search engines give you the most likely hits first, so search those carefully. You may have to try various keyword combinations. For example, if you are seeking information about the effect of college-age gambling on academic success, you may have to try "college sports gambling," "gambling," "academic success," and so forth.

Be particularly careful to evaluate information you derive from the Internet. *Anyone* can put *anything* on the Internet; no review procedure evaluates the information for accuracy or truth. *Wikipedia,* a user-written online encyclopedia, could be edited by anyone with access to the Internet, although new edits of particular articles have to be verified before they appear. Wikipedia is very popular with students and can be a good place to start for an overview of a new topic. However, neither of us allows it as a main source of information for group projects because its editing policy is questionable, potentially compromising the credibility of its information.

The invisible web is another way to access information on the Internet. This "deep" web contains information that is not accessible to standard search engines. Your own library, for example, probably cannot be accessed unless the user has a password thus they are not putting it out of reach of standard search engines. You can get to this information in a couple of ways.[46] When you search for "college sports gambling" add "database" to the search and other relevant databases might show up. GoshMe (goshme.com) is one of a few specialized tools built to search the invisible web.

Any claim, even outrageous ones, can be made on the Internet. Online information has been compared to "fast food"—you can quickly find the information but all too often it is poor for your academic health![47] Websites can be created that contain outright lies and misinformation. We found a website that advertised manbeef, or human meat, for consumption; it was a spoof, but some people had accepted it as true. To help you use your best critical thinking skills to evaluate online information, we have provided some criteria in Table 7.5.[48] In addition, you can go to the following websites to learn more about evaluating Internet information:

www.virtualsalt.com/evalu8it.htm

www.library.cornell.edu/olinuris/ref/research/webeval.html

http://gemini.lib.purdue.edu/core/files/evaluating3.html

After all, on the Internet no one knows you are a dog! (see p. 173 for cartoon)

**TABLE 7.5** **Criteria for Evaluating Web-Based Sources**

**AUTHORITY**
Can you find the source of the information? If not, how can you trust the information? If you can, ask whether you would trust that authority and whether the authority is held to any standards for information, like the American Medical Association.

**AUDIENCE**
Could the audience slant the information, and if so, in which way? Web designers do not design just for the fun of it; they have an audience in mind and tailor the information for that audience. In addition, determine if the information is too technical, simplistic, or jargon-filled for your purposes.

**PURPOSE**
Why is the information being offered? Is it offered to inform, persuade, entertain, or advocate? You can get some clue to its purpose by noting what comes after the dot. The ".gov" government notation is probably intended to inform whereas the ".com" or commercial notation may bring with it something to sell. The ".edu" or education notation will identify faculty and sources at colleges and universities that inform and persuade. Be careful because there are no restrictions on who can use these notations.

**RECENCY**
Can you determine how current the site is? The Internet allows for instant posting, but often sites are not updated regularly. Be careful with information from a site in which you cannot find when or how often it is updated. Many sites have e-mail contact information for the authors of the site. Use that information to ask questions about updating.

**COVERAGE**
Does the site provide the depth you need on your topic or issue? Sites will often have links to other sites. If you find those links credible use them because the use of a variety of sources is preferred.

© Andresr/Shutterstock RF

***Electronic Databases.*** Electronic databases available at most academic and public libraries provide a very efficient way to find printed information and can now be accessed at home via the Internet. Electronic databases contain titles, abstracts, and often the full text of magazine and journal articles, newspaper articles, and books on thousands of topics. Commonly used databases include InfoTrac, a general-purpose database that accesses business and trade journals; ERIC, which holds education-related materials gathered by the U.S. Department of Education; LexisNexis, which accesses legal and business resources; Communication & Mass Media Complete, which contains information from all communication-related journals; and EBSCOhost, another general-purpose database of thousands of periodicals. In addition, many newspapers, such as *The New York Times,* can be accessed electronically. As with Internet search engines, electronic databases typically operate using keywords or author names.

***Interviews.*** Members of your group may need to conduct several interviews. These may be face-to-face individual interviews, group interviews, or those conducted over the phone or via electronic mail. For example, the curriculum committee members interviewed their colleagues in person, phoned or e-mailed colleagues at other schools, and called a sample of alumni to ask for their perceptions and opinions.

***Other Sources.*** Useful information may come when you least expect it. Listening to the radio, watching television, conversing with family or friends, browsing through electronic bulletin boards, stumbling onto relevant information in a magazine while waiting to get a flu vaccine—all are potential sources. Be prepared to take advantage of these sources by recording the information as soon as possible so you don't forget it. Once you have gathered the information you need, you must decide how useful it is to you.

## EVALUATING INFORMATION

Now that you have been sponges and soaked up all the relevant information you can, you can begin evaluating what you have gathered. Now you must "pan for gold" by trying to find the nuggets of information that are valuable to you.[49] If a group bases its decision on inaccurate or outdated information, its decision will be flawed, no matter how systematic the gathering process has been. For example, the curriculum committee described earlier recommended that communication majors take several writing courses offered by the English department. However, even though the recommended courses were listed in the school's previous catalogue, the English department had revised its curriculum, eliminating several courses and changing others. This mistake was not a disaster, but it would not have occurred if curriculum committee members had checked with the English department to determine whether any course changes were anticipated.

How can you tell whether a piece of information is accurate and up-to-date and whether a source is credible? Evaluation of available information is perhaps the most crucial step in the critical thinking process. Several factors play a role in evaluating information: determining what someone means, distinguishing fact from opinion, clarifying ambiguous terms, assessing the source's credibility, and assessing the information's accuracy and worth. M. Neil Browne and Stuart Keeley's eleventh edition of *Asking the Right Questions: A Guide to Critical Thinking* is an excellent summary of how you can assess the value of information.

**Determining the Meaning of What Is Being Said.** The first thing you must do is decide exactly what the speaker or writer means—no easy task. Frequently, people bury the meaning of what they are saying among a jumble of opinions and irrelevant statements. You should identify the author's conclusion, reasons for the conclusion, and evidence to support the reasons. First, ask yourself what conclusion the author is drawing. What does he or she want you to do, think, or believe? Is there an action (such as voting for a particular candidate, writing letters to a Senator, or buying a particular product) that the author wants you to take? Next, determine what main arguments the author provides to support the conclusion or recommended action. For instance, look at the sample letter provided in the Apply Now box on page 178. What conclusion does the author want you to reach, and why?

Often, keeping track of the arguments and evidence that support them is easier if you outline the argument. Write the main conclusion at the top; then list each argument beneath it with space after each one. In this space list every piece of evidence the author or speaker offers in support of the claims. This will simplify your later task of evaluating how good the author's evidence and reasoning are and how valid the conclusions are.

When you gather information from a variety of sources, you must keep track of where the information came from and how it was stated, exactly, in the original source, so that you do not plagiarize. You are responsible for familiarizing yourself with your own school's plagiarism policies and their examples of plagiarism. In addition, visit the following websites:

http://www.plagiarism.org/index.html

http://owl.english.purdue.edu/owl/resource/560/01/

These sites provide detailed examples and concrete tips on how to avoid plagiarism in your group oral as well as written work.

***Distinguishing Fact from Opinion and Inference.*** You must be able to recognize the difference between a statement of fact and statements of opinion or inference based on that fact. **Facts** are descriptions that can be verified by observations and are not arguable. For example, we can verify that the population of Greene County, Missouri, in 2014 was approximately 285,865 by looking in any of several government publications that record population data. Be careful, though—some statements presented as facts are not facts at all but false statements. You need to determine whether statements presented as facts are actually true and up-to-date.

Opinions and inferences go beyond what was observed directly and imply some degree of probability or uncertainty. **Opinions,** unlike facts, are not all equal, although everyone has an equal right to express an opinion. Some opinions are more valid than others. Stephen Hawking's opinion about the way the universe operates should carry more weight than the opinions of the authors of this book because we are not theoretical physicists. The value of an opinion depends on the evidence supporting the opinion and the quality of the reasoning that ties the evidence and opinion together. Determining an opinion's value is part of your job as a critical thinker. For example, someone might say, "Greene County, Missouri, is growing rapidly." That is not a fact; that is an opinion. It is your responsibility to determine the validity of the opinion by asking questions such as the following: What was Greene County's population 10 years ago? What is the average annual rate of growth in the United States? In Missouri? How does Greene County's rate compare with that of other cities in Missouri? If you learn that Greene County's annual rate of growth from 2010 to 2014 has been 3.9 percent, compared to Missouri's 1.2 percent, you can reasonably conclude that "Greene County is growing quickly." Thus, opinions are arguable and should be evaluated systematically during a group's deliberations. Groups that make poor decisions do so in part because inferential errors impair their critical thinking.[50]

***Identifying and Clarifying Ambiguous Terms.*** Authors and speakers often make it hard to evaluate information because they use terminology that is **ambiguous,** or unclear. For example, candidate Beasley in the Apply Now box is termed "experienced." What does that mean? What kinds of experiences has she had? Is she experienced as a teacher, a parent, or an administrator? Is she experienced at working in a small group? Each of these experiences is different and paints a slightly different picture of the candidate.

**GLOSSARY**

**Fact**

*Something that can be verified by observation and is not arguable*

**Opinions**

*Inferences that go beyond facts and contain some degree of probability*

**Ambiguous**

*Refers to a term that has more than one possible meaning*

## Should You Support Mary Alice Beasley for School Board?

APPLY NOW

Your local parent-teacher organization has received the following letter from one school's site council. The executive committee, of which you are a member, is meeting to decide what to recommend to the entire PTO. Practice evaluating the information and arguments in the letter.

*Dear Parent-Teacher Organization Member,*

*As you know, the vote to elect a new member to the school board will occur on April 5. We want you to know that the Parents' Excellence in Schools Committee supports candidate Mary Alice Beasley for our school board.*

*Mary Alice Beasley is the best candidate we have running for the Central City school board. We need people like her who care about our kids. She has lived in Central City all her life and now has three children of her own in the school system. She has been an active member of the P.T.O. for the past six years and was chair of the fund-raising committee for Westwood School. Her experience will be invaluable.*

*In her second term as city councilwoman, she was the chief author of the plan to desegregate the city schools; as we all know, other cities have used this plan as the model for their own desegregation efforts. Mary Alice can represent the entire community well—she taught for nine years before she ran for city council, and she has a master's degree in education. Hers is exactly the kind of caring, experienced leadership we need on the school board. Mary Beasley deserves your endorsement. Remember to vote on April 5.*

Either individually or in groups of four to six, answer the following questions and then discuss them as a class:

1. What conclusion are you being asked to reach? Is there an action you are being asked to take in this letter?
2. Like most letters of this type, this letter interchanges fact and inference, or opinion. Make a list of all the facts presented in the letter and a list of all the inferences presented.
3. Ambiguous terms are sometimes difficult to spot because we each think we know what words such as *experienced* mean. Make a list of all the ambiguous terms (terms that can reasonably be understood in more than one way) presented in the letter. Before you assess how the letter's writer interprets each of these terms, what do you mean by each of them? For instance, what does *experienced* mean to you?

***Concluded***

APPLY NOW

4. For each of these terms, what evidence is presented in the letter that supports the author's opinion about Beasley? For example, what facts are presented to support the author's view that Beasley is "experienced"?
5. Would you vote for Beasley on the basis of this letter? Why or why not? What other information about this candidate would you like to have to help you make your decision? Where would you go for the information you need?

Earlier in the chapter, we evaluated the decision made by NASA officials to launch the *Challenger*. In their analysis of the decision-making process, Gouran and his associates discovered that failure to clarify ambiguous terms contributed to that terrible decision. They explain:

> *No one went so far as to say, "We recommend that you do not launch." Instead, they claimed making such statements as, "We do not have the data base from which to draw any conclusions for this particular situation"; "We did not have a sufficient data base to absolutely assure that nothing would strike the vehicle."*[51]

What do those statements mean? This kind of doublespeak confuses issues because it leaves room for a variety of interpretations by permitting others to read their own favorite interpretations into the message. At NASA no one asked explicitly for clarification of the ambiguous terms.

***Evaluating Opinions by Determining the Credibility of the Source.*** How can you tell whether an author or a speaker is someone whose opinions are worth your attention? Ask yourself several key questions to help you decide how much trust to place in an opinion.

- For example, if you find a source debunking the idea that climate change related to global warming is due in large measure to human activity, you should treat it with suspicion especially if it comes from the research out of the George C. Marshall Institute funded by ExxonMobil. On the other hand, if that statement were to come from the scientifically respected Intergovernmental Panel on Climate Change (IPCC), you would have greater reason to expect objectivity.
- Is the source a recognized expert on the subject? Is this someone whom other experts respect? Would you feel proud or silly quoting this person? We may feel comfortable citing LeBron James opinions about basketball but very uncomfortable citing Aunt Tilly's.
- Is the opinion consistent with other opinions expressed by the same source? Media sometimes misquote people. Are you reasonably sure the opinion stated is accurate? Is there a later interview or quote that reverses the inconsistent

**TABLE 7.6 Evaluating Information in the Critical Thinking Process**

**DETERMINE WHAT THE SPEAKER OR WRITER IS SAYING**
- What is the conclusion?
- What does the author want you to do?
- What are the main arguments in support of the conclusion?

**DISTINGUISH FACT FROM OPINION AND INFERENCE**
- What are the facts?
- What are the opinions?

**IDENTIFY AND CLARIFY AMBIGUOUS TERMS**
- What are the ambiguous terms?
- What do you think the author means by each term?
- If you can't decide with confidence, what problems does this create?

**DETERMINE THE CREDIBILITY OF THE SOURCE**
- Who is the author or speaker? What are his or her credentials on this issue?
- Is this a recognized expert?
- Is this a biased source or one with something to gain by expressing this opinion?
- Is the information consistent with other credible sources?

**ASSESS THE ACCURACY AND WORTH OF THE INFORMATION**
- What type of evidence (e.g., personal experience, statistical support, opinions of experts) is being offered in support of the author's arguments?
- Is the evidence supported by other experts or authorities, or just this author?
- Is the information based on the scientific method?
- If the information is based on interviews or questionnaires, was the sample large enough and representative enough? Were the questions clear and not biased or loaded?

opinion? Sometimes people do change their minds for good reasons. What is the reason given for the change of opinion? Does the evidence offered to explain the change seem reasonable to you? If not, suspect inaccuracy or some unknown bias.

***Assessing the Accuracy and Worth of the Information.*** Now that you have established a context for evaluating the information by determining exactly what is being said and how credible the source is, you are in a position to evaluate how good that information is (see Table 7.6). After all, it could be misinformation. You should ask yourself a number of questions about the information before using it during group discussions.

- What types of evidence are offered to support the argument? Is it a personal experience? Statistical support? The combined opinions of a number of recognized experts? Although many people do so, it is unsafe to accept personal experience as the sole basis for supporting an opinion. For example, assume you were once in a successful and productive group led by a dominant leader who decided everything and delegated these tasks to other members. Thus, your personal experience may lead you to believe that groups work best under strong, controlling leaders. But someone else's experience may differ. Assume a fellow group member worked in a democratic group, in which there was no one leader but all members contributed to leadership based on their areas of expertise. This member thinks that the only good group is a democratic one. Which of you is right? Each of you is right, for the particular circumstances of your experience, but neither of you is right to try to apply your experience to everyone else.

- Is the information based on the testimony of a number of experts in the field? If so, you can place greater trust in it, especially if these experts are widely recognized and accepted by their peers. Be sure to determine whether other experts disagree and why. Be especially careful about accepting information from an expert in one field about another field. For example, movie stars frequently express strong opinions about the American political scene. While some may be well informed, others are not.
- Is the information based on valid scientific or statistical reasoning? You should ask how the information was gathered, how the questions were worded, whether the data came from a properly designed survey, and so forth. Information must follow strict guidelines before it can legitimately be termed *scientific*. First, such information must be verifiable by others. Thus, although an experience that happens to someone may be true, it is not scientific unless the event is observed or can be re-created by other people. Second, scientific information must be obtained under controlled conditions by controlled observations. Having an informal conversation with your classmates about student loan debt and concluding that "American college students have the following attitudes toward student loans..." may be interesting, but it is not scientific. But if you surveyed a representative sample of students, asked each of them the same questions, and systematically analyzed their answers, you could reasonably conclude: "Students at my college believe the following about student loan debt..." Finally, scientific information must be expressed precisely. Another researcher, after reading an account of a scientifically controlled research study, should be able to carry out a study in exactly the same way, using the same procedures, equipment, and statistical tests.

Information gathered by questionnaires or interviews poses additional questions regarding the individuals who were queried. Were there enough of them, and were they representative of a larger population? In most cases random sampling is most likely to ensure a representative response. For example, assume your committee is charged with making recommendations regarding the high rates of student stress on your campus, and you decide to poll students who have sought help on your campus. If you survey only students who have actually sought help, your results are not likely to reflect the views of the entire student population. Making health recommendations that will affect thousands of students on the basis of responses from a few students is

**What Would You Do?**

ETHICAL DILEMMA

You and your group have been working on your panel presentation about the death penalty for several weeks, with one week to go before you are responsible for conducting the panel discussion in your class. This project represents a major portion of your grade in the small group class, and you are required to conclude your presentation by taking a position—your group must come out either in favor of or against the death penalty. After hashing this out for weeks, you have sorted through all your evidence and have almost reached consensus that you will come out in favor of the death penalty. This week, while doing library research for another class, you happen upon a new study, based on systematic examination of states with the death penalty, that strongly suggests the death penalty does *not* deter crime. The study seems well done; you don't think you can dismiss it as a piece of biased or poorly done research. But you know if you present it to your group, you'll push your emerging consensus further away, and you hate to do that! You are so close now to agreement, and you know this study will set you back. What do you do?

1. For what reasons would you *present* the article to your group?
2. For what reasons would you *withhold* the article?
3. What would you actually do?

irresponsible. On the other hand, if you systematically survey students who may or may not have sought counseling, your responses will be more representative and your conclusions more valid.

## CHECKING FOR ERRORS IN REASONING

The final element in the critical thinking process is assessing the quality of the reasoning people provide for their opinions or for supporting one conclusion over another. Unfortunately, most speakers and writers often make a variety of common reasoning errors, called **fallacies,** that makes assessing reasoning challenging. Fallacies tend to divert a listener's attention from the issue or sidetrack the discussion so that members of a group begin to debate something other than evidence and claims. However, critical thinkers working together in a small group should be able to spot each other's fallacies. The differing but complementary bases of information that individual members bring to a group discussion can help them compensate for each other's weaknesses to produce, on the whole, a superior group result.[52] There is no end to the kinds of fallacies you can find in a group discussion. The following ones are common ones and are offered as examples. For a more detailed list of fallacies and ways to correct them, see Richard Paul and Linda Elder's *The Thinker's Guide to Fallacies: The Art of Mental Trickery and Manipulation,* a useful resource.[53]

GLOSSARY

**Fallacies**

*Mistakes in reasoning and faulty reasoning*

**Overgeneralizing.** Generalizations are made when information about one or more instances is said to apply to many or all instances of the same type. For example, someone may read in the newspaper that a certain number of college students have defaulted on their government-guaranteed student loans. If that person concludes from this that "college students are irresponsible borrowers," he or she has made a generalization and implied that *all* college students are irresponsible borrowers. An **overgeneralization,** like the loan default example, is a conclusion that is not supported by enough data.

Generalizations by themselves are not automatically wrong. Conclusions based on carefully gathered data that were analyzed with appropriate statistical procedures are often very accurate and the goal of good scientific theory. Usually, such generalizations are qualified and not stated as applying to all cases. Remember, for a generalization to be factual for all cases, someone would have to observe all of those cases.

To decide whether a generalization is a valid conclusion or an overgeneralization, ask yourself a few questions:

- How many cases is the conclusion based on?
- Are there any exceptions to the conclusion?
- What form of evidence is the source asking us to accept: personal or other forms?
- Is the generalization expressed as probability or in "allness" terms?

**Attacking a Person Instead of the Argument.** Attacking a person instead of the argument, even if subtly done, is a form of name-calling used to direct attention away from someone's evidence and logic (or lack thereof). Sometimes called ad hominem attacks, such arguments take this form: "Because So-and-So is a ________ (woman, Catholic, foreigner, intellectual snob, atheist, liberal, etc.), you can't believe his/her opinions about the topic." Such an attack on the speaker moves the focus to the speaker and away from the merits of his or her opinion; more information is needed to critically evaluate the opinion.

**Confusing Causal Relationships.** Another common reasoning error occurs when the speaker or writer mistakenly states what caused an event. Frequently, people either imply that one cause exists for an event or reason or that because two events are related somehow they must have caused each other. For example, we have heard students say that if a manager implements quality control circles in a company, the company's profits will increase, implying that quality circles cause higher profits. In actuality, better employee training, lower costs of raw materials, increased prices for a company's products, improvements in technology, and improved upward communication and morale produced by the quality circle may each contribute to the increased profits.

Neither can we assume that, just because one event preceded another in time, the first caused the second. It may be that both are caused by a third event or condition. For example, one of us overheard someone mention statistics indicating that graduates of all-women's colleges are more likely to become members of the U.S. Congress and serve on the boards of Fortune 500 companies than are female graduates of coed schools. The person speaking was arguing that attendance at women's colleges *caused* this type

**GLOSSARY**

**Overgeneralization**

*A conclusion not supported by enough data*

## Gun Control

APPLY NOW

The shooting rampage on the Virginia Tech campus April 16, 2007, remains the largest mass shooting in our country's history. In a dorm and classroom building, 33 people lost their lives. This school shooting revived the ongoing debate over gun control.[54] While news of the tragedy was still fresh, many news programs featured reports about the national debate over how to solve the problem of gun-related violence on college campuses. A heated debate occurred in Virginia's own state legislature as representatives fought over whether concealed weapons should be allowed on their campuses. Virginia and 48 other states do issue gun permits allowing state residents to carry concealed weapons. The issue of whether to lift gun restrictions on college campuses is currently being hotly debated: Virginia voted not to, but Utah voted to allow students to carry concealed weapons on the University of Utah campus. Advocates for allowing firearms on college campuses argued that Virginia already has gun control laws that obviously do not work. If someone plans to kill a bunch of people and then themselves, regulations will not help, but coming face-to-face with another gun will. A concealed weapon is there for self-defense, and had faculty or students been armed, they could have used those weapons to stop the Virginia Tech killer. Opponents argued that allowing guns on college campuses is not going to solve the real problem, which is the *reason* for the violence; thus, we have to find ways to prevent people from using guns to express how disturbed they are. Opponents suggest attending to and treating the reasons for violence, not issuing gun permits to college students and faculty.

Try the following exercise. In a small group or as a whole class, to get a more vivid idea of the types of arguments made in this case, briefly research the issue of gun violence on college campuses and then simulate the point-counterpoint discussion, either between two class members or two large groups role-playing each position.

1. How many arguments can you create to support each position? Put them on the board for all to see.
2. What fallacies can you identify in the arguments presented?
3. Assume the two "debaters" are members of a small discussion group charged with identifying a policy to prevent college shootings. What would you say and do if you heard the kinds of fallacies being expressed during the discussion?

of career achievement. However, many women's colleges are academically selective as well as expensive. Women attending such schools are often both exceptionally bright and from families who own or are connected to Fortune 500 companies. It is plausible that these additional factors—ability and family connections—"cause" both the attendance at women's colleges and the career achievement. The relationship between college attendance and later achievement is likely to be a complex one that does not lend itself well to simple causal descriptions.

**Either-Or Thinking.** **Either-or thinking** (sometimes called a false dilemma) says that you must choose one thing or another, and no other choices are possible. Seldom is this the case. We talked about this kind of thinking and its consequences to group discussion when dealing with diversity in Chapter 6. In another example, assume your group is preparing a panel discussion about sex education in the schools, and you encounter the following statement: "Sex education is an important element of a young person's education. If the parents won't teach their children about sex, the schools have to." Most people would readily agree with the first sentence. The second, however, reveals either-or thinking; either the parents will teach the child about sex or the school will. In fact, other alternatives are possible. Perhaps churches, synagogues, or Camp Fire USA leaders could take on the job; or parents and school officials together could design a cooperative program. Do not be blind to other alternatives.

**Incomplete Comparisons.** Comparisons, especially **analogies,** help us understand issues more vividly. These play an important role in symbolic convergence (Chapter 6) and when the group is being creative. However, there are limitations to such comparisons when the group has moved into critical thinking. Comparing two things works to a point, but eventually the resemblance can break down. An incomplete analogy (sometimes called a faulty analogy) asks us to stretch a similarity too far. For example, assume you and other students are discussing how well the public relations major at your school prepares students to be public relations professionals. One student says, "You really can't learn much about public relations from school anyway. It's like trying to ride a bicycle by reading books about it but never getting on an actual bicycle."

At first glance, this remark hits home with many of us who complain that school can't prepare us for the "real world." However, let's look more closely. Yes, there are public relations experiences that cannot be duplicated in school. But there are many activities that *do* prepare students for professional practice. Designing flyers and brochures, writing news releases, taking photographs, planning a mock public relations campaign, and designing a survey are all examples of typical activities that public relations students perform in school that are also necessary on the job. Thus, whenever you see or hear someone make a comparison, first determine in what ways the two things being compared are similar, but also look for ways they are different. Does the analogy break down at any point. If so, where? How does this affect the reasoning you are being asked to accept?

These fallacies are some of the most common ones. Be alert for fallacies by asking the right probing questions about the ideas, opinions, interpretations, and conclusions someone is asking you to accept. Then pay careful attention to the answers you receive (or don't receive).

## AVOIDING GROUPTHINK

We introduced groupthink in Chapter 5 when we discussed the consequences of excessively high cohesiveness in which disagreement is seen as disloyalty or as "making

**GLOSSARY**

**Either-Or Thinking**

*Asking members to choose between only two options, as if no other choices existed*

**Analogies**

*Comparisons that help clarify ideas and issues*

### The 1999 Major League Umpire Resignation

CASE 7.3

Baseball fans will remember the summer of 1999 as the summer major league umpires took on Major League Baseball (MLB) and lost. Their decision to submit mass letters of resignation, met with disaster. Several umpires quickly took back their letters and MLB accepted the remaining letters from those who did not pull their letters. In an attempt to strike first, in a looming labor battle between umpires and league officials, the umpires made a poor strategic choice during a four-hour meeting July 14, 1999 in Philadelphia. In a rare look at the emergence of groupthink in a sports organization, Koerber and Neck show us how individuals can be so taken by peer pressure and groupthink that they would leave jobs they dearly love and have worked for all their lives.[57]

Major league umpires are a close-knit group of professionals. It is very hard to become a league umpire and once in you stay for a long time. You travel with each other and share a love for the game. Their work, like others, is governed by contracts negotiated between union and management. In 1999 the relationship between the umpires and MLB was strained making an imminent labor battle between them understandably messy. Neither group saw eye-to-eye on salary or the use of amateur umpires in the minor league, and there were rumors that several low-skilled umpires were facing "pink slips." Led by a very successful and popular general counsel for their union, "Richie" Phillips, the umpires decided to make the first move and 50 of the 60 umpires signed letters of resignation. Prevented by contract from striking, they were led to believe a mass resignation would so cripple baseball that MLB would bend over and give them what they wanted at the negotiation table. So what happened? How did a "sure bet" turn so wrong?

waves." Coined by Irving Janis and initially applied to the disastrous Bay of Pigs decision by the John F. Kennedy administration, *groupthink* commonly refers to bad decision making due to poor information processing in groups. Here, we examine this group phenomenon further to help us summarize our discussion of critical thinking in groups and to reinforce its importance to effective decision making. We will use primarily Case 7.3.

Groupthink is a failure of critical thinking and leads to flawed decisions grounded in partial information ineffectively analyzed. The umpires neglected a key piece of information regarding resignations; once a resignation is submitted it cannot be rescinded. Also during groupthink behavior, some members may privately have had doubts about the group's direction. There were umpires who opposed the resignation strategy yet censored themselves. In fact, about 20 opposed the resignations and instead of voicing their concerns in the July 14th meeting, they either did not submit their letters or pulled them immediately, effectively destroying the collective strength of the strategy.

Self-censorship is not unusual—few people want to be perceived as nuisances. A study of upper-management teams in 26 American corporations found that 19 percent of members said they went about company business by not making waves.[55] Nine percent prefer to maintain good relationships with their co-workers at the expense of getting the job done. That suggests a lot of flawed decision making happening at all levels! Let's look at how this kind of group dynamic can happen.

**Symptoms of Groupthink.** We have emphasized that group members, perhaps counterintuitively, do not automatically share information that runs counter to what appear to be group preferences.[56] They "seize and freeze" on early positions expressed by members and on those they think most members prefer, as well as resist positions that may be different from those earlier positions. One reason groupthink is most likely to occur in highly cohesive groups is the pressure to achieve consensus. In particular, cohesiveness based on interpersonal attraction is related to groupthink, but task-related cohesiveness is not.[58] Members of groups that exhibit high degrees of cohesiveness based on their interpersonal attraction to each other tend to be more psychologically connected to each other, and so they resist challenging each other.[59] This is a problem because groups *in general* tend to favor discussing what they already know as opposed to discussing new information.[60] Under conditions of groupthink, this tendency is even harder to monitor. In addition, groupthink is more likely to occur in groups with a long history, groups strongly embedded in their larger organizations, and groups that insulate themselves from their outside environments.[61] Spotting groupthink thus becomes crucial if decision-making groups are to be effective as they critically analyze problems and draw conclusions. Here are three important symptoms to help you spot groupthink.

1. **The group overestimates its power and morality.**

   Group members believe their cause is so right that nothing can go wrong with their plans. The umpires in Case 7.3 were not only a tightly knit group and prone to the downside of cohesion, they had also developed a collective belief that they were indispensable to MLB. Believing they had the upper hand, the umpires never considered any alternative strategies for dealing with management.

2. **The group becomes closed-minded.**

   Closed-minded people, instead of looking open-mindedly at all relevant information, consider only information that supports their beliefs. Group members, too, may have a preferred course of action and ignore any information that contradicts their preference. In the umpire case, a considerable number of them never spoke up during the July 14th meeting. They latched on to a singular strategy, never talking about what else they could do among themselves or even with family, friends, or outside counsel.

3. **Group members experience pressure to conform.**

   The pressures to conform show up in several ways. First, members censor their own remarks without apparent pressure from other members. When all the other

GLOSSARY

**Devil's Advocate**

*A group member who formally is expected to challenge ideas to foster critical thinking*

members of a group favor a certain action or even appear to, most people are hesitant to express their doubts. This is natural—you want the people in your group to like and respect you, and you don't want to be seen as "popping others' balloons." This self-censorship, although understandable, can block conflicting opinions from problem-solving discussions.

Second, a member who does voice a contradictory opinion can be seen as a deviant, as "making waves," and receive overt pressure from the group. Groups are uncomfortable with deviants (even idea deviants) and pressure them to go along with the group.

Finally, because self-censorship and group pressure suppress disagreement and doubt, the group experiences the illusion that members unanimously support the decision or proposal. In the case of the umpires, an estimated 20 did not support the resignation strategy. The actual test of their "consensus" cost them dearly.

**Preventing Groupthink.** You can take a number of steps to prevent groupthink from occurring. Following are suggestions for both group leaders and members, also summarized in Table 7.7.

1. **Encourage members to "kick the problem around" before they start focusing on a solution.**

   One group behavior that fosters groupthink is arriving at premature consensus.[62] The group has shortchanged the recommended first step of most structured problem-solving procedures, which is exploring the problem fully before trying to solve it. In addition, encouraging disagreement at this stage can help group members understand the problem better. Active disagreement at an early stage of problem exploration promotes increased knowledge and understanding. Family and friends of umpires learned after the fact of their decision to resign. No outside group, even lawyers, were brought into the discussion of their strategy.

2. **Establish a norm of critical evaluation.**

   The most important thing a group leader and other members can do to prevent groupthink is to establish a group norm (Chapter 5) to evaluate carefully and critically all information and reasoning. Such a norm can offset the proven human tendency to ignore or reject information that contradicts one's existing beliefs and values.

   Especially helpful is a norm promoting members' expressions of all disagreements. A norm supporting open expression of doubts and disagreements makes it OK for members to be in conflict with each other. One study found that, in a group in which everyone seems to hold the same viewpoint, even one member who is willing to share an opposing view can redirect the group's attention so that members examine their decision more thoughtfully.[63]

   Another way of encouraging honest disagreements is to assign the role of devil's advocate to one or more members of the group. A **devil's advocate** is a person who has been assigned the task of arguing against a popular proposal.

**TABLE 7.7** **Preventing Groupthink**

**ENCOURAGE MEMBERS TO "KICK THE PROBLEM AROUND"**

1. Be alert to prevent premature consensus.
2. Explore the problem thoroughly before attempting to develop a solution.
3. Encourage freewheeling argument before settling on a solution.

**ESTABLISH A NORM OF CRITICAL EVALUATION**

1. Encourage members to express disagreement.
2. Encourage critical thinking rather than the appearance of harmony.
3. Assign a devil's advocate to argue against popular proposals.
4. Be sure the leader accepts criticisms of his or her ideas open-mindedly.

**PREVENT LEADERS FROM STATING PREFERENCES AT THE BEGINNING OF A GROUP'S SESSION**

1. Let other members express opinions first.
2. Offer an opinion only as another alternative (not the alternative) to be considered.
3. Encourage the group to meet without the designated leader present.

**PREVENT INSULATION OF THE GROUP**

1. Invite outside experts to present information.
2. Discuss tentative solutions with trusted outsiders to get an unbiased reaction.
3. Be alert to information that contradicts the prevailing opinion of the group.

Thus, this person serves as an "official" idea deviant because the devil's advocate helps spot potential flaws in a plan or holes in arguments.

Groups have also used group support systems and computer-mediated communication (CMC) to encourage honest opinions. We have mentioned that computer use in group problem solving is valued for its anonymity. Users believe that this produces less pressure to conform and thus encourages more honesty. However, a member operating from behind a computer is still aware of expectations from others. Thus, CMC can both enhance and limit the impact of individual members' influence and power.[64] Sometimes the effect of perceived status differences is actually stronger in CMC.

The norm of critical evaluation must also be supported by the leader's behavior. One of us worked with a boss who asked staff members to identify any problems

### Contemporary Media and Groupthink

MEDIA AND TECHNOLOGY

After the deadly bombings during the Boston Marathon in April 2013, many Americans turned to the Internet to gather as much information as they could about the still-emerging story. A number of news and image-sharing websites allowed anyone interested to review photos from the marathon and attempt to locate the perpetrators. Users marked up photos to point out suspicious activity and eventually identified three suspects. None of these guesses were correct. Despite its attempts, the online community that formed in this situation was led astray by a serious case of groupthink.

Instead of allowing users to look at images independently and then vote on those that seemed suspicious, websites like Reddit sought a more exciting online experience. They encouraged users to work together to identify odd activity and to comment on one another's postings. The fact that viewers had to consider others' comments when evaluating photos influenced their own thinking, and some comments were given more weight because they were more noticeable than others. Additionally, after the first photos were posted, it is possible that users found ways to spot suspicious activity within them instead of forming their own opinions first. Instead of being allowed to think independently, the crowd fell victim to groupthink.

Consider your own experiences watching TV or reading online reports of terrorist actions. To what extent do you think mediated reports of these events make the public susceptible to groupthink? Are there ways that our culture can reduce the effects of groupthink on the way we assign meaning to mediated messages?

we saw with a plan he had devised to improve the working environment. Taking the boss at his word, a couple of staff members began to question various elements of the plan. As they spoke, the boss became defensive, minimized their concerns, defended his proposal, and appeared to view the questioning members as disloyal. The rest of the members remained silent without voicing their objections to the plan. The meeting concluded with the boss thinking the staff supported the plan, although it did not. In the future, whenever the boss asked for honest reactions to proposals he favored, no one was willing to go on the "hot seat" by expressing a criticism.

3. **Prevent leaders from stating their preferences at the beginning of a group's decision-making or problem-solving session.**

One important source of groupthink is a strong or charismatic leader's preference. "Richie" Phillips was the umpire union's general counsel. He had been very successful dealing with management in the past and was well liked. Although he denies it, several umpires stood firm in their recollections that from the start of the meeting he pushed for the resignation strategy.

As group leader, in addition to not stating your preferences early in a group's discussion, ask the group to meet without you, especially if you are the supervisor rather than an elected chair. If you suspect that your presence or personality inhibits the group members from saying what they really feel and think, schedule one or two meetings that you do not attend. This will make it easier for other members to express their opinions freely.

4. **Prevent insulation of the group.**

Groupthink often occurs when group members become so cohesive and caught up in their own ideas that they are insulated from external opinion and expertise. The umpires only ever considered information from Phillips and the union. They did not even consider that once their resignations had been submitted, they could not be rescinded. Not only did they block out alternatives, they also never discussed contingency plans.

Leaders and members of the group can offset this tendency. They can encourage members to present tentative decisions to trusted associates outside the group, then report back to the group with the feedback. They can hold public hearings, at which any interested person can speak on the issues facing the group, as zoning commissions do regularly. They can also arrange for outside experts to talk to the group. Most importantly, they can be alert themselves for any relevant information from outside the group, rather than protecting the group from outside influence.

Groups get caught in groupthink because they do not promote a constructive "show me" skepticism, which thwarts openness to new information, damages the evaluation of gathered information, and limits questioning of the reasoning behind arguments. Additional pressure to conform by ineffective leaders and by members not listening to outside sources of support can inhibit both creative and critical thinking in groups. Getting caught in groupthink leaves groups open to paying a heavy price, sometimes one paid in human life, as we saw in the *Challenger* disaster and other national tragedies.

## RESOURCES FOR REVIEW AND DISCUSSION

### SUMMARY

- To be effective problem solvers, group members must do a good job with both creative and critical thinking. Creative individuals are willing to communicate, to be unconventional, and to play in the group. Creative groups are willing to examine their norms and change those that interfere with creativity.
- Creativity requires freedom from judgment and can be enhanced through the use of three techniques: brainstorming, synectics, and appreciative inquiry. Brainstorming explicitly suspends criticism, and synectics works by attempting to make the familiar unfamiliar. Appreciative inquiry seeks to unleash creativity by focusing

on an organization's strengths and creating a shared vision within the team.

- Critical thinking involves a concentrated effort to assess the value of ideas and conclusions by gathering relevant information, examining that information carefully, and judging the reasoning that supports the conclusions and decisions. Critical thinking in small groups involves knowing when to use critical thinking and requires certain attitudes of group members, a methodical search for information, thorough evaluation of the information, and careful assessment of the reasoning behind opinions and beliefs based on that information.
- In gathering information, group members first should pool their knowledge and identify any gaps that are apparent. Then they should fill those gaps by using appropriate research methods, including direct observation, reading, using electronic databases, interviewing individuals or groups, and consulting other sources such as television, the Internet, and radio.
- When members evaluate information, they first should determine what is being said, which statements are facts and which are inferences or opinions, what terms are ambiguous, how believable the source is, and how accurate and valuable the information is.
- When they check for errors in reasoning, group members should be especially alert to the common fallacies. Critical thinking consists primarily of asking the right probing questions, which can prevent harmful throughput processes such as groupthink.
- Groupthink is the tendency of highly cohesive groups not to examine critically all aspects of a decision. Groups experiencing groupthink overestimate their power, evaluate information in a closed-minded and biased way, and experience pressures to conform.

EXERCISES

1. Form groups of four to six students. Each of you should be given some ordinary, tangible object, such as a clothespin, an alarm clock, or a ballpoint pen. Find a new use for the item that has nothing to do with the item's ordinary use. To do this, you must perceive the item in entirely new ways. To help you do this, your instructor can lead you in a guided meditation. For instance, imagine that the clothespins are alive and are sending you messages about what they would like to be used for. After you have discussed the problem in your groups for 15–20 minutes, present your favorite solution to the class. Then all of you should vote to select the most creative idea. (Perhaps your instructor will award prizes to the winning group.)
2. The following exercise helps clarify the difference between statements of fact and statements of inference. Place a familiar item (such as a coffee cup, a chair, or a ballpoint pen) in front of the class so everyone can see it easily. Make statements of fact about it. Each statement should be written on the board. After about 15 statements, identify as a class those statements that go beyond what was actually observed. Discuss why these statements are inferences rather than facts.
3. Videotape one of the many television programs that feature panel interviews with public figures (such as *Meet the Press*). Look for errors in reasoning, places where the interviewee seemed to camouflage what she or he was saying, or places where the interviewee was evasive. Discuss the program in class. It will be particularly helpful if you can show your tape in class.

KEY TERMS • CONCEPTS

Ambiguous
Analogies
Appreciative Inquiry
Arguments
Brainstorming
Creative Thinking
Critical Thinking
Devil's Advocate
Either-Or Thinking
Evidence
Fact
Fallacies
Open-minded
Opinions
Overgeneralization
Probing Questions
Synectics

CHAPTER 8

# Group Problem-Solving Procedures

## CHAPTER OUTLINE



## CHAPTER OBJECTIVES

After reading this chapter you should be able to:

1. Explain why using a systematic procedure for group problem solving usually produces better solutions than random or haphazard problem solving.
2. Define key terms such as *problem solving, decision making,* and *area of freedom* with examples.
3. Describe five characteristics of problems.
4. Explain why and how you would adjust the problem-solving process to accommodate any of the characteristics of problems.
5. Describe the functional theory of problem solving and decision making.
6. Describe each step of P-MOPS.
7. Explain how you could use techniques such as *focus groups, group support systems, RISK,* and *PERT* to help at various stages of P-MOPS.
8. Apply P-MOPS to fit a simple or complex problem.

## Relocating the Department of Music

CASE 8.1

The Department of Music at Missouri State University was housed in a 1950s building that was falling apart! Funds were found to remodel the building, but the building needed to be empty during the construction and remodeling period. The problem: where could 25 faculty and staff and 300 students be relocated for a year during the remodel? This relocation was complex, requiring moving not just desks, chairs, and filing cabinets, but about 50 pianos, 20 practice rooms (each with a piano), and about 6 classrooms.

The campus Space Committee charged Krista, a Facilities Management staff person, and her subcommittee to develop options. Krista was told she had to find space on campus—leasing external space would not be allowed. This initial problem question—Where on campus can the Music Department be relocated?—constrained the committee deliberations. If just regular offices had to be found, various nooks and crannies across campus could likely have been found for the 25 faculty and staff affected by the move. But those darned pianos! Where could they go?

Krista and her committee considered several options: relocating practice rooms in the open space of lobbies in existing buildings; distributing pianos and offices to spaces that had not yet been built out into smaller offices; using existing buildings the university leased in Springfield's downtown area that weren't fully occupied; and combinations of all these options. That would have meant, of course, that the department would be spread out across campus for a year, with faculty offices not anywhere near faculty teaching studios. No single or combined option could accommodate all the faculty, staff, practice rooms—and especially the pianos—that needed to be moved.

Krista told her bosses what her committee had discovered. Although they weren't happy, they changed the nature of the problem question: Where can we relocate the Music Department that will cause the least disruption in as cost-effective a way as possible? Rephrasing the problem question opened up several possibilities: two nearby defunct grocery stores provided ample space that could be built out temporarily; a local organization that had gone out of business had space that was already built out into offices and classrooms (although this was several miles from the campus); and a nearby strip mall had huge open space a previous tenant recently vacated. This last option was selected. Other criteria in favor of this option were that the owner was a responsible landlord; he was willing to build out the open space into offices, practice rooms, and classrooms; the lease was affordable; and, importantly, after Music moved out, the space could be used to relocate people from another building scheduled for remodeling.

This situation is a typical one faced by organizations every day. Krista's committee took months to solve this problem. Although more complex than most problems, it entailed the same process of evaluating the issue, looking for options, evaluating them, and finally selecting the best option.

**The challenges faced by the Space Committee in our opening case highlight the sort of issues groups face as they tackle the work of problem solving together. People pool their talents and resources to overcome a situation they find problematic. Although the desire is there, members may differ about priorities and approaches. In addition, groups are constrained by outside factors like large organizations, which provide parameters within which the group must work as was true with the initial charge of Krista's bosses, to find space on campus. Circumstances change and groups can find their ability to function altered for the better or for the worst. In our case, Krista's bosses recognized that the committee had genuinely tried to find campus space; they finally agreed to loosen their parameters. The process though took months of perseverance; many groups lack that patience.**

In Chapters 1 and 7 we maintained that groups can produce solutions to complex problems that are better than solutions produced by individuals (see Table 8.1); they also produce greater member understanding and more satisfaction.[1] The *assembly effect* is achieved when the group solution is superior both to the choice of the group's most expert member and to an averaging of opinions of all members—an example of the whole becoming greater than the sum of the parts. That is because group discussion can help members collectively recall information some may have forgotten, correct flawed information, help members understand information so that it is more useful, identify gaps in the information base, and help each other appropriately evaluate and weigh the importance of information.[2] However, this kind of synergy and its benefits do not happen if group members work independently.[3] They must work *inter*dependently and value each other's contributions as important to finishing the task at hand.[4] Working alone on group assignments is okay; however, as we learned in Chapter 7, although generating ideas alone during brainstorming has its benefits, the group is

**TABLE 8.1** **Advantages and Disadvantages of Solving Problems in Groups versus as Individuals**

| Advantages | Disadvantages |
|---|---|
| • Solutions for complex problems are usually superior.<br>• Groups have more resources, including information and methods.<br>• Members accept the solutions more readily; satisfaction is higher.<br>• Members understand the solution more completely. | • Groups take more time.<br>• Participation may be uneven; some members may dominate, and others withdraw.<br>• Interpersonal tension, disagreements about the task, and conformity pressures may interfere with critical thinking. |

responsible for merging those ideas and assessing them (see Table 8.1). Thinking you can simply string together a bunch of smaller assignments into a final project without discussion by the entire group and get the benefits of the assembly effect is naïve. The synergy of the assembly effect is possible only when members communicate with each other throughout the entire process.[5]

We have emphasized throughout Chapters 6 and 7 especially that the advantages of group work are not automatic. Groups experience a kind of production loss due to all sorts of reasons: Members dominate the group, members become fatigued during discussion, some members are quieter than others, members do not help each other see the connections between their ideas, and so on.[6] Simply because a group has been charged to solve a problem does not guarantee success. As with any effective group throughout process, you are advised to remain vigilant of your actions and follow systematic procedures to avoid as best you can any production loss. Systematic procedures usually produce better decisions than unsystematic ones.[7]

## A Systematic Procedure as the Basis for Problem Solving

There are a number of ways to solve problems. One way is by turning to an expert or someone you consider to be an authority, the way many people turn to doctors for dealing with illnesses. Or, you may solve problems at an intuitive level. For example, you may be wondering what to do about an assignment, and suddenly the answer occurs to you while you're taking a shower.

There's nothing wrong with these methods, particularly for problems that will affect only you. However, intuition can have serious limitations for group problem solving if you don't *also* use a systematic procedure for checking out the hunch. Careful, critical analysis of information, like the kind detailed in Chapter 7, is important too.

**GLOSSARY**

**Problem**

*The difference between what exists presently and what you expect or want*

What would you say if you went to the doctor because of chest pains and, without doing any tests, she said, "My intuition tells me you need a shot of penicillin"? Ideas derived only through intuition must be examined critically before they are implemented because critical thinking can reveal flaws in the ideas that may not be apparent at first. It's possible the hunch is terrific and may only need to be tweaked to solve your problem, but it's also possible that the hunch may cause more problems than it solves. Thus, no matter how a group discovers the possible solutions to a problem—through intuition, logic, or authority—the group must use a systematic process and the best creative and critical thinking it can muster to develop solutions and assess how well they will work.

There is also an ethical imperative to systematic problem solving. The National Communication Association's Credo of Ethical Communication, introduced in Chapter 1, tells us that one component of ethical communication involves taking responsibility for the short- and long-term consequences of our communication. Being systematic in our problem solving means being responsible. This shows we are willing to carefully consider our choices, realizing that our group decisions have consequences both to the group and to those outside the group who are affected by those group decisions. Those consequences can range from a poor evaluation on a project to the loss of life, as we saw in the *Challenger* case from Chapter 7.

This chapter is divided into two main sections, each dealing with group problem solving. The first section concentrates on describing the specifics of any problem a task group could face. We define what problems are, describe how they vary, and illustrate how good problem questions are created for discussions. The second section describes how to manage the entire problem-solving process carefully, with a systematic and flexible procedural model of problem solving, or P-MOPS.

## Capturing the Problem in Problem Solving

We have been discussing problem solving throughout this book as the central task of secondary groups. We have not yet discussed a key factor: just what is it that groups are solving? The opening case shows us that even well-intentioned individuals can make mistakes trying to figure out how best to word their problem and what they need to do to solve it. This section will clarify what a problem is, and how different characteristics of problems can influence the degree of systematic planning necessary to solve them effectively, and how you can generate sensible problem questions for group work in order to best facilitate creative solutions. This section is important because how a problem gets defined initially can have a profound impact on how the group treats the problem and its assessment in later stages of problem solving,[8] a recurring theme from Chapter 7.

### HOW DO WE KNOW A PROBLEM WHEN WE SEE ONE?

**Problem** refers to the difference between what you want or expect and what actually is the case. For example, you need your entire group to show up for a class presentation, but on the day of the presentation three members are no-shows. You have a problem!

Every problem—whether it is about dealing with absent members, lowering child neglect and abuse, improving campus safety, or decreasing student loan debts for college students—has three components that a group needs to understand before members start trying to solve something. Neglecting to do this can set your group up for failure.

1. **An undesirable existing situation.**

   If people believe that something is perfectly satisfactory as it is, there is no problem. For example, when Grupo Latino Americano's meeting place was accessible and affordable, it had no problem. But when the landlord suddenly tripled the rent, it needed to find a new place to meet. The undesirable present situation in this case was the loss of an affordable place to meet.

2. **A desired situation or goal.**

   At the start a goal can vary from a vague image of a better condition (being able to meet) to a very precise, detailed objective (finding a meeting place that is affordable, large enough to hold 30 people, close to walking distance of downtown, and allows food to be brought in). Effective problem solving involves establishing a precise goal that is achievable, doesn't suggest a solution, and is understandable to all members. Outstanding groups have clear goals that all members support.[9]

3. **Obstacles to change.**

   These are conditions and forces that must be overcome by the chosen solution to achieve the desired situation or goal. Typical obstacles include insufficient information, the competing interests of other people, lack of tools or skills, and insufficient funds. For example, when the Grupo Latino Americano's rent tripled, members had no idea what other facilities were available, what similar facilities rented for, how soon another facility could be located, whether members would be willing to move, what the group could afford, and so forth.

**GLOSSARY**

**Area of Freedom**

*The amount of authority and the limitations given to a group*

## AREA OF FREEDOM

Once you have a better handle on what the problem is, where you might like to go, and what stands in your way, your group needs to talk about the extent of its power to do anything about the problem. The **area of freedom** is the amount of authority and the limitations given to a group charged with solving a problem. A fact-finding group, for instance, may be asked only to investigate a problem, not carry out the solution. Another small group may have authority only to interpret information, as in the case of a jury that can decide guilt or innocence but not the penalty for guilt. Many advisory committees can recommend a solution but not make it binding. For example, a committee one of us observed was charged with making recommendations about the types of student activities on campus. Instead, this committee created a sweeping proposal to fire certain individuals and restructure the student activities department. Even though committee members worked long and conscientiously to develop the plan, it was not accepted because the committee went far beyond its area of freedom. In our opening case, the Space Committee was bound by the directives of that governing body, which initially allowed only on-campus space to be considered.

### Improving Airport Security

APPLY NOW

Far-reaching changes in airport safety in the United States were implemented after the terrorist attacks of September 11, 2001. The Transportation and Security Administration (TSA) was created to help enforce stricter airport safety procedures. Yet problems with airport safety keep surfacing. Map this problem according to the problem components described above.

1. An undesirable current situation: What is undesirable about safety procedures? What is undesirable about the equipment used in the safety screenings? What is undesirable about machine or human body searches? What is undesirable about the training and working conditions of TSA agents?
2. A desired situation or goal: What would this desired situation look like? For instance, passengers would like to board safely and quickly without unnecessary scrutiny.
3. Obstacles for change: What are the obstacles to achieving a desired situation or goal? For instance, do we lack appropriate training of TSA agents? Are airports equipped with proper equipment?

## CHARACTERISTICS OF PROBLEMS

We have shown you the three components that together constitute a problem: unhappiness over present conditions, a more desirable future goal, and obstacles that impede movement toward that goal. These need to be talked about by the group, as well as the assignment and any limitations to its problem solving. By discussing these matters, you begin to shape your overall problem-solving procedures to fit the unique details of your problem. To finish this assessment of your problem, you need to ask several questions about the particular nature of your problem so that you can adapt the problem-solving procedures that will follow.

Some problems are complex while others are relatively simple. Using a systematic process for problem solving doesn't mean force-fitting the procedure onto every kind of problem. Rather, it involves modifying that procedure to fit the particular problem your group faces because a problem's specific characteristics vary. The five we discuss here are among the most important.

**Task Difficulty.** How complex is the issue or problem? A complicated task with many dimensions and no clear solution is more difficult than a simpler task. The *Arizona Republic* news staff faced the difficult problem of whether to publish the photo of 19 flag-draped bodies of the firefighters lost in the summer 2013 Arizona fire.[10] The problem of publishing the news and respecting the loss of life was so difficult that they called on a local ethicist for feedback. Difficult tasks are often given to groups because their solution is beyond what one person can do. They require extensive problem mapping to help members fully understand the nature of the problem, unearth all the information, and coordinate their efforts—and this will take a lot of deliberation.

**Solution Multiplicity.** Are there many possible ways to solve the group's problem, or is there one correct answer? For instance, there are many fun and appropriate ways to plan your high school class's tenth reunion, but there may be only one solution to a math problem. When a problem has high solution multiplicity—in other words, has many possible solutions—you will want to make sure that your group identifies as many of those solutions as possible. This focus on creatively generating ideas (see Chapter 7) will be the key to success.

**Intrinsic Interests.** Are group members really interested and excited about working on this problem (high intrinsic interest), or would they rather go to the dentist than have to tackle the problem? You learned in Chapter 6 about different member characteristics and motivations that affect group processes. When members are excited and interested, they want to talk about the problem or issue, tell their own stories about it, or vent their feelings. Intrinsic interest is what helps members stick with an issue, sometimes for years.

**Member Familiarity.** Has the group ever confronted a similar problem? Did it solve the problem successfully? If so, the members have high familiarity with the problem. They may want to focus on establishing criteria for evaluating options. But if they have never undertaken anything similar, or if they have just formed a new group, they will need some time to get to know each other and to familiarize themselves with all aspects of the problem (particularly if it is complex). Initially, group members tend not to share all their information about a problem but share only information commonly known by the group.[11] Groups need to find out not only what members know in common but what they also know *uniquely* if they hope to find that best solution. Groups cannot build on member contributions if they are not shared. Joan Rentsch and her colleagues found that teams working on military problem-solving tasks were better able to share and assimilate information from their experts if they had explicit training on how to express their information and how then to connect the information.[12] Detailed problem mapping involving placing ideas on information boards really helped these groups.

**Acceptance Level.** Is acceptance of the solution by people who will be affected by it critical for success? For instance, if a company is considering changing its overtime policies, lack of employee acceptance can derail the "solution" and cause lasting bad feelings. In such a case, the acceptance level needs to be high, making it crucial for the group to solicit the opinions and ideas of those who will be affected. Before committing fully to the solution, the group may want to suggest partially implementing the solution and reevaluating it with those who are affected. But if the solution won't matter much to most people—such as which party favors to buy for that high school reunion—then members don't need to spend time seeking outside opinions.

Table 8.2 lists these five characteristics of problems and also offers suggestions for modifying any problem-solving procedure your group is using. Having a clear picture of the nature of your problem and how it varies in relationship to other problems is necessary prior to moving ahead with your systematic procedure.

TABLE 8.2 **Problem Characteristics and the Problem-Solving Process**

**TASK DIFFICULTY**

*Adaptation for high difficulty:*

1. Plan to meet often.
2. Use detailed problem mapping.
3. Include many subquestions to the problem-solving procedure.
4. Form a detailed implementation plan, in writing.

**SOLUTION MULTIPLICITY**

*Adaptation for high multiplicity:*

1. Use brainstorming or one of its variations to generate many ideas.
2. Use synectics or another creativity-enhancing technique to help members relax and be creative.
3. Leave plenty of time for generating ideas; don't rush the process.

**INTRINSIC INTEREST**

*Adaptation for high interest:*

1. Set aside a "ventilation" period early in the problem-solving process for members to express their feelings.
2. Leave plenty of time for early ventilation.
3. Don't overcontrol the ventilation process or introduce structured procedures too early.

**MEMBER FAMILIARITY**

*Adaptation for high familiarity:*

1. Focus on establishment of clear criteria.
2. Focus on evaluating the options using the criteria developed.

*Adaptation for low familiarity:*

1. Use detailed problem mapping.
2. Use consultants and outside experts for help.

**ACCEPTANCE LEVEL**

*Adaptation for high acceptance requirements:*

1. Include representatives in your group from groups that must accept the decision.
2. Use techniques to spot potential problems before finally deciding on a solution.
3. Pretest a solution by partially implementing it and agreeing to pull back if it doesn't seem to work.

## GETTING THE DISCUSSION QUESTION RIGHT

Formulating the right kind of question to launch the group's discussion is an important first step to an effective solution. Different types of questions and the ways they are phrased lead a group's discussion along different paths, as you saw with the Space Committee; you want to ensure that your group takes a path that doesn't close off potentially effective options. The **discussion question** is the central problem, question, or issue the group must answer. For discussions to be effective, a group's discussion question must be clear, must not suggest the solution in the question, and each member should be able to state what it is. Having a clear discussion question helps the group begin its task in the right way, whatever the task may be.

Unfortunately, many groups start with a question that limits them, is vague, or steers them into a particular direction.

In our opening case, only after the Space Committee hit a dead end were Krista's bosses open to broadening the initial problem question.

Establishing an effective discussion question can determine whether the group produces a good or poor solution. For instance, imagine your group decides to tackle overcrowding on campus. Consider the following two discussion questions developed by members to try and capture their problem: "How can we raise money to build another classroom building?" versus "How can we relieve the overcrowding in classrooms?" One form biases the group toward a particular solution. The first question focuses on an already-decided solution, which may or may not be the best solution to the problem. The second question focuses on the problem (overcrowding) without biasing the solution in advance. Building more classrooms may work, but perhaps the problems are due to poor scheduling of existing facilities. Maybe holding classes at off-campus locations such as shopping centers, theaters, and offices throughout the city would be more effective in reducing the overcrowding as well as provide better service to students. However, these options will never be discovered if the discussion question causes the group to pre-determine the solution.

As an input variable, the discussion question has a far-reaching effect on the system's throughput process and its subsequent output. The following guidelines help you phrase discussion questions that will focus and facilitate group interaction.

1. **Unless the group has already narrowed a list of alternatives to two, avoid either-or questions.** Usually, these oversimplify the issue by treating questions as if there were only two legitimate answers instead of a wide range, a type of fallacy we discussed in Chapter 7. In the list that follows, the first question of each pair is poorly worded in either-or terms; the second version is worded as an open-ended question:
   - **a.** Should our university's central administration be more diverse? (Implied is a yes or no answer.) To what extent is our central administration's gender, racial and ethnic diversity adequate?
   - **b.** Should we implement more exams or decrease papers? (Provides only two options.) How should we improve how students demonstrate knowledge in a subject?
2. **Word questions as concretely as possible.** Double-barreled questions that combine two questions in one are confusing. For example, "Do you

**GLOSSARY**

**Discussion Question**

*The discussion question is the central question of policy facing the group.*

### Takata's Reputation on the Line

APPLY NOW

Takata, a Japanese supplier, makes many of the airbags used in nearly two dozen car brands in the United States. The airbags may spontaneously inflate, sending shrapnel into the car's interior. Takata accepted fault in 2013, but claimed that only six makes were involved. However, a *New York Times* article in 2014 reported 139 injuries, including two deaths, from all automakers. At first, Takata said that its propellants were improperly handled and caused the airbags to burst. But later reports revealed long-standing problems with unacceptable defect rates at some plants and propellant problems. The *Times* article alleged that Takata knew about the defects as early as 2004, conducted secret tests to understand the problem, and later destroyed the data and physical evidence. It took Takata four years to acknowledge the problem. Takata called the *Times* article inaccurate, but as of 2015, had recalled 34 million vehicles . . . . Now, Takata's reputation has taken a hit. Think of yourself as a small crisis management team hired to help Takata restore its reputation. Conduct an analysis of the problem, using the following blog post by Clifford Atiyeh and Rusty Blackwell in *Car and Driver*: "Massive Takata Airbag Recall: Everything You Need to Know, Including Full List of Affected Vehicles," June 10, 2016: http://blog.caranddriver.com/massive-takata-airbag-recall-everything-you-need-to-know-including-full-list-of-affected-vehicles/.

1. Identify the elements of this problem: the undesirable existing situation, goal, and obstacles.
2. Craft a clear discussion question to focus your problem-solving process.
3. Using Table 8.2 as your guide, evaluate Takata's problem in terms of each characteristic:

   Task difficulty: high, medium, or low? Why?

   Solution multiplicity: high, medium, or low? Why?

   Intrinsic interest: high, medium, or low? Why?

   Member familiarity: high, medium, or low? Why?

   Acceptance level: high, medium, or low? Why?

think we should increase funding to the public schools by instituting casino gambling in the state?" is a double-barreled question. Listeners may want to respond differently to each part—maybe someone wants to increase funding to the schools but doesn't want to allow casino gambling in the state. Perhaps both issues need to be addressed. If so, each question should be asked separately: "First, do you think funding to the public schools should be increased? Second, should we approve a measure to allow casino gambling in our state?"

3. **Avoid suggesting the answer in the question.** This was exactly the issue with the Space Committee. In addition, some questions actually are sneaky ways to make a point. For instance, "Don't you think we should save money by limiting our search to on-campus space?" is actually a statement in favor of on-campus space.

Taking time to really talk about the nature of the problem helps a group avoid becoming solution-minded too quickly. This is a common problem in business groups.[13] Jumping into discussions of solutions without a comprehensive, initial understanding of the problem is like a car mechanic telling you that you need new valves without even looking under the hood! Defining the problem, detailing its specifics, and wording it into a clear discussion question enables you to make modifications in your problem-solving procedure and provides important initial insight into the problem before you begin the detailed work outlined in the next section of the chapter. The procedure described below is easily modified so you can take advantage of its flexibility and adapt it to the particulars of your group problem that have already been discussed.

## Effective Problem Solving and Decision Making

Problem solving and decision making are related but not identical. Problem solving is a more comprehensive process that includes decision making (choosing). **Problem solving** includes all those actions you have to do to move from the existing situation to your goal, including defining the problem, creating possible solutions, and choosing the best solution. **Decision making** explicitly refers to the act of selecting one or more available options; it does not involve creating possible options. The larger problem-solving process often involves making several decisions, such as how to define the problem, what solutions to consider, which to suggest or act upon, and how to implement the best solution. Let's now turn our attention to the larger problem-solving process, which you will note initially involves the task of understanding the problem we discussed earlier.

In the early 1900s, American philosopher John Dewey described the mental steps people take when they solve problems. His reflective thinking model described problem solving as a systematic rather than haphazard process. The steps look like this: First, we become aware of a difficulty; then we define and describe it, think of some possible solutions, evaluate these potential solutions, and make a decision about what to do. If possible, when we implement the solution, we monitor it to see how it's working, then keep it, adjust it, or replace it after testing it.[14] Group problem-solving procedures adapted from Dewey's sequence go under such names as the standard agenda, ideal solution, and single-question formats.

As Dewey did with individuals, Dennis Gouran, Randy Hirokawa, and their associates have examined problem solving and decision making in *groups*.[15] Their **functional theory** describes how communication helps or hinders group problem solving and decision making. It is called "functional" because it focuses attention on the communicative functions that must be performed if a group is to do a good job. Gouran and Hirokawa assume that group members *want* to make a good decision, have all the information and other resources they need to do so, and have the communicative and

**GLOSSARY**

**Problem Solving**

*Everything you need to do to move from your present undesirable situation to what you want, including creating solutions and choosing among them*

**Decision Making**

*Choosing from available options*

**Functional Theory**

*A description of how communication affects group problem solving*

**TABLE 8.3 Three Factors for Effective Problem Solving**

| |
|---|
| Meet all five task requirements. |
| Extract and use all information relevant to the task. |
| Remain willing to evaluate decisions and make alterations. |

thinking skills necessary to do a good job. If those conditions are present, whether a group solves problems effectively depends on three factors (see Table 8.3).

1. **The first factor pertains to the task requirements.**

   Functionally, five task requirements must be met for a group to succeed. First, members must understand the problem or issue, a necessity discussed in the previous section of this chapter. Second, they must discuss the minimum requirements of a successful solution, including what criteria it must meet. For instance, is there a budget members cannot exceed or an outside group whose support is essential? Third, the group must identify the alternatives from which it will make its choice. Recall that many groups stop identifying or creating alternatives too soon; without sufficient realistic alternatives to choose from, the group may miss the best one. Fourth, the alternatives must be thoroughly evaluated, for both strengths and weaknesses, against the agreed-upon criteria. Finally, the solution that best meets the criteria should be chosen.

2. **The second factor pertains to how well members use their communication to overcome obstacles to effective problem solving.**

   For instance, sometimes members fail to discover information pertinent to their problem or fail to share relevant information. We discussed earlier how members tend to share and believe information they have in common (that they all know), but to hold on to unique information that only one or a small number of them know.[16] Sometimes members consider their relationships with each other more important than finding the best solution; in that case members will refrain from disagreeing with each other and may try to pressure others to conform. The opposite may also be true—member dislike and distrust of each other often gets in the way of members listening to each other, even to the ideas from group experts.[17] Shirley Wang found that when members elaborate on information—discuss, expand, ask questions, and so forth—groups perform better.[18] She further noted that when members have a high degree of emotional intelligence, they are more likely to encourage informational elaboration. Another factor that encourages effective information processing is **team reflexivity,** an intentional discussion of a team's goals and processes.[19] Such deliberate discussion encourages information sharing and can function to correct problem-solving errors. Some members may be more self-interested than interested in helping the group. How the rest of the group deal with such members directly affects

**GLOSSARY**

**Team Reflexivity**

*A team's intentional discussion of goals and processes, which encourages information sharing*

the quality of decisions the group makes. Finally, how skilled members are at communication can affect how well members are willing to listen and be influenced. For example, in groups where high-status members communicated collaboratively, members were more willing to work together and were more willing to be influenced by their peers.[20]

3. **The third factor pertains to the degree of willingness members have to review their process and reconsider their decisions.**

   If they find flaws, members must be willing to second-guess themselves, even to the point of starting over. They must not remain committed to a solution when it is clear the solution is flawed. Their communication to each other should remind members of the importance of reviewing the process and of being fair in making the ultimate choice.

Many researchers have found that following a planned problem-solving procedure helps groups make better decisions and solve problems more effectively. Much like the focus facilitators can provide a group during critical thinking activities (see Chapter 7), such procedures can minimize the bad habits typical of small groups, including getting off track, being pressured by domineering members, prematurely rejecting ideas, and focusing on solutions too early in the process. The procedures help balance participation, improve a group's reflectiveness, coordinate members' thinking, and establish important ground rules for proceeding.[21]

It doesn't seem to matter which problem-solving procedure a group uses; *any* systematic procedure or outline produces better decisions than using no procedure.[22] Step-by-step procedures improve the quality of solutions because they provide logical priorities and steps that must be taken; they remind members of things they might otherwise forget.[23] Evidence suggests that groups arriving at high-quality solutions have made a thorough analysis of the problem, generated a variety of solutions, and conducted a detailed assessment of both the positive and negative aspects of their alternatives.[24] In addition, these groups have focused on a solution's possible problems and have avoided pitfalls.[25]

Group members have said that one of their most urgent needs is for guidance about methods and procedures to use during group work.[26] In particular, participants want methods that help them generate and organize their ideas about complex problems. One such guideline, the procedural model for problem solving, has been used with good success.

**GLOSSARY**

**Procedural Model of Problem Solving (P-MOPS)** *A flexible framework to guide each phase of the problem-solving process*

## THE PROCEDURAL MODEL OF PROBLEM SOLVING (P-MOPS)

Several different guidelines can help groups solve problems effectively; we favor the **procedural model of problem solving (P-MOPS)** because it focuses a group's attention on the essential tasks outlined by the functional theory. P-MOPS is a flexible framework that can guide each phase of problem solving.

P-MOPS reminds the group to analyze the problem thoroughly before trying to solve it and to think critically about the positive and negative outcomes likely to occur with each alternative solution. We shortened the name to remind you that it will help you "mop up" the details needed for good problem solving. The five steps in this general problem-solving procedure are: (1) describing and analyzing the problem, (2) generating and explaining possible solutions, (3) evaluating all solutions, (4) choosing the best solution, and (5) implementing the chosen solution.

**1. Describing and Analyzing the Problem.** During the first stage of problem solving, the group concentrates on thoroughly understanding the problem. Members should consider all three major elements of the problem: what is unsatisfactory, what is desired, and what obstacles exist. This phase of problem solving may require nothing more than sharing the knowledge members now have, illustrated by the mapping procedure depicted in Figure 8.1. That's easier said than done, though. Group members are apt to share freely that information they already hold in common.[27] Shared information can appear more credible and creates common ground among members, who then tend to withhold more diverse information later. Sharing information known to others is socially validating—other members will agree with you and support you, but they may look at you skeptically if you share information that is new to them.[28] Making the best use of any expert knowledge in the group is not an obvious endeavor. Group members can miss this divergent information for all sorts of reasons.[29] Simple dislike of members can get in your way of listening to expert members. Sometimes experts describe the problem in ways more novice members do not understand. Complicated tasks with no obvious answers make it harder for expert members to make their case.

To complicate matters, Charles Pavit and Lindsey Aloia discovered that members in business groups blurt out their individual preferences regarding possible solutions to their problem prior to even understanding their problem.[30] This leads to first impressions about those solutions that inhibit later critical thinking in steps two and three of P-MOPS.

**FIGURE 8.1** Maps of a Problem Before and After Members Discuss It

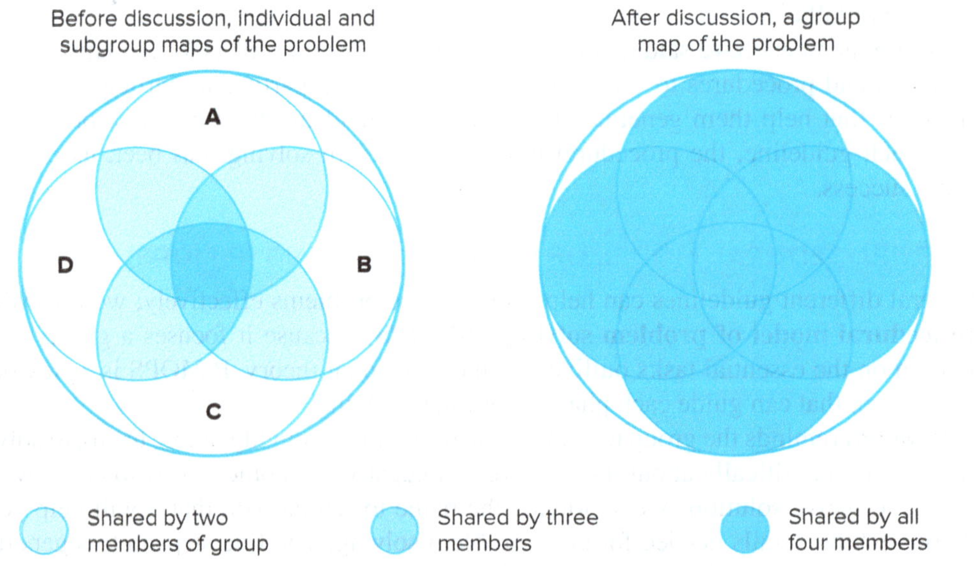

Groups with the time should consider letting individual members think about the problem first before even talking about it as a group.[31] Members have to overcome their natural reluctance to share certain kinds of information (where they diverge) and natural urge to share other kinds of information (where they agree) and be willing to make sure *all* information is shared and owned by the group.[32] The description and analysis of a problem should never be rushed—it is crucial to effective problem solving. If this stage sounds familiar to you, it *should* because it refers to the preliminary work of understanding the problem that we talked about in the first section of this chapter. As we move into a detailed discussion of a systematic procedure for problem solving, we bring this initial work into the first stage of P-MOPS.

Following are several principles to guide your thinking and discussion in step 1 of problem solving.

1. **Be sure you understand the charge precisely.**

   The **charge** is your assigned responsibility and limitations, given by the organization or person who created the group. Clarifying the charge means that you make sure you understand an assignment exactly as intended. Get the charge in hard copy if possible and ask the person presenting the charge to clarify any unclear terms. For instance, you need to know what form your final product is to take: a recommendation, a research report, a blueprint with perspective drawings, or any other tangible object. You will certainly need to know what limitations are placed on your area of freedom, such as information you can obtain from company records, legal restraints, and spending limits. You will want to know when your work must be done; deadlines are part of most charges to groups.

2. **State the problem as a single, clear problem question.**

   A well worded discussion question is essential. A question that suggests the solution, remember, biases the group and limits its effectiveness. "How can we convince the administration to put in a new parking lot?" is a *solution question* that assumes the solution to the parking problem is to create a new parking lot. This *problem question* is better: "How can we improve the parking situation on campus?"

3. **Focus on the problem before discussing how to solve it.**

   We have talked consistently about the fact that one common source of poor solutions is getting solution-centered before the problem has been thoroughly investigated, described, and analyzed. If a group member suggests a solution too early, the discussion leader or another member should then remind the group to refrain from any talk about what to do until after the group has completed its analysis of the problem.

4. **Describe the problem thoroughly.**

   Be sure to answer all questions about what is going on and what you hope to accomplish, as well as possible obstacles to that goal—the way a successful investigative reporter or detective does. A good way to describe the problem is to think of it as an uncharted map with only vague boundaries. Your first job as a group is to make a complete, detailed map of the problem. As we mentioned

**GLOSSARY**

**Charge**

*The group's assignment*

**TABLE 8.4** **Questions to Ask as You Analyze the Problem**

**WHAT ARE ALL THE RELEVANT FACTS?**

1. Who is involved? When? Where? How?
2. What complaints have been made?
3. What is the difference between what is expected and what is actually happening?
4. What harm has occurred?
5. What exceptions have there been?
6. What changes have occurred?
7. What other information do we need?

**WHAT MAY HAVE PRODUCED OR CAUSED THE UNSATISFACTORY CONDITION?**

1. What events precipitated the problem?
2. What other factors may have contributed to the problem?

**WHAT DO WE HOPE TO ACHIEVE?**

1. What form will our solution take?
2. What would be a minimum acceptable solution for each person concerned?

**WHAT ARE THE CHARACTERISTICS OF OUR PROBLEM?**

1. How difficult is our problem?
2. How many possible solutions are there to our problem?
3. How interested are we personally in this problem?
4. How familiar are we with the problem?
5. How important is it that those most affected accept the solution?

earlier, this process of information sharing is critical—don't be tempted to short-change it! Table 8.4 outlines questions you will need to answer.

5. **Make an outline and a schedule based on the procedural model of problem solving.**

   This is especially important if it is a major problem requiring extended work over several meetings. This outline and schedule can be modified later if needed, but at least now the group will reap the benefits of a plan before getting too deeply into the problem analysis.

6. **Summarize the problem as a group.**
   This helps build an interdependence between members; together they understand the problem and see how everyone is important to solving it. In the case of a large problem, this summary may be done in writing by one member and edited by the entire group until all members are satisfied with it.

Sometimes the problem you are addressing will affect a number of people, and you may need information about what is important to them. Other times a particular problem may have several aspects, and you may need to know which ones are the main issues or concerns. It was important for the Space Committee to know, for instance, that most music faculty, not just the piano faculty, needed to be near their pianos in order to teach their students. Thus, just finding typical office space to hold a desk and chair was not going to be adequate. One technique you can use to find out what is important to others is the focus group.

***Spotlighting Key Issues with Focus Groups.*** The **focus group** technique, which encourages unstructured discussion about a given topic, is often used to analyze people's interests and values. It is a great way for a group or an organization to find out what the important issues are regarding a problem facing the group; however, it is such a flexible procedure that it can be used at several steps in the problem-solving process.

In a focus group discussion, the facilitator introduces a topic to the group and instructs group members to discuss the topic any way they choose. The facilitator gives no further direction to the group but may probe or ask questions. Usually, the group discussion is tape-recorded for later analysis. After the group is finished, the facilitator or representatives of the parent organization listen to the tape for usable ideas. For example, a public relations officer at a small campus used a focus group to discover more effective ways of scheduling and promoting evening classes. A group of evening students was instructed simply to talk about what it was like to be an evening student. From the discussion it was clear that evening students were often trying to juggle full-time jobs, families, and other responsibilities in addition to school. The school's schedule was forcing them to come to the campus four nights a week to complete two courses. But the focus group discussion indicated that the students would be happy to stay later in the evening if they could take those two courses by coming to the campus only two nights a week. Campus officials found a way to "stack" the evening classes to allow this. In addition, the student comments spurred many imaginative ideas for advertising and promoting the evening offerings.

**2. Generating and Explaining Possible Solutions.** The quality of the solution to a problem will not be better than the quality of the pool of ideas the group considers. Studies of problem solving have shown that the ideas discovered later are more likely to be innovative and of higher quality than the ideas first mentioned.[33] You want to avoid what is commonly called the "group communication flaw" we have addressed most seriously since Chapter 7; groups close down prematurely their problem-solving activities as a consequence of early agreement.[34] This is why the *observation* in the participant-observation perspective we introduced you to in Chapter 1 is so critical. You have to remain vigilant to your processes and use procedures like problem-solving agendas to help you remain focused on things such as the creative generation of solutions and their critical assessment. Thus, the major issue of step 2 is not "What *should* be done to solve

**GLOSSARY**

**Focus Group**
*An unstructured technique in which members freely explore thoughts and feelings about a topic*

GLOSSARY

**Criteria**

*Standards and guidelines used to evaluate ideas and solutions*

the problem?" but "What *might* be done to solve the problem?" This subtle change in wording is important.

During step 2 the group focuses on creatively finding and listing possible solutions, not on critically determining their relative merits or on trying to decide what to do. Creative thinking is crucial to this step and was discussed in detail in Chapter 7. The leader may need to remind the group not to argue (yet) the relative merits of proposed solutions.

No criticism should be allowed during step 2, but ideas may be explained and clarified. Someone may ask, "What do you mean?" or "Could you please explain how that would work?" Descriptive explanations help everyone understand the idea and may even stimulate further ideas. Use the rules for brainstorming present in Chapter 7.

Sometimes, while generating ideas, a member will recognize details of the problem that ought to be explored more fully. The group may then cycle back to the P-MOPS step 1 for further exploration of that issue. For example, faculty on a committee charged with revising the communication major realized, in the middle of evaluating options for the revision, that they had forgotten to solicit feedback from an important group—their alumni. The members conducted a quick telephone survey of selected alumni, thus temporarily setting aside their evaluation to return to analysis of the problem. When they finish the additional analysis for step 1, members return to listing alternatives.

Once a group has completed its list of alternatives, it is ready to proceed with evaluating them.

**3. Evaluating All Possible Solutions.** During the third stage of problem solving, *all* proposed solutions should be evaluated. Critical thinking, as discussed in Chapter 7, is especially crucial during this stage, and you want to avoid groupthink. For instance, arguments in undergraduate groups tend to consist of simple assertions almost half of the time, and members seldom cite rules of logic or criteria as standards.[35] The options must be tested against the criteria the group has established, and members must be sure the solution is consistent with the facts brought out during discussion, the goals of the group, and the restrictions imposed by the group's area of freedom. It is especially important to consider all possible negative consequences of each solution, or new problems it might create for the group or other people.

***Criteria for Evaluating Solutions.*** **Criteria** are statements that set standards and limits for comparing and evaluating ideas. For example, search committee members assessing applicants for a library dean's position streamlined their evaluation process by using criteria sheets the members developed. Committee members made a list of the essential qualifications (e.g., academic degrees required, years of experience required) and the other desirable characteristics (e.g., fund-raising experience, team approach to managing). Then they decided which of the criteria were most important and placed them in a priority listing. This gave each member a set of specific guidelines to use as he or she read each application.

Serious secondary tension (see Chapter 5) may arise as people argue and disagree while they discuss the pros and cons of proposed solutions. Having agreed-upon criteria helps make arguments as constructive as possible and keeps personal defensiveness to a minimum. Establishing criteria is very important—groups that spend time discussing and establishing criteria are more effective than groups that don't.[36]

For example, a public utility where one of us lives recently was criticized by the public for its "excessively" generous employee compensation and benefits packages. To determine fair compensation and benefits, the utility's board of directors examined compensation of other public utilities and private companies of similar size and complexity. The directors used this information to develop objective criteria, based on evidence rather than their own hunches, in redesigning the benefits package. Thus, group members should discuss, agree upon, and possibly rank (from most to least important) the criteria for judging their ideas and solutions.

Some criteria are absolute, which means they *must* be met (e.g., "The library dean must have at least a master's degree in library science from an American Library Association-accredited school"). Other criteria are important but give the group some flexibility (e.g., "A Ph.D. is a preferred qualification for the library dean").

Some criteria are virtually universal in judging among solutions: Will the proposed solution actually solve the problem? Can the proposed solution be done? Will the benefits outweigh the costs? Is this solution within our area of freedom? and How acceptable is this idea to the people most likely to be affected by it? Such criteria encourage the group to consider whether the ideas proposed are legal, moral, workable, within the competence of the group or organization, within the control of the parent organization, and so on.

There is some debate over whether groups need to discuss criteria explicitly. When groups are given their criteria as part of their charge and the criteria are understood by the group, some evidence suggests that groups do not need to discuss criteria.[37] We believe, however, that it is never wrong to discuss criteria because discussion can confirm how much members both understand and agree to the criteria. In addition, discussing criteria exposes the values held by group members, and these value discussions are central to effective consensus building in groups.[38]

***Narrowing a Long List of Proposed Solutions.*** When a list of ideas has been generated by brainstorming or any other technique, the group will need to reduce this list to a manageable size for discussion. This can be done in a number of ways after the group has established its criteria. Here are three useful techniques:

1. Combine any ideas that are similar or overlapping. For example, "Hold a goodwill party" and "Have a get-acquainted cocktail party" could be combined into "Plan a social event."
2. Allow every member to vote for his or her top three choices. Tally the votes. Any proposed solutions that do not have at least two votes may be removed from the list.
3. Give each member a set of 10 or 15 stickers and ask them to "vote" on their preferred solutions. Members can distribute their stickers any way they want. They can put all their stickers on one item, if they strongly prefer that item, or put each sticker on a different item. The items receiving stickers are easy to spot and list in priority order. The group then discusses the pros and cons of the options that received at least one sticker.

***Charting the Pros and Cons.*** During the evaluation discussion, a recorder can help greatly by creating a chart of the ideas being discussed, with the pros and cons

TABLE 8.5 **Charting the Pros and Cons of Two Proposed Solutions**

| HOW TO REDUCE PASSENGER INJURIES IN AUTOMOBILE ACCIDENTS | |
|---|---|
| **Pass Federal Law to Require Use of Seat Belts** | **Require New Cars to Be Equipped with Airbags** |
| **Pros** | **Pros** |
| • Would reduce or eliminate many injuries.<br>• Would be inexpensive.<br>• Precedent exists in many states. | • Would be extremely effective.<br>• Technology currently exists. |
| **Cons** | **Cons** |
| • Infringes on individual rights; expect heated legal fight.<br>• Difficult to enforce.<br>• Some injuries could be worse with seatbelts. | • Would increase the cost of cars.<br>• Infringes on individual rights; expect heated legal battle.<br>• Airbags might inflate incorrectly and cause accident. |

mentioned for each idea, as shown in Table 8.5. Instead of *Pros* and *Cons,* the chart headings might be *Advantages* and *Disadvantages, For* and *Against,* or even + and –. Using such a chart that everyone can see helps the group remember major arguments and think critically about the proposals under consideration. This, too, can be done electronically, either with specialized software or by ordinary e-mail, with someone compiling the comments.

***Using Technology to Help Group Problem Solving.*** In previous chapters (especially Chapters 1, 3, 4, and 7) we have talked about computer technology and small group processes. We have compared computer-mediated communication with face-to-face communication and discussed face-to-face group use of electronic communication and how best to search for and use Internet information for group tasks. As you may remember, groups range from those that conduct business only face-to-face to those that mix face-to-face with some computer-mediated communication, to those that conduct business only in virtual space. Considering this range, we know groups use a broad mix of computer tools and programs designed for the exclusive purpose of helping groups with their problem solving. First, let's look at some of the broader tools of computer-mediated communication available to group members.

Electronic mail (e-mail) allows members to talk to each other asynchronously using their electronic tablets, cell phones, or personal computers when it is convenient, rendering meeting "time" much more flexible.[39] Electronic writing systems, like Dropbox and wiki (addressed in Chapter 3), permit members to co-author their writing simultaneously by allowing them to create, analyze, edit, and revise a single document.[40]

Instant messaging (IM) is popular in virtual groups because it allows for more rapid-fire message exchanges than e-mail. This kind of messaging cannot be archived like e-mail and its impact on work productivity is unclear.[41]

Instructors use asynchronous electronic bulletin board services (BBS) and synchronous chat environments, like the Internet Relay Chat (IRC), to facilitate classroom learning or as part of an online course.[42] More and more instructors are using services such as Blackboard as platforms for their classes that also allow students the opportunity to talk to each other. These technologies allow teachers and students to talk to each other when it is convenient and can equalize participation, increase student self-responsibility, allow students to see each other's perspectives, give students time to think about their responses, and teach valuable computer-mediated skills for their future professions.

We touched on different teleconference options in Chapter 3. The common audio conference allows members only to hear each other. Although limited in its nonverbal cues, if it is used well it can equalize participation.[43] Video conferencing, although still more expensive than audio conferencing, is preferred when members wish to see each other's nonverbal cues but is not cost effective for routine meetings.[44] Desktop video conferencing makes use of members' computers. The IRC we just discussed is a form of computer conferencing as are the tools found in a site like wiggio (www.wiggio.com/).

In general, these kinds of tools, like most computer tools, work best when you understand how they are meant to operate. Instant messages are quick but do not work for detailed messages that should be documented. Group experts still recommend that extended teleconferences be mixed with face-to-face conferencing to improve members' sense of "groupness."[45] Even effective teleconferencing requires setting and following guidelines for participation.[46]

**Group support systems (GSS)** are computer technologies designed to improve the quality and speed of group problem solving. Specifically, GSS exists to help groups with such tasks as idea generation, information organization, evaluation of options, and decision making. Many are designed to allow group members to work collaboratively on a problem even though they may be meeting in different locations at different times. Two of the more well-known support systems for problem solving are GroupSystems and Software Assisted Meeting Management (SAMM). Both include modules created to help groups in every area of problem solving.[47] They are particularly helpful during the evaluation stage because they structure the procedure by which members can honestly react to each other's suggestions and ideas.

Such systems have rapidly increased in number, ease of use, and effectiveness, especially as more and more organizations use local area networks that allow several computers to be connected to each other. People can employ GSS for either long-term use or for one problem-solving task. For example, workers in geographically dispersed areas can connect via computer to perform group work even though they may be far apart. Often, however, people meet electronically in the same room, each at his or her own computer terminal. This allows several members to "talk" at once by entering their messages into the computer, which compiles them quickly. It also permits anonymity; who submitted a particular comment, idea, criticism, and so forth is not recorded. Some GSS are highly specialized such as those designed to improve the idea-generation step of brainstorming. Others, are more general and are designed to improve the entire problem-solving and decision-making process, in part by providing structure.

**GLOSSARY**

**Group Support Systems (GSS)**

*Computer-based systems designed to improve various aspects of group work*

## The School Board Breaks a Deadlock

CASE 8.2

The school board in a city near where one of us lives had been stymied for several meetings over an issue related to a tax increase for schools and what arguments members should make in the local media to support the tax increase. Most of the members wanted to stress that the tax increase would mean higher salaries for teachers, more teachers in the system, and smaller class sizes. One very vocal member wanted to emphasize the deterioration of the buildings and the necessity for basic facility maintenance. The board was stuck over this and other issues. Members didn't want to alienate the "buildings" member so, wanting to be polite, they worked hard to find positive things to say about his arguments. However, this just fueled his enthusiasm. The school board president decided to use the university's "Decision Room," a room that had 20 terminals with capacity for full group support systems (GSS).

Two faculty members assisted the school board; one served as "chauffeur" to run the software while the other served as a neutral facilitator. The school board members typed their ideas into a terminal, where they appeared on a large, overhead screen that all could see. They were able to make anonymous comments about each idea. Finally, they rated each idea on a scale of 1 to 5 and rank-ordered each one as well. The ratings and rankings were instantly tallied, and a bar chart was produced that visually reproduced their numerical assessments. It was clear from the ratings and rankings that the "buildings" member was an outlier in the group. His ideas were not supported at all, which became obvious to everyone in the group, including him. This visual representation on the computer screen got through to him when the members' gentle oral comments had not. He dropped his insistence on the building maintenance platform for the tax levy.

1. What do you think are the advantages and disadvantages of using GSS?
2. Why do you think members were direct and clear using GSS where they had not been in face-to-face discussion?
3. What was persuasive about the visual representation that was not persuasive about the oral discussion?
4. For what other kinds of decisions do you think GSS would be helpful?
5. Are there situations in which you would not want to use GSS?

Group decision making using computer support systems seems to be at least as good as traditional group decision making.[48] Members are often more satisfied and like the fact that the computers permit simultaneous talk. Studies on GSS in organizations suggest that bigger groups are even more satisfied than smaller ones, that the systems seem to help group members sustain their task focus better and that less time seems to be spent in meetings. GSS also helps improve organizational record keeping and memory. In addition, the anonymity such systems provide is important, more so for groups with individuals of widely varied status than for groups of peers. In mixed-status groups, members use the anonymity feature of GSS to their advantage.[49] For example, sex is a status characteristic that, left hidden, can level the influence of members' sex in group interaction. Males generally enjoy more status. Online they tend to reveal that they are male, which circumvents the anonymity feature of GSS, making it more like face-to-face communication. Females, on the other hand, try to preserve their anonymity, hiding their sex so as to be more influential in the group.

Group members should recognize that using GSS is not always beneficial. Problems include some group members' discomfort with using computers, GSS procedures that may structure group interaction too tightly, and managers who may not want group members under their supervision to have full access to information easily obtained via computers.[50]

Be careful with any conclusion drawn about GSS. They are changing daily. They seem to be especially beneficial for certain types of tasks, such as idea generation and decision making.[51] However, face-to-face groups seem to be superior for negotiation and complex, cognitive tasks. Whether GSS improves performance depends on a variety of factors.[52] Groups using support systems generally make better decisions; such groups generate more alternatives; and participation among members is more even. As with face-to-face groups, virtual groups do better when they use a vigilant decision-making process and when they are reminded—via e-mail or other messages—to share all their information.[53] On the other hand, groups take longer to reach decisions, experience less consensus, and are less satisfied than face-to-face groups. An important key to satisfaction appears to be user familiarity—users' reactions are usually negative at first. Several reviews of GSS have found that group members need time to become familiar with the spirit or intention of GSS. As long as a GSS program is used consistently with its intentions, it can be very effective; however, merely using a GSS program without considering its intent may lead to failure. GSS do not do the work *for* the group, nor do they work if group members fail to use good communication skills. The same communication skills crucial to traditional face-to-face problem solving are still needed when groups use GSS as tools. For example, anonymity is usually beneficial; however, members who never see each other may not come to identify with the group or each other like they can in face-to-face groups. Groups should combine both face-to-face and computer-mediated communication.[54] The most we can say definitively is that GSS is generally good for groups although not in every circumstance.[55]

After all proposals have been thoroughly evaluated, the group has set the stage for the emergence of a final decision on a solution or policy. A favored solution may already have begun to emerge during the discussion.

**4. Choosing the Best Solution.** Decision making or choosing options is an integral part of the overall process of problem solving. Just as groups experience identifiable phases in their development (see Chapter 5), they also go through decision-making phases. Several well-respected researchers have contributed to our understanding of group decision-making phases.[56] For example, Donald Ellis and B. Aubrey Fisher found that many groups first enter an *orientation* phase, proceed to a *conflict* phase when they argue about their various options, and finally enter the phases of *decision emergence* and

### Using Chat Rooms

MEDIA AND TECHNOLOGY

Groups can use computer tools as simple as e-mail to facilitate information exchange between members or as complex as specialized group meeting software programs. An important characteristic of some of these tools is anonymity. Group members can therefore feel free to share ideas without fear of reprisal or ridicule. Unfortunately, many e-mail systems make anonymity difficult, and specialized meeting software can be expensive.

One alternative is to create a chat room and have group members log on using anonymous nicknames. Aside from anonymity, an advantage of chat rooms is that they allow for synchronous communication. Many online services allow users to create free chat rooms that can be used for private discussions among friends or for anonymous group discussions.

To begin a discussion, have one group member (or your teacher) create a new group. As you will discover, many groups provide more resources than simply chat rooms, including the ability to create polls, share files, and create databases. You should create a public group so that other group members can easily find it. Let other group members know the name of the group and, if applicable, the category (e.g., School and Education—Classmates—Our Group) you placed the group in.

Resources like these provide an easy way to use computer technology for your group. Using online chat rooms is easy once you are familiar with their many features. Group members should familiarize themselves with the chat room or group interface before using this technology to facilitate a discussion.

*reinforcement.*[57] Decision emergence may begin during step 3, as members gradually move toward a consensus and coalesce around one proposal. The members will usually know when this has happened. Often a discussion leader can hasten this by asking something like, "I think we may have decided on a solution. Is that right?" If members agree aloud or nod their heads, having a straw vote or simply asking, "Does everyone agree?" or "Does anyone disagree?" can confirm this consensus.

*Reinforcement* refers to the complimenting and back patting that members give each other after a job well done. They will say things like, "That took a long time, but we really came up with a workable solution," "I really think we did a fine job with that," or "We done good, folks!" Such back patting expresses and reinforces the positive feelings members have toward each other.

Not all groups experience exactly the same phases during decision making. That would be too simplistic. Marshall Poole, for example, found that many factors influence the types of phases groups experience and the order in which they occur.[58] We present the idea of group phases to help you analyze what may be occurring in groups you belong to, yet remember that the subject is more complex than we have described here (see Chapter 5).

***Methods of Making Decisions.*** A group can make decisions in many different ways, but some methods are likely to produce worse results than others. In some groups the leader has authority to make decisions and may do so frequently for the group. One person may be perceived as the most expert member on the problem the group is discussing; that person may be asked to make the decision for the group. As a way of avoiding conflict, the group can use a method of chance, such as flipping a coin, drawing straws, or rolling dice. Sometimes numbers can be averaged to produce a decision, such as averaging individual applicant rankings to decide who should be offered a job. Often groups decide by voting, which is mandatory in committees governed by Robert's Rules for Committees.

Common ways of making group decisions are for the leader or another designated member to decide without consulting the group, for the group leader to consult with other members but then make the final decision, for members to vote, or for the group to make the decision by consensus. The first method, decision by leader or designated member, is appropriate for minor decisions, such as where to meet, what refreshments to serve, what color notepads to put in the meeting room, or even whom to ask to type the report. It is also appropriate for those decisions for which the leader (or designated member) has all the information needed to make the decision, and support from group members is expected. The second method, the consultative method, is appropriate when the leader does not have all the needed information, when the group members are likely to accept the decision, when members cannot agree but a decision *must* be made, or when time is short. The third method, voting, occurs when the majority decides for the group. This method merely weighs the power of numbers, not the relative merits of ideas. The majority may be wrong and a minority of one member may have the best idea. Further, voting may split a group, with some members resenting the decision and trying to sabotage it. Voting can be used to get a sense of where members stand on an issue or to confirm that a decision has been reached.

A **consensus** decision is one that all members agree is the best one they can make that is acceptable to all; it doesn't necessarily mean that the final choice is anyone's first choice! Do not confuse consensus decision making with a haphazard, coincidental convergence of member opinions. *Consensus* as we mean it here is about both a method of careful, open decision making and a product (or decision) that everyone supports but that may not be the top choice for one or more members.[59] It is a form of decision making preferred by individuals if they have the time and the resources it requires. Consensus decision making is pervasive across all kinds of groups. Consensus decision making, done well, builds community and support for the final decision.[60]

We noted earlier that once a solution has been tentatively adopted, it is a good idea to test that decision among the people who will be most affected. It is especially useful to identify any negative consequences that may occur to others but that the committee may have overlooked; this can include the impact on the group as well. Groups that make risky decisions like death penalty juries, emergency response teams, personnel committees, crisis management teams, and medical donor selection committees (to name a few) can experience anxiety over what they see as unavoidable consequences to their decisions.[61] Imagine being a part of a small

**GLOSSARY**

**Consensus**

*A decision all members agree is the best they can all support but isn't necessarily everyone's first choice*

**GLOSSARY**

**RISK Technique**
*A technique to help a group assess potential problems or risks with a potential solution*

emergency response team coming upon a horrific traffic accident. You may all decide whom to treat first and in what manner but at the same time realize that some victims may not make it. Fifty of the 60 Major League Baseball umpires discussed in a case in Chapter 7 seemed ready to leave their jobs in mass until they actually went to resign and 20 of them, highly anxious over the decision, rescinded their letters, thereby destroying the leverage the umpires believed they had over management. The RISK technique is a procedure groups can use to explicitly identify decision risks so they can be addressed and planned for.

***Testing a Tentative Solution with the RISK Technique.*** The **RISK technique** is designed to help an organization assess how a proposed change or new policy will negatively affect the individuals and groups most involved. Suppose you are responsible for implementing a new employee benefits program at your company. Before you start putting the plan into effect, you want to make sure all problems that could come up have been identified and, if possible, dealt with in advance. RISK will help you do this. The steps for a face-to-face RISK meeting are summarized in Figure 8.2. Like other group techniques, RISK can also be conducted electronically.

A group may have selected an alternative and discovered, with RISK or some other technique, that the solution is acceptable to all concerned. However, its job still isn't finished! Most groups are then responsible for seeing to it that the solution is implemented. Sometimes, that task is given to another group. Nevertheless, the problem-solving process is not complete until the solution has been put into effect.

**5. Implementing the Chosen Solution.** The final step in group problem solving is implementing the solution. Good leaders see that the group works out the details of implementation. During this stage of problem solving, the group answers questions such as the following:

- Who will do what, when, and how so that our decision is enacted?
- How will we write and present our report?
- How will we word our motion to the membership meeting, and who will speak in support of it?
- What follow-up should we conduct to monitor how well this solution is working?

**FIGURE 8.2** Steps for Conducting the RISK Technique in a Face-to-Face Meeting

Proposed solution presented in detail; members identify risks or problems with it. → Risks posted without evaluation on a chart in round-robin fashion. → Master list of risks compiled and circulated to participants. → Second meeting held to discuss the list; problems perceived as serious retained. → Retained problems processed into an agenda and handled as in the problem census.

Some implementation plans are simple, but others are complicated and detailed, especially if the solution involves many people and numerous assignments. Program evaluation and review technique (PERT) is a procedure designed to help group members track the implementation of a complex solution; however, it is useful for implementing simple solutions as well.

***Using PERT to Implement a Solution.*** **PERT** is a set of concrete suggestions to help a group keep track of who will do what by when (See figure 8.3). Some of you may be familiar with GANTT charts which are popular with program managers in a variety of different professions. It can be difficult to follow a complicated implementation plan that involves many people, groups, and tasks. PERT helps do this by asking those responsible for implementation to make a chart showing deadline dates for completion of various tasks and the names of individuals or groups responsible.

Following are the main parts of the process:

1. Determine the final step by describing how the solution should appear when it is fully implemented.
2. List all the events that must occur before the final goal is realized.
3. Order these steps chronologically.
4. For complicated solutions, develop a flow diagram of the procedure and all the steps in it.
5. Generate a list of all the activities, materials, and people needed to accomplish each step.
6. Estimate the time needed to accomplish each step; then add all the estimates to find the total time needed for implementation of the plan.
7. Compare the total time estimate with deadlines or expectations, and correct as necessary by assigning more or less time and people to complete a given step.
8. Determine which members will be responsible for each step.[62]

Another way to construct a PERT chart is to work backward from a target date. For example, students in an upper division small group class, acting as small group consultants, were charged with observing an on-campus group of their choice. They would eventually deliver a written report to their "client" group, showing them the strengths and weaknesses of their group dynamics. Their PERT chart worked backward from the date of their presentation, taking into account how long each major step of their process would take. By doing that, they had a clearer picture of when they'd have to start working on the project to get it completed without undue haste. We recommend PERT to our students whenever they have complex group assignments to complete.

Although groups rarely stick *exactly* to the P-MOPS (or to any problem-solving guidelines), if you attempt to follow this sequence in the form of an outline of questions written about the problem, you will help guarantee that no important question, issue, or step is overlooked, and thereby increasing your chances of creating a good solution. The flexibility of the procedure lets you tailor it to the characteristics of any problem. So that you can understand better how such adaptations are made, we next present examples of outlines written, adapted, and followed by problem-solving groups.

**GLOSSARY**

**PERT**

*Program evaluation and review technique that helps group members manage and keep track of a complex task*

**FIGURE 8.3 Sample PERT Chart for a Student Group Project**

| Date | Aretha | Barney | Candy | Denzil | Entire Group |
|---|---|---|---|---|---|
| Tues Apr. 4 | Report on prelim observ. | | Report on prelim observ. | | Decide group to observe; decide variables |
| Thu Apr. 6 | | Prelim report, conflict | Prelim report, leadership | Prelim report, roles | Discuss prelim reports; decide methods of analysis |
| Tues Apr. 11 | | Complete lib research, Conflict | Complete lib research, Leadership | Complete lib research, Roles | |
| Thu Apr. 13 | | Observe group, 8 PM | Observe group, 8 PM | Have observ materials ready: survey, SYMLOG | |
| Tues Apr. 18 | | Complete SYMLOG of group | Complete SYMLOG of group | | Meet after class, discuss preliminary findings |
| Thu Apr. 20 | | | Observe group, 8 PM | Observe group, 8 PM Have tape recorder ready | |
| Tues Apr. 25 | | | | | Discuss overall observations; listen to tape |
| Thu Apr 27 | | Complete first draft, Conflict | Complete first draft, Leadership | Complete first draft, Roles | |
| Mon May 1 | Begin overall editing and typing | Final draft, Conflict; Intro done | Final draft, Leadership; Conclusion done | Final draft, Roles | Look at each other's sections to improve style |
| Tues May 2 | ↓ | | | | |
| Wed May 3 | ↓ | | | | |
| Thu May 4 | ↓ | | | | |
| Fri May 5 | Editing and typing done | Tables and charts to Aretha (conflict) | Tables/Charts to Aretha (leadership) | Tables/Charts to Aretha (roles) | |
| Sat May 6 | Proof: make copies | | | Proof; make copies | |
| Sun May 7 | Distribute copies to all by 8 PM | Assemble full report by 5 PM | Assemble full report by 5 PM | Make large charts for class presentation | |
| Mon May 8 | | Read full paper | Read full paper | Read full paper | Rehearsal at Aretha's, 7 PM |
| Tues May 9 | | | | | Final presentation to their "client" group |

© robertsrob/Getty Images RF

## Applications of P-MOPS

Use the information about problem characteristics in Table 8.2 to help you determine how to modify the P-MOPS to suit your particular problem.

The first example of a procedural outline, shown in Table 8.6, was created by a self-appointed advisory committee of students concerned about pedestrian safety on a street just east of campus. The group of students first decided on the general problem they wanted to tackle, then created an outline to guide their investigation over a 6-week span. They devised possible solutions, decided on what to recommend, and finally presented their report to both the city council and the president of the university. You will notice that it closely follows P-MOPS. The students' work was tragically timely—shortly after their presentation, a student was killed crossing that very street.

The outline in Table 8.7 is much shorter and simpler; it is designed to be used for a brief class discussion.

**TABLE 8.6** **Sample Outline Using P-MOPS for a Complicated Problem**

**Discussion question: What shall we recommend that city council and university administration do to reduce pedestrian injuries on National Avenue east of campus?**

**I.** What is the nature of our problem involving vehicle-pedestrian accidents on National Avenue east of campus?

A. How do we understand our charge?

**1.** What freedom do we have in this matter?

**2.** What limits do we have (such as cost, structure of report, etc.)?

**3.** To what does the general problem question refer?

**B.** How do we feel about this problem?

**C.** What do we find unsatisfactory about the way traffic and pedestrians currently affect each other on National Avenue?

**1.** Diagram of present street, buildings, crossing, medians, lights, and so on.

**2.** How serious is the problem of injuries to pedestrians?

**a.** What kinds of accidents and injuries have occurred?

**b.** When do these accidents happen?

**c.** Do they tend to occur at any specific times?

**d.** What kinds of persons are involved?

**e.** How does this compare to accidents and injuries elsewhere?

**f.** Are there any other facts we need to learn?

**D.** What seems to be causing these accidents?

**1.** Characteristics of the location?

**2.** Human behavior?

**3.** Other factors?

**E.** What do we hope to see accomplished?

**1.** In reducing the number of accidents and injuries?

**2.** In practices of city council and administration?

**3.** Any other features of our goal?

**F.** What obstacles exist to prevent achieving our goal?

**1.** Financial?

**2.** Priorities of council or administration?

**3.** Vested interests, such as businesses?

**4.** Other?

**II.** What might be done to improve the safety of pedestrians crossing National Avenue east of campus?

**A.** Brainstorm for ideas.

**B.** Do we need explanations or descriptions of any of these proposed solutions?

**TABLE 8.6** ***Continued***

**III.** What are the relative merits of our possible solutions to accidents and injuries on National Avenue?
- **A.** What criteria shall we use to evaluate our list of possible solutions?
  - **1.** Costs?
  - **2.** Acceptability to involved persons?
  - **3.** Probable effectiveness in solving the problem?
  - **4.** Appearance?
  - **5.** Other?
- **B.** Shall we eliminate or combine any ideas?
- **C.** How well does each remaining potential solution measure up to our criteria and the facts of the problem?

**IV.** What recommendation can we all support?
- **A.** Has a decision emerged?
- **B.** What can we all support?

**V.** How shall we prepare and submit our proposal?
- **A.** In what form shall we communicate with council and administration?
- **B.** How will we prepare the recommendation?
  - **1.** Who will prepare the recommendation?
  - **2.** How will we edit and approve this report?
- **C.** How will we make the actual presentation?
- **D.** Do we want to arrange for any follow-up on responses to our recommended solution?

**TABLE 8.7** **Sample Outline Using P-MOPS for a Simple Classroom Discussion**

**I.** What sort of final exam would we like for Communication 315?
- **A.** What is our area of freedom concerning the exam?
- **B.** What facts and feelings should we consider as we discuss what sort of exam to request?

**II.** What are our criteria in deciding on the type of exam to recommend?
- **A.** Learning objectives?
- **B.** Grades?

*(continued)*

**TABLE 8.7** ***Continued***

C. Preparation and study required?

D. Fairness?

E. Other?

III. What types of exams are possible?

IV. What are the advantages and disadvantages of each type?

V. What will we recommend as the type of final exam?

## RESOURCES FOR REVIEW AND DISCUSSION

### SUMMARY

- Effective group problem solving uses guidelines to help members think critically rather than relying on their intuition, overrelying on expert authority, or overrelying on personal experience.
- A problem consists of a situation perceived to be unsatisfactory, a desired situation or goal, and obstacles to reaching that goal.
- Five characteristics of problems should be considered by members when they adapt their problem-solving procedures to fit the specific problem: task difficulty, solution multiplicity, intrinsic interest, member familiarity, and acceptance level.
- The functional theory of effective problem solving and decision making identifies important functions that must be fulfilled for a group to solve problems effectively. Members must do a thorough job of meeting the task requirements, use their communication skills to help the group overcome potential problems, be willing to review their process, and even reconsider their solution if necessary.
- The procedural model of problem solving (P-MOPS) provides a flexible sequence of steps, based on extensive research, for effective problem solving. These steps include thoroughly describing and analyzing the problem, listing a variety of solutions, carefully and critically evaluating their positive and negative elements, selecting the one that best meets the criteria, and planning how to implement the chosen solution.
- Several specific techniques can help at each step. For instance, focus groups can help identify key issues pertaining to the problem; group support systems can help, especially with evaluation; the RISK technique can identify problems with a proposed solution the group is seriously considering; and PERT helps a group follow its path while implementing its solution.
- Group decisions can be made by the leader, by voting, or by consensus.

## EXERCISES

1. Think of a current or recent problem you have encountered. Analyze your problem by identifying its component parts (present situation, obstacles, and goal). Pay particular attention to the obstacles you identify. Form into groups of four to six, and discuss each of the problems. Ask your team members to help you brainstorm ways of overcoming the obstacles you have identified.

2. As a class, choose two problems, one that is relatively simple and has few options and one that is relatively complex with high solution multiplicity (such as how the university should spend its contingency reserve money of $500,000). Write a leader's outline for structuring a discussion of each of these two issues by adapting P-MOPS to fit the discussion topic.

   After everyone has created an outline, select two leaders, one to guide each of the discussions using his or her outline. After the discussion, talk about what worked and what did not in the outline. How would you modify each outline to improve it?

3. View Part 3 ("An Ineffective Problem-Solving Discussion") of the videotape *Communicating Effectively in Small Groups* that was designed to accompany this text. This segment depicts a group doing a terrible job of problem solving. After viewing the tape, explain what you would do to correct the deficiencies. The following can guide your critique:

   *a.* Give specific examples of either poor or excellent problem-solving skills demonstrated by the group members.

   *b.* Examine the behavior of the leader, Alyce. What could she have done to improve the discussion process?

   *c.* Ask what specific behaviors helped the problem-solving process and what behaviors hurt it. Why did they have such an effect?

## KEY TERMS • CONCEPTS

Area of Freedom
Charge
Consensus
Criteria
Decision Making
Discussion Question
Focus Group
Functional Theory
Group Support Systems (GSS)
PERT
Problem
Problem Solving
Procedural Model of Problem Solving (P-MOPS)
RISK Technique
Team Reflexivity

CHAPTER 9

# Managing Small Group Conflict Productively

## CHAPTER OUTLINE



## CHAPTER OBJECTIVES

**After reading this chapter you should be able to:**

1. Define conflict.
2. Discuss the three prevailing myths about small group conflict.
3. Differentiate between task, relational, and process group conflict.
4. Explain how computer-mediated communication influences the three types of group conflict.
5. Compare and contrast the five major conflict styles.
6. Explain how group members can disagree ethically.
7. Discuss how members can maximize their chances to influence the group.
8. List and explain the steps of the nominal group technique.
9. Describe the four steps in principled negotiation, and explain how to use them to help manage a conflict.

## The Cask and Cleaver Work Crew

CASE 9.1

The Cask and Cleaver is a local restaurant in California's Central Valley. Its servers (usually students) meet semiannually to select their shifts. At these meetings eight or nine servers take turns, in round-robin fashion, picking a shift. The server with the most seniority picks first, and so on, until all shifts are covered. The servers want to choose shifts that make the most money in the least time so that they can survive financially and still have enough time to study and play. The stakes are higher for those with greater financial needs because they must live with the schedule for six months.

One meeting has become legendary as the most contentious in the restaurant's history. Mark, the senior server, took charge and chose first. At his fourth turn, he realized an earlier turn had been skipped and servers with less seniority had taken one more turn than he had. Mark suggested that they start over again. Some supported his idea, but Tom and Paul did not. They were pleased with their shifts after having lived with very poor schedules during the previous six months. After discussing it, the group decided to start over. During the second round it became apparent that the members were choosing differently; furthermore, the new schedule heavily favored Mark and Beth (Mark's wife), whereas Tom and Paul were not faring well at all. Opposition to starting over was voiced again with greater emphasis. Mark and Beth became defensive, arguing that it was not their fault Tom and Paul had two night classes. Tom and Paul perceived this reaction as callous and reminded Mark and Beth that they had no alternative class sections to choose from. Mark replied, "That's not my problem." Another server, Nathan, sided with Paul and Tom, forming a clique that characterized Mark and Beth as self-centered and unsympathetic to the financial needs of others. Mark, Beth, and another server, Maria, all believed that the others' school schedules were not their concern and that shift scheduling was a hit-or-miss process anyway: Sometimes you do well and sometimes you don't. To them, Tom and Paul were "crybabies" who wanted special treatment because they were university students. Tracey and Jeremy, two other servers, remained neutral, moving between the two cliques, listening to both sides, and conferring between themselves without ever sharing their views of the conflict.

**By now you should realize the benefits of small group decision making and problem solving. Yet these benefits do not just happen—they come after hard work, thoughtful modifications, and the knowledge that conflict will be a part of the process. Members have to work with their collective knowledge and skills, which will sometimes complement each other and sometimes clash. When group members do the work of vigilant problem solving and the critical thinking it requires, disagreement will occur. Conflict, expressed and managed well, can help members sharpen their thinking and decide wisely. In contrast, unexpressed disagreement contributes to groupthink (discussed in Chapters 5 and 7), harms group task and social processes, and can destroy a group. We discuss conflict in this chapter—its myths, the different types and styles you will encounter in your groups, the effects it can have on a group, and ways it can be managed well.**

## What Is Conflict?

Joyce Hocker and William Wilmot, two leading conflict scholars, define **conflict** as "an expressed struggle between at least two interdependent parties who perceive incompatible goals, scarce resources, and interference from the other party in achieving their goals."[1] Certainly group members, like Tracey and Jeremy in our opening case, experience conflict without saying a word.[2] Our interest is in expressed conflict and the central role of communication during conflict.

You have probably observed conflict expressed in a small group, such as when two or more people express different ideas, fight with each other over group procedures, or simply do not like each other. These kinds of primary and secondary tensions (see Chapter 5) in groups are common and have to be managed. In our opening case, the conflict began to surface initially over the way servers determined their shifts. Once the crew began to start over and other options emerged, the conflict over a group norm got very personal. Some conflicts will become heated and others will pass with little notice. If conflict is handled well, it can help improve a group's performance.

## Myths about Conflict

You have learned from previous chapters that group members often do not freely express their unique opinions about the task and tend toward early closure, eliminating any detailed discussion of the reasons behind different member preferences for certain options. Group members do this for all sorts of reasons, which range from general reasons associated with members' personalities and cultures to the specific demands of the situation, such as running out of time. Another reason pertains to the common myths about conflict members bring into the group. We would like to dispel three of the most familiar ones (summarized in Table 9.1).

1. **Conflict is harmful to a group and should be avoided.**

   This harm is evident in our Cask and Cleaver crew, with servers throwing all sorts of blame around and showing defensiveness because they believe they are being faulted maliciously. It is not uncommon for people to see conflict as harmful.

**GLOSSARY**

**Conflict**

*Occurs when discordant ideas or feelings are expressed or experienced between two interdependent parties*

**TABLE 9.1 Myths about Conflict and the Reality**

| Myth 1 | Myth 2 | Myth 3 |
|---|---|---|
| • Conflict is harmful and should be avoided. | • Conflict represents a misunderstanding or breakdown in communication. | • Conflicts can be resolved if parties are willing to discuss the issues. |
| **Reality** | **Reality** | **Reality** |
| • Conflict can help members understand an issue more clearly.<br>• Conflict can improve group decisions.<br>• Conflict can increase member involvement.<br>• Conflict can increase cohesiveness. | • Many conflicts occur over differences in values, goals, methods of achieving goals, and limited resources, not communication. | • Conflicts over basic values and goals may not be resolvable.<br>• Conflicts over limited resources and methods of achieving goals may be resolvable through communication if the basic values and goals of the parties are compatible. |

Shannon Kerwin and her colleagues found that members of nonprofit groups, in this case boards of sport organizations, were hesitant to call their contentious talk "conflict," preferring instead to label it a "disagreement."[3] However, conflict is beneficial to the group *if it is expressed and managed properly.*

Conflict can help members understand the issues surrounding a decision or problem more completely. When members disagree, they discover that there are perspectives other than their own. Karl Smith and colleagues found that when students in learning groups heard other opinions, they became uncertain about their own, sought out information about the different positions, and were better able to remember information about both their positions and those of others.[4] Expressed disagreement early in the problem-solving process and at the beginning of meetings can help facilitate learning about the issues.[5] There is a difference between sharing your preference for an option (e.g., I want a different shift) and sharing your reasons for the preference (e.g., I need a different shift because I cannot find a babysitter). In groups that agree early, members tend to share only their preferences whereas groups who express disagreement are more apt to go in to the reasons for their preferences.[6]

One of us served on an advisory board for a nonprofit organization. The administrative officer of the organization wanted to fire an employee immediately, without issuing a warning or giving the employee a chance to correct the offending behavior. One member, experienced with personnel laws, disagreed strongly. When the other members understood the legal and ethical problems with discharging employees before giving them a chance to improve their performance, they agreed to give the employee a clear set of guidelines and expectations to be followed. One group member's willingness to disagree enabled the others to understand the issue more completely.

Conflict also can improve a group's decision, which is a logical outcome of members understanding an issue more clearly. In the previous example, the dismissed employee could have sued the organization and the board for arbitrarily firing him. Clarifying his job duties and the board's expectations gave him the best possible chance to perform effectively. What if some board members initially agreed with the administrative officer? Hearing this agreement early probably would have led to members hearing a consensus and ending their discussion without talking about the reasons for their preferences. Why discuss more when we all agree? This group communication flaw can be avoided by sharing instead different reasons for member preferences.[7] Only after they had argued, over the course of several meetings, did they truly appreciate that giving the employee a chance to improve both was fair to him and protected them in case of legal challenge. Expressed conflict over the reasons for member preferences is a much more effective way to influence each other compared to simply agreeing to an option because it looks like it is an option most members prefer.[8]

Conflict also tends to increase member involvement and participation. In the previous advisory board example, members who had begun to skip meetings started to come regularly again. Usually, members become more interested when they believe their opinions can make a difference in the group's outcomes.

Finally, conflict can increase cohesiveness. Have you ever had an argument with your dating partner, spouse, or friend, then observed how close you both felt after you had talked through it? After the Cask and Cleaver crew eventually managed to deal with their issues constructively, lighthearted banter about this meeting being the "ugliest scheduling meeting of all time" followed, as well as the promise never to let such contention happen again. Both task success and interpersonal tolerance can combine to strengthen cohesiveness. During the advisory board's discussion about firing the employee, members expressed strong feelings on several sides of the issue, yet as consensus emerged, members became closer than ever. Several members expressed their appreciation to the member who initially spoke up against the firing. They believed that her comments forced the group to anticipate possible problems and to create a better solution, although at the time they did not see her disagreement as helpful. Consensus decision making, introduced in Chapter 8, is not superficial agreement on issues. It emerges out of members working through often difficult discussions of their values, which eventually converge in collective support of a solution.[9]

Appreciating that conflict itself is not the problem, but how it is handled helps shift members away from avoiding it altogether to focusing on how to best communicate about it as it emerges in group discussions.

2. **Conflicts stem only from misunderstandings and breakdowns in communication.**

Certainly, *some* conflicts occur due to misunderstandings and communication failures, but others do not. Often conflicts occur when individuals understand each other perfectly well but disagree on basic values or the distribution of rewards. For example, a classroom group trying to agree on whether to recommend the repeal of the *Roe v. Wade* court decision making abortions legal in the United States was unable to arrive at an answer acceptable to everyone. Several members believed that life begins at conception and that abortion is murder. Other members believed that a woman's life should take precedence over the fetus, at least until the fetus reaches a certain stage of development. Each subgroup fully understood the position of the other subgroup. Misunderstanding and communication breakdown did not occur. However, the subgroups' differing values and assumptions made agreement seem impossible.

Managing conflict well entails figuring out *why* the conflict is occurring; assuming that all conflicts occur because communication is the problem is dangerous.[10] When we do this, we trivialize communication by turning it into a cure-all and come to believe that more communication will solve the problem. Too often, increasing communication may do little to help and may even make a situation worse.

3. **All conflicts can be resolved if parties are willing to discuss the issues.**

Conflicts vary in their degree of perceived resolvability, which depends on the underlying reason for the conflict. Conflict over basic *values* is highly subjective. The abortion question is not resolvable at the present time because the two assumptions represented—(1) a fetus is a person from conception and has rights equal to those of the mother, versus (2) a fetus becomes a person sometime after conception, until which time the woman's rights take precedence—are not reconcilable. Conflicts over perceived *scarce resources* are also difficult to resolve. If a university has limited funds to disperse to a variety of student groups then discussion of how best to distribute those funds can be filled with acrimony. Members may very well agree that other groups deserve funding, but if it is at the expense of their own group, discussion could get difficult. Conflicts over *goals* can sometimes be difficult to resolve as well. Assume that you want an A on your group project while someone else is satisfied with a C. If you can't convince the other person of the value of striving for excellence, and the other person can't persuade you to lighten up, you are at an impasse.

Simply discussing the issues does not automatically guarantee a satisfactory outcome. Our Cask and Cleaver crew initially thought they were at an impasse, yet with patience and careful analysis they figured out how to best manage their issues. The interdependence of the group system guarantees that conflict will emerge because it is key to effective mutual influence during discussion of issues. We prefer to talk about managing conflict than resolving it, recognizing that conflict is fluid in groups and rarely goes away. The real issue then is *how* members communicate about the conflict in their groups. Before we discuss explicitly how to manage conflict in groups, let's take a closer look at the different types of conflict you may find in your groups. Identifying the cause of the conflict is important to talking about it effectively.

GLOSSARY

**Task Conflict**

*Conflict resulting from disagreements over ideas, information, reasoning, or evidence*

**Relational Conflict**

*Conflict resulting from personality clashes, likes, dislikes, and competition for power*

## Types of Conflict

Group conflict will often start out as one thing and then branch off into other types of conflict. The Cask and Cleaver crew had previously established a group norm for fair distribution of resources—shift times. Mark, however, used his seniority (another resource) to pressure other members to redo the shift selection procedure thus altering the group norm. Some members did not see a problem with the schedules, but others did. Coalitions formed, blame was tossed around, and others just kept quiet. Most obviously, the underlying resources at issue for the servers were money, time, and power. Conflict over an established procedure moved quickly into more interpersonal ones. Interestingly, these procedural and interpersonal conflicts are the two most common workplace conflicts encountered by college students in their early workplace experiences.[11] In addition, college students report that it is common for procedural conflicts, such as how to decide shift schedules, to turn into interpersonal conflict.

Conflict in and of itself is neither automatically helpful nor harmful to a group. What *does* matter is what the conflict is about, how it is initiated, and how it is managed. Learning the nuances of the types of conflict in groups can help with their identification and addressing how you might approach dealing with them. The three most common types are task, relational, and process conflict. All three are readily recognized by group members.[12]

### TASK CONFLICT

**Task conflict** is commonly known as *substantive* or *intrinsic* heard most often when members clash over ideas, meanings, issues, or other matters relevant to its task.[13] Secondary tension, introduced in Chapter 5, is the discomfort members feel when in task conflict, the *what* of group conflict. This work-related conflict is the basis for effective problem solving and decision making. Managed well, task conflict allows group members to challenge and evaluate ideas, proposals, evidence, and reasoning. Doubts are brought out into the open. It is not unusual for group members themselves to report that task conflict is necessary for good decisions to emerge.[14]

### RELATIONAL CONFLICT

**Relational conflict** is also known as *affective* or *extrinsic* conflict. It originates from interpersonal power clashes or likes and dislikes unrelated to the group's task.[15] It represents the *who* in the conflict and is associated with the tertiary tension discussed in Chapter 5. This type of conflict is usually detrimental to the group and as you will recall from Chapter 6, it is often found to be one of the key factors in whether a group can effectively manage its perceived diversity.[16] Much of the Cask and Cleaver server conflict involves power struggles between them—who gets to decide the rules and change them. Clashes emerge over such factors as personalities, learning styles, priorities, openness to experience, or perspectives due to age and culture. Mahmut Bayazit and Elizabeth Mannix found that relational conflict, not task conflict, was the main reason team members gave for wanting to leave the team.[17] Relational conflict is associated with stress, dissatisfaction, frustration, and burn out.[18]

Our observations of numerous groups suggest that much relational conflict is rooted in acts of superiority that are rejected by other members. Most of this "I am better, more important, more knowledgeable" signaling is nonverbal, projected by subtle patterns of vocal tones, postures, and head/body angles. Group members are quite capable of telling the difference between task (depersonalized) and relational (personalized) conflict and recognizing that personal conflict harms consensus building.[19] Members who destructively get in the way of group processes, compared to those who constructively voice different ideas, are perceived less favorably by others, seen as harming cohesion, and tend to have their influence blocked.[20]

GLOSSARY

**Process Conflict**

*Conflict over how to do something and members' contributions to the group*

## PROCESS CONFLICT

**Process conflict,** otherwise known as *procedural* conflict, is now described as involving both task and relationship dimensions.[21] When the conflict is about the *how* of group work or how to accomplish work goals, then you have conflict over logistics; or a more task-oriented conflict. Members may clash over how to make their decisions, how best to spend their time, how to distribute their work, how best to run meetings, and so on. The Cask and Cleaver crew conflict began over a procedure decided in previous months. Members who disagree over procedures and use ineffective behaviors to manage this conflict will find themselves triggering a nasty relational conflict, as the Cask and Cleaver crew found out.

The second dimension of process conflict is the *how much* of group work because it involves *coordination* of member responsibilities and workloads.[22] This type of process conflict is more relationally oriented because it involves issues of fairness or equity between members. Inequity reduces satisfaction with the group and is associated with high levels of conflict.[23] This is why equitable distribution of speaking turns is so important to effective decision making.[24] Returning to our case, Mark set off a firestorm by using his seniority to force reconsideration of a procedure already judged fair by the others. Coalitions formed between members to counter Mark's behavior. Coalitions often form in groups between members with few resources and minimal power in their attempt to level the playing field and often disappear when the balance returns. The Cask and Cleaver crew threw themselves into disarray when they altered an accepted norm of fairness, which they in turn had to manage to prevent servers from quitting or working conditions from deteriorating.

Although we talked about these three types separately, they are all interrelated and often blend into one another.[25] In our case, Mark's reconsideration of their procedure (process conflict) was really not the issue—it was *how* he went about reconsidering the it (relational conflict). Process conflict with its task and relational dimensions can hide either type of conflict. Members do genuinely disagree over procedures; however, sometimes they can use procedural conflict to avoid another task conflict by forcing a vote.[26] The reality of group conflict is that task and process conflicts can easily become personal especially if members perceive they are being treated unfairly or members are not coping well with the type of conflict facing them.[27] Members more readily accept their task conflict if it does not turn personal.[28] This relational conflict then derails the task and process conflict. Interestingly the group itself can show a collective coping strategy to their conflict and if properly matched to the types of conflict can not only reduce relational conflict, but also prevent the task conflict from moving into a relational conflict.[29] Task conflict needs a focus on the problem at hand rather than the feelings of the members and relational conflict calls for a focus on emotions. Coping with task conflict with a problem focus helps group separate their task issues from their relational ones.

## Conflict Types and Computer-Mediated Communication (CMC)

Small groups often use a blend of face-to-face and computer-mediated communication (CMC). Group members can use computers to talk to each other online, and some may use group support systems (GSS) to help them during their problem-solving discussions. Early research comparing conflict in CMC with face-to-face (FtF) groups produced inconsistent results.[30] For example, CMC groups engaged in more inflammatory, profane, and negative communication than FtF groups. However, groups that used GSS, like the ones discussed in Chapter 8, exhibited less substantive and affective conflict if members used the methods as they were meant to be used. Thus, we might conclude that if groups using CMC gave members time to get to know each other (a common recommendation when using CMC) and adapted GSS appropriately, then computer use could lessen the potential damaging effects of conflict.

In a rare study comparing type of conflict in CMC and FtF groups, differences were found.[31] While both kinds of groups do experience similar amounts of task conflict, the CMC groups showed more relational and task conflict early on over their procedures. These groups have fewer social norms initially, given their anonymity, to support positive self-images and issues of how to use their technology gave rise to early task conflict. Over time though this conflict lessened especially as members became familiar with how to use their technology.[32]

Although CMC groups do not follow the same pattern of conflict types as FtF groups, they do go on to reach comparable levels. If you use any type of CMC for informal or formal group interaction, make sure you give yourselves time for social development. Groups whose members primarily connect using computers should consider times for meeting face-to-face, especially early on, to give themselves the opportunity to create social and procedural norms acceptable to their group.[33]

CMC groups initially show an interrelationship between procedural-based task conflict and relational conflict—struggles with technology get tied into interpersonal struggles—whereas FtF groups show a blending of procedural with broader task conflicts.[34] Learning about these different conflict types and how they are manifested in groups is essential to understanding how conflict can help or hinder a group.[35] Groups as we pointed out have been shown to be rather adept at creating ways to help manage task conflict and steer clear of negative emotions.[36]

## Managing Group Conflict

We hope we have convinced you of the value of constructive task conflict during small group problem solving. Trying to squelch conflict does not eliminate it—it just sends it underground. If managed inappropriately, conflict can hurt the group and its members and, we would argue, is unethical. All the ethical principles of the National Communication Association's Credo for Ethical Communication (see Chapter 1) remind us that conflict mishandled destroys respect and trust, shuts down honest and open communication, and can be degrading, coercive, and irresponsible. In this section we discuss how to manage conflict productively and ethically.

## CONFLICT MANAGEMENT STYLES

There are many different ways of describing how people manage conflict. Common models describe from two to five styles. We have chosen a typical five-style conflict management model because we believe that it better captures subtle nuances among the styles that can be lost in other, popular three-style models.[37] The five styles we discuss here were described by Kenneth Thomas.[38] Whatever style an individual chooses is based on the answers to two questions: (1) How important is it to satisfy your own needs? and (2) How important is it to satisfy the other person's needs? Figure 9.1 shows how these two needs intersect to produce the five common conflict management styles of avoidance, accommodation, competition, collaboration, and compromise. Table 9.2 gives examples of statements illustrating each style. *No one conflict style is best to use in all circumstances.* Factors to consider include how important the issue is, how serious the consequences will be if the group makes a mistake, whether

**FIGURE 9.1 Conflict Management Styles**

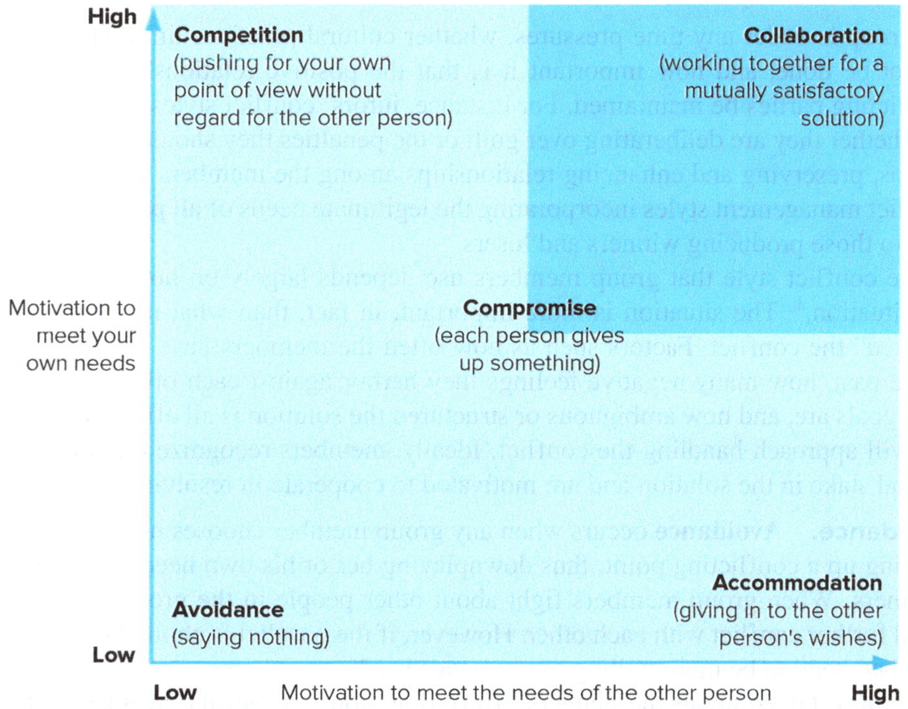


SOURCE: Adapted from K. Thomas, "Conflict and Conflict Management," *Handbook of Industrial and Organizational Psychology*, ed. by Marvin D. Dunnette (Chicago: Rand McNally, 1976).

TABLE 9.2 **Statements That Illustrate the Five Conflict Management Styles**

Mary, the college chief financial officer, wants the snack shop to close at 5 P.M. Roger, the evening student counselor, wants it to stay open until 8 P.M. Following are examples of how Roger might respond to Mary, using each of the conflict management styles discussed in the chapter:

**Mary:** We'll have to close the snack shop at 5. There isn't any money to keep it open later.

| Avoidance | Accommodation | Competition | Compromise | Collaboration |
|---|---|---|---|---|
| **Roger:** [Says nothing; accepts Mary's statement, even though he disagrees.] | **Roger:** I'd really like to keep it open, but, if there's no money, I guess there's nothing else we can do. | **Roger:** I won't accept that! We can't let the evening students down that way. Cut something else to get the money! | **Roger:** I would accept keeping it open just until 6:30 if you could cut some money from another program. | **Roger:** I understand that it's necessary to contain costs. It's also important to serve evening students. Is there some way we can provide them food service without increasing costs? |

This was an actual problem faced by a student services committee. The solution? Provide vending machine service. This maintained constant labor costs but gave students food service after 5 P.M.

the group is under any time pressures, whether cultural practices limit what can and cannot be done, and how important it is that the positive relationship between the conflicting parties be maintained. For instance, jurors' conflict styles shift depending on whether they are deliberating over guilt or the penalties they should give.[39] In most groups, preserving and enhancing relationships among the members is important. So conflict management styles incorporating the legitimate needs of all parties are preferable to those producing winners and losers.

The conflict style that group members use depends largely on how they perceive the situation.[40] The situation is more important, in fact, than what members believe "started" the conflict. Factors such as how often the members have been in conflict in the past, how many negative feelings they harbor against each other, how mutual their goals are, and how ambiguous or structured the solution is all affect how a member will approach handling the conflict. Ideally, members recognize that they have a mutual stake in the solution and are motivated to cooperate in resolving the conflict.

**Avoidance.** **Avoidance** occurs when any group member chooses not to disagree or to bring up a conflicting point, thus downplaying her or his own needs and the needs of others. When group members fight about other people in the group, they tend to avoid further conflict with each other. However, if the conflict is about the task, group members tend to be more willing to work together.[41]

We have talked about the dangers of avoiding conflict, but the avoidance style is sometimes appropriate. If the issue is not very important, and you are certain that the

**GLOSSARY**

**Avoidance**
*Conflict style describing a person's unwillingness to confront or engage in conflict*

group's decision will not be hurt by your failure to speak up, avoiding a possible conflict is appropriate. One of us served on a committee planning an awards banquet. The rest of the members favored a different restaurant from the one your author preferred. Both restaurants were comparable in price, service, and atmosphere. This was not an important enough issue to argue about, because there was no risk of making a serious mistake. In Mary and Roger's case (Table 9.2) Roger could certainly avoid challenging Mary's stand on the snack shop; after all what serious mistake could ensue to the student services committee if the shop closes? However, no other options had been presented and avoidance could close down the discussion, thus preventing other voices to emerge.

**Accommodation.** **Accommodation** (also called *appeasement* or *giving in*) occurs when one person or faction gives in to the other without arguing strongly for a different point of view. In our student services example, Roger does speak up, reinforcing Mary's point that there is no money and, although he wishes the snack shop would remain open, concedes to Mary. This style is similar to avoidance in that a person downplays her or his own needs, but it differs in that the person works harder to meet the needs of others. You should be honest with yourself if you choose to accommodate. Don't give in if the issue really is important to you. The question Roger would have to ask himself, as a voice for students, is how important food service is to students after 5 P.M. We realize this could be hard for those group members who fear talking in front of others.[42] However, if you give in but privately resent it, in the future you are likely to find yourself arguing with the other person for no apparent reason. On the other hand, if the issue is not crucial to you but you know it is important to the other person, then accommodation is appropriate.

**Competition.** **Competition,** sometimes called the *win-lose style,* occurs when you fight hard to win and you don't care whether the other person is satisfied with the solution. Most of the time, highly competitive ways of handling conflict are harmful to a group. If one person tries to impose his or her will on a group, the other members will probably fight back. Competitive tactics often escalate a conflict, especially when people stop listening to understand each other. For example, at an advisory board meeting, one member, Sherman, argued strongly for one solution to a particular problem. Two members disagreed with Sherman, who then began to use a variety of tactics to win the argument, starting with persuasion but moving quickly to attempted coercion and intimidation. The group retaliated and voted against his suggestion.

When a group is doing something you believe is harmful or wrong or goes against your values and beliefs, then competition is appropriate. Don't accommodate or avoid conflict if you think your basic values are being compromised or if you think the group is about to make a major mistake. Roger's competitive response to Mary shows he obviously is against closing down the snack shop, yet look at how he presents this position to Mary—if he had said this to you, how would you feel? Compare this competitive response to the member opposed to firing the employee, described earlier in this chapter. She was willing to face the group's disapproval because she genuinely believed they were about to make a big mistake, and she was not willing to compromise. Remember, though, that a conflict where one person wins but others feel like a

**GLOSSARY**

**Accommodation**

*Conflict style describing a person's willingness to engage in conflict; however, she or he backs away from the conflict by giving in to appease the other party*

**Competition**

*Conflict style showing a preference for coming out ahead in the conflict at the expense of the other party*

© John Lund/Blend Images RF

decision has been forced down their throats will almost certainly erode a group's cohesion or members' affinity toward one other.

**Collaboration.** **Collaboration,** the win-win style of conflict management, occurs when the people in the conflict want to meet opposing parties' needs along with their own. Like competition, collaboration assumes individuals may argue strongly for their points of view. Unlike competitors, collaborators take care not to attack each other as people or to say or do anything that will harm the relationship. They behave ethically by treating each other as peers. They invest a great deal of energy in searching for a solution that will satisfy everyone. Group members whose communication is collaborative are more satisfied with their group outcomes than members who avoid conflict.[43]

Collaboration can reveal options that other styles miss. For example, the student services committee that served as the model for Table 9.2 initially struggled with two apparently competing goals—making sure that evening students had food available and making sure overhead costs stayed the same. During the discussion, characterized by genuine attempts to help both Mary and Roger achieve their goals, another member suggested the creative option of expanding vending services. This would meet student needs while costing the college nothing, since the vending company would pay for machine costs. But if the committee had voted without discussing the issues, or if either Mary or Roger had kept quiet, this option would never have surfaced.

Collaborative solutions to conflict often take time and energy so groups have to judge whether some decisions are worth the time and energy. If they are then groups should strive for collaboration.

**GLOSSARY**

**Collaboration**
*Conflict style showing a preference for working with the other to find a solution that pleases both parties*

**Compromise.** **Compromise** represents a middle-ground conflict management style that can be called a *partial-win/partial-lose solution* for each party. Unlike collaboration, parties using compromise give up something to get something in return. This type of horse-trading is typical of labor-management and government bargaining: "I'll settle for a $1-per-hour raise if you give up the demand for mandatory overtime," or "I'll vote for your bill if you support my amendment." If you know you are going to have to compromise, you will be tempted to inflate your original demands. For instance, if you know you will have to settle for less money than you want, you'll ask at first for a higher figure than you really need.

When collaboration is impossible due to time pressures or differences in values, compromise may represent the best option available. With compromise each party does not completely receive what it wanted to begin with. However, if what each party had to give up seems balanced and the solution appears *fair* to all sides, then compromise can work quite well. *We cannot emphasize too strongly the importance of fairness.* Had Mary accepted Roger's compromise offer, the student services committee would have to ask whether the compromise would be fair to the area that would lose money. A compromise can work only if all parties feel the solution is fair, and that no one has *won.* But parties cannot assume they know what "fair" means. Instead, both parties should explain honestly what they believe is fair, and these individual conceptions of fairness should be included as absolute criteria by which to evaluate the final decision.

**GLOSSARY**

**Compromise**
*Conflict style showing a preference for giving a little and gaining a little to manage the issue*

**Working with Conflict Management Styles.** There are appropriate times and situations to use each of the conflict management styles described here. However, approaches that are *integrative*—in other words, that focus on helping participants integrate their goals and needs—generally lead to better group decisions for complex tasks. Tim Kuhn and Marshall Scott Poole looked at naturally occurring groups in two major U.S. organizations.[44] Integrative conflict styles—collaboration and sometimes compromise—were more effective than avoidance and confrontational styles.

Their observations of these groups also revealed important insight into how they were able to productively manage their conflict styles. Members worked to establish stable roles, relationships, and norms for accomplishing their tasks. They formulated norms for handling conflict early in their development and generally didn't change their patterns much. The lesson here is to pay attention to your group's emerging norms for handling conflict and to discuss them if you believe they could be counterproductive to good problem solving.

In an insightful study of the process of consensus in a naturally occurring group, Mary Ann Renz showed how groups that value consensus develop norms that allow them to deal with the push and pull between their efforts to be open with each other and the demands to finish the task.[45] This kind of tension can produce frustration and conflict in consensus decision-making groups. Building consensus over time involves making lots of little decisions and requires that groups maintain a willingness to review their process and make adaptations. So what happens when a previous proposal has been accepted but someone now wants to challenge it? Renz discovered that one particular group used C. T. Butler and Amy Rothstein's 1991 book *On Conflict and Consensus,* which they called their "little white book," as a procedural guide to help them decide what they should do if someone was blocking consensus on a proposal. This worked for them because they had all decided on the validity of the little white book and agreed to follow its recommendations; the guidelines had already been determined to be fair. This is one example of how a group effectively developed its own norms for managing conflict—in this case procedural conflict—fairly.

Your group norms are a way of productively managing different conflict styles in your group. This discussion reveals an important insight into how groups judge which style is best for its dynamics. Each one can be evaluated not only in terms of its effectiveness but also in term of its appropriateness.[46] Effectiveness is judged by the person engaging in the action, and appropriateness is judged by the other members in accordance with social norms. For instance, more collaborative styles are seen as both effective and appropriate, whereas competition can be effective in reaching your goals but probably will not be seen as appropriate by others. In our Cask and Cleaver server group, Mark probably thought he was being effective in pursuing his interests, but others certainly did not see his behavior as appropriate. Often we fail to see that what is happening in our group conflicts is a clash between effectiveness and appropriateness.[47]

Conflict management styles are based on cultural norms and expectations like the ones we talked about in Chapter 6. The advice we give you here, particularly about openly expressing your disagreement, is consistent with norms for the individualistic cultures of the United States and Western Europe. An analysis of conflict management studies has questioned the view that it is always better to express conflict directly.[48] In Asian cultures, which tend to be collectivist, preserving harmony, and helping others save face are paramount in group work. A more direct, competitive behavior may be effective in getting something done in a group but would not be seen as appropriate by those who are more collectivist or interdependent with others. Open disagreement is considered rude, in part because it can damage relationships. Avoidance, accommodation, and indirect expression of disagreement are considered appropriate responses.

Although more collectivist cultures such as Japan may prefer collaborative styles that value harmony and preserving the self-esteem of others, they may change the style depending on whom the conflict involves and what it concerns. In conflicts over values and opinions, Japanese tend to avoid conflict with acquaintances more than with close friends; they are more collaborative with close friends.[49] They can act collectivist and interdependent with members of their in-groups but can turn very competitive toward members of out-groups; thus, their intergroup communication is not the same as their intragroup communication.[50]

Each style is appropriate under certain circumstances, but having a more collaborative style is preferred in most problem-solving discussions. You may have found yourself in temporary task groups like the ones found in many small group courses. You usually have not met your group members before, do not plan on seeing them after the class is finished, and have only a short amount of time—at least it certainly feels like it—to finish your task. In temporary, highly task-focused groups, members generally perceive collaborative styles as more competent and avoidance styles as incompetent.[51] However, time may leave little room for collaborative styles. Confrontational, competitive styles may be effective for finishing the task under the gun, yet other members do not perceive them as appropriate. It is not enough to simply understand that your differences

## When Relational Conflict Gets in the Way

ETHICAL DILEMMA

We often assign our student groups to observe and gather information about other real-life groups. One of our groups observed another group of students working on a project for a marketing class. This group of six included two men and four women, one of whom was lesbian. When other group members talked about their girlfriends and boyfriends, Robin talked about her wife as well. Charlotte, one of the women, snickered and smirked whenever Robin shared personal information—though this behavior was expected and accepted for the other students in this group. Our observing group couldn't help noticing Charlotte's disdain for Robin and became really upset when Charlotte's antagonism toward Robin escalated. Charlotte made fun of Robin and her wife when Robin wasn't there. She labeled Robin's ideas for the project "stupid" even though, according to the observing group, Robin had the most creative ideas for the marketing project and was able to back up her suggestions with factual information. In addition, Charlotte forgot to tell Robin about a meeting the group had scheduled. In one particularly hostile instance, the marketing group had planned to meet in one room but decided to change rooms after they got there. Robin had told them she would be a little late because she was coming from work. After the group changed rooms, Charlotte e-mailed Robin about the change but did not tell Robin where they had moved. Robin eventually found the right room, after wandering all over the building searching for her team. Instead of apologizing, Charlotte yelled at her for being later than she had said. Through all this, Robin remained polite, engaged, and friendly. The observing students were horrified! They felt bad for Robin, couldn't believe how badly Charlotte treated her, and also were distressed that no one in the group called Charlotte on her hostile behavior or came to Robin's defense. We have discussed in several places how conflict over the task and procedures can turn into relational conflict rather easily. In this case, we see a situation where, from the start, a relational conflict consistently interfered with the effective management of group task work.

1. Although we did not address sexual orientation in the diversity chapter, it is an individual difference that can elicit strong feelings. Charlotte obviously felt strongly opposed to working with someone of Robin's sexual orientation. What do you think Charlotte should have done, knowing that she felt so strongly?
2. This situation was a no-win one for Robin. If she kept silent about the mistreatment, she seemed to be condoning it. But if she said something, she would have put herself in a vulnerable position—her grade depended on the team's work. What do you think Robin should have done about being bullied?

*(continued)*

***Concluded***

ETHICAL DILEMMA

3. The other members of the marketing group stood by and watched Charlotte bully Robin. What options did they have? What would you have done if you had been a member of this group?
4. The observing group was a guest, in a way. They had permission to observe, but were not expected to interfere in the marketing group's interactions. What choices did they have? What would you have done if you had been on the observation team?

are clashing into task or relational conflict.[52] You have to consider, as well, how you are dealing with your differences. Are you avoiding or competing over them to uphold one or more member preferences? Or are you collaborating and openly talking through those differences? How you engage in your conflict has been shown to have more of an impact on your group's outcome and your desire to work together than simply the type of conflict you are in. Remain aware of how you are using your collaborative, collective efforts to leverage against any member views of difference (e.g., "we are just too different" or "we have too many differences on this point") that stand in the way with dealing with both task and relational conflict. Keep this in mind as we discuss more specifically how to ethically express disagreement.

## EXPRESSING DISAGREEMENT ETHICALLY

When you express disagreement, the *how* is just as important as the *what.* This distinction is significant; no matter how valid your disagreement is, if you express it in a tactless or arrogant way, you hurt your chance of benefiting the group. A legitimate concern (the *what*) can be expressed so insensitively (the *how*) that even a rational group member becomes defensive rather than receptive to what you have to say. The following suggestions, summarized in Table 9.3, will help you disagree without damaging relationships with other group members.

1. **Express your disagreement.**

   A disagreement has no chance of helping a group if it is not expressed. An unexpressed disagreement does not disappear—it goes underground, to resurface in inappropriate ways. Avoiding a conflict is only a temporary "solution." Issues can pile up so that eventually a large blowup occurs when each issue could have been handled individually. Groups with a variety of approaches to gathering and processing information can work through their disagreement if they willingly talk through their disagreement.[53]

2. **Express your disagreement in a timely way.**

   Research demonstrates that *when* you disagree is an important consideration.[54] When group members approach a deadline or have already decided on a proposal, they are less tolerant of a member who introduces a dissenting opinion or wants to reconsider a previous decision because this threatens closure.[55] Members can respond rather emotionally to a late disagreement. Another idea is to

**TABLE 9.3 How to Disagree Productively**

**EXPRESS YOUR DISAGREEMENT**

1. Remember that failure to express doubts and disagreements deprives the group of potentially valuable information and reasoning.

**EXPRESS DISAGREEMENT IN A TIMELY WAY**

1. Don't wait until the deadline is near to speak.

**EXPRESS DISAGREEMENTS WITH SENSITIVITY TOWARD OTHERS**

1. Disagree with the idea, but do not criticize the person.
2. Use neutral, not emotionally charged, language.
3. Be respectful of different face needs of members.

**REACT TO DISAGREEMENT WITH A SPIRIT OF INQUIRY, NOT DEFENSIVENESS**

1. Ask for criticism of your ideas and opinions.
2. Show you are interested in the other's opinion by listening actively and sincerely.
3. Clarify misunderstandings that may have occurred.

hold smaller informal meetings specifically to talk about proposals, which encourages more reticent members to voice their concerns. Some groups also use "second-chance" meetings to try to avoid late disagreement.

3. **Express your disagreements with rhetorical sensitivity toward the rest of the group.** Disagree with the idea, or parts of the idea, without criticizing the person. Suppose you have just suggested that your campus shut down its snack bar at 5 P.M. to cut costs. Which response would you rather hear: "That's stupid! What are the evening students supposed to do, starve?" or "One problem I see is that your suggestion does not consider evening students' needs for food service"? The first response implies that the speaker is stupid, arouses defensiveness, and cuts off further examination of the issue. The second response describes a major problem with the suggestion and leaves room for discussion regarding how to cut food service costs. The second response is more collaborative, considering the group as a whole, while the first attacks a person to the detriment of the person and the group.

   Another way to show your sensitivity is to use neutral instead of emotionally charged language. Name-calling or otherwise pushing people's emotional buttons is never helpful. One of us recently attended a meeting where one member, John, who disagreed with another member, Janos, made a snide play on words using Janos's last name. Naturally, Janos was offended, and the atmosphere remained tense until John apologized. Disagreeing by making fun of others does not improve the group's decision-making process. Review Chapter 4's lessons on the powerful ways our language creates the climate and tone of group interaction.

The material on managing tensions in your group in Chapter 5 and on working with diversity in Chapter 6 offers additional suggestions for being rhetorically sensitive to others. Recall that the central feature of working with diversity is human respect and the belief that fairness applies to everyone.[56] We all, no matter what our cultural backgrounds, have face needs, but we achieve them differently. Stella Ting-Toomey suggests that more of us need to "give face" more often to others.[57] This suggestion addresses again the importance of considering how your group is working through its conflict. How you deal with your differences influences your outcomes and how you view your differences (collaborative or competitive) impacts whether you see your group efforts as worth it or not.[58]

4. **React to disagreement with a spirit of inquiry, not defensiveness.**

Whether you are the group's leader or just a member, every group member contributes to the climate of the group through their behaviors. When someone disagrees with you, if you show that you are interested in what the other member is saying and in his or her reasons for disagreeing, you send the right message to the rest of the group. Even if the disagreement was expressed poorly, you do not have to let someone else's insensitivity control your reaction. Group members' reactions to argument are more important than the arguments themselves in creating group divisiveness over issues.[59] Listen actively (Chapter 3) to the person who disagrees, make sure that person has understood your position accurately, clarify any misunderstandings that may have occurred, and show that you are willing to work together to find the best possible solution.

For example, Kareema's committee had worked for several months on a proposal to change the criteria for promotion in her department. A new member, appointed to the committee to replace someone who had left the department, questioned the committee's preliminary investigation, saying, "I don't see how that's going to work. Seems to me you'll have more problems than you had before." Although Kareema *felt* defensive, she reacted calmly and asked, "Derek, what problems do you see with the proposal?" Derek explained his concerns, several of which uncovered problems Kareema's committee had overlooked. The committee's revised proposal accommodated Derek's concerns. The final proposal was much stronger and was overwhelmingly approved by the rest of the department.

## MAXIMIZING YOUR CHANCES TO INFLUENCE THE GROUP

Expressing your disagreement is the only way to make your ideas and reasoning available to the group. Even so, it is often difficult for people who are perceived as group deviants, even beneficial idea deviants, to influence the other members of the group. Whether you stand alone as an idea deviant or belong to a minority subgroup, the following suggestions will help you maximize your influence when you express your disagreement.

1. **Make sure your arguments are of high quality.**

   This is the single most important thing that you can do. Rick Garlick and Paul Mongeau found that, although several factors—including the idea deviant's expertise, attractiveness, and job status—affect that person's status within the group, only the quality of the deviant's argument directly influences the other members' attitude change.[60] That means you must think the problem through carefully and be willing to listen to the objections others may have.

2. **Make sure your arguments are consistent.**

   Lisa Gebhart and Renee Meyers found that subgroups expressing minority opinions are more successful if they generally stick to a consistent message.[61] This is especially important during the latter part of a discussion. These authors recommend, however, that a minority subgroup not be so consistent that it appears rigid and unable to understand others' views.

3. **If you are a member of a subgroup, make sure all the subgroup members publicly agree with each other.**

   Subgroups, or coalitions, are a powerful way group members have of influencing each other in conflict.[62] They occur for a variety of reasons as we saw earlier in our Cask and Cleaver case. Some form around popular members, some because members are not sure who has the power and who does not. Often, group members form coalitions because they lack resources or power and hope to increase their influence—"power in numbers." However, coalitions containing members who disagree with each other are less influential than coalitions presenting a united front.[63] The subgroup members should meet privately and hash out any disagreements among themselves before they meet with the rest of the group so that they can agree on a consistent message.

## THE NOMINAL GROUP TECHNIQUE

A major advantage of group over individual problem solving is that several heads can be better than one. But capitalizing on that advantage can be difficult. While the number of ideas increases with additional members, the opportunity for conflict also increases. The **nominal group technique** is a group idea-generation technique to help members reach a decision on a controversial issue without bitterness from a win–lose conflict. This technique extends the process of brainstorming by incorporating a voting step into the process allowing members to rank and discuss the brainstormed alternatives.

Nominal means "in name only." The nominal group technique capitalizes on the finding that sometimes people working individually while in the presence of others generate more ideas than while interacting as a group. In addition, sometimes dominant members inhibit the participation of quieter members. The nominal group technique gets around this potential problem by alternating between solitary work and group interaction. One organization used the nominal group technique as part of a detailed decision analysis procedure to decide what type of computer system to buy. This complex organization consisted of many different units and subunits that coordinated work with each other, but it also had unique computing needs that had to be satisfied. The nominal group technique helped all these individual units achieve consensus about the best computer system to buy. Participants were satisfied with both the process and the outcome.[64]

### GLOSSARY

**Nominal Group Technique**

*A technique that alternates between individual work and group work to help a group hear from every member when discussing a controversial issue*

FIGURE 9.2 Steps for Conducting the Nominal Group Technique

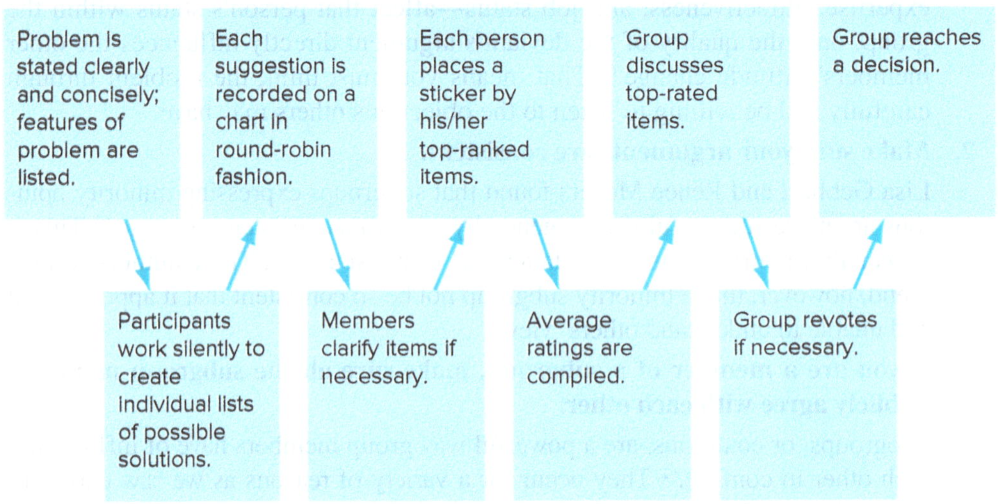


In the nominal group technique, members (usually six to nine) work individually in each other's presence by writing their ideas. Then members record the ideas on a chart, discuss them as a group, and finally evaluate them by a ranking procedure until members reach a decision. The following steps, summarized in Figure 9.2, make up the process.

1. **The problem, situation, or question is stated clearly and concisely.**

   Elements of the problem or question are described, and discrepancies between what is desired and what currently exists are explained, often by a member of top management. Care must be taken not to mention possible solutions. Group members can ask questions to clarify or add information about the problem. If the group is large, it may be subdivided into smaller groups, each with its own facilitator.

2. **The coordinator asks participants to generate a list of the features or characteristics of the problem or question.**

   Steps 1 and 2 may be combined; the facilitator presents the problem and moves the group directly to step 3.

3. **The coordinator gives the group 5–15 minutes to work silently.**

   Each person brainwrites as many solutions or answers to the original question as possible.

4. **Each suggestion is listed and recorded in round-robin fashion on a chart visible to all members.**

   The first person gives one item from his or her list, and the recorder lists it. Then the next person gives one item, and so forth, until the master list is complete. If any additional ideas or items occur to people while the list is being compiled, they should add them to the master list. During this step no discussion of the merits of the suggestions is permitted.

5. **Members clarify the items but do not yet evaluate them.**

   The group discusses each item on the list, but only to clarify or elaborate on it. Any member may ask what a particular item means, but arguing, criticizing, and disagreeing are not permitted during step 5.

6. **Each person chooses his or her top-ranked items.**

   The easiest way to do this is to give each person a set of stickers to place next to his or her most important items. Sometimes participants are instructed to place one sticker by the five most important items. Other times participants are told they can distribute their stickers however they want, including placing all five on one item. Then the items with the most stickers become the agenda items for the group's discussion.

7. **The group engages in full discussion of the top-rated items.**

   This discussion should be a freewheeling and thorough evaluative discussion. Critical thinking, disagreement, and exhaustive analysis of the items are encouraged.

8. **A decision is reached.**

   Often the discussion in step 7 will produce a consensus decision. If so, the group's work is completed. If not, group members can revote on the items and continue their discussion. Steps 6 and 7 may be repeated as often as necessary until support for one idea, or for a combination of ideas, emerges. The decision is then acted on by the group or the parent organization that established the group.

Both of us have used this technique, or modifications of it, with great success. One of us employed it to help a major manufacturer identify problems with package instructions for a product and to suggest possible solutions for these problems. Recently, we used a modification of the nominal group technique with students to help plan changes to the communication curriculum. In each case it was not important for the group members providing the information to develop a sense of cohesiveness; thus, the nominal group technique was ideally suited for the situations.

Working to balance the effectiveness and appropriateness of our behaviors when we express disagreement and attempt to maximize our influence in our groups is central to productive conflict. The nominal group technique helps to facilitate this balance. In addition, another technique has been found to be useful to groups.

## STEPS IN PRINCIPLED NEGOTIATION

Each member of a group, along with the group's leader, is responsible for helping manage the conflicts that arise within the group. However, even though you may want to resolve a conflict effectively, you may not know how to proceed or previous attempts have not worked. The following helpful steps are suggested by Roger Fisher and William Ury in their book *Getting to Yes: Negotiating Agreement Without Giving In.*[65] Following these suggestions will help a group engage in **principled negotiation,** a conflict management procedure grounded in the premise that without communication there simply is no negotiation, and that communication must allow individuals to be heard in ways that do not damage relationships. Members can use this procedure collectively, or the designated leader or other facilitator can guide members through the process to a solution.

**GLOSSARY**

**Principled Negotiation**

*One way of dealing with conflict that promotes finding ways to meet the needs of conflicting parties and respecting their relationship*

### Helping the Cask and Cleaver Crew

APPLY NOW

The Cask and Cleaver work crew still must come up with the next six-month shift schedule. They almost had their schedule until Mark discovered he had been skipped. Now they are taking sides, acting defensive, and calling each other names. Your job is to take the role of each crew member and use the nominal group technique to create a shift schedule that is satisfactory to all the crew. Mark and Beth are married, and Beth has major health problems. Mark is a full-time student, and Beth works full time. Maria is married and recently started her own business. Tom and Nathan are students at a local university working toward a teaching credential. Paul is a graduate student and single. Tracey is an undergraduate and recently divorced. Jeremy, an undergraduate, is single and lives at home with his parents.

Select a facilitator to help the "crew" go through the eight steps of the nominal group technique. After a solution is derived, the class can discuss the following:

1. What was difficult about the procedure?
2. Did the "crew" think that the technique helped in any way? If so, how? If not, why?
3. Read ahead and see if this crew's solution is anything like the one the real crew devised.

1. **Separate the people from the problem.**

   Sometimes conflict produces such strong emotions that people cannot be objective. What may start as a disagreement about how to get something done becomes a personal declaration of war in which combatants try to hurt each other. Earlier, when we discussed conflict types, we explained how important it is to dislodge the task issues from the relational ones. The administrative headquarters of a church recently experienced serious conflict among administrators. Members on both sides of the fence began to talk about the other side as *the enemy.* After several long sessions with a trained mediator, people on each side began to listen carefully to those on the other side. Each side learned that the other side cared deeply about the issues; they also realized that they shared many concerns. Eventually, the conflict was resolved and the bad feelings healed. This occurred in part because both sides demonstrated that they cared about each other and because they focused on the *issues* that divided them rather than on personalities.

2. **Focus on interests, not positions.**

   Group members are tempted to stake out positions from which they cannot be budged. If Roger says, "I insist that we keep the snack bar open in the evening," and Mary says, "We have to close the snack bar in the evening to save money," there is no way to reconcile those positions—they are incompatible. The harder individuals cling to them, the more difficult it will be to resolve the conflict. However, people stake out positions for reasons that seem good to them. It is

### Should He Go Back to School?

APPLY NOW

Sam and Tashie have been married for 12 years. Sam wants to quit his job because he is bored and believes they had an agreement that he would be able to complete his education after they had been married a few years. Tashie owns her own company, which is finally getting off the ground, and she doesn't believe they have the money for Sam to leave his job. Select two students to role-play the discussion between Sam and Tashie in front of the class. After the role-play, use the principled negotiation procedure with the entire class to help Sam and Tashie manage the conflict.

1. **People:** Ask the role-players how they feel about the argument, themselves, and the other person. Emphasize the importance of recognizing feelings.
2. **Interests:** Distinguish between the irreconcilable positions and the interests behind each position. Have the class and the role-players participate in discovering what each person's interests may be.
3. **Options:** Ask the class and the role-players to brainstorm creative options for this couple. Emphasize the point that interests may be met in a variety of ways, one of which is bound to be acceptable to both.
4. **Criteria:** Explore whether any objective criteria might apply to this couple's dilemma.

the *reasons* for the positions (personal interests) that should be the focus of the negotiation. In our earlier example, Mary wanted to save the campus money while Roger wanted to make sure the evening students were provided with food service. Not only are these legitimate interests, but they also are probably interests common to *both* Roger and Mary. Roger cared about financial solvency, and Mary cared about serving evening students, but each of them emphasized a different priority. One way to reframe this issue was to close the snack shop at 5 P.M. (thereby saving on labor and utility costs) but provide vending machines with a variety of sandwiches and snacks. In this way, the legitimate interests of each individual were served.

3. **Invent new options for mutual gain.**

Group members should become creative at inventing alternatives. A number of techniques, such as brainstorming, are designed to help groups become more inventive.

Initially the only options our Cask and Cleaver crew presented were to start all over again or keep going and ignore Mark's skipped turn. Another option, one that the crew did not consider, was to go back to the point where Mark was skipped, keep everything the same up until then, and start anew from Mark's skipped turn. In fact, Tracey's option effectively solved the problem. She pointed out that while it was not

Mark and Beth's fault that Paul and Tom had night classes, it also was not Paul and Tom's fault that Beth needed surgery. She suggested that Mark give his night shift to Tom so he and Beth, who didn't work that night, could spend some time together. Mark saw the logic in Tracey's solution and gave his valued shift to Tom. All members apologized to those whom they had offended. The crew was able to come up with an option that gave them mutual gain given their reasons for their positions.

4. **Insist on using objective criteria.**

   Much wasted time can be saved if members use criteria they agree are fair and appropriate for evaluating solutions, much like the "little white book" in an earlier example.

   The same use of objective criteria occurs in other situations too. One of our students, a residence hall adviser, used the principled negotiation technique with four roommates having problems devising an equitable schedule for leaving their suite clean at the end of the school year. Instead of doing what she normally would do (that is, assigning specific responsibilities to each roommate), Amanda met with all four women together and asked them what was most important to each regarding this end-of-year task. It turned out that each woman wanted the tasks to be divided fairly and to be assured that the last woman to leave the suite would not be stuck with tasks the others had not completed. Amanda asked them how they would divide the tasks and establish consequences to ensure that each woman completed her assigned duties. The roommates themselves divvied up the work and suggested several options for holding one another accountable. Amanda was delighted because the women owned the solution and were more likely to carry it out than one she had imposed on them.

Even with the best of intentions, sometimes a group becomes deadlocked in its conflict. We recommend that groups try to resolve their own conflicts first, but if that isn't possible, a group can try mediation or arbitration. The principled negotiation procedure can be used by an outside facilitator. This may be necessary if the leader has been actively involved in the conflict. Finally, a group may bring in an outside arbitrator with power to settle the dispute. However, these are last resorts. It is far better if a group can resolve its own conflicts.

## RESOURCES FOR REVIEW AND DISCUSSION

### SUMMARY

- Three common myths about conflict are that conflict is always harmful, it is due to misunderstandings, and it can be resolved by good communication.
- Two conflict types in groups involve the task and relationships between group members.
- The five common conflict management styles of avoidance, accommodation, competition, collaboration, and compromise are each appropriate in certain circumstances, but styles that encourage members to look for ways to satisfy all participants are usually preferable.

- Group norms for expressing disagreement and influencing each other should balance both the demands of effectiveness and appropriateness especially during conflict.
- Group members can use the nominal group technique, which balances solitary and group work, to help work through potentially contentious discussions.
- Group members can also use procedures such as principled negotiation, which focuses on people's interests rather than positions, finding creative options, and using objective criteria to resolve conflicts.

## EXERCISES

1. Rent either *Twelve Angry Men* or *Lord of the Flies.* Watch the movie and observe types of conflicts: how these conflicts were handled, what the effects of the conflicts were on the group, how decision making was affected by the various conflicts, and what the group could have done to improve its ability to manage conflict. You can do this yourself, or you can discuss your observations with others in class who have also watched the video.
2. Think of a group you currently belong to. Recollect two recent conflicts in the group. Write an essay describing the conflict, labeling the type of conflict, and reporting how it was managed. Draw some conclusions about conflict in group interaction from these observations.
3. Divide yourselves into groups and come to a consensus regarding what you would do about each of the following group problems.
   *a.* Ann has missed the first three meetings of the group. For the first two she said she had to work, but she offered no reason for missing the last one. She also has completed none of the work she agreed to do for the group.
   *b.* Bob is a domineering individual who attempts to control the direction of the group. He evaluates each idea as soon as it is presented. As a result, the rest of the members have stopped volunteering suggestions and ideas.
   *c.* The members of the group have fallen into two subgroups, and competition has arisen between the subgroups. If you didn't have to work together, you would have split apart long ago.

## KEY TERMS • CONCEPTS

| | | |
|---|---|---|
| Accommodation | Compromise | Process Conflict |
| Avoidance | Conflict | Relational Conflict |
| Collaboration | Nominal Group Technique | Task Conflict |
| Competition | Principled Negotiation | |

CHAPTER 10

# Applying Leadership Principles

## CHAPTER OUTLINE

Leadership and Leaders

Myths about Leadership

Figuring Out the Dynamics of Leadership

What Good Leaders Do

Encouraging Distributed Leadership

Ethical Guidelines for Group Leaders

## CHAPTER OBJECTIVES

After reading this chapter you should be able to:

1. Distinguish between leadership and a leader; differentiate a designated from an emergent leader.
2. Describe the seven sources of a leader's power, and give an example of each.
3. List and discuss the myths of leadership.
4. Discuss different approaches to understanding leadership.
5. Describe the administrative duties leaders are expected to perform, and explain how leaders can perform these effectively.
6. List and explain six factors involved in leading group discussions.
7. Explain how establishing a climate of trust, developing teamwork, and promoting cooperation can help develop the group.
8. Define *distributed leadership* and discuss what it means to encourage it.
9. List and explain the ethical guidelines for group leaders.

### The College Service Club

CASE 10.1

TerryAnn was so envious of the close, cohesive executive committee of her service club that she decided to run for office so she could be part of the team. When she was elected president as a junior, she was thrilled. She wanted the club and the executive committee to continue experiencing the same success she had witnessed as a member. Unfortunately, things didn't turn out that way. TerryAnn and the rest of the executive committee met soon after the spring election to make plans for the upcoming fall. Although many good ideas surfaced at this meeting, no one wrote them down. TerryAnn was somewhat intimidated by all the seniors on the executive committee, and she was reluctant to assign tasks or even ask the other members to do things. No one else picked up the ball either. Consequently, no one remembered what they had decided or knew who was supposed to do what. Committee members lost valuable summer planning time because they weren't organized. When fall came, they had to scramble to catch up.

TerryAnn's reluctance to guide the process affected both the executive committee and the regular organizational meetings. She made no effort to start the meetings on time, so members got into the habit of coming late. Because there was no agenda, members did not know what they would be discussing or what materials they should bring to the meetings. Discussion was haphazard, jumping from one topic to the next without ever finishing a single subject. No meeting minutes were ever compiled or distributed, so members weren't sure what actions had been decided or who was assigned to what tasks. As a result of the disorganization in the executive committee, service club members became disenchanted with the organization. Membership decreased. As the frustrating year drew to a close, TerryAnn was increasingly depressed because her high hopes for the club had not come close to being realized.

**This story could have had a different ending if TerryAnn had known what the other members expected of her. Because she was afraid to be seen as a dictator, she did the exact opposite. But the group members were practically begging for TerryAnn to give them structure and organization so that the club's jobs would get done. TerryAnn's "leadership" did not match what the group needed and expected from her.**

**GLOSSARY**

**Leadership**
*The use of communication to modify attitudes and behaviors of members to meet group goals and needs*

**Influence**
*The use of interpersonal power to modify the actions and attitudes of members*

**Legitimate Power**
*Influence based on a member's title or position in the group*

In this chapter we will differentiate leadership from leaders, describe the sources of a leader's power, discuss myths about leadership and different ways to understand effective leadership, and explain the typical duties of designated small group leaders. In addition, we suggest guidelines to encourage distributed leadership and describe ethical leader behavior.

# Leadership and Leaders

A group's leader is a person who helps the group attain its goal, and leadership refers to behaviors which direct the group to its goal. Successful groups must have effective leadership, something every member including a leader is capable of demonstrating. We now look more closely at how leaders and group members can provide leadership to the group.

## WHAT IS LEADERSHIP?

Michael Hackman and Craig Johnson define **leadership** as "human (symbolic) communication which modifies the attitudes and behaviors of others in order to meet shared group goals and needs."[1] Communication (see Chapter 1) involves people creating, interpreting, and negotiating shared meaning and that includes leadership and what it means to a group. Communication is the central defining activity of leading and implies three things. First, leadership is accomplished through communication—what a group member actually says and does in group interaction. Second, leadership consists of those behaviors that *help* the group achieve shared goals. A rebel—even a popular one—would not be considered a group leader if the rebellious actions interfered with the group's accomplishment of its goals. Finally, the term *modifies* in the definition suggests that group leaders must be adaptable to the changing conditions of the group. Thus, leadership is a dynamic process between leaders and followers, which is created through communicative interaction.

## SOURCES OF POWER AND INFLUENCE

The central defining characteristic of leadership is **influence,** or the use of power to modify the thoughts and actions of group member.[2] Where does this social influence come from? Why do some people have an easy time getting others to work for them, but others do not? Bertram Raven and John French identified five sources of interpersonal power that capture the different kinds of influence between leaders and followers: legitimate, reward, punishment, expert, and referent.[3] Although these five sources of power are the most widely cited, we will also include two other sources of power recognized in theories of leadership: informational and ecological.[4] Table 10.1 summarizes these seven.

A member's title or position confers **legitimate power.** Just having the title of "chair," whether the individual was appointed or elected to the position, gives that individual the ability and right to influence the others. TerryAnn did not recognize that she had the legitimate power, as president, to do such things as asking another member to take meeting notes or assigning tasks.

**TABLE 10.1 Sources of Power and Influence**

| |
|---|
| **LEGITIMATE POWER**<br>Leader is elected or appointed; has a title (chair, coordinator). |
| **REWARD OR PUNISHMENT**<br>Leader can give or take away items of value; may be tangible (money, promotion, titles) or intangible (praise, acceptance). |
| **EXPERT POWER**<br>Leader has information, knowledge, or skills needed and valued by the group. |
| **REFERENT POWER**<br>Leader is admired and respected; other group members try to copy his or her behavior. |
| **INFORMATION POWER**<br>Leader has access to information and controls distribution of information. |
| **ECOLOGICAL POWER**<br>Leader directs how a task is organized and can alter a group's working physical environment. |

**Reward power** comes from someone's perceived ability to give others what they want and value, and **punishment power** comes from the perceived ability to take those things away. Both rewards and punishments can be tangible or intangible. For instance, Sandra rewards her fellow members with praise and encouragement, which have great power to influence others. Similarly, frowning, ignoring someone, asking a member to redo an assignment, and so forth are intangible ways of punishing group members. Tangible rewards can include such things as special privileges, monetary bonuses, and promotions. Tangible punishments may include taking away special privileges, giving someone undesirable assignments or work shifts, or even firing a member. **Coercion** is one extreme form of punishment involving threats or force to make a member comply. Such tactics can breed resentment, sabotage, and rebellion and are inappropriate to use in small groups.

An individual with **expert power** is perceived by other members to have valuable knowledge or skill. For instance, Tashie, her group's "PowerPoint Queen," found her advice was often followed whenever they had to design a public presentation of any kind. Tashie's abilities were recognized by the group and they were willing to incorporate her strengths into their projects.

A person with **referent power** is someone others admire and want to be like. In high school one of us belonged to a social group led by a "cool" informal leader with considerable referent power. Members of her group accepted Mia's opinions about a variety of issues: how to dress, whom to date, what school activities to join. One day Mia suggested that the group ditch school for the afternoon. Group members did—much to their dismay when they all got caught!

**GLOSSARY**

**Reward Power**
*Influence derived from someone's ability to give members what they want and need*

**Punishment Power**
*Influence derived from someone's ability to take away what members want and value*

**Coercion**
*Using threats of force to make a member comply*

**Expert Power**
*Interpersonal influence that stems from someone's perceived knowledge or skill*

**Referent Power**
*Influence due to a person's ability to be liked and admired*

GLOSSARY

**Information Power**

*Influence based on a person's ability to control information*

**Ecological Power**

*Influence derived from a person's ability to manipulate the logistics of the task as well as the physical environment of a group*

**Leader**

*Any person in the group who uses interpersonal influence to help the group achieve its goals*

**Designated Leader**

*An appointed or elected leader whose title (chair, president) identifies him or her as leader*

Two other sources of power extend our understanding of the influence leaders enact in groups.[5] **Information power** involves the degree of control a member can have over information. This control can involve the actual amount of information a leader has as well as the leader's access to information useful to the group, which can impact the leader's perceived expertise. The degree to which a leader is the only source of information relates to the members' dependence on the leader. For instance, managers may resist the adoption of new technology because they do not want others having access to that information. Further, a leader can sway members' support of ideas by editing out information that could weaken support for the idea.

Finally, **ecological power** involves a form of indirect influence stemming from a person's ability to control the organization of work and the physical environment of the group. We often do not recognize that something as simple as being able to arrange a group's working environment can influence member behavior. Recall from Chapter 4 that who sits next to whom, for example, guides who has access to whom in a group. In addition, directing the procedures a group will use or influencing the kind of technology the group will use influences members' satisfaction and their relationships to each other. Because TerryAnn did not want to jeopardize her acceptance by others, she was reluctant to take charge by organizing the group's processes. This lack of ecological power then reduced her power in other ways—such as her legitimate power as designated leader.

A leader's social influence often involves more than one source of and leadership involves mutual influence between leaders and the other members of the group. "The only person who practices leadership alone in a room is the psychotic."[6] Whether a leader's efforts to influence a group toward its shared goal is effective can be answered only in the actions of the other group members.[7] Now we turn our attention to those specific persons who are recognized by group members as their leader.

## WHAT IS A LEADER?

A **leader** is *any* person who exercises interpersonal influence to help a group attain its goals. That's what makes distributed leadership, discussed in Chapter 1, possible. There are several important implications to this statement. First, this definition of *leader* implies that all individuals in a group can (and should) supply some of the needed leadership services to the group. Second, any member of a group, with or without a title, can at times function as a group's leader. Third, the definition assumes that *communication* is the process through which a person actually leads others. Rather than assuming that leaders are born or must have particular titles, this definition suggests that leaders *perform behaviors* that help a group achieve its goals. We next discuss the two types of leaders found in groups.

**Designated Leader.** The **designated leader** holds a title (e.g., chair, coordinator, moderator, facilitator, president) that identifies his or her specific position in the group. They are either elected by the group or can be appointed by someone else such as a manager or teacher. Group members typically expect the designated leader will act to help them be successful. For example, Michael Kramer found in his study of a community theater group that members expected their designated leader to provide the directions for completing the task, coordinate other secondary leaders in the group, and provide them with a vision.[8]

**Emergent Leader.** An **emergent leader** starts out with the same status as other members in a group of peers, but gradually emerges as an informal leader. Mia, in our earlier example, was an emergent leader—her group didn't elect her to the post, but by virtue of her personality and influence, she emerged as the group's leader. You may have experienced working in groups, like those in your courses, where there is no designated leader. Understanding how informal leaders emerge also sheds light onto the behaviors that make up effective leadership.

Studies conducted at the University of Minnesota reveal how informal leaders emerge over time in groups without any designated leader.[9] First, all members initially have the potential to be recognized as leader by the others. However, members who don't speak up or are uninformed are quickly eliminated from consideration. Next to be eliminated are members who, compared to the rest, are overly bossy or dogmatic. Those who remain as potential leaders speak frequently, are well informed on the issues facing the group, and are open-minded, democratic, sensitive, and skilled in expressing ideas for the group. The emergent group leader is ultimately the member who seems able to provide the best blend of task and people skills. Especially important is the ability to coordinate the work of other members by communicating effectively with them. Subsequent studies have found that communication relevant to the group's task is the one factor that significantly predicts leadership emergence.[10]

Other behaviors or characteristics related to leadership emergence have been found. They include effective listening,[11] self-monitoring (the ability to pay attention to how others are responding to you and to adjust your own behavior in response),[12] being extraverted and sociable,[13] and intelligence.[14] Even members who act on positive images of themselves as leaders get recognized as leaders more often than those who do not, and this in turn strengthens those self-views of leadership.[15]

Although a prevailing assumption has been that males usually emerge as leaders, biological sex now seems irrelevant, although psychological gender is not. Task-oriented women emerge as group leaders as often as task-oriented men. In one study of all female groups, women who emerged as leaders combined intelligence with the personality trait of androgyny (i.e., exhibiting both masculine and feminine characteristics).[16] In mixed-gender groups, regardless of sex, masculine and androgynous members emerged as leaders more often than feminine and undifferentiated members.[17] Groups appear to choose leaders based on performance, especially if they delay naming a leader until after they have had a chance to get to know each other and work on their task.[18] Research into gender and leadership shows that men and women lead equally well, and group members are equally satisfied with both male and female leaders.[19]

The process of leadership emergence speaks to the effectiveness of designated leaders as well. First, emergent leaders influence primarily through referent, expert, reward, informational, and ecological power. By definition, they have the support of other group members. So, even though you may hold the title of leader (or chair, president, coordinator, and so forth) in your group, it will benefit you to

GLOSSARY

**Emergent Leader**

*A person who starts out with the same status as other members but gradually emerges as informal leader in the eyes of the other members*

act like the kind of person who would also emerge as the group's leader. Second, the person who emerges as a leader in one group may not emerge as leader in another. Each group's situation is different, requiring a different blend of leader skills. The type of task as well as the personalities and preferences of the members influence what type of leadership is comfortable to a given group. For example, in graduate school one of us participated in a group where all other members were engineers. They were highly task-oriented and impatient with chitchat, which they saw as irrelevant to the task. In contrast, many groups of communication students are sociable and would perceive an exclusively task-focused leader as hostile or uncaring. As leader, pay attention to the group's needs so you can adjust your behavior appropriately.

Most of what we know about leadership emergence is taken from studying face-to-face groups. With the growing influence of computer-mediated communication, we have grown increasingly interested in how leaders emerge in groups that use varying degrees of computer technology. Wicham and Walther, in the first study of its kind, compared how leaders emerged in virtual leaderless groups and in those with a designated leader.[20] They discovered that leaders do emerge, and members quite easily identify their emergent leaders. In fact, the leaderless groups showed more agreement on who the leaders were than the designated leader groups. The single most important behavior these leaders displayed was frequency of communication, similar to findings from face-to-face groups. Encouraging behaviors from individuals also mattered to perceptions of leadership.

Now we will turn our attention to several misconceptions people have about leadership.

### Informal Leadership in the Group

APPLY NOW

Think of a group you belong to that does not have an official leader. Most such groups will have an informal leader. Picture that person as you answer the questions below. When you are finished, divide into groups of five or six, and share your observations with one another. Are there any common characteristics or behaviors that the emergent leaders demonstrate?

1. What are the sources of power that give your informal leader the ability to influence? List as many as apply, and provide specific examples of how your leader used his or her power.
2. If you found yourself in a high-stakes project group with this person (e.g., in a group that had to complete a project for a major portion of a course grade), would this person emerge as leader in that group? Would this person's leadership skills be a good fit for the project group? Why or why not?
3. Are there other individuals in the group who demonstrate leadership skills? If so, who are they? What sources of power do they possess? Provide examples.

## Myths about Leadership

Students usually say that leaders "control the actions of the other members," "give orders," and generally "tell people what to do." We examine this and several other pervasive myths about leadership here.

1. **Leadership is a personality trait that individuals possess in varying degrees.**
   Up until the 1950s, the study of leadership consisted of a search for the traits that make people leaders, including intelligence, attractiveness, psychological dominance, group size, and, most recently, communication traits such as communication apprehension, verbal aggressiveness, and ability to argue a position well, or argumentativeness.[21] However, strict trait approaches to studying leadership have three drawbacks. First, there is no trait or set of traits that leaders have but followers do not. No trait differentiates leaders from members.

   A second drawback to this approach is the underlying assumption that all leadership situations call for the same trait or set of traits. Does the leader of a classroom discussion group need the same traits as the leader of a military platoon? No single set of traits will identify the best leader for any given group or situation.

   A third drawback to this approach is the assumption that these traits are located within a person, which ignores the idea that leadership is found in the interaction between leaders and group members. If you aren't born with the characteristics of a leader (whatever those may be), you will not become a leader. Instead, leadership consists of *behaving in ways that can be learned* (at least up to a point). Consider, for a moment, Judy Shepard, the woman who created the Matthew Shepard Foundation. Shepard's son, Matthew, was murdered in Wyoming. She created the foundation to advance social justice and equality for lesbian, gay, bisexual, and transgender (LGBT) people to honor her son. Her efforts led eventually to the passage of the Matthew Shepard and James Byrd Jr. Hate Crimes Prevention Act in 2009. Nothing in her previous background or experience could have predicted that she would become a prominent spokesperson for LGBT equality and impact national law as she has. There are no set of traits that will guarantee leadership in every situation.[22]
2. **There is an ideal leadership style, no matter what the situation.**
   If there is no set of traits that guarantees leadership, is there a style of leadership that will? Several studies indicated that leaders perform both *task-oriented* and *relationship-oriented* behaviors.[23] Many organizations developed training programs to teach employees how to engage in both of these kinds of behaviors.

   Other researchers have examined different kinds of leadership styles, summarized in Table 10.2. The three most common styles are: autocratic (authoritarian), democratic (participatory), and laissez-faire (noninvolved). *Autocratic* leaders decide the group's agenda, select procedures the group will follow, and decide who will speak when. Highly authoritarian leaders can stifle group members who are expert, creative, and enthusiastic, but their groups can be very productive.

   *Democratic* leaders want all the group members to participate in decision making, and so their communication is more relationship-oriented than autocratic leaders.

**TABLE 10.2** **Styles of Leadership**

**AUTOCRATIC LEADERSHIP**
Characterized by decisions made solely by the leader, with little to no consultation with group members and a primary focus on the task but not relationships. "Here is what I've decided we're going to do . . . ."

**DEMOCRATIC LEADERSHIP**
Characterized by decisions made by leaders in consultation with group members and a primary focus on both task and social dimensions of the group. "What ideas do you have for solving our problem?"

**LAISSEZ-FAIRE LEADERSHIP**
Characterized by a passive, hands-off attitude that translates into behavior providing little leadership; requires that others step in and take over if the group is to succeed. "Do what you want, it doesn't really matter to me."

**TRANSACTIONAL LEADERSHIP**
Characterized by the exchange of resources between the leader and followers as a way to influence member behavior.

**TRANSFORMATIONAL LEADERSHIP**
Characterized by a leader's ability to inspire followers to act toward a greater good beyond their own self-interests.

**CHARISMATIC LEADERSHIP**
Characterized by a leader whose power is connected to his or her perceived extraordinary qualities.

They try to discover the wishes of the group members and help them achieve their common goals. They encourage members to develop the group's agenda and to determine what procedures the group will use. Members of groups with democratic leaders tend to be more satisfied, to participate more actively in meetings, to demonstrate more commitment to group decisions, and to be more innovative than members of groups with either autocratic or laissez-faire leaders.[24]

*Laissez-faire* "leaders," who consider themselves to be no different from the other members, are hands-off. They avoid influencing the group, thus laissez-faire styles are in fact not leadership at all. Occasionally, the other members of groups led by laissez-faire leaders blend their efforts to lead the group successfully, but more often such groups end up wasting a lot of time or following the structure provided by an autocratic leader who emerges and takes charge. Kramer's study of the community theater group supported this conclusion.[25] When this group's designated leader failed to lead, other members stepped up to fill the void. Kramer noted, however, that these members were highly motivated and speculated that had they not been motivated from the beginning their production probably would have failed.

Finding an ideal style to fit all situations is futile because leadership is a function of a variety of factors. A review of the research does suggest that several other factors work in combination with democratic and autocratic styles to influence group productivity.[26] Democratic leadership seems to be more productive when it occurs in natural, real-life settings and when the group's task is a complex one. In addition, member satisfaction with democratic leadership is not guaranteed.

Other leadership styles have also captured the attention of organizational and management researchers.[27] You may have heard, for instance, about transactional, transformational, and charismatic leadership styles. All three of these styles provide a way for people to capture the more emotional and symbolic attributes of leadership. Leaders, after all, are not only a part of group experience, they also influence the meaning given that experience (see, e.g., the process of symbolic convergence in Chapter 7). *Transactional leadership* involves a leader's willingness to trade or exchange one resource for another. Political leaders, for example, trade votes for funding of hometown pet projects. *Transformative leadership,* in contrast, involves a higher degree of symbolic behavior in that the leader is able to rally others to buy into and support a common good beyond that of any one person. These leaders are often called visionary leaders who inspire and motivate their followers such as Martin Luther King Jr. and Senator Bernie Sanders. Closely related and often used interchangeably with transformational leadership is charismatic leadership. Former president Bill Clinton, the late Steve Jobs of Apple Computer, and Sarah Palin are often referred to as charismatic. While both involve leaders who communicate a vision to followers, *charismatic leadership* is more focused on the leader and his or her extraordinary qualities that move followers to act.[28] These styles involve sets of behaviors relevant to leadership: trading resources, encouraging members to work for something greater than themselves, and reflecting the power of one person's character to move people.

The styles approach oversimplifies the complexities of groups as open systems. For example, consider the following two groups: (1) an advertising agency's creative team, in which the members have worked together successfully for two years, and (2) an outdoor survival group of adolescent boys, strangers to each other, none of whom has ever been camping. Would you recommend the same style of leadership to the coordinator of the creative team and to the adult adviser of the survival group? But just as different groups vary in their needs for different leadership services, a single group's needs will change greatly over time as well. Early in a group's history, the more inexperienced members expect a take-charge leader, but as group members become more experienced, they may prefer less control and more shared responsibility for the group.[29] TerryAnn, in our opening case, failed to first assess what the new group needed and ask herself if she was the right person for the job.

3. **Leaders get other people to do the work for them.**

When some students are elected or appointed to leadership positions, they assume that their job is to tell other people what to do and often seem surprised that it doesn't work. Recently, the president of a campus organization was disgusted

**TABLE 10.3 Three Approaches to Leadership**

| | |
|---|---|
| **Functional Concept** | Central task and social actions or functions must be identified and carried out by leaders and group members in their pursuit of group goals. |
| **Contingency Concept** | Appropriate leadership actions must match the situational characteristics of the group including the type of task, member readiness, and the group's interpersonal climate. |
| **Distributive Concept** | Leadership is a function of the group's efforts found in the inseparable relationship between leaders and followers. |

that a colleague failed to complete an assignment for the organization. "I told her what to do, and I told her we needed the information for today's meeting," she said. She didn't understand that just telling someone to do something doesn't ensure that it will happen.

## Figuring Out the Dynamics of Leadership

Now that you know that small group leadership isn't a trait, a style, or the act of bossing people around, let's discuss what it *does* involve. Several leadership approaches will help understand that leadership is a dynamic process and not something found solely in a person (see Table 10.3).

### THE FUNCTIONAL CONCEPT OF GROUP LEADERSHIP

The **functional concept** of leadership promoted the idea that essential functions must be carried out in a group to ensure success, and these functions are the responsibility of all group members. Both task-related functions connected with getting the job done (e.g., shaping the task, offering suggestions, creating agendas, gathering information, keeping the group on task) and people-related functions (e.g., harmonizing, relieving tension, helping members become a team) must be performed and adjusted to changes in the group.[30] All members should carry this load because one person cannot do it all and involving members creates greater commitment.

For example, one project manager at a Fortune 500 corporation was terrific at motivating and developing her staff. Staff member Tina was a fabulous presenter. Carol could interpret data and incorporate it effectively into the group's reports. Roger was a gifted writer, and Ty was super-organized, with the ability to keep track of where everyone was on a project. Tamika had a quirky sense of humor and could always lighten things up if meetings got tense. These staff members worked as a *team,* with no one member dominating and the leader encouraging them to use all their talents on behalf of the team.

**GLOSSARY**

**Functional Concept**

*The idea that groups need to have certain functions performed, and all group members can and should perform needed functions*

When all members take on the responsibility of meeting these two functions, the leader's job is *completing* the group by supplying any needed functions (services) that other members are not providing or at least seeing that someone supplies them (see Chapter 1).[31] A leader should be able to constantly monitor the group's progress, identify what the group needs at any time, decide whether those functions are currently being performed adequately by other members, and, if not, provide them or encourage someone else to do so. For example, when John notices that Rada has not offered an opinion about an important issue, he deliberately asks Rada her opinion. If the group seems confused, John summarizes and clarifies or calls on Kim, the group's recorder, to reorient the group. When he sees the group becoming tense, he may offer a joke or suggest a 10-minute break.

Kramer's study of the community theater group provides support for the ability of a good leader to call on others to help with the task of meeting these functions.[32] Even when the designated leader failed to lead, the other group members were capable of stepping in at various times to supply the needed guidance and attention the group needed to mount a successful production. Group members attended to both task and relational functions by stating what needed to be done, how it could be done, or by jumping in and starting the task.

GLOSSARY

**Contingency Concept**

*The idea that features of the situation determine appropriate leadership behavior*

## THE CONTINGENCY CONCEPT OF GROUP LEADERSHIP

Related to the functions approach, the **contingency concept** holds that appropriate leadership behavior depends on the situation. TerryAnn's laid-back manner of leading did not work in her particular service club, but with a group of experienced pros, it could have been quite effective. There are several contingency approaches; we will focus on those developed by Paul Hersey and Kenneth Blanchard because their approach is representative of the ones that recognize leaders adapt to meet the changing needs of their groups.

Contingency approaches suggest that leaders should consider several factors before deciding on the specific leadership services appropriate for the group. Among these factors are the type of task, how well the members work together, and how well members work with the leader.[33] A major factor that affects the way a leader should act is the maturity level, or readiness, of the followers.[34] Hersey and Blanchard have provided a model, shown in Figure 10.1, to help match leadership style to the readiness level of the followers. In general, the more experienced, interested, and motivated the members are, the less direction is needed from the leader.

Hersey and Blanchard's model, tempered with your common sense and knowledge of group leadership, helps you know how to adapt. If group members are unable or unwilling or don't have enough information to complete the task on their own, they are low in readiness. *Telling* (high-task and low-relationship orientation) can be an effective leadership style. The leader needs to give them specific instructions and provide close supervision of their work: "Our goal is to increase sales by 15 percent, and here's what I want you to do . . . ." The leader tells the members what, how, and when to do something.

With low to moderate readiness, group members are usually willing but do not have the skills or experience necessary to perform well. In this case the leader takes a *selling* (high-task and high-relationship orientation) approach by providing much of the

FIGURE 10.1 Model of Situational Leadership

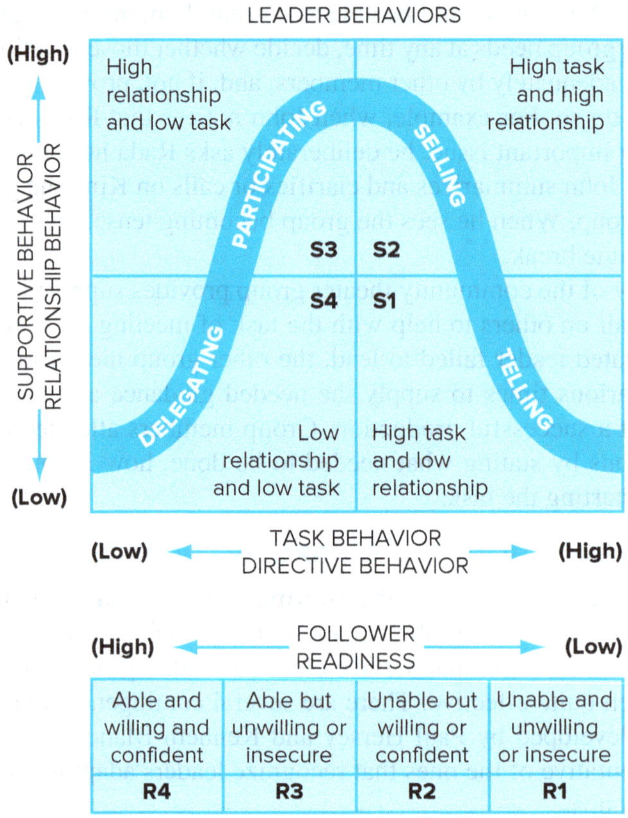


SOURCE: 2006 The Center for Leadership Studies, Inc. Escondido, CA 92025.

direction but seeking members' support for this direction: "One of our goals is to increase sales by 15 percent, and I'd really like your input about how we can do that." The leader encourages members to ask for explanations and additional information. The leader's goal is to promote member enthusiasm while providing the guidance needed to complete the task well.

With members of moderate to high readiness, the leader can pay less attention to the demands of the task and concentrate instead on the relationships among members: "How is the sales campaign going? What can I do to help you?" Here, followers have the skills to perform the job but may need encouragement to act or coordination to work out a division of labor. The leader's supportive, democratic style is called *participating* (low-task and high-relationship orientation) because decision making is shared and the leader's role is mostly one of facilitation and coordination. All members share in leading the group and any member could probably serve as its designated leader.

In a fully ready, mature group, members are both able and willing to perform. They need little task-related supervision or encouragement. In this situation the *delegating* (low-task and low-relationship orientation) style is appropriate; the leader turns the responsibility for the group over to the group: "Let me know if you need anything." Delegating is appropriate where a more active leadership style might be perceived as interference. However, even when the group is fully ready, the leader must still monitor the changing conditions of the group and be ready to step in to perform additional services the group may need. This was TerryAnn's style, but her followers were not at this level of readiness.

The contingency approach, while used widely in the military, management, and education, has produced mixed research results.[35] For instance, there is not conclusive evidence that if leaders follow the guidelines in Hersey and Blanchard's model they will be more effective. However, studies of this model have shown the importance of paying attention to members who are low in readiness and mentoring them into higher levels of maturity. Leaders are warned not to make oversimplified generalizations from the model and force-fit members into categories but to remain flexible and alert to the nuances of interpersonal relationships between themselves and their followers.[36] Central to this model is understanding that leaders must adapt differing styles to match their members' readiness, their ability and willingness to tackle the group task.[37] Eventually, leaders who were "tellers" should become partners so the leadership can be distributed.

**GLOSSARY**

**Distributed Leadership**
*The idea that each group member can and should provide leadership services to a group*

## THE DISTRIBUTED CONCEPT OF GROUP LEADERSHIP

In both the functional and contingency concepts we emphasized that leadership is the property of the *group* and not the individual who happens to have the title of "leader." Yet both approaches, while recognizing leadership as a group phenomenon, still tend to focus directly on leader behaviors adapting *to* members and the situation. **Distributed leadership** explicitly acknowledges that leadership is the property of the group and that leadership and followership are so intertwined that they cannot be separated from each other.[38]

Studying leader behaviors is not wrong, but it is only part of the puzzle. Traditional approaches to leadership overplay the singular influence of a leader. Members are equally important to understanding group leadership. They are also smart, resourceful, and quite capable of being just as influential in a group as a leader and just as capable of influencing a leader's actions.

Overall leadership activity by all members has been found to be more related to productivity than activity of the designated leader alone.[39] Distributing leadership functions is good not only for members, but also for the group. Distributed leadership, however, is not simply a matter of everyone pitching in. As leaders and members mutually influence each other, contradictions or contrary demands between them will emerge.[40] Galanes, for instance, in her study of leadership discovered contrary demands felt between control from the leader and control from the group as well as the tensions between the demand of task work and nontask work.[41] Leaders often talk about trying to figure out when to be more controlling and when to let others exert control. In addition, we have constantly addressed the competing demands of staying on task and going off task. Work groups are notorious for going off track to talk about other issues, relationships in the group, their own processes, and to simply gossip. The challenge for a group's leadership is not to push a group to either side of these contrary demands but to realize group dynamics are about both leader and group control and task and off-task interaction. The key is balancing these demands, not getting rid of one or the other.

We have discussed major myths surrounding group leadership, and presented alternative insights into leadership. It is now time to investigate the general expectations all members bring to a group concerning their leader.

## What Good Leaders Do

A group leader has a lot of work to do, sometimes more than any other member. Research gives us insight into what good group leaders do to help their teams succeed.[42]

1. **Good leaders establish the group's goal and make sure the group starts in the right direction.**

   Usually, the goals are put into writing, perhaps as part of a team charter that spells out the charge, area of freedom, and scope of the project. They take the time to ensure that everyone understands and supports the goal, even to the extent of asking a completely unsupportive member to leave the team. Do not be afraid to set your standards high initially—members are expecting this early on in the group process.[43]

2. **Good leaders mold the group members into a team with a collaborative climate for working together.**

   They take team building seriously and recognize that to accomplish good group work, members must trust one another and feel free to contribute. Good leaders constantly monitor the group's interactions to ensure that members are working collaboratively, provide positive feedback, and intervene when they perceive a problem.

3. **Good leaders never lose sight of the group's task and its progress toward completion of that task.**

   That means they keep track at all times where the group is in relation to its goals. Along with keeping the group moving forward, they are able to paint the "big picture" so that members know what has been accomplished and what still needs to be done. Group members will show a desire to talk about side issues to the main issue, social issues of the group, and the actual process they are using to accomplish their task or goal. Good leaders meet the challenge of balancing the contradictory demands of both task work and off-task interaction.[44]

4. **Consistent with the leadership approaches discussed earlier, good leaders develop their members' talents by encouraging them to assume leadership responsibilities for the group.**

   Good leaders understand that often they need to exert more control initially, but as the group progresses they can ease up on control allowing members to build confidence in themselves and the team.[45] This is no easy task. Good leaders have to learn not only to encourage members in their work but also to train them in the tasks that are being asked of them.

**TABLE 10.4 Four Areas of Leadership Competence in Virtual Groups**

| | |
|---|---|
| **Leadership is key to virtual group success.** | Members expect leaders to help them become a group. In virtual groups, though, they have to be skilled in the technology. |
| **Virtual group leaders have to carefully manage meetings.** | Meetings are central to virtual groups because they are the only place these groups get together. |
| **Virtual group leaders do not lose sight of the social dimension of their group.** | Computer-mediated communication is highly task focused. Leaders have to pay more attention to nurturing this dimension. |
| **Virtual group leaders use multiple technologies in their group work.** | Virtual groups use all sorts of media to communicate (e.g., e-mail, telephones, instant messaging, teleconferencing) and leaders have to be effective in all of them. |

5. **Good group leaders do not take their leadership for granted.**
   They work at it, think about it, and consciously try to improve their own leadership skills realizing the interdependent relationship between them and the rest of the group.

What good leaders do in virtual groups is no less important and may be even more complicated given that members may be spread out all over the world, speak different languages, and work in different time zones.[46] Add to this the fact that not everyone is proficient with technology and computers. Some have even proposed that virtual groups can lead themselves and do not need designated leaders. However, research by Hambley, O'Neill, and Kline tells us otherwise. Table 10.4 describes the leadership skills needed in virtual groups.

## Which Contingency Style Is Most Appropriate?

APPLY NOW

You have been asked to conduct a workshop on group leadership for a major corporation in your city. You have selected the contingency approach to leadership as the focus of your workshop. The corporation has asked that your workshop contain several activities to give the participants "hands-on" experience with current thinking about group leadership. You have decided that one of those activities will involve application of the contingency model to several different kinds of groups. Your task now is to construct the activity. To do so, you need the materials to set up the activity and the answers to the activity.

You first will ask the participants to create a matrix that lists the four Hersey and Blanchard leadership styles (participating, selling, delegating, and telling) across the top. Under each style, list the contingencies that make that style appropriate, along with how each contingency is

(*Continued*)

***Concluded***

APPLY NOW

likely to affect the style. Next, you will give participants a list of situations and ask them to determine what style is most appropriate using their matrix. The list of situations includes the following:

- A group of college students studying together for a final exam
- A heart transplant team
- A task force of neighbors trying to rid the neighborhood of crack dealers
- A group of student senators planning the senate agenda for the following month
- A self-managed work group of employees assembling an automobile
- A group of four grown children planning their parents' fiftieth wedding anniversary party

You will ask participants to use their matrix to determine the appropriate style for each of these. To be prepared to direct discussion after the participants have finished this part of the activity, you must first participate in the activity yourself.

1. Construct the matrix, as you will ask the participants to do.
2. Apply the matrix to the six situations listed.

## DUTIES GROUP MEMBERS EXPECT LEADERS TO DO

Group members expect that their leaders will be competent and committed and will work for the good of the group. In particular, most group members in the United States assume that their designated leaders will provide services in three major categories, described briefly in Table 10.5: performing administrative duties, leading group discussions, and developing the group.[47] The behaviors of good leaders presented

**TABLE 10.5 Major Duties Leaders Are Expected to Perform**

| | |
|---|---|
| PERFORMING ADMINISTRATIVE DUTIES | Planning and preparing for meetings; keeping members informed; following up between meetings; making sure the group keeps complete written records |
| LEADING GROUP DISCUSSION | Starting discussions and keeping them on track; encouraging participation; stimulating members' creative and critical thinking |
| DEVELOPING THE GROUP | Fostering a productive and supporting climate; developing teamwork, cooperation, and trust |

earlier guide the carrying out of these specific services. The following information can serve as your concise leader's manual whenever you find yourself elected or appointed designated leader of a group.

## PERFORMING ADMINISTRATIVE DUTIES

The value of group meetings, while bothersome to many, should not be underestimated. The group's problem solving, decision making, and overall sense making occur during meetings. In 2001 it was estimated that corporations spent 7 to 15 percent of their personnel budgets on them; which can translate into millions of dollars.[48] In a study of one "large company" it was discovered that a single weekly meeting took up 300,000 hours a year of manager and team time: personal time, team time, preparatory time, and time in related meetings![49] Wasting time in meetings costs in employee fatigue and stress, job dissatisfaction, lost opportunities, and even time spent after meetings cooling off or just trying to make sense of what happened in the meeting. Wasted meeting time is particularly harmful to virtual groups, given that meetings are the only time members come together to do their work. Meetings are essential to all groups and their mishandling can be prevented with thoughtful management. Table 10.6 provides guidelines for conducting productive meetings.

**TABLE 10.6** **Performing Administrative Duties**

### PLANNING FOR MEETINGS

1. **Define the purpose of the meeting and clearly communicate it to the members.**
   "To talk about what we are going to do this year" is too vague; "To establish a list of priorities we want to accomplish in the next 6 months" is clear and specific.
2. **Make sure members know the place, starting time, and closing time for the meeting.**
   "At the library" is not clear; "In room 302 of the library" eliminates confusion.
3. **If special resource people are needed at the meeting, advise and prepare them.**
   Any invited guests such as specialists in areas of concern to your group need to know when to attend, where, what to bring, and what to expect at the meeting.
4. **Make all necessary physical and technological arrangements.**
   Tools like Wikispaces (www.wikispaces.com) and Wiggio (www.wiggio.com) are user friendly and allow members to connect with each other during and after meetings.

### FOLLOWING UP ON MEETINGS

1. **Keep track of member assignments.**
   Member assignments can be recorded in meeting minutes and progress on them can be checked between meetings.

*(Continued)*

**GLOSSARY**

**Agenda**
*The list of items to be discussed at a meeting*

**Minutes**
*Notes of what occurred at a meeting*

**TABLE 10.6** ***Concluded***

2. **Serve as liaison with other groups.**
   Leaders are the spokespersons for the group and are responsible for answering inquiries about the group and its work.

3. **Evaluate the worth of group meetings.**
   Periodic review of the value of meetings and making any necessary changes to their conduct increases their productivity.[50]

MANAGING THE GROUP'S WRITTEN COMMUNICATION

1. **Send a meeting notice and agenda to each member before each meeting.**
   Sixty-three percent of meetings are reported to have no **agenda** or a list of items to be discussed at a meeting.[51] Any special reports noted in the agenda should be sent along with the agenda.

2. **Keep personal notes to keep track of what is going on.**
   These notes are brief or just enough to help you keep track of those items important to the discussion.

3. **Keep minutes of each meeting so you will have a record of what you did.**
   **Minutes** are notes of what occurred at each meeting and summarize important actions, conclusions, and assignments. More confidential and sensitive information, for example, how a member voted unless this is required by law, is not recorded. They are sent to members after the meeting and take on different forms like those shown in Figure 10.2.

4. **Keep in a permanent file copies (hard copy or electronic) of any reports, resolutions, or recommendations made by a group.**
   Along with the minutes, these documents need to be a part of the group's permanent record.

## LEADING GROUP DISCUSSIONS

One of your most important duties as designated leader is coordinating discussions so that they are productive. Plan how you will start the meeting, keep the discussion organized, encourage all members to participate, and stimulate both creative and critical thinking. Monitor what was accomplished so that unfinished business can be taken up in the next meeting. This sounds daunting when faced with trying to do it all yourself and letting group members take responsibility as well. Galanes found all the leaders she studied emphasized that, despite being torn in different directions, they all planned for group work and remained flexible.[52] Guidelines for leading group discussions are found in Table 10.7.

© Purestock/Superstock RF

**FIGURE 10.2 Examples of Group Minutes Using Two Different Formats**

**Minutes of November 16, 2017, Meeting of Committee A (Version 1)**

Committee A held a special meeting at 1:30 p.m. on Thursday, November 16, 2017, in room 14 of the Jones Library.

Attendance: Walter Bradley, Marlynn Jones, George Smith, Barbara Trekheld, Michael Williams

Absent: Jantha Calamus, Peter Shiuoka

1. The minutes of the November 9 meeting were approved as distributed.
2. Two nominations for membership in the graduate faculty were considered. A subcommittee of Bradley and Trekheld reported that their investigation indicates that Dr. Robert Jordan met all criteria for membership. It was moved that Professor Jordan be recommended to Dean Bryant for membership in the graduate faculty. The vote was unanimously in favor.

   The nomination of Professor Andrea Long was discussed; it was concluded that she met all criteria, and that the nomination had been processed properly. It was moved that Professor Long be recommended for appointment to the graduate faculty. The motion passed unanimously.

(*Continued*)

**FIGURE 10.2** *Concluded*

**Minutes of November 16, 2017, Meeting of Committee A (Version 2)**

3. Encouragement of grant activity. Discussion next centered on the question of how to encourage more faculty members to submit proposals for funding grants. Several ideas were discussed. It was moved that we recommend to President Yardley that
   *a.* A policy be established to grant reduced teaching loads to all professional faculty who submit two or more grant proposals in a semester.
   *b.* Ten percent of all grant overhead be returned to the department that obtained the grant for use in any appropriate way.

This motion was approved unanimously.

Attendance: Walter Bradley, Marlynn Jones, George Smith, Barbara Trekheld, Michael Williams (chair)

Members absent: Jantha Calamus, Peter Shiuoka

| **Topic** | **Discussion** | **Actions/ recommendations** |
|---|---|---|
| Minutes of 11/16/17 | None | Approved as distributed |
| Nominations for graduate faculty membership | Subcommittee of Bradley and Trekheld reported that both Dr. Robert Jordan and Dr. Andrea Long meet all criteria and should be recommended to Dean Bryant for membership. | Recommendation passed unanimously, for Drs. Jordan and Long |
| Grant activity | Discussion centered on how to encourage faculty members to submit pro-posals for funding grants. After discussion of several proposals, motion was made to recommend to President Yardley that<br>1. Professional faculty who submit two or more grant proposals in a semester be given reduced teaching loads.<br>2. Ten percent of all grant overhead be returned to the department that obtained the grant, to use in any appropriate way. | Motion to submit the two recommendations to Pres. Yardley passed unanimously |

Respectfully submitted,

George Smith, Secretary

**TABLE 10.7** **Leading Group Discussions**

INITIATING DISCUSSIONS

1. **Help reduce primary tensions, especially with new groups.**
   Icebreakers or a social event can be used to help members get to know one another.
2. **Briefly review the purpose of the meeting, the specific outcomes desired, and the area of freedom of the group.**
   Clarification before the meetings helps to prevent mishaps during the meeting.
3. **Give out or post electronically informational and organizational handouts.**
   These may include agendas, outlines for discussion, or reports. Google Docs, for instance, can be used for posting and editing handouts.
4. **See that special roles are established as needed.**
   Establish what if any roles, like recorder, will be needed for the discussion.
5. **Suggest procedures to follow.**
   Offer suggestions for how decisions will be made (e.g., consensus or voting) and ask if a small group procedure such as *Robert's Rule of Order Revised* will be used. Allow the groups accept or modify their procedures.
6. **Ask a clear question to help members focus on the first substantive issue on the agenda.**
   For instance, "At this meeting we must decide which two of our five job applicants we should interview in person. You all received copies of their resumes prior to the meeting. Unless you would rather proceed differently, I suggest we go in alphabetical order and talk about each strengths and weaknesses against our criteria. Does this sound OK? {wait for feedback} Fine, then let's begin."

STRUCTURING DISCUSSIONS

1. **Keep the group focused on the goal; watch for digressions and topic changes.**
   Digression from the task as well as topic shifts are normal; however, you want to avert a lengthy digress. Bring the group back with something like, "We seem to be losing sight of our objective" or "We are jumping ahead, let's finish one topic before going to another."
2. **Display the discussion or problem-solving procedure electronically or in a hard copy for all the members to see.**
   Procedures like brainstorming and nominal group technique flow better when members have the steps in front of them.
3. **Summarize each major step or decision.**
   Members can lose track of their discussion and good summaries after completion of step or decision helps to link to the next one. "If I may summarize, we believe that alternative one should be eliminated because it is too costly, given our allotted budget." {wait for response} "I sense agreement, which means we have narrowed our discussion to alternative two and three, let's move on."

(*Continued*)

TABLE 10.7

4. **Structure the group's time.**
   Pay attention to the time given for the meeting. Frustration often ensues when members believe they have run out of time to discuss one or more important issues.

5. **Bring the discussion to a definite close.**
   This is done at the designated end time and should include a summary of the progress made during the meeting, a review of assignments, comments about the next meeting, and support of the member efforts.

EQUALIZING OPPORTUNITY TO PARTICIPATE

1. **Address your comments to the group rather than individuals.**
   Unless you are specifically directing a comment to one person, speak to the group as a whole and make eye contact with everyone including the quieter members.

2. **Control dominating or long-winded speakers.**
   You can redirect a member who is monopolizing time by first avoiding eye contact, sitting where you can look out to other members, and interject requests for comments from other members. In addition, groups can establish their own rules for discussion including how long members have to speak.

3. **Encourage less talkative members to participate.**
   Those who are more talkative can overwhelm quiet members. Encourage quiet members, "Maria, would you like to add your opinion to our discussion?" Watch for nonverbal cues that indicate someone has something to add to the conversation. Sometimes giving quieter members assignments based on their expertise and request they report back to the group is helpful, "Kim you are a statistical whiz, will you take charge of data analysis for the project and tell us how we might best proceed with this research?"

4. **Avoid commenting after each member's remark.**
   Commenting too much sets up an expectation that a leader will do so with every suggestion and interrupts the flow of conversation. Listen and speak when really needed.

5. **Bounce questions of interpretation back to the group.**
   Wait for members to express their views on issues before interjecting your own tentatively as simply an alternative. If directly asked for your opinion, you can reply with, "Let's see what everyone else thinks first. What do the rest of you think about . . .?"

6. **Remain neutral during arguments.**
   When you are heavily involved in an issue, it can be hard to remain objective. Guard against behaviors that may stifle other's opinions and remain as neutral as you can and encourage critical thinking by everyone.

STIMULATE CREATIVE THINKING

1. **Suggest discussion techniques that are designed to tap a group's creativity.**
   Several techniques, such as brainstorming, appreciative inquiry and synetics, are designed especially to help a group create inventive solutions.

*(Continued)*

TABLE 10.7 ***Concluded***

2. **When the flow of ideas stops, encourage the search for a few more alternatives.**
   This often happens late in creative discussion, help with, "What else can we think of to . . .?" or take a break and return to discussion.
3. **Discuss the components of the problem one at a time.**
   For instance, ask, "Is there any way to improve the appearance of . . .?"
4. **Watch for suggestions that open up new areas of thinking and then pose a general question about them.**
   If someone, for instance, suggests putting up signs in the labs to prevent users from eating or drinking in the lab you might capitalize on the idea with "How else could we publicize the no food or drink in our labs?"
5. **Encourage an alternative perspective or switch senses.**
   For instance if a your problem is visual ("How can we create an eye-catching graphic for our new store?"), think in sound ("What would an attention-getting ad for the new store *sound* like?")

STIMULATE CRITICAL THINKING

1. **Encourage the evaluation of information and reasoning.**
   Questions should address sources of evidence, its relevance, its accuracy, and the reasoning of the arguments.
2. **See that all group members understand and accept the standards, criteria, or assumptions used in making group judgments.**
   Fair judgments are based on clear criteria for evaluation. Ask members, for instance, "Are there any other concerns we wish to insist on?" or "Do we accept this assumption of criteria number 2?"
3. **See that all proposed solutions are tested thoroughly before they are accepted as final group decisions.**
   Ensure that all solutions have been challenged. For a major problem, consider a second-chance meeting, where all doubts, concerns, or untested assumptions are heard.
4. **Establish a devil's advocate individual or competing subgroup to poke holes in potential solutions.**
   Assign one or more members the task of looking for flaws in solutions. Assign two or more groups to a friendly competition of seeing who can find the most deficiencies in the solutions being considered. Critical thinking can be fun!

Given the importance of meetings to virtual groups, it should not be surprising to learn that virtual group members do complain often about leaders who do not run meetings effectively.[53] Teleconferencing, discussed in previous chapters, is the primary tool used for virtual group meetings. Table 10.8 highlights effective ways leaders can run these meetings.

We now consider specific areas in which the designated small group leader can help group members develop, a topic we explored in detail in Chapter 5.

## Red Ribbon Committee and Sober Graduation

APPLY NOW

The Red Ribbon Committee is a community group in California's Central Valley. The committee develops, plans, and presents several community events each year that promote a sober and drug-free lifestyle. Each year the committee debates whether the sober graduation party should last all night or end at 2 or 3 A.M. Students, noting that their parents would not approve of an all-night event, have said they'd be willing to go even if it was not all night. Lupe (a 50-year-old Latina woman with strong community ties) and Tracy (a divorced Caucasian woman in her late 40s who is quite vocal about how things should be done) argue that it should end early because the students and chaperones get too tired. In addition, they note that the majority of problems usually happen after 2 A.M. They suggest that the main goal of sober graduation is to get as many students as possible to attend, and that means guaranteeing their safety. The other four members of the group (a Caucasian female and former school board member, a wealthy female Portuguese dairy owner who is feared in the community, a Portuguese man who is very active in the community, and a young Caucasian man employed by the school district) argue that the goal is to ensure the kids are safe *all* night. Traditionally, they add, these events have been all-night affairs. Lupe and Tracy have become increasingly adamant; they want the others to try their idea at least once to see how it would work.

You are the leader of this group. At this point, how would you stimulate creative and critical thinking in this group?

1. Offer suggestions, relevant to this committee, about how members can stimulate creative thinking?
2. Offer ways the group can critically examine the suggestions generated by creative thinking?

**TABLE 10.8** **Leading Virtual Group Discussions**

Know how to use computer tools like teleconferencing.

Set the rules for the use of any computer tools and model best practices.

1. If instant messaging (IM) is used, how will it be used during the meeting? (IM is good for short messages but content cannot be archived.)
2. If chats will occur, how will they be used? (Chat content can be archived.)

Support equitable participation.

1. Keep track of who speaks.
2. Notice if a member has dropped out of the conversation.

*(Continued)*

**TABLE 10.8** ***Concluded***

Monitor your own behavior.

1. Be careful not to jump in too quickly.
2. Be patient listening to others, the lag time between messages can be delayed.
3. Be prompt in checking for the meaning of messages. Nonverbal behavior, like silence, can be read negatively during computer-mediated communication.

## DEVELOPING THE GROUP

One of the most important functions of the leader is to assist in the group's development from a collection of individuals to a productive unit. This involves such things as establishing a climate of trust, promoting teamwork and cooperation, and evaluating the group's progress. We provide guidelines for your consideration in Table 10.9.

**TABLE 10.9** **Developing the Group**

ESTABLISHING A CLIMATE OF TRUST

1. **Establish norms that build trust.**
   Too many leaders do not speak soon enough to members who act in ways to harm the group.[54] Work on norms that encourage, for instance, freedom to disagree, active listening, timely work, and cooperation.
2. **Function as a coordinator rather than a dictator.**
   Serve the needs of the group by asking rather than demanding, for instance, that members share in the work of the group.
3. **Encourage members to get to know each other.**
   Members trust each other when they know one another and feel safe. Unstructured social events are an easy way to promote teamwork.

DEVELOPING TEAMWORK AND PROMOTING COOPERATION

1. **Speak of *us* and *we*, rather than *I* and *you*.**
   "We" implies a commitment to the whole group.
2. **Develop a name or another symbol of group identification.**
   Fun logos, T-shirts, tweet handles, and even "inside" jokes show a shared identity.
3. **Watch for evidence of hidden agenda items that conflict with group goals.**
   If you suspect a hidden agenda that is interfering with the group, bring it to the group's attention; ignoring it only makes it worse in the long run.

(*Continued*)

**TABLE 10.9** ***Concluded***

4. **Use appropriate conflict management approaches and procedures.**
   Keep member conflict focused on the issues and not on each other by stopping members from attacking each other. Understanding reasons for group conflict and the different ways to manage it is invaluable to a leader (see Chapter 9).
5. **Share rewards with the group.**
   Wise leaders always share praise for the group's work with members. Cohesiveness grows out of display of pride in the group and acknowledging the service of all members.
6. **Have fun; share a laugh or joke with the group.**
   The appropriate use of humor and fantasy helps ease tensions and helps people feel good about each other.

## Marcos and His Fraternity

APPLY NOW

Marcos was appointed chair of the service committee of his college fraternity. He and Luis were the only experienced members on the committee; the other three members were new to the fraternity. His committee was responsible for organizing the fraternity's service projects and recruiting frat members to participate. The inexperienced members were excited about working on the committee, but they were not aware of all the fraternity's activities, procedures, and past efforts. Marcos faced a challenge. He did not want to stifle the enthusiasm, dominate the group, or do most of the work for the group. On the other hand, he did not want to lose valuable time while the new members felt their way along. He preferred working on a committee where all members could contribute equally, but he believed that, at least at first, these members weren't ready to contribute fully—they needed strong direction.

He and Luis worked together between the committee meetings to establish an agenda and select some of the early goals and service activities for the committee. During these meetings Marcos kept close control over the agenda and the discussion. He assigned specific tasks, always making sure the tasks were acceptable to members. He also encouraged newer members to contribute to the group until they could speak on their own. As he recognized that the newer members were becoming capable of acting on their own, he began to encourage

(*Continued*)

***Concluded***

APPLY NOW

them to take over more planning and decision-making responsibilities. He eventually became less involved in the details of committee work, focusing more on the process of discussion and decision making during meetings. He moved from functioning as a director to functioning as a coordinator.

Marcos recently heard about TerryAnn's problems with her service club from a disgruntled committee member. Concerned that he may not be as effective as he thinks he is, he comes to you, a buddy, for advice. He knows you are taking a small group communication course.

1. What are his strengths, and what may be his weaknesses?
2. Given the information Marcos has provided and the material you have read about performing administrative duties, leading group discussions, developing the group, and managing the group's written communication, devise a list of specific questions you think are important to ask if you want to get a good handle on Marcos's situation.

Although virtual groups pose unique challenges to virtual group leaders, members do expect leaders to help the group develop over time.[55] Successful development requires, just as it does in face-to-face groups, a balance between task and social activities. Table 10.10 shows how virtual group leaders can balance the demands of both in virtual groups.

As you can see, any group's designated leader is expected to perform a variety of duties associated with the title *leader*. Far from being the person who orders others around, the leader serves the group by making sure it has what it needs.

**TABLE 10.10** **Helping Virtual Groups Develop**

**When possible have face-to-face contact with members.**

**Nurture online relationships.**

1. Personalize e-mails to members.
2. Avoid use of e-mail to manage conflicts.
3. Avoid the overuse of impersonal "reply-all" function.
4. Use blogs and chats to have social talk.

**Model principled behavior.**

1. Connect with members during site visits, over the phone, and by e-mail.
2. Help members understand best practices of work.
3. Explicitly honor member work.

## Encouraging Distributed Leadership

We have encouraged you to think about group leadership in a way that may be different from how you've thought about it in the past; not so much what a person does to a group but how leaders and followers mutually define each other as well as share in the process of moving a group toward its goal. We suggested that you as leader encourage other group members to assume responsibility for leading the group. Distributing the leadership in this way helps you, in the long run, by using all members' abilities and talents to the fullest. It helps the other members develop leadership skills and also makes a wider scope of abilities available to serve the group.

Distributive leadership is challenging and requires a level of maturity and self-confidence by everyone. That can take time to develop, as Marcos recognized. You can't assume, as TerryAnn did, that members are fully ready to take over and run the group! Until members achieve this level of skill and maturity, you'll need to be astute in supplying just the right amount of direction, particularly as members try to grapple with the initial ambiguity that typically faces a newly formed group. Kramer's study of the community theatre group taught us that shared leadership does not resemble equal distribution at all times.[56] Instead, who is doing what for the group shifts, and over time a sense of "sharedness" and "equity" emerges—the key is balance and distribution.

This section contains several suggestions for effectively leading a group where leadership is distributed. These suggestions do not ask you to change your personality. Instead, they ask you to focus on your *communication behavior* and adapt it appropriately.

1. **Be perceptive; analyze the needs of the group.**

   Effective leaders understand people. They know how to help others motivate themselves to contribute their best.[57] In part they do this by listening carefully—actively—to what is going on in the group. For example, if group members appear confused, you know that the group should spend some time clarifying the discussion. Consider the following dialogue:

   **Jerry:** Yeah, we've got to finish everything Monday night, the charts and all, with the easel, and get the stuff to Maryann. Our presentation on Tuesday should be pretty good.

### The Great Leader

APPLY NOW

The following quote is attributed to Chinese philosopher Lao Tse:

*The wicked leader is he whom the people despise.*

*The good leader is he whom the people revere.*

*The great leader is he about whom the people say, "We did it ourselves."*

What do you understand this quote to mean? How can a leader lead and still have people say, "We did it ourselves"?

SOURCE: Quote from Peter M. Serge, "The Leader's New Work: Building Learning Organizations," *Sloan Management Review*, Reprint Series 32 (Fall 1990), p. 22.

**Maryann:** [Becoming agitated and visibly upset] That's not going to give me nearly enough time to type them! I have to have them by Friday at the latest! How can you expect me to type the charts, fix the table of contents, copy the paper, and have it ready to turn in by Tuesday if I don't get the stuff before Monday night?

**Sheri:** [Trying to calm Maryann but also somewhat annoyed at her tone of voice] Lighten up, Maryann. It won't take that long—we've only got two charts to do, and I can help you.

**Terrell:** [The group's coordinator, sensing this argument stems from a misunderstanding] Hold on, guys. I think we're talking about two different sets of charts. If I remember right, we promised we'd get the data tables that are supposed to go into our written report to Maryann by Friday so she can type them over the weekend. But I thought Sheri and I were supposed to make the two chart posters for our class presentation on Monday night. Isn't that what we decided?

Here, Terrell senses that the argument is over a misunderstanding and attempts to clarify it for the group. Notice that he states his clarification ("If I remember right" and "Isn't that what we decided?") provisionally, so others can disagree or improve on his understanding if he has been mistaken. Terrell can perform this function for the group only because he has been paying attention and listening actively.

2. **Adapt your behavior to fit the needs of the group; be a completer.**

   Groups need different things at different times. In addition to being able to analyze your group's needs, you must be able to adapt your behavior to perform a variety of functions, but it doesn't make sense to perform functions that others are already performing well. In the previous example, if Sheri had clarified Maryann's and Jerry's misunderstanding, there would have been no reason for Terrell to do so. Terrell jumped in because clarification was needed and no one else was providing it. He served as a completer by "plugging in the holes" for the others.

3. **Focus primarily on task needs rather than social relationships.**

   The person most likely to emerge as a leader is a task-oriented individual who clearly helps the group achieve its goal. This doesn't mean you should never tend to relationship issues, but it does mean that you should always keep one eye on the task. This helps you make the best use of the members' time and provide the appropriate amount of coordination and structure for your group.

4. **Balance your active participation with good listening.**

   Emergent leaders are active group participants; your fellow members expect you to take an interest and contribute. However, balance your talking with good listening so you don't dominate the group. Don't feel you have to comment on everything. Let the discussion flow freely without overcontrolling it.

5. **Express yourself clearly and concisely.**

   When you do talk, get to the heart of the matter being discussed, clarify, and summarize what is being said. Don't ramble; be well organized, coherent, and relevant. The ability to verbalize the group's goals, procedures, ideas, values, and ideals is an important leadership skill.

6. **Be knowledgeable about group processes and group techniques.**
   This point may seem obvious, but many designated group leaders are clueless about how to lead a group. Too often, a committee head is appointed without anyone checking that the individual has had adequate training to perform well. Like TerryAnn you may be willing to do the job, but if you don't know what you are doing, you can make a shambles of what could have been a productive group. To be effective, know what to expect, what your skills are, and what your group needs.
7. **Be willing to plan, improvise, and adapt.**
   Distributed leadership is not about either controlling a group or letting a group do what it wants. It is about mutually influencing each other toward the group's goal, which means it is about both controlling when necessary and letting go when necessary. To effectively do this, leaders must find a balance between competing demands and remain flexible.

You also should be familiar with a variety of small group techniques, including computer-based group support systems, and suggest them when appropriate. Using GSS successfully depends on several factors, such as whether the group has good facilitative leadership with a leader sensitive to group dynamics.[58] Sometimes members can become caught up with the "bells and whistles" of GSS and lose sight of its purpose. Effective group leaders use these computer programs wisely and help members overcome their anxiety or lack of interest in computer technology.

## Ethical Guidelines for Group Leaders

The essence of leadership is interpersonal influence and power. The issue most germane to leadership is not power itself but how that power is used and the ethics of leadership. Michael Hackman and Craig Johnson suggest that leaders be held to the highest possible ethical standards.[59] We refer to the National Communication Association's Credo for Ethical Communication, introduced in Chapter 1, for the following guidelines to help you maintain the highest ethical standards as a group leader.

1. **Do not lie or intentionally send deceptive or harmful messages.**
   Not only should leaders tell the members the truth, but they also should hold truth to be the standard for the group's decision making. That means, for instance, that you should welcome all relevant information in the group, whether it supports your preference or not. It also means that you must be willing to subject your ideas to the same standards of evaluation as the others' ideas.
2. **Place your concern for the group and for others ahead of your own personal gain.**
   In addition to willingly committing your time and energy to serving the group, never take advantage of your power as leader for personal gain or advantage.

Leaders' hidden agendas are as counterproductive to the group as members' hidden agendas are.

3. **Be respectful of and sensitive to the other members.**

   Groups are effective problem solvers because several heads are better than one, but only if the members feel free to share their thoughts and ideas within the group. Never do anything intentionally to ridicule members or their ideas or to discourage their participation. Homans and Greer have discovered that in especially diverse groups, leaders need to show considerate leadership: build trust, step in and manage conflict, and help members nurture their relationships. Of particular importance is the ability of considerate leaders to see members as unique individuals.[60] Most of what is written and studied about leadership is centered on an American perspective.[61] A leader's importance and whether leadership behaviors are effective do vary across cultures.[62] While there is evidence that being dynamic and encouraging is favored across cultures and being self-focused is not, we know little about the specific cultural variables that impact how leaders and leadership are judged across cultures. This much can be said, good leaders adapt to their circumstances and this means all group members are sensitive and committed to their set of circumstances.[63]

4. **Stand behind the other members when they carry out policies and actions approved by the leader and the group.**

   Don't try to enhance your own position by betraying your fellow members. If something goes wrong with a decision the group has made, assume personal responsibility for the decision.

5. **Treat members with equal respect, regardless of sex, ethnicity, or social background.**

   Respond to members without regard to their sex, ethnicity, social background, age, or other personal or social attributes. Members should be valued for their contributions to the group, not their sex or race. As an ethical leader, minimize status differences to encourage everyone's participation.

6. **Establish clear policies that all group members are expected to follow.**

   Group rules and procedures should be clearly understood. Group members should be encouraged to participate in establishing the group's procedures and policies.

7. **Follow the group rules, just as you expect the others to do.**

   Because of your status as the group leader, you may be given some leeway to violate rules others are expected to follow. Do not abuse this privilege. If others are expected to arrive on time, so should you. If you reprimand members for failing to complete assignments, make sure your own assignments are completed well and on time. As much as possible, be a model member for the group.

As Lao Tse said: "The great leader is he about whom the people say, 'We did it ourselves.' " Will you be that kind of leader?

## Your Needs or the Team's Needs?

ETHICAL DILEMMA

In 1971, after the *Swann v. Charlotte-Mecklenburg Board of Education* decision that permitted busing to achieve racial integration, schools were required to become integrated immediately.* In Alexandria, Virginia, the previously all-white high school was closed, and students were absorbed into the previously all-black school. Bob Yardley, who had been the winning, successful head football coach of the all-white school, expected to be named head football coach of the integrated school. However, Horace Bond, a young African American coach new to the community, was offered the position. At first reluctant to accept the offer, Bond was encouraged by town leaders; he eventually accepted. Bond considered for a long time what he might do to bring his black and white players together—particularly when neither set of students wanted to be brought together! He offered an assistant coaching position to Bob Yardley.

If you were Bob Yardley, what would you do? You think you should have had the head coaching spot, and it's not fair that you didn't get the offer. But you also think that achieving racial integration is a positive step, and you want to help the school achieve it. You have several choices.

1. You could accept, refuse, accept and try to sabotage Coach Bond's efforts, and so forth. List at least five options in this situation.
2. Assume you decided to accept Coach Bond's offer. What would be your communication behavior toward him? Respectful? Disdainful? How would you show your feelings through your communication behavior?
3. You truly believe the top spot should have been yours, but assume that you've decided you want to make a positive contribution here. What would you do? How would you behave toward Bond and the players?
4. How would you describe the ethical dilemma you face and on what basis would you make your ethical decision?

*This story is used with permission of Robin Swanson. Names of the schools and individuals have been changed. The actual outcome was positive—the coaches found a way to work together, the players were forced to operate as a team (although they initially resisted), and the team won the regional championship in an undefeated season.

## RESOURCES FOR REVIEW AND DISCUSSION

SUMMARY

- Leadership consists of using communication to modify others' behaviors to meet group goals; a leader is anyone who exerts influence to help a group. Designated leaders are appointed or elected, whereas emergent leaders surface naturally from within a group of peers.
- Leaders derive their ability to influence others from seven sources of power: reward, punishment, legitimate, expert, referent, informational, and ecological. The more sources of power a leader has, the greater is that leader's ability to influence the other group members.

- Three common myths about leadership are that leaders have special traits that followers don't, that there is an ideal leadership style, and that leaders get other people to do all the work for them.
- The functional approach to leadership encourages all group members to perform whatever functions a group needs. The contingency approach assumes that the type of leadership a group needs depends on the group's situation. The distributed approach recognizes the interdependent relationship between leaders and followers and the often messy contradictions faced by leaders.
- Group members in all types of groups including virtual ones expect leaders to perform four broad types of tasks: providing administrative services for a group, structuring a group's discussions, helping a group develop as a team, and managing a group's written messages.
- Distributed leadership involves both leaders and followers enacting leadership behaviors and defining each other. This kind of leadership is often characterized by contradictory demands on the leader and members of the group.
- Ethical leaders tell the truth, are sensitive to and respectful of others, support the other members, establish clear rules that they expect to follow themselves, and put group concerns ahead of their own personal gain.

EXERCISES

1. View Part 1 ("Leadership") of the video *Communicating Effectively in Small Groups,* and discuss the following questions:
   *a.* What functions did the leader perform?
   *b.* How effective was each function? How appropriate?
   *c.* Were there any points during the discussion where the leader failed to supply needed leadership service? Did anyone else step in to provide it? Was the group hurt?
   *d.* On a scale of 1 to 10, how effective was the leader? Why do you say this?
2. Select five members from your class to act as a problem-solving group. Assign one of the members to be the leader of the group. Ask the group to tackle the following problem:

   **The Teacher's Dilemma**

   *An English teacher in a consolidated, rural school has had extensive dramatic experience. She was chosen by the principal to direct the first play in the new school. The play will be the first major production for the school. Its success may determine whether there will be any future plays produced at the school, and if well done, it could bring prestige to both the teacher and the school. As a result, the teacher is exhausting every means available to her to make the play an artistic success. She has chosen all the cast except for the leading female part. The principal's daughter wants the part, and the principal told the teacher he really wants his daughter to have it. But she is a poor actress and would jeopardize the success of the show. Tentatively, the teacher has chosen someone who should do an excellent job in the role, but the principal has implied that if his daughter is not selected, he will appoint another director in the future. What should she do?*

   Place the group of five in the middle of the class and surround it with the rest of the class members. They are to watch this group's discussion and to evaluate the leader on his or her ability to lead the group discussion. How well did he or she do? On what do you base your evaluation?
3. Form small groups of four to six members. Discuss the "ideal" group leader. Each group is to address not only the specific duties leaders should perform but also the communicative skills leaders should exhibit and

the ethical principles they should both exhibit and uphold. Each group should create a "Guidelines for Group Leaders" manual that could be distributed to student leaders at your school. Discuss each group's guidelines to determine which ones tend to be common to all groups. Why do you think these tend to be the most common?

## KEY TERMS • CONCEPTS

| | | |
|---|---|---|
| Agenda | Emergent Leader | Leadership |
| Coercion | Expert Power | Legitimate Power |
| Contingency Concept | Functional Concept | Minutes |
| Designated Leader | Influence | Punishment Power |
| Distributed Leadership | Information Power | Referent Power |
| Ecological Power | Leader | Reward Power |

# Small Group Public Presentations (also available online)

PART

# FIVE

# Small Group Public Presentations

Just as it is important to figure out how best to pursue a group task, groups must often make oral presentations of their work. In Part Five, we discuss a three-step process to prepare your group's oral presentation, by focusing on the planning, organizing, and presenting stages of these presentations.

CHAPTER

# 11 Planning, Organizing, and Presenting Small Group Oral Presentations

## CHAPTER OUTLINE



## CHAPTER OBJECTIVES

**After reading this chapter you should be able to:**

1. Explain the different choices members can make in planning, organizing, and presenting their work.
2. Compare and contrast the three types of public discussions.
3. Discuss the role of the moderator in any type of public discussion.
4. Explain the essential parts of the introduction, the body, and the conclusion of an oral presentation.
5. Compare and contrast the four methods of presenting a speech.
6. Describe and apply relevant criteria to evaluate an oral presentation.

### Food for the Homeless

CASE 11.1

Six students in a small group communication class spent more than half the semester discussing the problems faced by a local homeless shelter. One especially significant problem they noted was the great reduction in contributions, especially of food, during the economic recession. The shelter seemed to get more than enough donations during the healthy economic times, but contributions dropped significantly during the recession when many people were losing their jobs and their homes. As part of the solution section of their report, the students recommended a way of getting more edible leftovers from local restaurants to the shelter, a program they had discovered already in operation in a few other communities across the nation.

The students' written report earned them an A. Their instructor was so impressed that he showed the report to a close friend, the president of the local restaurant association. She, too, thought the students were on to something and invited them to make a 15-minute presentation about their project at the association's monthly meeting. The students were excited that their work might become something more than a classroom exercise and that they might be able to help the homeless shelter, but they did not know how they should respond to this invitation. Should they let their leader represent them? Should they all go and each say a few words? Should they let their most talkative member make the presentation or the one who seemed to be the best critical thinker? The meeting was coming quickly, and they did not know what to do.

**We spend so much time focusing on the work that group members engage in while problem solving that we can forget many problem-solving groups are not finished when they select a solution to their problem. Groups of all kinds must publicly present their group work to others. Now the group must turn its attention to figure out how best to create and deliver an oral presentation to a specific audience.**

## The Planning Stage

The moment your group knows you must give a presentation, you should schedule a planning meeting to work through key details. Often, you may know in advance that a group project will culminate in a public presentation. If this is the case, when you lay out

**GLOSSARY**

**Audience Analysis**
*Studying the unique character of who will receive a presentation in order to adapt how a speech will be delivered and what will be presented*

your project schedule, it needs to include preparation for this presentation. Practicing engineers, for instance, report that while oral presentations are a key part of their jobs, often the time and effort they spend preparing for these presentations is more important to and demanding on them than the actual presentation.[1] To do a good job, the group must consider its occasion, purpose, topic, member strengths/difficulties, and supplemental logistics. This initial overview, as well as plenty of preparation, is essential for a smooth production. In this section we look at each element and describe different types of oral presentations that groups often deliver.

## YOUR AUDIENCE

Assessing your audience is important for creating a comfortable speaking environment for both your group and your audience. Although we usually *think* about our audience when giving presentations, too often we do not carefully figure out who this group of listeners is to us.[2] **Audience analysis** is a systematic approach to gathering as much information as possible about the audience for the purpose of tailoring your presentation to the information you uncover in that analysis.[3] Audience members listen to material presented to them through their *own* perspectives, not those of the person presenting the material. In professional contexts such as engineering, for instance, the ability to communicate main ideas in a multitude of ways is critical.[4] Engineers speak to audiences that can include clients, engineers like themselves, staff members, and federal and local agencies—all with varying technological competence. Engineers thus need at least "a dozen ways to state and clarify any individual idea or piece of technical information."[5]

How might audience perspectives affect how they listen to your group presentation? Consider audience attitudes toward topics.[6] If you know that your audience is not familiar with your topic, then you should stay with basic facts and provide background information. If your group's topic is new to the audience, such as hydraulic fracturing or "fracking," then you should show why listeners should care about the topic and demonstrate how this issue relates to energy issues they *do* know about. If your audience holds attitudes against your topic, then create a common ground with the audience and relate your group's main points to audience perspectives. For example, suppose your group believes it is necessary to use marijuana for medical purposes; however, you know your audience is against drug use. Show how your group and the audience care about health care for loved ones, and then relate your main points to the audience's beliefs about health care for those they love. If your audience is strongly against your group's main points, then make sure you build a sound case for your points. All these recommendations are grounded in *knowing* your audience.

You can learn about your audience in a variety of ways.[7] If you want targeted information about a particular audience, interview them or conduct a survey. This is easy if your audience will be members of your class. Interviews can be composed of open-ended questions and closed-ended questions. For example an open-ended question might be something like, "How are you planning on managing the tuition increase the university is proposing?" A closed-ended question would look like, "Do you agree with the recent decision to increase student tuition? Yes or No?" You can also answer your questions by giving your audience a written survey. If you want only general information about your audience, you can access published polls, which can give you information about attitudes on current topics. For example, the Roper Center for Public Opinion holds the largest collection of polls and surveys in the United States (www.ropercenter.uconn.edu). A variety of demographic statistics about the United States can be found on the U.S. Census Bureau's website (www.census.gov). Finally, if someone has invited you to speak, as happened in the opening case, you can ask that person to share information about the audience.

Once you are aware of *who* your audience is, you can determine the knowledge they may or may not have about the topic. As a group you should answer specific questions about your audience. Will you be speaking only to your class, or will your instructor be part of the audience? Will it be the entire membership of your fraternity or just the executive committee? Will it be people you know, or will most of them be strangers? Will the audience members be there voluntarily, or is someone forcing them to attend? The mood of your audience can depend on whether your audience feels required to be there.

Up to now, we have been talking about voluntary audiences. These audiences come to presentations because of a desire to listen to the presentation. Often, however, you might face an involuntary audience like the one in college courses or ones mandated for employees.[8] Some audience members may very will wish to listen to your presentation, but many may not and may even be upset that they are required to sit through a group presentation on a topic they care little for or dislike. You probably have already been a part of a course where you had to sit through lots of presentations. You watched as audience members texted each other, worked on material for other classes, rolled their eyes in boredom. Now you find yourself having to give a presentation to an audience required to attend. What should you do?

A captive or required audience member is going to need a presentation with lots of enthusiasm and reasons why they should listen. Use the reasons for being required to be present as part of your presentations. If your audience is required to attend, address this in your introduction, and consider making light of it. If you know some people will not like your topic, find out why and work with their objections. Use yourself! Have a group discussion about how it has been for your group to sit through required presentations and use this information to create a better presentation. Bottom line—show the audience you thought about them.[9] Remember, for more opportunities of audience inclusion, find out as much as possible about the audience before you start writing your presentation, especially if your audience is an involuntary one.

## YOUR OCCASION

Depending on who has invited your group to speak, you may be able to get much of your information about the audience and the occasion from this lead contact person. Ask if you can visit the facility and room you will be speaking in before the event occurs; also doublecheck the time, major purpose, and context of the event. How many people are expected? Where will you be placed in the speaking lineup, and how much control do you have over your setting? Before your group begins serious purpose and topic planning, make sure you clarify <u>why</u> you have been asked to speak to this audience and whether there is a specific goal that needs to be met. If you are preparing for a classroom presentation of your small group project, you already know the time and place for your presentation. Clarify with your instructor the purpose and requirements

GLOSSARY

**Informative Speech**

*A speech given with the primary purpose of teaching something to an audience*

**Persuasive Speech**

*A speech containing a call to action by the audience*

**Entertainment Speech**

*A speech with the main purpose of amusing the audience*

of the presentation and how you can use the room for the presentation. Many classrooms are not very inviting for presentations. Do not be afraid to alter the environment to suit your purposes if you can. Move furniture, open or close blinds, bring in props that support your task, and so on. The important point to make is that your group take control of as much of the occasion as you can—be proactive.

## YOUR PURPOSE

Typically, a speaker wants to have a general purpose of informing, persuading, or entertaining an audience. Knowing what you are trying to accomplish is an essential step in any effective presentation. If your group doesn't know what the presentation is supposed to accomplish, how can the audience members make sense of what they are supposed to do with the information you present? The **informative speech** is used when your group wants to educate, enlighten, or inform. For example, if your group is reporting on a new community service group that has just moved into the area, and you are offering information that describes who they are, where they come from, and what they offer, your purpose is to inform. If your group wanted the audience to donate time or money to this community service organization, your purpose would be to persuade.

A **persuasive speech** is defined by the call to action. Your purpose is to get your audience to do something with the information your group gives them. An example of a persuasive purpose would be trying to influence your fraternity or sorority to try a new fund-raising technique. You want your audience members to agree with you and adopt your suggestion(s). Often a group's purpose is a combination of both informing and persuading—you tell about the problem and persuade the audience to adapt your solution.

On occasion you may be asked to give an **entertainment speech,** such as to wrap up the year's events or "roast" a colleague at the annual company picnic. You want the audience members to enjoy themselves, to laugh and have a good time. Sometimes it is hard to get an audience to warm up to jokes and different types of humor, so be prepared if you do not get the response you want. Also, be aware that most jokes are directed at the expense of others, so be very careful that your humor is appropriate and tasteful, and does not turn off audience members. What is funny on Comedy Central may not be appropriate for your audience. You're speaking to make a connection with your audience, not to alienate them.

Although your purpose may be to entertain, this speech could easily inform or persuade as well. The presentation in our opening case had two purposes: to inform restauranteurs about how other communities handled left-over food and to persuade them to adopt this practice in their own community.

## YOUR SUBJECT OR TOPIC

As soon as you determine the general purpose, establish a specific subject or topic of your presentation. Your instructor or employer may give you a topic, but sometimes, the choice of a specific topic will be left up to you. This step is often one of the most difficult. Where do you start? The best topics come from your own experiences, beliefs, or skills. As a group, sit down and brainstorm different topic ideas from your own individual experiences. What are your interests and hobbies? What subjects do you enjoy, read about, and find interesting? Often you are selected to speak because of some expertise you possess. You can also ask whoever asked you to speak which of several topics the audience would find most appealing. When you are giving a presentation as part of a project for a course, then your project topic is your presentation's topic. If for instance, you have just completed a problem-solving project on how to reduce suicides in the American military, the topic of your presentation is your problem (high suicide rates in the American military) and the steps in the P-MOPS (see Chapter 8) are your sub-areas.

Undoubtedly, there will be a time limit for your presentation. You may have 5 minutes or 20, or you may be told simply to "be brief" or to "fill us in." Keep your time limit in mind when selecting what to say about your subject. Inexperienced speakers often make the mistake of coming to the podium with enough material for two or three speeches. As a result the audience gets restless or your instructor tells you to stop so that others in the class have time to speak. Don't try to cover everything you know about a subject; select those matters that are most important to you and of special interest to your audience. One of the hardest tasks facing a problem-solving group is turning a comprehensive written project into an oral presentation. Your group has to consider carefully what material has to be covered to give your project justice, address instructor guidelines, and meet time limits.

## MEMBER STRENGTHS AND FEARS

Knowing the strengths and fears that your members may have with oral presentations will help in the organizing and presenting stages. What information does each individual group member have about the topic that has been chosen for discussion? What contacts or research leads do you have as a group? What is the attitude of the group toward the topic? After assessing the strengths of group members, deciding who will present different points will be easier. Also, if a question-and-answer period will follow your presentation, knowing members' strengths will help in determining who is best qualified to answer the specific questions that are asked.

In addition to looking at the strengths of four to five members, the group has to focus on member difficulties in making oral presentations. Anxiety can prevent members from having a confident and effective delivery. A group must not rely on the stereotype that "any leader can lead an effective oral presentation." Anxiety is normal and may be experienced in different ways. Just because your group leader or president has no problem speaking to *your* group as a whole doesn't mean she or he will be comfortable speaking to a group that may be larger or unknown to the speaker. Knowing a member's difficulty with or enjoyment of public speaking will allow your group to organize different presenting strategies that take the focus off of one person. This knowledge will also be a helpful reminder that your group should practice the delivery to ease tensions.

## SUPPLEMENTAL LOGISTICS

Near the end of your planning stage, your group should be more knowledgeable about what you need. Will you need supplies to set up your speaking environment? Are you using a visual aid? What will you need to run this visual aid properly (e.g., TV, DVD player, laptop, computer, projector, audio player, access to the Internet)? Is this hardware already in the room you will be presenting in? If it isn't, then how do you make

**GLOSSARY**

**Panel Discussion**
*One of three kinds of group public discussions, in which panel members often bring different points of view to the discussion*

sure it will be there? Speakers often forget a simple item, such as tape, and end up worrying about the poster that will not stand up straight instead of focusing on the words that are just as important as the visual aid. Do not expect a member of your audience, your teacher, or a contact person to provide you with these items. The lesson here is to be proactive. Even if your presentation is a required element of a course project, it is nonetheless still your presentation—act like it is yours. It never hurts to be overprepared. A good rule of thumb: be prepared enough to give your group presentation without any audio and visual aids should something go wrong. Remember, these tools only supplement your presentation; they do not take the place of your presentation.

Take, for example, the community service story discussed earlier. If your group hasn't gone the extra mile to find pamphlets, booklets, handouts, buttons, balloons, fact sheets, or other items that this homeless shelter has for distribution, then you may be missing out on updated information. Many organizations would be happy to have a volunteer group inform others about their needs and services, and your presentation would look that much more professional because you obtained original, from-the-source information about your topic.

## TYPES OF GROUP ORAL PRESENTATIONS

Once you have completed your presentation assessment, you must decide which presentation format best fits the purpose and occasion of your presentation. These formats allow for differing viewpoints to be expressed and are often followed by comments and questions from the audience. The three most common group presentation formats are the panel discussion, symposium, and forum (see Table 11.1).

**Panel Discussion.** A **panel discussion** is a public interaction between a small number of people, often selected because of their knowledge of a topic and usually holding conflicting viewpoints. The purpose of a panel is to make the audience more aware of a significant topic or to persuade them to act in a certain way (e.g., vote for a specific issue or candidate). For example, your group may be asked by your instructor to serve as a panel and explain your semester project and conclusions to the rest of your class.

**TABLE 11.1 Types of Group Presentations**

| Panel: Conversation among Experts | Symposium: Individual Uninterrupted Presentations | Forum: Questions and Comments from Audience |
|---|---|---|
| Topics outlined in advance | Different aspects of topic discussed by panelists | Different viewpoints encouraged |
| Controversy encouraged | No interaction among panelists | Questions directed at individuals or at entire group |
| Moderator acts as traffic cop | Moderator introduces topic and panelists | Moderator selects audience participants |

The procedure to follow for a panel discussion includes the following:

1. Select a **moderator** to maintain order, see that all the major issues are covered, and ensure that everyone gets to speak. The moderator introduces the members of the panel and keeps the discussion moving by calling on speakers as necessary. The moderator acts as a conversational traffic cop, directing questions to the appropriate panelists and clarifying issues and statements as necessary. The moderator also makes appropriate opening and closing remarks and directs any subsequent audience participation.
2. Before the discussion, make an outline of all the important points the group wants to cover, and decide in what order to cover them. Follow this outline closely during the panel discussion. What might this outline look like? Often your presentation outline mirrors whatever problem-solving agenda your group used to arrive at a solution for your problem—if that was your task. For instance, if you used the procedural model of problem solving (P-MOPS), detailed in Chapter 8, then your presentation agenda would look like the outlines found in Tables 8.5 and 8.6.
3. Make appropriate physical arrangements:
   *a.* Seat panelists so they can see each other and make eye contact with the audience; a semicircle is appropriate.
   *b.* Seat panelists at a table or desk so it is easy for them to write notes.
   *c.* Identify panelists with a name card on the table in front of them or their names on a blackboard behind them. The audience can then address questions to specific panelists easily.
   *d.* If the discussion is to be held in a large auditorium, place microphones on the table for the panelists to share. If audience participation will follow, strategically locate at least one standup microphone in the auditorium.
   *e.* Make provisions for panelists to present visual aids. Provide an easel or chalkboard that is easy to reach and will not block the view of the audience or panel.
4. Recognize that the panelists should not hesitate to disagree with each other, but should do so politely. Even when they are not talking, the audience can see them, so they should refrain from inappropriate nonverbal communication. Remember that just because you might not be speaking at the moment, you are still an active part of the presentation and should look as if you are attentive to the event.

**Symposium.** A **symposium** is much more structured than a panel discussion. Instead of a relatively free interchange of ideas, the topic is divided into segments, and each discussant presents an uninterrupted speech on a portion of the topic. The purpose of a symposium is similar to that of a panel: to enlighten an audience on a subject of importance. For example, in 2009, Fargo, North Dakota experienced record flooding of the Red River Valley.[10] Because an earlier 1997 flood of that valley had caused extensive damage and displaced 50,000 people, it was important this time to let the public know what was being done to coordinate flood control efforts. City officials (the mayor, vice-mayor, and city manager) along with representatives of the National

GLOSSARY

**Moderator**

*A participant in a public group presentation whose main responsibility is to regulate the discussion and guide any audience participation*

**Symposium**

*One of three kinds of group public discussions, in which participants deliver uninterrupted speeches on a selected topic*

GLOSSARY

**Forum Discussion**

*Structured audience participation after a speech, symposium, panel, or debate*

Guard and the Federal Emergency Management Agency (FEMA) provided regular 8 A.M. meetings, televised to the public, to keep everyone informed until the danger had passed. People physically present at the daily briefings, including the press, could ask questions that the presenters would address, according to their expertise. Citizens needed accurate and clear information about what to do, what not to do, how they could help, and what officials were doing, which the daily briefings provided. This type of symposium allowed officials—each from his or her own perspective—to communicate with the public, to keep citizens from panicking, and in this case to present a united front. Procedures for a symposium are as follows:

1. Select a moderator to introduce the speakers, introduce the topic, and make concluding remarks.
2. Select a small group of experts to present different aspects of the issue. Because each individual presentation is uninterrupted, make sure there will not be much repetition among the speakers. Pay particular attention to how you will transition between speakers so that the overall presentation is coherent.
3. As with the panel presentation, make appropriate physical arrangements. In a class group presentation, this means knowing what in the classroom can be moved, how the room can best be arranged, and where the group will be placed relevant to the audience. Do not wait for others, including your instructor, to make these physical arrangements for you. At the Fargo briefings, equipment had to be set up to broadcast the meetings.
4. If necessary, work through any conflict or disagreement in advance, particularly if it is important to present a united front. In the Fargo briefings, officials reasoned that it was critical to prevent public disagreement, such as was common during the Hurricane Katrina disaster in 2005 when local and national officials fought publicly over decisions and recommendations.[11] Such public in-fighting hampered rescue efforts. To prevent that, the Fargo team had a daily pre-meeting before the public meeting to iron out any disagreement privately before going public.

**Forum Discussion.** A **forum discussion** allows members of an audience for a speech, symposium, panel discussion, debate, or other public presentation an opportunity to comment on what they have heard and to ask questions of the speakers. All sides of the question should be given an equal amount of presentation time, and no speaker should be allowed to monopolize the floor. The moderator's role is crucial. Some suggestions for the moderator are:

1. Let audience members know that a forum will follow the panel or symposium so they can prepare their questions or comments.
2. Make sure everyone understands any special rules of the forum segment. How will audience members be recognized? They might raise their hands or step forward to an audience microphone. Will speakers from the audience be allowed to ask a follow-up question? Will someone who has not spoken have preference over someone who has already spoken? If there is a time limit for questions, make sure it is announced and followed.
3. Make sure everyone knows when the forum will end, and do not accept questions once that time has been reached. Offer a warning before the last question or two.

**What Type of Group Presentation Should the Group Make to the Restaurant Association?**

APPLY NOW

Form groups of about six people, and discuss how you feel about making oral presentations. Next, pretend that you are the members of the discussion group described in Case 11.1, and decide how you would respond to the invitation from the restaurant association.

1. Would you prefer to work together and put on a panel or a symposium? If so, whom would you select to be the moderator? Why?
2. Would you prefer to send a single representative? If so, which of you would you send? Why?
3. Compare your group's answers to these questions with those of the other groups in your class. How do you account for differences and similarities?

4. Try to ensure that a diversity of views is offered. Ask for comments opposed to those that have just been expressed. On a very controversial issue, the moderator might deliberately alternate between a spokesperson from one side and the other.
5. Make sure everyone can hear questions or comments. If necessary, repeat them for the audience.
6. Following the last question or comment, offer a brief summary and thank everyone for their participation.

## The Organizing Stage

The success of the organizing stage depends on how well group members interact and listen to one another. If the group allows one person to take the lead, expecting that this person will plan and organize the presentation, many problems will arise. Not only will only one person know what is going to be discussed, but resentment may arise. As with every other stage, it is important to have every member present during the organizing stage. In this section on organization, we focus on the importance of delegating member duties, we explain different types of verbal and visual materials that the group can use, and we provide a speaker's blueprint for organizing these materials and the presentation.

### DELEGATING DUTIES

Although the delegation of duties may sound like a function of the leader, this is not always the case. After assessing the strengths and fears of each member, it is important to determine what each member feels most comfortable with and where his or her presentation strengths lie. If you don't speak up at this crucial time of organizing, you might be stuck with a job that you don't know how to perform or have no desire to do. When presenting on specific areas, examine the different backgrounds and experiences of your members, and analyze where their strengths lie. Think about the different majors in a college classroom. If these students had to build a presentation about the green spaces on their campus, which areas of the presentation would be best delegated to whom? For example, math majors could demonstrate, with the use of numbers, green/nongreen space ratios, or funding issues. History majors could give background to this ongoing problem. An art major would be our first choice when deciding on visual aids, and communication majors might have the duty of surveying students and administration on solutions to this problem.

Knowing each group member's responsibilities will help when you plan speaking duties and each member's order in the presentation. After you are aware of who is speaking when and about what, you will want to discuss who will obtain verbal and visual aid materials. Who will be required to set up the computer projector or TV/VCR, turn the lights off during the slide show, or set up a meeting with an outside agency? Each duty is extremely important to the success of the group and its presentation and should be planned *before* the day of the event. Do not hesitate to use a PERT chart (see Chapter 8) again here when laying out your presentation. This chart can give you a visual depiction of duties with a time line.

## GATHERING VERBAL AND VISUAL MATERIALS

**Verbal Materials.** Once your group is aware of each member's duties, you can now conduct much more focused research on each person's item for discussion. Often speakers will try to take the lazy way out and craft their talks without obtaining supporting material. Listed are three of the most important types of verbal supporting materials: examples, statistics, and statements by authorities, or testimony.

- **Examples:** Aristotle said that examples become "witnesses and a witness is everywhere persuasive."[12] Examples are used in inductive reasoning, where a generalization is drawn from a number of specific instances. Examples can range from detailed factual ones (the story of a rape victim, complete with dialogue, names, and dates), to undeveloped factual examples (a listing of the countries in the world where war is presently occurring), to hypothetical ones (how much a dollar will be worth in 10 years given a certain rate of inflation). You should choose typical examples and offer enough to make your point believable.
- **Statistics:** Statistics are numbers or quantification used to explain or support your position. Audience members can be easily confused by statistics, so make your statistics clear and meaningful. For instance, it is hard to imagine how large a country is if the speaker tells us only that it is 200,000 square miles in area. More helpful is a comparison: about the size of California and Oregon combined. To emphasize how large the state budget in California was in 2013 ($145 billion), point out that to spend that much, the state had to spend $397.3 million a day, $16.6 million per hour, or $4,598 per second.
- **Testimony:** Some people are recognized as authorities on certain issues. To support your position, you may want to quote directly or paraphrase what these authorities have said or written about your topic. Obtain this from library research or interviews or over the Internet. The group mentioned in Case 11.1 got useful materials from interviewing the director of the homeless shelter and from newspaper articles about similar shelters across the country.

Three common types of testimony are lay, expert, and celebrity. *Lay testimony* is a statement taken from an ordinary individual. Information that is reported by a person who has special training or knowledge about the topic is *expert testimony.* A person who is famous would offer *celebrity testimony.* Let's imagine that your group has decided to give an informative presentation on tips for a long-lasting, happy marriage. Who might you interview for lay, expert, and celebrity testimony? Think about the problems that might arise if you chose testimony from someone who is known too well by the audience. For example, picking Arnold Schwarzenegger as your celebrity testimony might cause problems. Although he might offer interesting tips for your presentation, the public knowledge of his "love child" and divorce from Maria Shriver might taint the message.

The bottom line when assessing verbal supporting material is to be aware of the attitudes that your audience might have toward your research—who or what is seen as more credible? If your oral presentation is based on a comprehensive written project already full of supporting material your group needs, assess the supporting material from the perspective of the audience and select material accordingly.

**Visual and Auditory Materials.** Careful use of both visual and auditory aids will enhance your presentation (see Table 11.2). Keep in mind, for instance, what successful attorneys know: A visual aid helps your audience remember your main points. Most lawyers know that juries pay closer attention, understand technical points better, and remember more when oral testimony is coupled with a visual

**TABLE 11.2 Simple Rules for Using Presentation Aids**

1. Ensure that any equipment your group will be using is in operating order prior to your presentation.
2. Be prepared to give the presentation even if the equipment fails.
3. Create aids that are large enough for entire audience to see and loud enough for them to hear.
4. Display the visual aid long enough to make your point.
5. Pass out materials before and after the presentation with instructions to audience on how to use the materials. Keep attention on presenters.
6. Only select presentation aids that complement the content of your presentation—they should not be the presentation nor distract from the presentation. The presenter needs to remain "front and center" always.
7. While using presentation aids, maintain eye contact with the audience—do not read from the slide.
8. Practice using the visual aids before the presentation; know when to use them, how to use them, and how to remove them when finished with your point.

prop. The classic courtroom example is the image of Johnnie Cochran slipping on the leather glove while repeating, "If it doesn't fit, you must acquit" in the courtroom while he was defending O.J. Simpson, on trial for murder. If visual images were not important, we would not have an obsession with television. Imagine listening to your news, sports, and favorite television programming only on the radio.

Now that you have a better understanding of the importance of these images, here are a number of possibilities that can enhance your presentation.

- **Object:** If what you are speaking about is small enough, bring it with you. A calm dog is an effective prop to illustrate pet therapy for nursing homes or hospitals. If your subject is too large or noisy to bring with you, use a model or picture instead.
- **Model:** A plastic model of the object can allow the audience to see what you are talking about when the real object is too large. The space shuttle will be unable to land on your campus, but a model can easily be displayed on a small table in the front of the classroom.
- **Demonstration:** It can be effective to <u>show</u> your audience what you mean. One of our students gave a great presentation about how to mix a great-tasting margarita. She demonstrated her steps as she went along.
- **Picture or video:** A photograph, slide, or videotape can focus the audience's attention on your topic. To show the problem of traffic congestion in your city, for instance, take a video of rush hour on a busy street. Slide shows need to be planned and rehearsed well in advance of the performance. Your group does not want to be known as the group with the upside-down slides.
- **Map:** Most Americans' knowledge of geography is weak. Don't assume that just because you know where a city is, everyone in your audience will, too. Give them a map of the place itself, and show it in relation to other familiar points of interest.
- **Transparency:** Placing an outline of your presentation on a PowerPoint slide allows you to address the audience while you show them the image. Any image on a PowerPoint slide or even one projected onto a screen with an overhead camera needs to be kept simple. Overloading the slide with too much information, fancy fonts, and special effects is a common mistake.
- **Chart:** Charts are especially useful for showing statistics. Numbers are sometimes hard to grasp in a speech, especially when there are a lot of them. Make it easy for your listeners by putting the figures on a chart. If you are going to compare statistics, consider making a pie chart to demonstrate percentages, a bar graph to exhibit comparisons, and/or a line graph to illustrate increases and decreases.
- **Handout:** Many items mentioned earlier can be put on a handout and given to the audience before the presentation begins. If you distribute an outline, leave some blanks so listeners can take notes and stay involved with your presentation. Don't forget to look into free handouts that might be provided by local organizations or businesses.

### Using Presentation Technology

MEDIA AND TECHNOLOGY

The availability and simplicity of presentational software such as Prezi or Microsoft PowerPoint have increased audience expectations for the use of professionally created visuals to aid in understanding presentation content. Prezi is a newer online tool that allows users to create slides within a much larger "canvas" and zoom in on items as desired. While PowerPoint offers many presentation effects, it demands that slides play in a more linear fashion. Despite the pervasiveness of this type of technology, many public-speaking professionals question whether multimedia visual aids help or hinder speakers. Thus, practitioners recommend using the following guidelines:

1. **Don't let technology dictate content.** Determine the most appropriate content, and then begin to think about how you can use the presentation software to enhance how the material is conveyed to your audience.
2. **Ensure that special effects have a purpose.** Although they may be fun to include (and show off your knowledge of the software), they distract from your content.
3. **Keep wording clear and simple.** Abbreviate your message by outlining thoughts that provide a memory trigger for you and the audience. Use a consistent font size and style with a combination of upper- and lowercase lettering. Cramming too much text on a slide is a common PowerPoint mistake.
4. **Keep a consistent design.** Use color sparingly, with backgrounds that allow your text to stand out. A slide is of little use if the audience can't read the material.

- **Chalkboard:** Use the board only to illustrate something you are saying at the same time. For example, if you use an unfamiliar technical term, write it on the board. But audiences should not have to watch you make a chart on the board of the increase in automobile accidents over the past 30 years. Make a chart of this the night before, and have it ready to go when you get to that part of your speech.
- **Multimedia:** Presentation software, such as Microsoft PowerPoint, Apple Keynote, Google Docs, Adobe Flash, Prezi, and GoAnimate, can make your presentation polished and professional. You can program everything from charts and slides to video clips with sound for presentation in your speech. You can even create a link to the Internet that the audience can view on your screen. You will need access to a television monitor, a computer-projection table, or an LCD panel that can be placed on a regular overhead projector.

## ORGANIZING MATERIALS AND THE PRESENTATION

The verbal and visual information you have gathered will be a valuable asset as you plan the organization and writing of your presentation. Think of this as drawing a

**GLOSSARY**

**Introduction** *The first of three components of a speech, designed to catch the attention of the audience, show a need to listen, and clarify the main point of the speech*

road map of how the audience should follow your speech. As with any road map, directions must be clear, so the audience can understand how and why you are taking them through your chosen topic. Every speech should have an introduction, a body, and a conclusion, with clear transitions between major ideas. Earlier we pointed out that presentation outlines often follow the problem-solving agenda used by the group to arrive at a solution to their problem question. Again you can refer to Tables 8.5 and 8.6 to get an idea of how you might organize your oral presentation. Plan to get the audience's attention, explain what you are going to be talking about, talk about it, and then summarize what you have said.

**Introduction.** An **introduction** has three essential elements: an attention step, a need step, and a thesis statement. First, your goal is to motivate your audience to listen. This is called the *attention step,* and you can choose from a number of ways to capture an audience's attention.

1. **Use humor.**

   One way of getting audience members to listen to you is to make them laugh. However, be careful if you use this approach. First, what you say must be funny to others, not just to you. Preview the joke or story to other people before you use it in your presentation. If your friends enjoy it, chances are your audience will, too. The humor also must be in good taste. You do not want to offend or alienate anyone. You want favorable attention, with people wanting to listen to you. Finally, your humor should be relevant to your topic, the audience, or occasion. Something that James Corden said on the Late Late Show the night before may be humorous, but if it is not related to what you want to talk about, find something more appropriate and relevant.

2. **Ask a question.**

   A second way of getting attention is by asking the members of the audience a question. If you are going to talk about parking problems on your campus, ask, "How many of you have been late to a class because you could not find a close place to park?" or "How many of you have gotten a parking ticket from the campus gestapo this semester?" If you want an answer, tell them how to respond: "Please raise your hand." However, don't make your question so personal that you won't get an accurate response. "How many of you use cocaine on a regular basis?" will probably get a laugh, but no hands will go up. Finally, use the information as a transition into the topic of your speech: "That's what I thought. Too many of us are spending too much money on parking tickets when the university should be building more parking structures." You must be able to use any answer as a transition. If no one raised a hand, say something like, "Well, you are lucky. In my research I've found too many of us spending . . ."

   A rhetorical question is a question that the speaker asks but does not want the audience to answer aloud. The speaker will answer the question as part of the speech: "Is there any way to stop cheating on college campuses? I think there is, and today I am going to offer you three practical solutions to what seems to be epidemic at our school and at other colleges across the country." The audience will think about the question, but the speaker will provide the answer.

3. **Make a striking statement.**

   Say something at the start of your speech to grab the audience's attention and make them want to listen. Saying, "I can guarantee you an A in this course and in every other course you take this semester" will probably gain the attention of every student in your class. Likewise, "Our division has been wasting at least $50,000 a year for the past three years" will gain the attention of your employer. You have to be able to carry out your promise in the rest of your speech, but you can be sure that for the first few minutes, at least, people will be listening to you. Another good example of a striking statement is the tagline used by news programs or talk shows to get you to stay tuned to an upcoming segment. This statement should make your audience feel like they want and need to listen to what your group has to say during the presentation.

4. **Offer a striking quotation.**

   Giving a vivid quotation can attract attention. For example, if your group has been doing research on date rape, quoting from the Stanford rape victim's open letter about how she felt during the attack will attract attention to your topic. Reading a quotation from a song or a poem is another way of attracting favorable attention. Quoting someone familiar and well liked or someone saying something unexpected or out of character can gain attention. For example, a student giving a presentation on myths in student academic performance began this way: "I've heard it said that 'a theory is a thing of beauty, until it gets run over by a fact.' Nowhere is this more true than in the field of education." Although the quote does not directly relate to education, the speaker makes the connection for the audience while grabbing their attention with vivid imagery.

5. **Tell a short story.**

   People are interested in other people. Telling a story related to your topic is a great way to gain attention. The story can be true or fictional, but it must help you make your point. If a character in the story is someone audience members can relate to, so much the better.

6. **Provide an activity.**

   Have your audience do something. During a presentation about bullying, one group demonstrated that words matter by asking each audience member to write his or her mother's name on a piece of paper, then to crumble that paper and stomp on it. Most audience members couldn't bring themselves to bring harm to their mothers—even if that just consisted of a name on a piece of paper! The group made its point that words are important.

The second essential part of an introduction is the *need step.* Follow your attention step with a short statement that shows audience members why they need or can benefit from the information you are about to give them. A direct purpose statement shows audience members how the presentation is relevant to their lives and how they can directly benefit by listening. If you are talking about a new medical discovery, tell the audience that your information could help save a life. If your topic is the outrageous prices at the college bookstore, tell them you can save them money. An indirect need step implies that, because the topic is so significant, everyone should know something

GLOSSARY

**Body**

*The second of three components of a speech, where the main ideas are introduced and developed*

about it: "What happens to Social Security will affect all of us no matter how young or old we are today."

The third element of a good introduction is the *thesis statement* and *preview.* Here you tell the audience what specifically you will be talking about. Like a road map, it shows your listeners where you are going, making it easier for them to follow along. Use enumeration (i.e., words like *first, second,* and *third*) so listeners know how many main points you will cover. A completed introduction will gain the audience's attention, establish the need to listen, and demonstrate the purpose and main points of your speech. You must do so in a short amount of time. If your presentation is 10 to 20 minutes long, your introduction should not exceed two minutes.

**Body.** The **body** of the speech is the main portion of the presentation, in which you actually talk about the ideas you want to cover. Present your ideas in an easily recognized pattern so your audience can see the relationship among them. If your group's task was to solve a problem, then the body of your oral presentation contains the most important information from your problem-solving agenda (see Chapter 8). Remember to use transition statements that help move your speech smoothly from one point to the next. The following are some of the most common patterns of organization.

- **Problem-solution:** The problem-solution pattern is especially important if you are trying to persuade your audience to accept your recommendation. You state the problem, discuss its causes and significance, and then present your proposal

Source: Jennifer Haliski/U.S. Food and Drug Administration

as a solution for the problem. This pattern is also easy to use if you want to inform, such as by showing how a problem has already been solved. "How the U.S. Coast Guard managed the worst oil spill in the nation's history" could be discussed using this pattern.

- **Chronological:** A chronological order is a discussion of things as they happen in time. Talking about how something is made, explaining a historical event, or listing the steps one needs to follow when searching for a job naturally calls for a chronological order. The history of your sorority or the development of the motion picture industry likewise calls for chronological order.
- **Spatial:** A spatial order is used to describe things as they exist in space. A presentation describing the best areas to ski in California could go from north to south within the state, for example.
- **Cause and effect or effect to cause:** Explaining how the Zika virus affects millions of people is an example of cause and effect organization. You describe how the virus was discovered and how it works and then discuss the suffering of the people who have contracted it. You can also reverse the process by first talking about the people who are suffering and then describing why this situation exists.
- **Topical:** A topical organization examines the inherent parts of a topic, its essential components. For instance, our American system of government is made up of the executive, legislative, and judicial branches. To cover the entire topic, you have to mention all three parts.

You may discover that pairing some of the organizational styles works more efficiently. No organization style is always the best, but using some type of systematic approach is essential to the development of your main purpose and ideas. A stream of consciousness is not considered a typical pattern. Members of the audience may not think along the same lines you do. Instead of presenting a topic in exactly the same way the ideas came to you, you are better off choosing a pattern with which audience members are likely to be familiar.

**Conclusion.** Your **conclusion** should be a summary of the main points you want the audience to remember and leave them with a strong impression. What do you hope listeners retain after they leave the room, even if they forget everything else? Your conclusion is similar to your introduction, but your final summary should be more concrete. Remind the audience of the specific items you covered and, while summarizing your position, explain what you want them to remember. Include in your summary some memorable clincher that relates back to your thesis statement in the introduction.

If your purpose is to persuade, this is your last chance to get the audience emotionally involved in your topic. Use this opportunity to reconnect with your audience, offer a challenge, or help them to see how things could change for better or worse if action is or is not taken. Conclusions are brief (about one minute) yet should not be underestimated in their potential to leave a lasting impression on the audience.

GLOSSARY

**Conclusion**

*The third of three components of a speech, that summarizes the ideas a speaker wishes the audience to remember*

GLOSSARY

**Manuscript**

*A speech read word-for-word from a prepared manuscript*

# The Presenting Stage

Surveys show that many Americans fear public speaking more than they fear spiders, snakes, or even death.[13] You may be in a group communication class because you were trying to avoid "the dreaded speech." However, as a group member, you are still faced with this feared endeavor. Many times in your career you may need to speak to a committee or larger audience, so it is wise to work through this fear of making an oral presentation now. We offer advice for checking your language, practicing your speech out loud, and, finally, evaluating your speech or the speeches of others.

## CHECKING YOUR LANGUAGE

In the English language we have approximately half a million words to express our ideas. The average college student can recognize 60,000 words and actually uses about 20,000.[14] The more word choices speakers have, the better able they are to make language do their bidding and fulfill their purposes.[15] Speakers often forget that writing the speech is only half the battle; the delivery is just as important. Speak to your audience in a conversational style, just as if you are giving the speech to friends, and not in a dry monotone or reading manner. Should you not know how to pronounce a word, learn it before the speech and avoid, "I think it's pronounced . . ." during the speech. Generally, speakers should strive for a style that is clear, vivid, and appropriate.

*Clarity* requires language that is concrete rather than abstract. Note the difference between explaining that last night you saw Tom "coming down the street" and saying you saw him "staggering" or "crawling" or "stumbling" or "skipping down the street." Clarity also requires that you avoid jargon and use words that your audience will understand.

*Vividness* attracts our attention. Using figurative language, repetition, and amplification (supporting details that develop or reinforce an idea) will add vividness to your presentation and make it easier for your audience to pay attention. Try to imagine Martin Luther King's famous "I Have a Dream" speech without repetition or figurative language—part of what made his speech so memorable.

Finally, make sure your language choices are *appropriate* for the audience and the occasion. A formal classroom presentation probably should not be filled with expletives or street language unless they are being used to illustrate something in the speech.

## PRACTICE ALOUD

There are four ways of delivering an oral presentation: manuscript, memorization, impromptu, and extemporaneous. Each method has advantages and disadvantages.

If you write out everything you want to say, word for word in a **manuscript,** you won't leave anything out when you present the speech. Everything you want to say is right there in front of you. Unfortunately, many speakers become so dependent on their manuscripts that they pay little attention to the audience. They have little eye contact with listeners and may not notice whether listeners understand the material presented. Listeners may feel that the speaker has little interest in them and may find the speech boring. News broadcasters and many political figures avoid this problem by using a TelePrompTer that makes it seem as if they are looking directly at their listener, but such equipment is probably not available to you. If you must use a manuscript, work diligently to make a connection with your audience through eye contact and body language while occasionally looking down to find your next point.

You could also **memorize** your speech. Thus, you make sure you don't leave anything out and at the same time maintain eye contact with your audience. However, this requires that you have a good memory and do not forget even minor points. No situation is more uncomfortable for a speaker than drawing a blank about what comes next. If you are going to attempt a memorized presentation, make sure it really is committed to memory and that it does not sound memorized. The delivery of a memorized speech often sounds robotic. Because the speaker spends many hours working on the memorization of the material, she or he doesn't have time to work on a natural, conversational delivery. Even good eye contact will not fool an audience if you do not sound interested in the subject or in them.

An **impromptu speech** is one delivered off-the-cuff. There are no notes and no specific preparation; you speak from the knowledge that you have gained over a lifetime. Not having to prepare in advance is an advantage, but a disadvantage is that such speeches can sound disorganized or incoherent. The perfect example that might have easily explained your second point may not come to mind until you are well into your third point. The audience is left to put all the little pieces of information together. In a panel presentation individual panelists may present impromptu when they answer a moderator's question if they do not have the questions beforehand. Anytime forums are involved, where audience members can ask spontaneous questions, a respondent's answer will be impromptu.

An **extemporaneous speech** is a prepared speech, but instead of writing out a manuscript or memorizing it, you write an outline of what you want to cover, using as few or as many notes as you need to present your ideas. This type of speech is one typically required of students in small group discussion courses and the most preferred because it can offer the most connection with the audience. You will first practice from a complete sentence outline of your presentation. Then reduce that outline into a speaker's topic outline that can be placed on note cards. This should contain only words or brief phrases that help you remember what to say. It should also contain presentation cues reminding you to look at the audience, pause, give emphasis, don't lean on podium and so on (see Figure 11.1 for an example of one note card for the first step in an introduction). The exact wording of the speech will be different every time you present it, but the main points will always be there. This method permits you to have much eye contact with the audience. It also allows you to react to your audience's feedback without fear of losing your place or forgetting something you want to say. If you realize that some of your listeners do not understand you, you can offer another example or repeat your point in a different way to make the point clear, then return to where you left off in your notes.

Once you have selected the method of delivery, practice your speech out loud. Thinking the speech silently to yourself does not take as much time as saying it

**GLOSSARY**

**Memorization**

*A speech delivered from memory*

**Impromptu Speech**

*A speech delivered without preparation or notes*

**Extemporaneous Speech**

*A speech that is prepared and delivered from notes and not read from a manuscript*

FIGURE 11.1 Note Card for Attention Step of Introduction

| Introduction | |
|---|---|
| 1 | (*Plant feet at podium and look around at the audience) |
| I. ATTENTION: | Show slide of 3 cities<br>Ask what they have in common.<br>(*Let audience respond)<br>Tell all in top 20 for human trafficking (Dept. of Justice) |

aloud does, so you may misjudge the length. You also need to hear what the speech sounds like, because you may find that something said easily in your head is a real tongue twister when said aloud. A colleague of ours remembers his embarrassment when he wanted to say "needy student" but "nudey student" came out. After a second and then a third unsuccessful attempt at "needy," he was forced to switch to "impecunious." If possible, get someone to listen to your speech before you present it to an audience. That person will be able to tell you what you can do to improve the speech.

Group presentations call for not only individual practice of speeches but also *group* practice. Find the time to go through your presentation together, concentrating on how you will shift between speakers, where you will stand or sit and how you will act while others are speaking, what members can do to help if someone forgets to say something, and so on. Showing a sense of continuity and togetherness during a presentation that involves more than one person is challenging and needs to be rehearsed. You would also do well to talk about how the group will handle any spur-of-the-moment failure of equipment and how the group can complete a presentation should a member be unable to attend and you cannot reschedule it.

## What Makes a Good Oral Presentation?

Since the time of the ancient Greeks and Romans, a number of criteria have been generally agreed upon as artistic standards to evaluate oral performances. These standards are called the *canons of rhetoric*. Karyn and Donald Rybacki write, "Because rhetorical theory was an outgrowth of observations of the practice of public speaking in classical cultures, the canons are particularly appropriate to the analysis of speeches."[16] The five classical canons were **invention, arrangement, style, delivery,** and memory. You can use these elements to render an overall evaluation of any presentation, to compare it to other presentations you have heard, or to offer

GLOSSARY

**Invention**

*A canon of rhetoric identifying the raw materials of the speech and how they are adapted to a particular audience*

**Arrangement**

*One of the canons of rhetoric, specifying how a speech is ordered or put together*

**Style**

*One of the canons of rhetoric, referring to the individual manner in which a speech is delivered*

**Delivery**

*One of the canons of rhetoric pertaining to how the presentation is given*

suggestions for improvement. We will concentrate on the first four canons because memory—the use of codes and mnemonic devices the speaker relied on to recall lengthy speeches—has generally been replaced by written notes and the use of TelePrompTers. The canons and questions to ask for each canon are summarized in Table 11.3.

**TABLE 11.3** **Criteria for Evaluation: the Canons and Questions to Ask**

**Invention:** the raw materials and how they are adapted to the audience

- Was the topic appropriate?
- Were interesting examples and illustrations included?
- Did the examples and statistics support the thesis?
- Did the speaker relate the topic to the audience?
- Was the speaker ethical (accurate, respectful of others, adapting to the audience)?
- Did the speech fit within the allotted time limit?
- If part of a panel or symposium:
  - Did the speakers work together to cover the issue?
  - Did the moderator keep the discussion focused?

**Arrangement:** the organization of the presentation

- Were the main points clear and easy to follow?
- Was the organization logical for the topic?
- Did the introduction capture the audience's attention?
- Were the transitions effective?
- Did the conclusion summarize the main points and recap the central idea?
- If part of a panel or symposium:
  - Were the introductions clear?
  - Did participants stick to the topic?
  - Did the moderator provide appropriate transitions?

**Style:** the choice of language

- Was the language clear and easy to follow?
- Was the language appropriate to the audience and occasion?
- Was the language vivid and did it hold the audience's attention?
- Did the speaker(s) use language ethically?

**Delivery:** the oral presentation

- Did the speaker(s) maintain eye contact with the audience?
- Did the speaker(s) avoid distracting mannerism and movements?
- Did the speaker(s) vary their pitch and rate? Did they seem engaged?
- Did the speaker(s) use appropriate and natural movements and gestures?
- Did the presentation flow naturally from speaker to speaker?

### Preparing an Individual Presentation

APPLY NOW

Congratulations! The group mentioned in Case 11.1 has selected you to make the oral presentation to the restaurant association. Although the other members will be present to help answer questions, the primary responsibility for the presentation rests with you.

1. Based on the information you already have, go through the planning stages of preparing an oral presentation. For example, decide whether you are going to try to persuade your listeners to act or to inform them of what your group has discovered. What do you think the audience will be like? How will audience members respond to you? What makes you think so?
2. List the verbal and visual materials you plan to use. Be specific. What types of visual aids would be effective? What kinds of statistics?
3. Assuming that all these materials are available, what pattern of organization would be most effective in presenting them? What type of introduction would best attract the audience's attention?
4. Compare your answers with those of the other members of your class.

### Using the Canons to Evaluate

APPLY NOW

Demosthenes, the great Greek orator of antiquity, is supposed to have claimed that the most important canon was delivery, the second most important was delivery, and the third most important was delivery.

1. Which canon do you think is the most important? How would you divide 100 points among the four canons to show their relative importance?
2. In a small group, discuss which of the canons you feel to be most important, rank them from 1 (most important) to 4 (least important), and figure out the average score for each based on the 100-point scale.
3. Can your group offer any examples of contemporary or historical public speakers who rate high on all the canons? Who rates poorly on all?
4. Compare your responses to those of the other groups in your class.

## RESOURCES FOR REVIEW AND DISCUSSION

### SUMMARY

- Small groups are often called upon to make oral presentations of their work, so members need to understand how to be effective presenters.
- Public presentation sessions include panels and symposiums, where speakers publicly discuss an issue before an audience; a forum often follows, where the audience can address or question the speakers.
- In preparing a speech, the speaker must first determine whether the purpose is to inform, persuade, or entertain.
- Speakers must analyze the audience to understand how to get their attention; find the most appropriate and interesting ideas, supporting materials, and visuals aids to present; and organize the material so that it is easy for the audience to follow the presentation.
- An effective presentation includes an introduction, body, and conclusion.
- Oral presentations can be evaluated using four criteria, based on the canons of rhetoric, which include invention, arrangement, style, and delivery.

### EXERCISES

1. C-SPAN is a nonprofit cooperative of the cable industry. C-SPAN programming covers a variety of political events, including congressional hearings, press conferences, public policy conferences, and so forth. Watch C-SPAN for examples of panels, forums, or symposiums.
   *a.* Could you distinguish which kind of public presentation was taking place?
   *b.* Was there a moderator? How effective was the moderator? Why?
   *c.* What did you find interesting about how the public presentation was conducted? What did you see that was problematic?
   *d.* Did the public presentation meet with your expectations? Were you surprised? Why?
   *e.* Did you get any ideas about how you might or might not conduct your own public presentation?
2. Take some time to listen to the persuasive speech of a car salesperson and a minister. Compare and contrast the "sales pitch" of both. Both presentations are persuasive in nature, but they are delivered to different audiences. How are their oral presentations the same? How are their oral presentations different?
3. Various videos and CD-ROMs contain the text of famous speeches. You can rent these at your local or school library. Find one with excerpts or the entire speech of someone famous who interests you. Watch the speech and evaluate according to the four canons: invention, style, delivery, and arrangement.

### KEY TERMS • CONCEPTS

Arrangement
Audience Analysis
Body
Conclusion
Delivery
Entertainment Speech
Extemporaneous Speech
Forum Discussion
Impromptu Speech
Informative Speech
Introduction
Invention
Manuscript
Memorization
Moderator
Panel Discussion
Persuasive Speech
Style
Symposium

APPENDIX A

# Techniques for Observing Problem-Solving Groups

## Consulting to the Technical College Executive Committee

CASE A.1

The technical college's executive committee meetings were boring. Members agreed that communication among the various departments was essential for the college to function effectively, but the weekly staff meetings somehow were not satisfying this need. Real communication about problems, solutions, and goals of the various departments was done outside the meetings. Members didn't complain much, but they showed little enthusiasm for the meetings. The chair of the committee, Basil, was concerned. He asked Gloria to observe the meetings, figure out what was wrong, make recommendations for improvement, and conduct training sessions to help members interact more effectively during the meetings.

For two months Gloria systematically observed, analyzed, and evaluated the staff meetings. First, she attended meetings, took notes, and completed a content analysis that showed Basil doing most of the talking. He was almost the only member to initiate new ideas during the meetings. Other members contributed only when addressed directly by Basil. Thus, a *wheel* interaction pattern (with Basil at the hub and everyone else as an individual spoke) had become the group's norm. On a questionnaire asking about effectiveness, Basil indicated that he believed the meetings were very effective, most other members thought they were moderately effective, and two members rated them completely ineffective. Gloria followed up the questionnaire by interviewing each staff member to determine how the meetings could be improved. She paid particular attention to the comments of the two dissatisfied members.

Gloria concluded that Basil dominated the meetings but that he was unaware he was doing so. Members felt stifled during the meetings but didn't know how to express those feelings to Basil or to change the pattern of their meetings. Members wanted to discuss freely the problems that had come up in their respective departments, and they hoped the staff meetings would provide an open forum for exchanging information and ideas. The two members who were most dissatisfied were quite knowledgeable about college operations and felt particularly ignored. Members were suppressing disagreements for fear of retribution by Basil; although Basil was not a tyrant, he made it clear from his behavior (rolling his eyes, interrupting people, speaking sarcastically) that he did not like it when others disagreed with his ideas. In short, this committee displayed some obvious and some hidden problems, all of which could be overcome with training and desire.

**This story highlights the value of having someone observe a group, describe its behavior, evaluate that behavior, and make recommendations to improve the functioning of the group. In this appendix we will present a variety of techniques to help you do that.**

## The Role of the Observer

The role of group observer can be valuable and helpful if the observer knows how to function. Knowledgeable observers function like athletic coaches, helping players improve their performance as a team.

In Chapter 1 we described the participant-observer, a group member who makes available his or her knowledge and skills to help a group perform more effectively. A second type of observer is the **consultant-observer,** an outsider brought in to observe, evaluate, and make recommendations to the group. The consultant-observer may be a member of the organization the group belongs to or an outside consultant trained in small group communication. That was Gloria's situation when she observed the technical college executive staff, and that may also be your position someday.

Participant- and consultant-observers have unique advantages and disadvantages. The consultant-observer may be able to see things about group members and their processes that insiders may miss, but the participant-observer may have inside information that gives insight regarding what is happening in the group. A group that has been experiencing serious conflict may view the consultant-observer as a hatchet person for an executive. On the other hand, a participant-observer may be seen as biased rather than objective, thereby undermining his or her effectiveness as an adviser to the group.

In general, observers seek to answer two questions: How well is this group performing? and How can it improve? However, *many* elements contribute to a group's performance. Observers cannot look at everything at once, or they will become overwhelmed. They plan their observation strategy in advance. Table A.1 lists questions you can use as a

**GLOSSARY**

**Consultant-Observer**

*An outsider who observes and evaluates a group*

**TABLE A.1 Questions to Guide Your Observations**

**GROUP GOALS**

- Are there clear and accepted group goals?
- How well does the group understand its charge?
- Does the group know and accept limits on its area of freedom?
- Do members know what output they are supposed to produce?

**SETTING**

- Does the physical environment (seating arrangements, privacy, attractiveness) facilitate group discussions?

**COMMUNICATION SKILLS AND INTERACTION PATTERNS**

- How clearly do members express their ideas and opinions?
- Do members complete one topic before they switch to another?
- Is verbal participation balanced equally among all members?
- Is the pattern of interaction evenly distributed or unduly restricted?

**COMMUNICATION CLIMATE AND NORMS**

- Does the group climate seem supportive and cooperative or defensive and competitive?
- What attitudes do the members exhibit toward themselves and each other?
- Do any hidden agenda items seem to interfere with group progress?
- Do any norms seem to interfere with group progress or cohesiveness?

**LEADERSHIP AND MEMBER ROLES**

- What style of leadership is the designated leader providing?
- Is the leadership appropriate for the group's needs?
- Are the roles performed by members appropriate both for their skills and for the needs of the group?
- Are there any needed functions not being provided by anyone?

**DECISION-MAKING AND PROBLEM-SOLVING PROCEDURES**

- Are members adequately prepared for meetings?
- Does the group use an agenda? How well is it followed? Does it serve the group?
- Is anyone providing periodic internal summaries so members can keep track of major points of discussion?
- Are decisions, assignments, and proposals being recorded?
- How are decisions being made?
- Has the group defined and analyzed the problem before developing solutions?
- Do members understand and agree on criteria in making decisions?
- How creative is the group in generating potential solutions?
- Do members defer judgment until all solutions have been listed and understood?
- Are information and ideas being evaluated critically or accepted at face value?
- Do you see any tendency toward groupthink?
- Has the group made adequate plans to implement decisions?
- Are special procedures (brainstorming, focus groups, etc.) being used as needed?
- Could procedural changes benefit the group?

general guide for observing. Don't try to answer all the questions; instead, use the list to screen out elements that seem to be working well so you can concentrate your observation on those that can be improved.

Both participant- and consultant-observers should follow several guidelines when they are giving feedback to a group:

1. **Stress the positive** and point out what the group or the leader is doing well.
2. **Do not overwhelm the group** by telling the members each and every thing you think should be improved. Instead, emphasize one or two things that most need improvement.
3. **Avoid arguing** when you present your observations and advice. Leave the group members free to decide whether and how your advice will be used.
4. **Do not interrupt the whole meeting** to give advice to the group's leader during a meeting. Instead, whisper or write your suggestions.
5. **Speak clearly and concisely** when you are giving feedback. Do not ramble or belabor your points. Consider the following remarks by Erina, who observed that group members were switching to new topics without completing the original one:

   *One of the problems I see is that you are having trouble staying on track with your discussion! In the past five minutes, you have talked about a pedestrian overpass at Grand and National, why money was spent on artificial turf instead of library books, how you can handle a landlord who won't repair plumbing, and several other topics. Your discussion would be more efficient if you helped each other focus on the original question: How can pedestrian/car accidents be eliminated on National Avenue?*

   In this example of giving feedback, Erina states the problem she has observed, gives a few (rather than 10 or 20) examples to clarify what she means, and provides a suggestion that makes the whole group responsible for solving the problem. She doesn't ramble endlessly about the problem or blame individual members.
6. **Prepare members to use special procedures** by explaining the procedure or giving them a handout that outlines the key steps. (Feel free to use the figures in this book, as long as you give credit to the source.)
7. **Make individual critical comments in private** to the appropriate person so that he or she will not feel attacked or publicly humiliated.

Now that you have an idea of what observers look for and how they present their findings, here are a variety of instruments to help you gather information about your group.

## Observation Instruments and Techniques

The following techniques and instruments may be used by group members as part of their group self-evaluation or by observers. They can be used as is or adapted to suit particular situations (e.g., face-to-face or online or both) and groups.

FIGURE A.1 Verbal Interaction Diagram

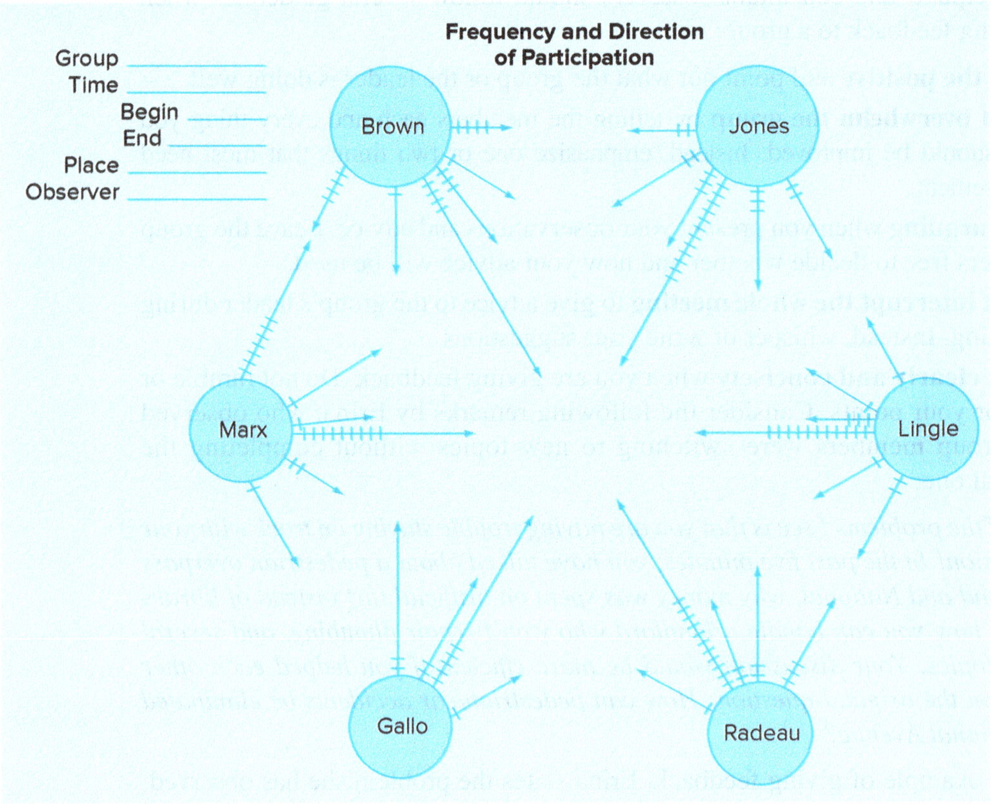


## VERBAL INTERACTION ANALYSIS

A **verbal interaction analysis** shows who talks to whom, how often each member speaks, and whether the group participation is balanced or dominated by one or more individuals. A model interaction diagram is shown in Figure A.1. The names of all participants are located around the circle in the same order in which they sit during the discussion. Whenever a person speaks, an arrow is drawn from that person's position toward the individual to whom the remark was addressed. Subsequent remarks in the same direction are indicated by the short cross marks on the base of the arrow. (For example, Gallo addressed three remarks to Brown in the model diagram.) The longer arrow pointing toward the center indicates remarks made to the group as a whole.

An interaction diagram can look messy or confusing. For easier interpretation, display the numbers and percentages in a chart (see Figure A.2). From the frequency of participation to the group as a whole and to specific members, who might you guess is the leader of this group? Do you consider the participation balanced? Does anyone appear to dominate the discussion?

GLOSSARY

**Verbal Interaction Analysis**

*A technique to discover who talks to whom*

FIGURE A.2 How to Display Data from a Verbal Interaction Diagram

Group *CURRICULUM COMMITTEE* Place *CRAIG HALL*

Observer *SMITH* Date *9-15-2017*

Beginning time *9:00 a.m.* Ending time *10:30 a.m.*

| FROM: \ TO: | | Brown | Jones | Lingle | Radeau | Gallo | Marx | Group | Total |
|---|---|---|---|---|---|---|---|---|---|
| Brown | | – | 5 | 2 | 4 | 2 | 5 | 5 | 23 / 16.1 |
| Jones | | 3 | – | 3 | 4 | 4 | 3 | 13 | 30 / 21 |
| Lingle | | 2 | 2 | – | 3 | 2 | 4 | 12 | 25 / 17.5 |
| Radeau | | 3 | 3 | 4 | – | 0 | 2 | 12 | 24 / 16.8 |
| Gallo | | 3 | 3 | 2 | 0 | – | 0 | 6 | 14 / 9.8 |
| Marx | | 8 | 2 | 2 | 3 | 2 | – | 10 | 27 / 18.9 |
| Total | number | 19 | 15 | 13 | 14 | 10 | 14 | 58 | 143 |
| | percent | 13.3 | 10.5 | 9.1 | 9.8 | 7 | 9.8 | 40.6 | 100 |

## CONTENT ANALYSIS PROCEDURES

**Content analysis procedures** examine the *type* of remarks being made by specific members. In Figure A.3 specific task, maintenance, and self-centered behaviors are listed along the left margin and the participants' names across the top (those listed here are more exhaustive than the list in Chapter 5). Each time a member speaks, the observer places a mark in the appropriate box according to the type of remark made. The tally marks are converted to percentages, as shown in Figure A.4. Who is probably the task leader of this group? Who is the maintenance leader? Are any individuals acting in self-centered ways?

Any category system can be used as the basis for a content analysis diagram. For example, you may want to focus on the defensive and supportive behaviors described in Chapter 5. In that case you would record all the individual defensive and supportive communication categories (control, superiority, provisionalism, empathy, etc.) along the left side.

GLOSSARY

**Content Analysis Procedures**

*Techniques to help analyze the types of remarks being made*

**FIGURE A.3 Content Analysis of Task, Maintenance, and Self-Centered Behaviors**

Group ____________ Place ____________ Observer ____________

Date ____________ Beginning time ____________ Ending time ____________

| | Behavioral Functions | Participants' Names | | | | | |
|---|---|---|---|---|---|---|---|
| | | | | | | | |
| Task-Oriented | 1. Initiating and orienting | | | | | | |
| | 2. Information giving | | | | | | |
| | 3. Information seeking | | | | | | |
| | 4. Opinion giving | | | | | | |
| | 5. Opinion seeking | | | | | | |
| | 6. Clarifying | | | | | | |
| | 7. Elaborating | | | | | | |
| | 8. Summarizing | | | | | | |
| | 9. Consensus testing | | | | | | |
| | 10. Recording | | | | | | |
| | 11. Suggesting procedure | | | | | | |
| Maintenance | 12. Gatekeeping | | | | | | |
| | 13. Supporting | | | | | | |
| | 14. Harmonizing | | | | | | |
| | 15. Tension relieving | | | | | | |
| | 16. Dramatizing | | | | | | |
| | 17. Showing solidarity | | | | | | |
| Self-Centered | 18. Withdrawing | | | | | | |
| | 19. Blocking | | | | | | |
| | 20. Status and recognition seeking | | | | | | |
| | 21. Playing | | | | | | |
| | 22. Acting helpless | | | | | | |

**FIGURE A.4** How to Display Data from Content Analysis of Member Behaviors

Group *EXECUTIVE COMMITTEE* Place *CU LOBBY*

Observer *ANDY* Date *10-13-2017*

Beginning time *4:30 p.m.* Ending time *6:30 p.m.*

| | Behavioral Functions | Participants' Names: Mary | John | Edna | Dave | Jodi | Total number / percent |
|---|---|---|---|---|---|---|---|
| Task-Oriented | 1. Initiating and orienting | 5 | 3 | | | | 8 / 5.7 |
| | 2. Information giving | 6 | 5 | | 2 | 3 | 16 / 11.4 |
| | 3. Information seeking | | | 3 | | | 3 / 2.1 |
| | 4. Opinion giving | 8 | 8 | 4 | 2 | 1 | 23 / 16.4 |
| | 5. Opinion seeking | | | 2 | | | 2 / 1.4 |
| | 6. Clarifying | | | 3 | | | 3 / 2.1 |
| | 7. Elaborating | 2 | 4 | | | 1 | 7 / 5 |
| | 8. Summarizing | 2 | | | | | 2 / 1.4 |
| | 9. Consensus testing | 8 | | | | | 8 / 5.6 |
| | 10. Recording | | | | 3 | | 3 / 2.1 |
| | 11. Suggesting procedure | | | 5 | | | 5 / 3.5 |
| Maintenance | 12. Gatekeeping | 3 | | 6 | | | 9 / 6.3 |
| | 13. Supporting | | | 1 | 5 | | 6 / 4.2 |
| | 14. Harmonizing | 2 | | 2 | 6 | | 10 / 7 |
| | 15. Tension relieving | | | | 3 | 2 | 5 / 3.5 |
| | 16. Dramatizing | | | | | 6 | 6 / 4.2 |
| | 17. Showing solidarity | | 5 | | | 3 | 8 / 5.6 |
| Self-Centered | 18. Withdrawing | | | | 4 | | 4 / 2.8 |
| | 19. Blocking | | 1 | | | | 1 / .7 |
| | 20. Status and recognition seeking | 2 | 5 | | | | 7 / 4.9 |
| | 21. Playing | | | 4 | | | 4 / 2.8 |
| | 22. Acting helpless | | | | | 2 | 2 / 1.4 |
| | Total number / percent | 38 / 26.8 | 31 / 21.9 | 30 / 21.1 | 25 / 17.6 | 18 / 12.6 | 142 / 100 |

GLOSSARY

**Rating Scales**

*Questions (scales) to help evaluate specific aspects of a group*

Other types of content analyses can be performed. For example, you might want to trace the development of any fantasy chains in the group, the progression of an idea from its original introduction by one member through all its modifications by the rest of the group, the types of conflicts, or the types of arguments members use to support their ideas. It is easier if you tape-record (with permission, of course) the group's interaction first.

## RATING SCALES

**Rating scales** are questionnaires that ask members or observers to assess any aspect of a group, such as group climate, cohesiveness, efficiency, satisfaction, freedom to express disagreement, and organization of discussion. For example, the question "How well did the committee chair keep the discussion organized?" asks you to rate the leader's ability to conduct a systematic discussion. Scale questions may be closed-ended, in which the responses are already provided for you (such as *very well, adequately,* and *very poorly*), or open-ended, in which you are free to respond any way you choose. The following figures provide a number of examples of rating scales. Figure A.5 is a general scale to evaluate any group discussion, and Figure A.6 is a scale

**FIGURE A.5** All-Purpose Discussion Rating Scale

Date ______________ Group ______________

Time ______________ Observer ______________

| Group Characteristic | 5 Excellent | 4 Good | 3 Average | 2 Fair | 1 Poor |
|---|---|---|---|---|---|
| Organization of discussion | | | | | |
| Equality of opportunity to speak | | | | | |
| Cooperative group orientation | | | | | |
| Listening to understand | | | | | |
| Evaluation of ideas | | | | | |
| Comments: | | | | | |

**FIGURE A.6** Problem-Solving Process Rating Scale

*Instructions:* Indicate the degree to which the group accomplished each identified behavior. Use the following scale for your evaluations:

| Poor | Fair | Average | Good | Excellent |
|---|---|---|---|---|
| 1 | 2 | 3 | 4 | 5 |

Circle the appropriate number in front of each item.

| | | | | | |
|---|---|---|---|---|---|
| 1 | 2 | 3 | 4 | 5 | 1. The concern of each member was identified regarding the problem the group attempted to solve. |
| 1 | 2 | 3 | 4 | 5 | 2. This concern was identified *before* the problem was analyzed. |
| 1 | 2 | 3 | 4 | 5 | 3. In problem analysis, the present condition was carefully compared with the specific condition desired. |
| 1 | 2 | 3 | 4 | 5 | 4. The goal was carefully defined and agreed to by all members. |
| 1 | 2 | 3 | 4 | 5 | 5. Valid (and relevant) information was secured when needed. |
| 1 | 2 | 3 | 4 | 5 | 6. Possible solutions were listed and clarified before they were evaluated. |
| 1 | 2 | 3 | 4 | 5 | 7. Criteria for evaluating proposed solutions were clearly identified and accepted by the group. |
| 1 | 2 | 3 | 4 | 5 | 8. Predictions were made regarding the probable effectiveness of each proposed solution, using the available information and criteria. |
| 1 | 2 | 3 | 4 | 5 | 9. Consensus was achieved on the most desirable solution. |
| 1 | 2 | 3 | 4 | 5 | 10. A detailed plan to implement the solution was developed. |
| 1 | 2 | 3 | 4 | 5 | 11. The problem-solving process was systematic and orderly. |

adapted from one developed by Patton and Giffin to identify deficiencies in problem-solving procedures. Figure A.7 is the Seashore Index of Group Cohesiveness, which measures cohesiveness of a work group.[1] We encourage you to modify these scales or create your own.

**FIGURE A.7 Seashore Index of Group Cohesiveness**

Check one response for each question.

1. Do you feel that you are really a part of your work group?

   ______ Really a part of my work group

   ______ Included in most ways

   ______ Included in some ways, but not in others

   ______ Don't feel I really belong

   ______ Don't work with any one group of people

   ______ Not ascertained

2. If you had a chance to do the same kind of work for the same pay in another work group, how would you feel about moving?

   ______ Would want very much to move

   ______ Would rather move than stay where I am

   ______ Would make no difference to me

   ______ Would want very much to stay where I am

   ______ Not ascertained

3. How does your group compare with other similar groups on each of the following points?

| | Better than Most | About the Same as Most | Not as Good as Most | Not Ascertained |
|---|---|---|---|---|
| a. The way the members get along together | ______ | ______ | ______ | ______ |
| b. The way the members stick together | ______ | ______ | ______ | ______ |
| c. The way the members help each other on the job | ______ | ______ | ______ | ______ |

SOURCE: From Stanley Seashore, *Group Cohesiveness in the Industrial Work Group* (Ann Arbor, MI: Institute for Social Research, University of Michigan, 1954).

## SYMLOG

SYMLOG is a special kind of analysis from rating scale data that can help a group "picture" its diversity. In Chapter 6 we talked explicitly about the critical role diversity plays in effective group interaction. We also have learned throughout this book that sometimes the very diversity that enhances group problem solving may become difficult or impossible to manage. Something is needed to help members diagnose their differences and plan how to reconcile those differences so that the group's diversity can help rather than hurt the group. SYMLOG provides a methodology that can "show" a group where its most acute differences are and in what directions members should move to get the group on track.

**SYMLOG** is an acronym for System for the Multiple-Level Observation of Groups; it is both a comprehensive theory and a methodology that produces a diagram of relationships among group members.[2] We present a simplified explanation here so you can understand how SYMLOG can be used to describe and help a group.

SYMLOG theory assumes that behaviors in a group can be classified along three dimensions: dominant versus submissive, friendly versus unfriendly, and task-oriented versus emotionally expressive. An observer uses a 26-item rating scale to categorize each member's behavior; the rating scale is then tallied in a special way so that each member can be placed on the SYMLOG diagram. An example of a SYMLOG diagram, or map, is shown in Figure A.8. The more a member is task-oriented, the closer he or she is to the top of the diagram; the more emotionally expressive, the closer to the bottom.

**GLOSSARY**

**SYMLOG**

*The System for the Multiple-Level Observation of Groups, a theory and methodology that produces a diagram of relationships among group members*

**FIGURE A.8 SYMLOG Diagram of a Noncohesive Group**

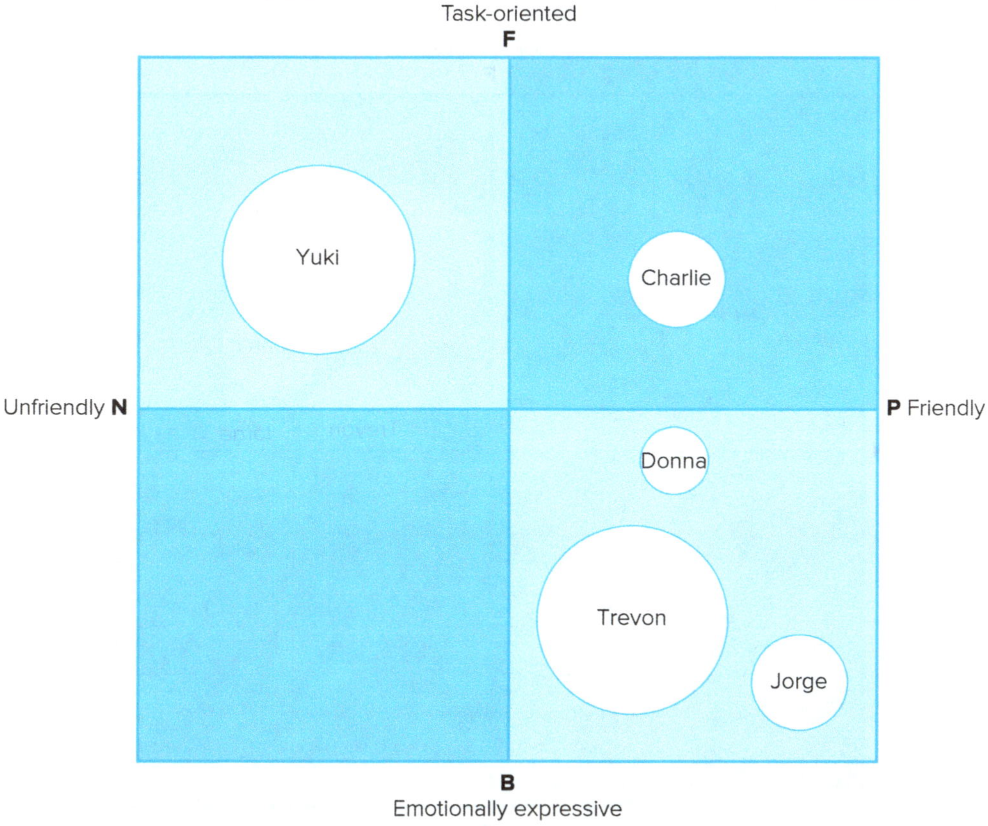

(The F stands for forward, or task-oriented behavior, and the B stands for backward, or emotionally expressive behavior.) The friendlier a member is toward the other members of the group, the closer he or she is to the right; the more unfriendly, the closer to the left. (The P stands for positive or friendly behavior, the N for negative or unfriendly behavior.) The third dimension, dominance or submissiveness, is shown by the size of the circle; a dominant member has a large circle, while a submissive one has a small one.

In the SYMLOG diagram in Figure A.8, Yuki is very dominant, task-oriented, and negative toward other members of the group. In contrast, Trevon is friendly and emotionally expressive, although he also is dominant. A group with two such strong, but opposite, individuals is likely to experience conflict during meetings. Charlie is moderately dominant, positive, and task-oriented. (This is how democratic leaders and members of productive, democratic groups often appear in SYMLOG diagrams.) If you were asked to describe this group, you would probably say that it is unproductive, lacks cohesiveness, and appears to waste a lot of time during meetings because there's a struggle between the most task-oriented and most emotionally expressive members.

The SYMLOG diagram in Figure A.9 shows a unified, cohesive group. All the members are in or near the upper right-hand quadrant (the decision-making quadrant),

FIGURE A.9 SYMLOG Diagram of a Cohesive Group

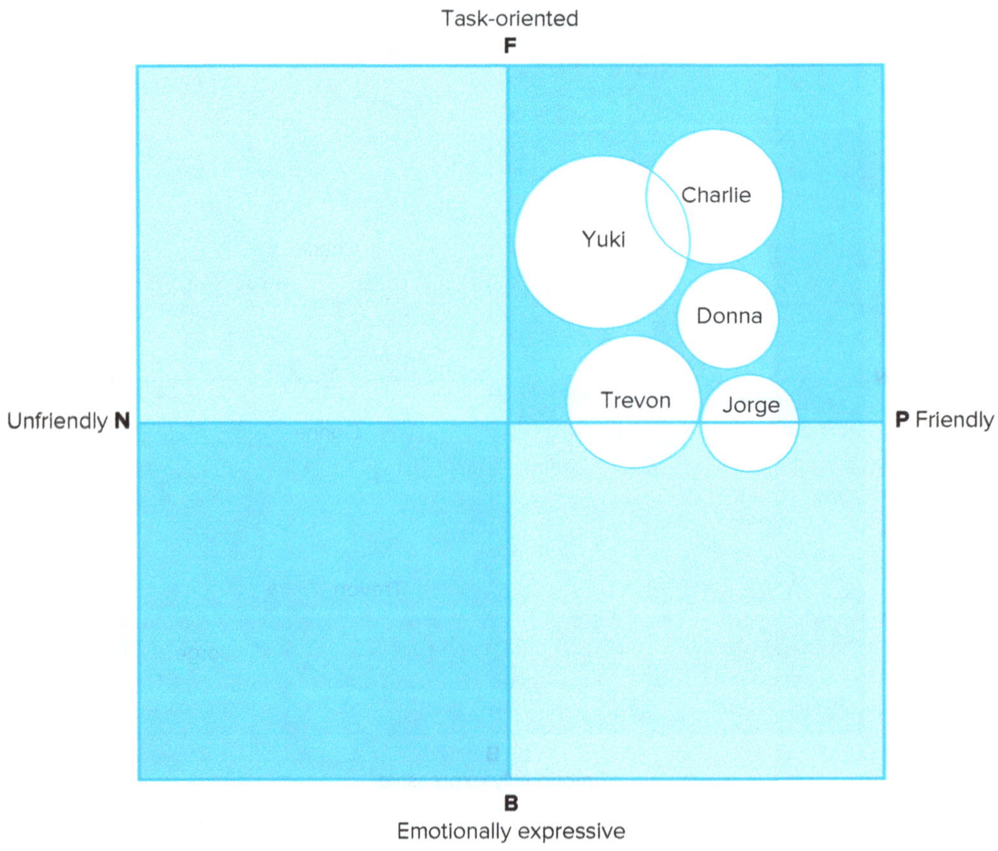

which shows that they are task-oriented enough to make progress toward the group's goal but friendly enough toward each other that interpersonal relationships are probably harmonious. This group is likely to be productive and efficient.

Thinking in SYMLOG terminology helps you manage the complexity of group interaction as you create a snapshot capturing the texture of a group. Because SYMLOG gives you that visual representation, it is easy to grasp several complex relationships at once. That makes this tool particularly effective in helping you and your fellow group members analyze and diagnose yourselves. It also gives you an idea of what you might do if problems are revealed. A SYMLOG diagram represents the perceptions of the person who constructed it; this provides potentially valuable information to help group members begin discussing their perceptions and preferences. For instance, those members whose SYMLOG diagrams show that they perceive Yuki to be unfriendly may be asked to share specific examples that led them to that conclusion. Likewise, those whose diagrams place Trevon in the emotionally expressive area can explain why they see him that way and what they feel about it.

If it is too threatening or frightening for group members to conduct such discussions on their own, a trusted facilitator can help manage the discussion. Consultants who use SYMLOG often ask members of the group being observed to complete the SYMLOG forms in advance. From these they create SYMLOG diagrams to distribute to the group. Having the SYMLOG "pictures" prompts members to talk about themselves and their relationships with each other in a relatively nonthreatening way. This can set the stage for tremendous growth and development in the group. Take a look at Figure A.10. Assume you are a consultant brought in to help Basil and his group. In preparation for meeting with the group you asked the members to fill out the SYMLOG rating scales and from those you constructed SYMLOG diagrams for each member. Basil's is on the left in Figure A.10

**FIGURE A.10** Data From a SYMLOG Analysis

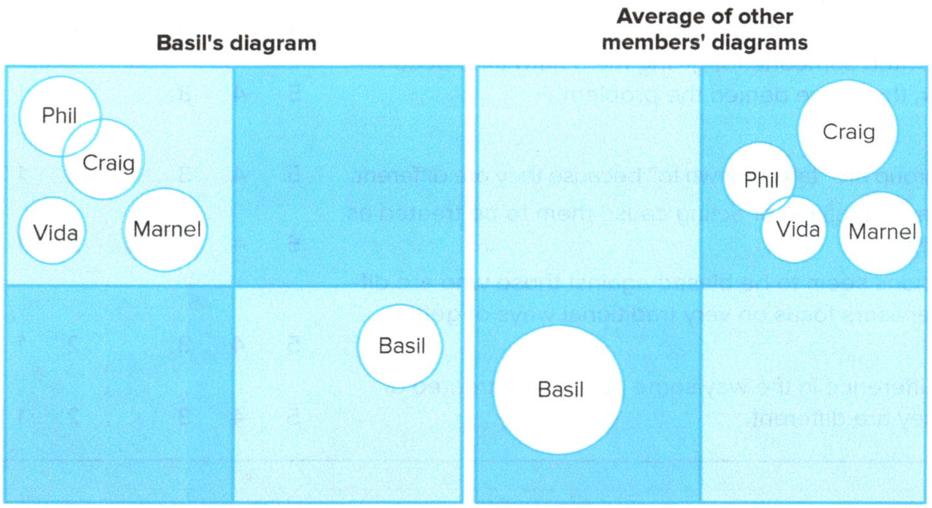

and since the other four were so similar you combined their responses into a single one on the right.

1. Interpret the group from Basil's perspective.
2. Interpret it from the others' perspectives.

**FIGURE A.11 Workplace Diversity Questionnaire**

| | Agree | | | | Disagree |
|---|---|---|---|---|---|
| **Inclusion** | | | | | |
| 1. If someone who is not included in the mainstream tries to get information or makes a request, others stall or avoid helping them out in subtle ways. | 5 | 4 | 3 | 2 | 1 |
| 2. It seems that the real reason people are denied promotions or raises is that they are seen as not fitting in. | 5 | 4 | 3 | 2 | 1 |
| 3. I have to prove myself more and work a lot harder to get into that next position because of my gender or ethnic background. | 5 | 4 | 3 | 2 | 1 |
| 4. It's hard to get ahead here unless you are part of the old boys' network. | 5 | 4 | 3 | 2 | 1 |
| **Ideation** | | | | | |
| 5. When people from different backgrounds work together in groups, some people feel slighted because their ideas are not acknowledged. | 5 | 4 | 3 | 2 | 1 |
| 6. People are reluctant to get involved in a project that requires them to balance ideas from different gender and racial points of view. | 5 | 4 | 3 | 2 | 1 |
| 7. Individuals with different backgrounds have a difficult time getting their ideas across. | 5 | 4 | 3 | 2 | 1 |
| 8. Individuals in our group have a difficult time really listening with an open mind to the ideas presented by those of another culture or gender. | 5 | 4 | 3 | 2 | 1 |
| **Understanding** | | | | | |
| 9. When people who are culturally different or of different genders work together in our group, there is always some amount of miscommunication. | 5 | 4 | 3 | 2 | 1 |
| 10. Women and people of color are interpreted differently than white males, even when they say the same thing. | 5 | 4 | 3 | 2 | 1 |
| 11. Whenever I've confronted someone for giving me a hard time because of my race or gender, they have denied the problem. | 5 | 4 | 3 | 2 | 1 |
| **Treatment** | | | | | |
| 12. Some people in our group are "talked down to" because they are different. | 5 | 4 | 3 | 2 | 1 |
| 13. People's different ways of talking or acting cause them to be treated as less competent or smart. | 5 | 4 | 3 | 2 | 1 |
| 14. Performance evaluations seem to be biased against those who are different, because supervisors focus on very traditional ways of getting work done. | 5 | 4 | 3 | 2 | 1 |
| 15. You can just feel a difference in the way some people are treated or talked to because they are different. | 5 | 4 | 3 | 2 | 1 |

3. How would you use this information to help the group?
4. What would be the focus of your work with this group and why?

There are a variety of ways to use SYMLOG. It is possible to construct a SYMLOG diagram by hand, and someone with skills on spreadsheet applications, such as Excel, can create a program to perform the necessary math for calculating the SYMLOG numbers. If this analysis appeals to you, we recommend that you purchase the *SYMLOG Case Study Kit,* which contains all the instructions and forms you need to produce a diagram by hand.

If you would like a less complex way to assess diversity in your group you can use the workplace diversity questionnaire (Figure A.11). This was created by Larkey to help members of diverse groups judge how well they manage their diversity.[3]

GLOSSARY

**Postmeeting Reaction (PMR) Forms**

*Questionnaires members complete after a meeting to evaluate that particular meeting*

## POSTMEETING REACTION FORMS

**Postmeeting reaction (PMR) forms** are questionnaires designed to get feedback from members about a particular meeting. PMR forms may focus on a particular aspect (such as leadership) or deal with several broad aspects (such as how effective members believe the meetings are). The leader, a member, or an observer distributes the PMR forms; members complete them anonymously, the results are tallied, and the findings are reported to the group as soon as possible. The findings provide a basis for the group to discuss how to improve its communication and effectiveness. Basil, the group leader in our introductory example, could have used PMR forms himself to get feedback from the other members about how the group's discussions could be improved.

PMR forms are tailored to fit the purposes and needs of the group. Questions may concern substantive items, interpersonal relationships, matters of procedure, or a mixture of all three. Two different examples of PMR forms are shown in Figures A.12 and A.13.

**FIGURE A.12 Postmeeting Reaction Form**

1. How do you feel about today's discussion?

   Excellent ___ Good ___ All right ___ So-so ___ Bad ___

2. What were the strong points of the discussion?

3. What were the weaknesses?

4. What changes would you suggest for future meetings?

(You need not sign your name.)

FIGURE A.13 Postmeeting Reaction Form

*Instructions:* Circle the number that best indicates your reactions to the following questions about the discussion in which you participated:

1. *Adequacy of Communication.* To what extent do you feel members were understanding each others' statements and positions?

   0 1 2 3 4 5 6 7 8 9 10

   Talked past each other; misunderstanding — Communicated directly with each other; understanding well

2. *Opportunity to Speak.* To what extent did you feel free to speak?

   0 1 2 3 4 5 6 7 8 9 10

   Never had a chance to speak — Had all the opportunity to talk I wanted

3. *Climate of Acceptance.* How well did members support each other, show acceptance of individuals?

   0 1 2 3 4 5 6 7 8 9 10

   Highly critical and punishing — Supportive and receptive

4. *Interpersonal Relations.* How pleasant and concerned were members with interpersonal relations?

   0 1 2 3 4 5 6 7 8 9 10

   Quarrelsome, status differences emphasized — Pleasant, empathic, concerned with persons

5. *Leadership.* How adequate was the leader (or leadership) of the group?

   0 1 2 3 4 5 6 7 8 9 10

   Too weak ( ) or dominating ( ) — Shared, group-centered, and sufficient

6. *Satisfaction with Role.* How satisfied are you with your personal participation in the discussion?

   0 1 2 3 4 5 6 7 8 9 10

   Very dissatisfied — Very satisfied

7. *Quality of Product.* How satisfied are you with the discussions, solutions, or learnings that came out of this discussion?

   0 1 2 3 4 5 6 7 8 9 10

   Very displeased — Very satisfied

8. *Overall.* How do you rate the discussion as a whole apart from any specific aspect of it?

   0 1 2 3 4 5 6 7 8 9 10

   Awful; waste of time — Superb; time well spent

## Evaluating Individual Participants

In addition to evaluating general group processes, it is often useful to evaluate behaviors of individual participants. An observer or the members themselves may complete the following forms. Figure A.14 is a simple rating form that focuses on

**FIGURE A.14 Participating Rating Scale**

Date ______________________

______________________ Observer ______________________

(Name of participant)

1. Contributions to the *content of the discussion?* (well prepared, supplied information, adequate reasoning, etc.)

| 5 | 4 | 3 | 2 | 1 |
|---|---|---|---|---|
| Outstanding in quality and quantity | | Fair share | | Few or none |

2. Contributions to *efficient group procedures?* (agenda planning, relevant comments, summaries, keeping on track)

| 5 | 4 | 3 | 2 | 1 |
|---|---|---|---|---|
| Always relevant, aided organization | | Relevant, no aid in order | | Sidetracked, confused group |

3. Degree of *cooperating?* (listening to understand, responsible, agreeable, group-centered, open-minded)

| 5 | 4 | 3 | 2 | 1 |
|---|---|---|---|---|
| Very responsible and constructive | | | | Self-centered |

4. *Speaking?* (clear, to group, one point at a time, concise)

| 5 | 4 | 3 | 2 | 1 |
|---|---|---|---|---|
| Brief, clear, to group | | | | Vague, indirect, wordy |

5. *Value* to the group? (overall rating)

| 5 | 4 | 3 | 2 | 1 |
|---|---|---|---|---|
| Most valuable | | | | Least valuable |

Suggestions:

**FIGURE A.15 Participating Rating Scale**

Participant's name ____________________

*Instructions:* Circle the number that best reflects your evaluation of the discussant's participation on each scale.

| Superior | | | | Poor | |
|---|---|---|---|---|---|
| 1 | 2 | 3 | 4 | 5 | 1. Was prepared and informed. |
| 1 | 2 | 3 | 4 | 5 | 2. Contributions were brief and clear. |
| 1 | 2 | 3 | 4 | 5 | 3. Comments relevant and well timed. |
| 1 | 2 | 3 | 4 | 5 | 4. Spoke distinctly and audibly to all. |
| 1 | 2 | 3 | 4 | 5 | 5. Contributions made readily and voluntarily. |
| 1 | 2 | 3 | 4 | 5 | 6. Frequency of participation (if poor, too low [] or high []). |
| 1 | 2 | 3 | 4 | 5 | 7. Nonverbal responses were clear and constant. |
| 1 | 2 | 3 | 4 | 5 | 8. Listened to understand and follow discussion. |
| 1 | 2 | 3 | 4 | 5 | 9. Open-minded. |
| 1 | 2 | 3 | 4 | 5 | 10. Cooperative and constructive. |
| 1 | 2 | 3 | 4 | 5 | 11. Helped keep discussion organized, following outline. |
| 1 | 2 | 3 | 4 | 5 | 12. Contributed to evaluation of information and ideas. |
| 1 | 2 | 3 | 4 | 5 | 13. Respectful and tactful with others. |
| 1 | 2 | 3 | 4 | 5 | 14. Encouraged others to participate. |
| 1 | 2 | 3 | 4 | 5 | 15. Overall rating in relation to other discussants. |

Comments Evaluator ____________________

some of the most important aspects of participation. A more detailed form is shown in Figure A.15. Figure A.16 is a scale to evaluate conflict styles, Figure A.17 is a scale to evaluate leadership, and Figure A.18 is a leader's self-rating scale.

**FIGURE A.16 Ross-Dewine Conflict Management Message Style Instrument**

Directions: Below you will find messages that have been delivered by persons in conflict situations. Consider each message separately and decide how closely this message resembles the ones that you have used in conflict settings. The language may not be exactly the same as yours, but consider the messages in terms of similarity to your messages in conflict. There are no right or wrong answers, nor are these messages designed to trick you. Answer in terms of responses you make, not what you think you should say. Give each message a 1–5 rating on the answer sheet provided according to the following scale. Mark one answer only.

In conflict situations, I

| 1 | 2 | 3 | 4 | 5 |
|---|---|---|---|---|
| **never say things like this** | **rarely say things like this** | **sometimes say things like this** | **often say things like this** | **usually say things like this** |

_______ 1. "Can't you see how foolish you're being with that thinking?"

_______ 2. "How can I make you feel happy again?"

_______ 3. "I'm really bothered by some things that are happening here; can we talk about these?"

_______ 4. "I really don't have any more to say on this . . . " (silence)

_______ 5. "What possible solution can we come up with?"

_______ 6. "I'm really sorry that your feelings are hurt—maybe you're right."

_______ 7. "Let's talk this thing out and see how we can deal with this hassle."

_______ 8. "Shut up! You are wrong! I don't want to hear any more of what you have to say."

_______ 9. "It is your fault if I fail at this, and don't you ever expect any help from me when you're on the spot."

_______ 10. "You can't do (say) that to me—it's either my way or forget it."

_______ 11. "Let's try finding an answer that will give us both some of what we want."

_______ 12. "This is something we have to work out; we're always arguing about it."

_______ 13. "Whatever makes you feel happiest is OK by me."

_______ 14. "Let's just leave well enough alone."

_______ 15. "That's OK . . . it wasn't important anyway . . . You feeling OK now?"

_______ 16. "If you're not going to cooperate, I'll just go to someone who will."

_______ 17. "I think we need to try to understand the problem."

_______ 18. "You might as well accept my decision; you can't do anything about it anyway."

Scoring:
Self-oriented: Add items 1, 4, 8, 9, 10, 16, 18
Other-oriented: Add items 2, 6, 13, 14, 15
Issue-oriented: Add items 3, 5, 7, 11, 12, 17
Roseanna G. Ross and Sue DeWine, "Assessing the Ross-DeWine Conflict Management Message Style (CMMS)," *Management Communication Quarterly* 1 (February 1988), 389–413.

**FIGURE A.17 Barnlund-Haiman Leadership Rating Scale**

*Instructions:* This rating scale may be used to evaluate leadership in groups with or without official leaders. In the latter case (the leaderless group), use part A of each item only. When evaluating the actions of an official leader, use parts A and B of each item on the scale.

## Influence in Procedure

*Initiating Discussion*

A.

| 3 | 2 | 1 | 0 | 1 | 2 | 3 |
|---|---|---|---|---|---|---|
| Group needed more help in getting started | | | Group got right amount of help | | | Group needed less help in getting started |

B. The quality of the introductory remarks was

| Excellent | Good | Adequate | Fair | Poor |
|---|---|---|---|---|

*Organizing Group Thinking*

A.

| 3 | 2 | 1 | 0 | 1 | 2 | 3 |
|---|---|---|---|---|---|---|
| Group needed more direction in thinking | | | Group got right amount of help | | | Group needed less direction in thinking |

B. If and when attempts were made to organize group thinking, they were

| Excellent | Good | Adequate | Fair | Poor |
|---|---|---|---|---|

*Clarifying Communication*

A.

| 3 | 2 | 1 | 0 | 1 | 2 | 3 |
|---|---|---|---|---|---|---|
| Group needed more help in clarifying communication | | | Group got right amount of help | | | Group needed less help in clarifying communication |

B. If and when attempts were made to clarify communication, they were

| Excellent | Good | Adequate | Fair | Poor |
|---|---|---|---|---|

*Summarizing and Verbalizing Agreements*

A.

| 3 | 2 | 1 | 0 | 1 | 2 | 3 |
|---|---|---|---|---|---|---|
| Group needed more help in summarizing and verbalizing agreements | | | Group got right amount of help | | | Group needed less help in summarizing and verbalizing agreements |

B. If and when attempts were made to summarize and verbalize, they were

| Excellent | Good | Adequate | Fair | Poor |
|---|---|---|---|---|

*Resolving Conflict*

A.

| 3 | 2 | 1 | 0 | 1 | 2 | 3 |
|---|---|---|---|---|---|---|
| Group needed more help in resolving conflict | | | Group got right amount of help | | | Group needed less help in resolving conflict |

B. If and when attempts were made to resolve conflict, they were

| Excellent | Good | Adequate | Fair | Poor |
|---|---|---|---|---|

*(continued)*

SOURCE: From D. C. Barnlund and F. S. Haiman, *The Dynamics of Discussion* (Boston, MA: Houghton-Mifflin, 1960), pp. 401–404. Used by permission of Robert Goldsmith, M.D., executor of Barnlund estate.[3]

**FIGURE A.17** *Continued*

## Influence in Creative and Critical Thinking

*Stimulating Critical Thinking*

A.

| 3 | 2 | 1 | 0 | 1 | 2 | 3 |
|---|---|---|---|---|---|---|
| Group needed more stimulation in creative thinking | | | Group got right amount of help | | | Group needed less stimulation in creative thinking |

B. If and when attempts were made to stimulate ideas, they were

| Excellent | Good | Adequate | Fair | Poor |
|---|---|---|---|---|

*Encouraging Criticism*

A.

| 3 | 2 | 1 | 0 | 1 | 2 | 3 |
|---|---|---|---|---|---|---|
| Group needed more encouragement to be critical | | | Group got right amount of help | | | Group needed less encouragement to be critical |

B. If and when attempts were made to encourage criticism, they were

| Excellent | Good | Adequate | Fair | Poor |
|---|---|---|---|---|

*Balancing Abstract and Concrete Thought*

A.

| 3 | 2 | 1 | 0 | 1 | 2 | 3 |
|---|---|---|---|---|---|---|
| Group needed to be more concrete | | | Group achieved proper balance | | | Group needed to be more abstract |

B. If and when attempts were made to balance abstract and concrete thought, they were

| Excellent | Good | Adequate | Fair | Poor |
|---|---|---|---|---|

## Influence in Interpersonal Relations

*Climate-Making*

A.

| 3 | 2 | 1 | 0 | 1 | 2 | 3 |
|---|---|---|---|---|---|---|
| Group needed more help in securing a permissive atmosphere | | | Group got right amount of help | | | Group needed less help in securing a permissive atmosphere |

B. If and when attempts were made to establish a permissive atmosphere, they were

| Excellent | Good | Adequate | Fair | Poor |
|---|---|---|---|---|

*Regulating Participation*

A.

| 3 | 2 | 1 | 0 | 1 | 2 | 3 |
|---|---|---|---|---|---|---|
| Group needed more regulation of participation | | | Group got right amount of help | | | Group needed less regulation of participation |

B. If and when attempts were made to regulate participation, they were

| Excellent | Good | Adequate | Fair | Poor |
|---|---|---|---|---|

*Overall Leadership*

A.

| 3 | 2 | 1 | 0 | 1 | 2 | 3 |
|---|---|---|---|---|---|---|
| Group needed more control | | | Group got right amount of control | | | Group needed less control |

B. If and when attempts were made to control the group, they were

| Excellent | Good | Adequate | Fair | Poor |
|---|---|---|---|---|

**FIGURE A.18 Leader Self-Rating Scale**

*Instructions:* Rate yourself on each item by putting a check mark in the "Yes" or "No" column. Your score is five times the number of items marked "Yes." Rating: *excellent,* 90 or higher; *good,* 80–85; *fair,* 70–75; *inadequate,* 65 or lower.

| | Yes | No |
|---|---|---|
| 1. I prepared all needed facilities. | ___ | ___ |
| 2. I started the meeting promptly and ended on time. | ___ | ___ |
| 3. I established an atmosphere of permissiveness and informality. I was open and responsive to all ideas. | ___ | ___ |
| 4. I clearly oriented the group to its purpose and area of freedom. | ___ | ___ |
| 5. I encouraged all members to participate and maintained equal opportunity for all to speak. | ___ | ___ |
| 6. I used a plan for leading the group in an organized consideration of all major phases of the problem. | ___ | ___ |
| 7. I listened actively and (if needed) encouraged all members to do so. | ___ | ___ |
| 8. I saw to it that the problem was discussed thoroughly before solutions were considered. | ___ | ___ |
| 9. I integrated related ideas or suggestions and urged the group to arrive at consensus on a solution. | ___ | ___ |
| 10. My questions were clear and brief. | ___ | ___ |
| 11. I saw to it that unclear statements were paraphrased or otherwise clarified. | ___ | ___ |
| 12. I prompted open discussion of substantive conflicts. | ___ | ___ |
| 13. I maintained order and organization, promptly pointing out tangents, making transitions, and keeping track of the passage of time. | ___ | ___ |
| 14. I saw to it that the meeting produced definite assignments or plans for action, and that any subsequent meeting was arranged. | ___ | ___ |
| 15. All important information, ideas, and decisions were promptly and accurately recorded. | ___ | ___ |
| 16. I actively encouraged creative thinking. | ___ | ___ |
| 17. I encouraged thorough evaluation of information and all ideas for solutions. | ___ | ___ |
| 18. I was able to remain neutral during constructive arguments and otherwise encourage teamwork. | ___ | ___ |
| 19. I suggested or urged establishment of needed norms and standards. | ___ | ___ |
| 20. I encouraged members to discuss how they felt about the group process and resolve any blocks to progress. | ___ | ___ |

## RESOURCES FOR REVIEW AND DISCUSSION

### SUMMARY

- A consultant-observer is an outsider brought in to observe a group; such observers may be more objective than participant-observers.
- Participant- and consultant-observers cannot look at everything at once, so they concentrate on those elements a group needs to improve most.
- When they give feedback, they focus on a few elements rather than risk overwhelming the group.
- Observers and group members themselves can use a variety of methods to gather information, including verbal interaction analyses, content analyses, and rating scales.

### KEY TERMS • CONCEPTS

Consultant-Observer
Content Analysis Procedures
Postmeeting Reaction (PMR) Forms
Rating Scales
SYMLOG
Verbal Interaction Analysis

**Chapter 1**

1. Synthesized from information in Samantha Glen, *Best Friends: The True Story of the World's Most Beloved Animal Sanctuary* (New York: Kensington Books, 2001), and from the Best Friends Animal Society website, accessed (again) on June 17, 2016: http://www.bestfriends.org.
2. Best Friends Animal Society website, accessed (again) on June 17, 2016: http://www.Bestfriends.org/About/Our-Story/History Best Friends
3. About Women's History website, accessed (again) on February 7, 2011: http://womenshistory.about.com/cs/quotes/a/qu_margaretmead.htm. The origin of this quote is unknown, but Margaret Mead is believed to have said this spontaneously and then been quoted in a newspaper report.
4. Michelle Tullier, "The Skills You Have . . . and the Skills They Want," accessed (again) on June 17, 2016: http://career-advice.monster.com/job-search/getting-started/skills-you-have-skills-they-want/article.aspx.
5. Sarah Haberman, "My Advice to a College Freshman: Showing Up to Class Is Great, But There's So Much More You Can Do," accessed June 17, 2016: http://www.monstercom/blog/b/advice-college-freshman-0902.
6. Rob Cross, Reb Rebele, and Adam Grant, "Collaborative Overload," *Harvard Business Review*, January-February 2016. http://www.Hbr.org/2016/01/Collaborative-Overload.
7. Gardiner Harris, "New for Aspiring Doctors, the People Skills Test," *The New York Times,* July 10, 2011. http://www.nytimes.com/2011/07/11/health/policy/11docs.html.
8. Ellen Neuborne, "Companies Save, but Workers Pay," *USA Today*, February 25, 1997, pp. 1B–2B.
9. Cross, Rebele, and Grant, "Collaborative Overload."
10. Daniel McGinn, "Mired in Meetings," *Newsweek,* October 16, 2000, pp. 52–54.
11. Steven G. Rogelberg, Linds Rhoades Shanock, and Cliff W. Scott, "Wasted Time and Money in Meetings: Increasing Return on Investment," *Small Group Research* 43 (2012), pp. 236–45.
12. Lawrence R. Frey, "The Call of the Field: Studying Communication in Natural Groups," in *Group Communication in Context,* ed. Lawrence R. Frey (Hillsdale, NJ: Lawrence Erlbaum, 1994), pp. ix–xiv.
13. Charles C. DuBois, "Portrait of the Ideal MBA," *The Penn Stater,* September/October 1992, p. 131.
14. Joann Keyton, "Relational Communication in Groups," in *Handbook of Group Communication Theory & Research,* ed. Lawrence R. Frey (Thousand Oaks, CA: Sage, 1999), p. 192.
15. Glen, *Best Friends.*
16. Ibid., p. 116.
17. This line of research began in 1928 and continues to the present. For a concise summary of the research, see Marvin E. Shaw, *Group Dynamics,* 3rd ed. (New York: McGraw-Hill, 1981), pp. 57–64.
18. Herm W. Smith, "Group versus Individual Problem Solving and Type of Problem Solved," *Small Group Behavior* 20 (1989), pp. 357–74.
19. Dana Powell and Robert G. Powell, *Classroom Communication and Diversity: Enhancing Instructional Practice* (Mahwah, NJ: Lawrence Erlbaum, 2016), pp. 230–44.
20. Charles Duhigg, "What Google Learned from Its Quest to Build a Perfect Team," *The New York Times Magazine*, February 25, 2016. http://www.nytimes.com/2016/02/28/magazine/what-google-learned-from-its-quest-to-build-the-perfect-team.html?smid=nytcore-ipad-share&smprod=nytcore-ipad.
21. Powell and Powell, *Classroom Communication and Diversity: Enhancing Instructional Practice.*
22. Dennis S. Gouran and Randy Y. Hirokawa, "Counteractive Functions of Communication in Effective Group Decision Making," in *Communication and Group Decision Making,* eds. Randy Y. Hirokawa and Marshall Scott Poole (Beverly Hills, CA: Sage, 1986), pp. 81–90.
23. Associated Press, "Second Opinion Can Spark Big Changes," accessed (again) on February 7, 2011: http://www.msnbc.msn.com/id/16430071/.
24. Shaw, *Group Dynamics,* p. 8.
25. Susan A. Wheelan, "Group Size, Group Development, and Group Productivity," *Small Group Research* 40 (2009), pp. 247–62.
26. Steven A. Beebe and John T. Masterson, *Communicating in Small Groups,* 7th ed. (Boston, MA: Allyn & Bacon, 2003), pp. 6–9.
27. Frank LaFasto and Carl Larson, *When Teams Work Best: 6,000 Team Members and Leaders Tell What It Takes to Succeed* (Thousand Oaks, CA: Sage, 2001), pp. xii–xiii.
28. Randy Y. Hirokawa, Robert S. Cathcart, Larry A. Samovar, and Linda D. Henman, "Part IV: Group Processes," in *Small Group*

*Communication: Theory and Practice,* 8th ed., eds. Randy Y. Hirokawa, Robert S. Cathcart, Larry A. Samovar, and Linda D. Henman (Los Angeles, CA: Roxbury, 2003), p. 83.

29. Stefanie K. Johnson, Kenneth Bettenhausen, and Ellie Gibbons, "Realities of Working in Virtual Teams: Affective and Attitudinal Outcomes of Using Computer-Mediated Communication," *Small Group Research* 40 (2009), pp. 623–49.
30. Sandra Ketrow, "Nonverbal Aspects of Group Communication," in *Handbook of Group Communication Theory & Research,* ed. Lawrence R. Frey (Thousand Oaks, CA: Sage, 1999), pp. 251–87.
31. Joseph B. Walther, Tracy Loh, and Laura Granka, "Let Me Count the Ways: The Interchange of Verbal and Nonverbal Cues in Computer-Mediated and Face-to-Face Affinity," *Journal of Language and Social Psychology* 24 (2005), pp. 36–65.
32. Will Schutz, *The Human Element: Productivity, Self-Esteem, and the Bottom Line* (San Francisco, CA: Jossey-Bass, 1994).
33. Thomas J. Socha, "Communication in Family Units," in *Handbook of Group Communication Theory & Research,* ed. Lawrence R. Frey (Thousand Oaks, CA: Sage, 1999), pp. 475–92.
34. Joann Keyton and Stephensen J. Beck, "The Influential Role of Relational Messages in Group Interaction," *Group Dynamics: Theory, Research, and Practice* 13 (2009), pp. 14–30.
35. Carolyn M. Anderson and Matthew M. Martin, "The Effects of Communication Motives, Interaction Involvement, and Loneliness on Satisfaction: A Model of Small Groups," *Small Group Research* 26 (February 1995), pp. 118–37.
36. Kevin Wright, "Perceptions of On-Line Support Providers: An Examination of Perceived Homophily, Course Credibility, Communication and Social Support Within On-Line Support Groups," *Communication Quarterly* 48 (Winter 2000), pp. 44–59.
37. Susan A. Wheelan and Alan R. List, "Cohort Group Effectiveness and the Educational Achievement of Adult Undergraduate Students," *Small Group Research* 31 (December 2000), pp. 724–38.
38. Henry P. Sims, Jr., and James W. Dean, Jr., "Beyond Quality Circles: Self-Managing Teams," *Personnel Journal* (1985), pp. 25–32.
39. Chuck Blakeman, "Why Self-Managed Teams Are the Future of Business," *INC*, accessed June 17, 2016: http://www.inc.com/chuck-blakeman/why-self-managed-teams-are-the-future-of-business.html.
40. Suggestions synthesized from Neil Clark, *Teambuilding: A Practical Guide for Trainers* (New York: McGraw-Hill, 1994); Glenn M. Parker, *Team Players and Teamwork* (San Francisco, CA: Jossey-Bass, 1991); and Glenn H. Varney, *Building Productive Teams: An Action Guide and Resource Book* (San Francisco, CA: Jossey-Bass, 1989).
41. *The Random House Dictionary of the English Language,* 2nd ed. unabridged (New York: Random House, 1987), p. 665.
42. Charles Duhigg, "What Google Learned from Its Quest to Build a Perfect Team."

#### Chapter 2

1. Dawn Steel (Producer) and Jon Turtetaub (Director), *Cool Runnings* [Film]. Distributed by Walt Disney Pictures (1993) and available on video.
2. Em Griffin, *A First Look at Communication Theory,* 2nd ed. (New York: McGraw-Hill, 2003), p. 4.
3. Daniel Katz and Robert Kahn, *The Social Psychology of Organizations,* 2nd ed. (New York: Wiley, 1978).
4. Benjamin J. Broome and Luann Fulbright, "A Multistage Influence Model of Barriers to Small Group Problem Solving: A Participant-Generated Agenda for Small Group Research," *Small Group Research* 26 (February 1995), pp. 25–55.
5. Linda Putnam and Cynthia Stohl, "Bona Fide Groups: An Alternative Perspective for Communication and Small Group Decision Making," in *Communication and Group Decision Making,* 2nd ed., eds. Randy Hirokawa and Marshall Poole (Thousand Oaks, CA: Sage, 1996), pp. 147–78.
6. Broome and Fulbright, "A Multistage Influence Model."
7. Randy Y. Hirokawa and Joann Keyton, "Perceived Facilitators and Inhibitors of Effectiveness in Organizational Work Teams," *Management Communication Quarterly* 8 (May 1995), pp. 424–46.
8. Deborah G. Ancona and David F. Caldwell, "Bridging the Boundary: External Activity and Performance in Organizational Teams," *Administrative Science Quarterly* 37 (December 1992), pp. 634–65.
9. Cynthia Stohl and Kasey Walker, "A Bona Fide Perspective for the Future of Groups," in *New Directions in Group Communication,* ed. Lawrence

R. Frey (Thousand Oaks, CA: Sage, 2002), pp. 237–52.

10. Paul Elias, "Courts Finally Catching Up to Texting Jurors," *Blue Ridge Now*, March 6, 2010, http://www.blueridgenow.com/article/20100306/NEWS/100309838.

11. Deborah G. Ancona and David F. Caldwell, "Beyond Task and Maintenance: Defining External Functions in Groups," *Group & Organization Studies* 13 (December 1988), pp. 468–94; Deborah G. Ancona and David F. Caldwell, "Bridging the Boundary: External Activity and Performance in Organizational Teams," *Administrative Science Quarterly* 37 (December 1992), pp. 634–65.

12. Anat Drach-Zahavy and Anit Somech, "From an Intrateam to an Interteam Perspective of Effectiveness: The Role of Interdependence and Boundary Activities," *Small Group Research* 41, no. 2 (2010), pp. 143–74.

13. Amy Tessler, Norm Wada, and Bob Klein, "Quality Function Deployment (QFD) at PG&E: Applying Quality Function Deployment to the Residential Services of Pacific Gas & Electric," accessed January 6, 2007: www.ams-inc.com/publications/reprints.asp?id=6.

14. Beth Bonniwell Haslett and John R. Ogilive, "Feedback Processes in Task Groups," in *Small Group Communication: Theory and Practice,* 8th ed., eds. Randy Hirokawa, Robert Cathcart, Larry Samovar, and Linda Henman (Los Angeles, CA: Roxbury, 2003), pp. 97–108.

15. Ibid.

16. Ibid.

17. Ibid.

18. Harold Carey and Patrick Laughlin, "Groups Perform Better Than the Best Individuals on Letters-to-Numbers Problems: Effects of Induced Strategies," *Group Processes and Intergroup Relations* 15 (2012), pp. 231–42.

19. David A. Harrison, Kenneth. H. Price, Joanne H. Gavin, and Anna T. Florey, "Time, Teams, and Task Performance: Changing Attitudes of Surface and Deep-Level Diversity on Group Functioning," *Academy of Management Journal* 45 (October 2002), pp. 1029–45.

20. Abran J. Salazar, "Understanding the Synergistic Effects of Communication in the Small Group: Making the Most of Group Member Abilities," *Small Group Research* 26 (May 1995), pp. 169–99.

21. Charles Duhigg, "What Google Learned from Its Quest to Build a Perfect Team."

22. Stephen W. Littlejohn, *Theories of Human Communication,* 7th ed. (Belmont, CA: Wadsworth /Thomson Learning, 2002).

**Chapter 3**

1. Richard West and Lynn H. Turner, *Introducing Communication Theory: Analysis and Application,* 2nd ed. (New York: McGraw-Hill, 2004).

2. John W. Howard, " Tower Am I Cleared to Land?": Problematic Communication in Aviation Discourse," *Human Communication Research* 34 (2008), pp. 370–91.

3. Paul Watzlawick, Janet H. Beavin, and Don D. Jackson, *The Pragmatics of Human Communication* (New York: Norton, 1967).

4. Charles Duhigg, "What Google Learned from Its Quest to Build a Perfect Team."

5. Michael Purdy, "The Listener Wins," http://content.comcast.monster.com/business-communication/The-Listener-Wins/home.aspx, accessed June 18, 2016.

6. Curt Bechler and Scott D. Johnson, "Leadership and Listening: A Study of Members' Perceptions," *Small Group Research* 26 (February 1995), pp. 77–85.

7. Lyman K. Steil, Larry L. Barker, and Kittie W. Watson, *Effective Listening: Key to Your Success* (Reading, MA: Addison-Wesley, 1983), pp. 21–22.

8. Purdy, "The Listener Wins."

9. Kittie W. Watson, "Listener Preferences: The Paradox of Small-Group Interactions," in *Small Group Communication: Theory and Practice,* 7th ed., eds. Robert S. Cathcart, Larry A. Samovar, and Linda Henman (Madison, WI: Brown & Benchmark, 1996), pp. 268–82.

10. Eva M. Lira, Pilar Ripoll, José M. Peiró, and Ana M. Zornoza, "The Role of Information and Communication Technologies in the Relationship Between Group Effectiveness and Group Potency: A Longitudinal Study," *Small Group Research* 39 (December 2008), pp. 728–45.

11. Charlene Solomon, "The Challenge of Working in Virtual Teams: Virtual Teams Survey Report 2010," *RW3 Culture Wizard*, http://www.communicationcache.com/uploads/1/0/8/8/10887248/the_challenges_of_working_in_virtual_teams.pdf.

12. Sebastian Bailey, "How to Best the Five Killers of Virtual Working," *Forbes/Entrepreneurs* (March 5, 2013), http://www.forbes.com/sites/sebastianbailey/2013/03/05/how-to-overcome-the-five-major-disadvantages-of-virtual-working/#b78086553d71.

13. San Bolkan and Jennifer Linn Holmgren, " 'You are such a great teacher and I hate to bother you but . . .': Instructors' Perceptions of Students and Their Use of Email Messages with Varying Politeness Strategies," *Communication Education* 61 (July 2012), pp. 253–70.

**Chapter 4**

1. Joseph A. DeVito, *The Communication Handbook: A Dictionary* (New York: Harper & Row, 1986).
2. Wendy Leeds-Hurwitz, *Communication in Everyday Life: A Social Interpretation,* 3rd ed. (Norwood, NJ: Ablex, 1992).
3. Charles Duhigg, "What Google Learned from Its Quest to Build a Perfect Team."
4. This example is a modification of a case where a Fresno, California, high school student was suspended from school for using "nigga" to greet a friend on school grounds.
5. Michael Watkins, "Making Virtual Teams Work: Ten Basic Principles," *Harvard Business Review* (June 27, 2013). https://hbr.org/2013/06/making-virtual-teams-work-ten.
6. Meredith May, "Talkin' off the Hizzle with Homeys," *San Francisco Chronicle,* April 29, 2001, pp. A1, A17.
7. Ibid., p. A17.
8. John Stewart and Carol Logan, *Together: Communicating Interpersonally,* 5th ed. (New York: McGraw-Hill, 1998).
9. Ibid.
10. Ray L. Birdwhistell, *Kinesics and Context: Essays on Body Motion Communication.* (Philadelphia, PA: University of Pennsylvania Press, 1970).
11. Dana R. Carney, Judith A. Hall, and Lavonia Smith LeBeau, "Beliefs about the Nonverbal Expression of Social Power," *Journal of Nonverbal Behavior,* 29, no. 2 (Summer 2005), pp. 105–21.
12. Timothy P. Mottet, Steven A. Beebe, Paul C. Raffeld, and Michelle L. Paulsel, "The Effects of Student Verbal and Nonverbal Responsiveness on Teachers' Liking of Students and Willingness to Comply with Student Requests," *Communication Quarterly,* 52, no. 1 (Winter 2004), pp. 27–38.
13. Kory Floyd and George Ray, "Adaptation to Expressed Liking and Disliking in Initial Interactions: Response Patterns for Nonverbal Involvement and Pleasantness," paper presented at the International Communication Association Conference, New York, May 26–30, 2005.
14. Sandra Ketrow, "Nonverbal Aspects of Group Communication," in *The Handbook of Group Communication Theory & Research,* ed. Lawrence R. Frey (Thousand Oaks, CA: Sage, 1999), pp. 251–87.
15. Ibid.
16. Edward T. Hall, *The Silent Language* (Garden City, NY: Doubleday, 1959).
17. Ketrow, "Nonverbal Aspects of Group Communication."
18. Ibid.
19. Judee K. Burgoon, Don W. Stacks, and Steven A. Burch, "The Role of Interpersonal Rewards and Violations of Distancing Expectations in Achieving Influence in Small Groups," *Communication: Journal of the Association of the Pacific* 11 (1982), pp. 114–28.
20. Ketrow, "Nonverbal Aspects of Group Communication."
21. P. Eckman, P. Ellsworth, and W. V. Friesen, *Emotion in the Human Face: Guidelines for Research and an Integration of Findings* (New York: Pergamon, 1971).
22. Mark Frank, Anastacia Kurylo, Kang Sinuk, AmyMarie Keller, Malgorzata Habasz, and Courtney Nolan, "I See How You Feel: Training Laypeople and Professionals to Recognize Fleeting Emotions," paper presented at the International Communication Association conference, New York, May 26–30, 2005.
23. A. E. Scheffler, "Quasi-Courtship Behavior in Psychotherapy," *Psychiatry* 28 (1965), pp. 245–56.
24. Edward A. Mabry, "Developmental Aspects of Nonverbal Behavior in Small Group Settings," *Small Group Behavior* 20 (1989), pp. 190–202.
25. Martin Remland, "Developing Leadership Skills in Nonverbal Communication: A Situational Perspective," *Journal of Business Communication* 3 (1981), pp. 17–29.
26. Judee K. Burgoon and Thomas Saine, *The Unknown Dialogue: An Introduction to Nonverbal Communication* (Boston, MA: Houghton Mifflin, 1978).
27. Joel D. Davitz and Lois Davitz, "Nonverbal Vocal Communication of Feelings," *Journal of Communication* 11 (1961), pp. 81–86.
28. Ketrow, "Nonverbal Aspects of Group Communication."
29. Pino Cutrone, "A Case Study Examining Backchannels in Conversations between

Japanese-British Dyads," *Multilingua,* 24, no. 3 (2005), pp. 237–74.

30. Han Z. Li, "Backchannel Responses as Misleading Feedback in Intercultural Discourse," *Journal of Intercultural Communication Research* 35, no. 2 (July 2006), pp. 99–116.
31. Donald Klopf, *Intercultural Encounters: The Fundamentals of Intercultural Communication* (Englewood, CO: Morion, 1987), p. 177.
32. R. G. Harper, A. N. Weins, and J. D. Matarazzo, *Nonverbal Communication: The State of the Art* (New York: Wiley, 1978).
33. Hall, *The Silent Language,* pp. 175–76.
34. Ketrow, "Nonverbal Aspects of Group Communication."
35. Ibid.
36. Amy L. Gonzales, Jeffrey T. Hancock, and James W. Pennebaker, "Language Style Matching as a Predictor of Social Dynamics in Small Groups," *Communication Research* 37 (2010), pp. 3–19.
37. Charlene Solomon, "The Challenge of Working in Virtual Teams: Virtual Teams Survey Report 2010," *RW3 Culture Wizard,* http://www.communicationcache.com/uploads/1/0/8/8/10887248/the_challenges_of_working_in_virtual_teams.pdf.
38. S. R. Hiltz and M. Turoff, "Virtual Meetings: Computer Conferencing and Distributed Group Support," in *Computer Augmented Teamwork: A Guided Tour,* eds. R. P. Bostrom, R. T. Watson, and S. T. Kinney (New York: Van Nostrand Reinhold, 1992), pp. 67–85.
39. Everett M. Rogers, *Communication Technology: The New Media in Society* (New York: Free Press, 1986).
40. Sebastian Bailey, "How to Best the Five Killers of Virtual Working," *Forbes/Entrepreneurs* (March 5, 2013): http://www.forbes.com/sites/sebastianbailey/2013/03/05/how-to-overcome-the-five-major-disadvantages-of-virtual-working/#5280d0fd53d7.
41. Joseph B. Walther, Tracy Loh, and Laura Granka, "Let Me Count the Ways: The Interchange of Verbal and Nonverbal Cues in Computer-Mediated and Face-to-Face Affinity," *Journal of Language and Social Psychology* 24 (2005), pp. 36–65; Social Information Processing Theory of Joseph Walther, Chapter 11 in *A First Look at Communication Theory,* 7th ed., by Em Griffin (New York: McGraw-Hill, 2009), pp. 138–50.

**Chapter 5**

1. Marshall Scott Poole, David R. Siebold, and Robert D. McPhee, "Group Decision Making as a Structurational Process," *Quarterly Journal of Speech* 71 (1985), pp. 74–102; Marshall Scott Poole, "Group Communication and the Structuring Process," in *Small Group Communication: Theory & Practice, An Anthology,* 8th ed., eds. Randy Y. Hirokawa, Robert S. Cathcart, Larry A. Samovar, and Linda D. Henman (Los Angeles, CA: Roxbury, 2003), pp. 48–58.
2. Simone Kauffeld and Nale Lehmann-Willenbrock, "Meetings Matter: Effects of Team Meetings on Team and Organizational Success," *Small Group Research* 43 (2012), pp. 130–58.
3. Robert F. Bales, "The Equilibrium Problem in Small Groups," in *Working Papers in the Theory of Action,* eds. Talcott Parsons, Robert F. Bales, and Edward A. Shils (New York: Free Press, 1953), pp. 111–61.
4. The terms *primary* and *secondary tension* were first used by Ernest G. Bormann; elaboration of the concepts may be found in Bormann, *Discussion and Group Methods: Theory and Practice,* 2nd ed. (New York: Harper & Row, 1975), pp. 181–90.
5. Donald G. Ellis and B. Aubrey Fisher, *Small Group Decision Making: Communication and the Group Process,* 4th ed. (New York: McGraw-Hill, 1994), p. 38.
6. Bormann, *Discussion and Group Methods.*
7. Ellis and Fisher, *Small Group Decision Making,* p. 38.
8. Joseph B. Walther and Judee K. Burgoon, "Relational Communication in Computer-Mediated Interaction," *Human Communication Research* 19 (1992), pp. 50–88.
9. Bruce Tuckman, "Developmental Sequence in Small Groups," *Psychological Bulletin* 63 (1965), pp. 384–99; Bruce Tuckman and Mary Ann Jensen, "Stages of Small-Group Development Revisited," *Group & Organization Studies* 2, no. 4 (1977), pp. 419–27.
10. Connie Gersick, "Time and Transition in Work Teams," in *Small Group Communication: Theory & Practice,* 8th ed., eds. Randy Hirokawa, Robert Cathcart, Larry Samovar, and Linda Henman (Los Angeles, CA: Roxbury, 2003), pp. 59–75.
11. Carolyn M. Anderson, Bruce L. Riddle, and Matthew M. Martin, "Socialization Processes in

Groups," in *Handbook of Group Communication Theory & Research,* ed. Lawrence R. Frey (Thousand Oaks, CA: Sage, 1999), p. 142.

12. Ibid., pp. 139–63.
13. Anderson et al., p. 149.
14. Stewart Sigman, "The Applicability of the Concept of Recruitment to the Communication Study of a Nursing Home: An Ethnographic Case Study," *International Journal of Aging and Human Development* 22 (1985–86), pp. 215–33. See also Melanie Booth-Butterfield, Stephen Booth-Butterfield, and Jolene Koester, "The Function of Uncertainty Reduction in Alleviating Primary Tension in Small Groups," *Communication Research Reports* 5 (1988), pp. 146–53.
15. Anderson et al., "Socialization Processes in Groups," p. 151.
16. K.E.W. Morrison, "Information Usefulness and Acquisition During Organizational Encounter," *Management Communication Quarterly* 9 (1995), pp. 131–55.
17. Anderson et al., p. 152.
18. Ibid., p. 164.
19. Joann Keyton, "Group Termination: Completing the Study of Group Development," *Small Group Research* 24 (1993), pp. 84–100.
20. Moira Burke, Robert Kraut, and Elisabeth Joyce, "Membership Claims and Requests: Conversation-Level Newcomer Socialization Strategies in Online Groups," *Small Group Research* 41 (2010), pp. 4–40.
21. Stephanie Zimmerman, "Social Cognition and Evaluations of Health Care Team Communication Effectiveness," *Western Journal of Communication* 58 (Spring 1994), pp. 116–41.
22. Peter E. Mudrack and Genevieve M. Farrell, "An Examination of Functional Role Behavior and Its Consequences for Individuals in Group Settings," *Small Group Research* 26 (November 1995), pp. 542–71.
23. Aitor Aritzeta, Barbara Senior, and Stephen Swailes, "Team Role Preferences and Cognitive Styles: A Convergent Validity Study," *Small Group Research* 36, no. 4 (August 2005), pp. 404–36.
24. Craig R. Scott, "New Communication Technologies and Teams," in *Small Group Communication: Theory & Practice,* 8th ed., eds. Randy Hirokawa, Robert Cathcart, Larry Samovar, and Linda Henman (Los Angeles, CA: Roxbury, 2003), pp. 134–47.
25. Susan B. Shimanoff, "Coordinating Group Interaction via Communication Rules," in *Small Group Communication: A Reader,* 6th ed., eds. Robert Cathcart and Larry Samovar (Dubuque, IA: Wm. C. Brown, 1992), p. 255.
26. Daniel Feldman, "Development and Enforcement of Group Norms," *Academy of Management Review* 9 (1984), pp. 47–53.
27. Stanley Schacter, "Deviation, Rejection, and Communication," *Journal of Abnormal and Social Psychology* 46 (1951), pp. 190–207; and Harold Leavitt, *Managerial Psychology,* 2nd ed. (Chicago, IL: University of Chicago Press, 1964), pp. 270–74.
28. Ronald R. Sims, "Linking Groupthink to Unethical Behavior in Organizations," *Journal of Business Ethics* 11 (September 1992), pp. 651–62.
29. Katherine W. Hawkins and Bryant P. Fillion, "Perceived Communication Skill Needs for Work Groups," *Communication Research Reports* 16 (Spring 1999), pp. 167–74.
30. Joseph P. Folger and Marshall S. Poole, *Working Through Conflict: A Communication Perspective* (Glenview, IL: Scott, Foresman, 1984), p. 84.
31. Hawkins and Fillion, "Perceived Communication Skill Needs for Work Groups," pp. 167–74.
32. Carl E. Larson and Frank M. J. LaFasto, *TeamWork: What Must Go Right, What Can Go Wrong* (Newbury Park, CA: Sage, 1989).
33. Sheila Simsarian Webber, "Development of Cognitive and Affective Trust in Teams: A Longitudinal Study," *Small Group Research* 39 (2008), pp. 746–69.
34. M. E. Johnson and J. G. Fortman, "Internal Structure of the Gross Cohesiveness Scale," *Small Group Behavior* 19 (February 1988), pp. 187–96.
35. C. N. Greene, "Cohesion and Productivity in Work Groups," *Small Group Behavior* 21 (February 1989), pp. 221–25.
36. Brian Mullen, Tara Anthony, Eduardo Salas, and James E. Driskell, "Group Cohesiveness and Quality of Decision Making: An Integration of Tests of the Groupthink Hypothesis," *Small Group Research* 25 (May 1995), pp. 189–204.
37. Claus W. Langfred, "Is Group Cohesiveness a Double-Edged Sword? An Investigation on the Effects of Cohesiveness on Performance," *Small Group Research* 29 (1996), pp. 124–43.

38. Stanley M. Gully, Dennis J. Devine, and David J. Whitney, "A Meta-Analysis of Cohesion and Performance: Effects of Level of Analysis and Task Interdependence," *Small Group Research* 43 (2012), pp. 702–25.

39. Irving L. Janis, *Groupthink: Psychological Studies of Policy Decisions and Fiascoes,* 2nd ed. (Boston, MA: Houghton Mifflin, 1983), pp. 14–47.

40. Bret H. Bradley, John E. Baur, Christopher G. Banford, and Bennett E. Postlethwaite, "Team Players and Collective Performance: How Agreeableness Affects Team Performance Over Time," *Small Group Research* 44 (2013), pp. 680–711.

41. Dejun Tony Kong, Lee J. Konczak, and William P. Bottom, "Team Performance as a Joint Function of Team Member Satisfaction and Agreeableness," *Small Group Research* 46 (2015), pp. 160–78.

42. Jack R. Gibb, "Defensive Communication," *Journal of Communication* 11 (1961), pp. 141–48.

**Chapter 6**

1. Jennifer J. Mease, "Reconsidering Consultant's Strategic Use of the Business Case for Diversity," *Journal of Applied Communication Research* 40 (2012), pp. 384–402.

2. Radostina K. Purvanova, "The Role of Feeling Known for Team Member Outcomes in Project Teams," *Small Group Research* 44 (June 2013), pp. 298–331.

3. Marvin E. Shaw, *Group Dynamics; The Psychology of Small Group Behavior,* 2nd ed. (New York: McGraw-Hill, 1971), pp. 219–36.

4. David A. Harrison, Kenneth H. Price, and Myrtle P. Bell, "Beyond Relational Demography: Time and the Effects of Surface- and Deep-Level Diversity on Work Group Cohesion," *Academy of Management Journal* 41 (1998), pp. 96–107.

5. Suzanne T. Bell, "Deep-Level Composition Variables as Predictors of Team Performance: A Meta-analysis," *Journal of Applied Psychology* 92 (2007), pp. 595–615.

6. William B. Johnston and Arnold E. Packer, *Workforce 2000: Work and Workers for the 21st Century* (Indianapolis, IN: Hudson Institute, 1987).

7. Rebecca Mitchell, Stephen Nicholas, and Brendan Boyle, "The Role of Openness to Cognitive Diversity and Group Processes in Knowledge Creation, *Small Group Research* 40 (2009), pp. 535–54.

8. Tanja Hentschel, Meir Shemla, Jurgen Wegge, and Eric Kearney, "Perceived Diversity and Team Functioning: The Role of Diversity Beliefs and Affect," *Small Group Research* 44 (2013), pp. 33–61.

9. James R. Larson, Jr., "Deep Diversity and Strong Synergy: Modeling the Impact of Variability in Members' Problem-Solving Strategies on Group Problem-Solving Performance," *Small Group Research* 38 (2007), pp. 413–36.

10. G. M. Parker, *Team Players and Teamwork: The New Competitive Business Strategy* (San Francisco, CA: Jossey-Bass, 1990); and R. A. Eisenstat, "Fairfield Systems Group," in *Groups That Work and Those That Don't,* ed. J. R. Hackman (San Francisco, CA: Jossey -Bass, 1990), pp. 171–81.

11. Hentschel, Shemla, Wegge, and Kearney, "Perceived Diversity and Team Functioning: The Role of Diversity Beliefs and Affect."

12. Carolyn M. Anderson and Matthew M. Martin, "Communication Motives (State vs. Trait?) and Task Group Outcomes," *Communication Research Reports* 19 (Summer 2002), pp. 269–82.

13. Ibid., p. 193.

14. Dirk Scheerhorn and Patricia Geist, "Social Dynamics in Groups," in *Managing Group Life,* eds. Lawrence R. Frey and J. Kevin Barge (Boston, MA: Houghton Mifflin, 1997), pp. 80–103.

15. Carolyn M. Anderson and Matthew M. Martin, "The Effects of Communication Motives, Interaction Involvement, and Loneliness on Satisfaction: A Model of Small Groups," *Small Group Research* 26 (February 1995), pp. 118–37.

16. John G. Oetzel and Keri Bolton-Oetzel, "Exploring the Relationship between Self-Construal and Dimensions of Group Effectiveness," *Management Communication Quarterly* 10, no. 3 (February 1997), pp. 289–315.

17. Torsten Reimer, Sascha Kuendig, Ulrich Hoffrage, Ernest Park, and Verlin Hinz, "Effects of the Information Environment on Group Discussions and Decisions in the Hidden-Profile Paradigm," *Communication Monographs* 74, no. 1 (March 2007), pp. 1–28.

18. David A. Kolb, *Experiential Learning: Experience as the Source of Learning and Development* (Englewood Cliffs, NJ: Prentice-Hall, 1984).

19. Synthesized from Isabel Briggs Myers, *Introduction to Type: A Description of the Theory and Application of the Myers-Briggs Type Indicator* (Palo Alto, CA: Consulting Psychologists Press,

1987); Otto Kroeger and Janet A. Thuesen, *Type Talk: The 16 Personality Types That Determine How We Live, Love, and Work* (New York: Dell, 1988); Otto Kroeger with Janet A. Thuesen, *Type Talk at Work: How the 16 Personality Types Determine Your Success on the Job* (New York: Dell, 1992); and Paul D. Tieger and Barbara Barron-Tieger, *Nurture by Nature: Understand Your Child's Personality Type—And Become a Better Parent* (Boston, MA: Little, Brown, 1997), pp. 5–62.

20. Abby L. Mello and Joan R. Rentsch, "Cognitive Diversity in Teams: A Multidisciplinary Review," *Small Group Research* 46 (December 2015), pp. 623–58.
21. Abby L. Mello and Lisa A. Delise, "Cognitive Diversity to Team Outcomes: The Roles of Cohesion and Conflict Management," *Small Group Research* 46 (April 2015), pp. 204–26.
22. Yan Zhang and Ming-Yun Huai, "Diverse Work Groups and Employee Performance: The Role of Communication Ties," *Small Group Research* 47 (February, 2016), pp. 28–57.
23. See, for example, John G. Oetzel, "Culturally Homogeneous and Heterogeneous Groups: Explaining Communication Processes through Individualism-Collectivism and Self-Construal," *International Journal of Intercultural Relations* 22, no. 2 (May 1998), pp. 135–61; John G. Oetzel, "Explaining Individual Communication Processes in Homogenous and Heterogeneous Groups through Individualism-Collectivism and Self-Construal," *Human Communication Research* 25, no. 2 (December 1998), pp. 202–24; Kim M. Shapcott, Albert V. Carron, and Paul A. Estabrooks, "Member Diversity and Cohesion and Performance in Walking Groups," *Small Group Research* 37, no. 6 (December 2006), pp. 701–20; Tanja Hentschel, Meir Shemla, Jurgen Wegge, and Eric Kearney, "Perceived Diversity and Team Functioning: The Role of Diversity Beliefs and Affect," *Small Group Research* 44 (2013), pp. 33–61; and Yuan Jiang, Susan E. Jackson, James B. Shaw, and Yunhyung Chung, "The Consequences of Educational Speciality and Nationality Faultlines for Project Teams," *Small Group Research* 43 (2012), pp. 613–44.
24. The following information about culture is synthesized from a number of sources, including Edward T. Hall, *Beyond Culture* (New York: Anchor Press, 1977); Geert Hofstede, *Culture's Consequences: International Differences in Work-Related Values,* 2nd ed. (Beverly Hills, CA: Sage, 2001); William B. Gudykunst and Stella Ting-Toomey, *Culture and Interpersonal Communication* (Newbury Park, CA: Sage, 1988); Myron Lustig and Jolene Koester, *Interpersonal Competence: Interpersonal Communication Across Cultures* (New York: Harper Collins, 1993); and Myron W. Lustig and Laura L. Casotta, "Comparing Group Communication Across Culture: Leadership, Conformity, and Discussion Procedures," in *Small Group Communication: A Reader,* 6th ed., eds. Robert S. Cathcart and Larry A. Samovar (Dubuque, IA: Wm. C. Brown, 1992), pp. 393–404.
25. Larry A. Samovar and Richard E. Porter, *Communication Between Cultures,* 4th ed. (Belmont, CA: Wadsworth, 2001), pp. 52–88.
26. Min-Sun Kim and William F. Sharkey, "Independent and Interdependent Construals of Self: Explaining Cultural Patterns of Interpersonal Communication in Multicultural Organizational Settings," *Communication Quarterly* 43 (Winter 1995), pp. 20–38.
27. This section is a summary of Oetzel, "Culturally Homogeneous," and Oetzel, "Explaining Individual."
28. This information is synthesized from Michael L. Hecht, Mary Jane Collier, and Sidney A. Ribeau, *African American Communication: Ethnic Identity and Cultural Interpretation,* vol. 2, Language and Language Behaviors series (Newbury Park, CA: Sage, 1993), especially Chap. 3, pp. 82–113, and Anita K. Foeman and Gary Pressley, "Ethnic Culture and Corporate Culture: Using Black Styles in Organizations," *Communication Quarterly* 35 (Fall 1987), pp. 293–307.
29. Rebecca Leonard and Don C. Locke, "Communication Stereotypes: Is Interracial Communication Possible?" *Journal of Black Studies* 23 (March 1993), pp. 332–43.
30. Mark P. Orbe, "Remember, It's Always Whites' Ball: Descriptions of African American Male Communication," *Communication Quarterly* 35 (Fall 1987), pp. 293–307.
31. C. Kirchmeyer and A. Cohen, "Multicultural Groups: Their Performance and Reactions with Constructive Conflict," *Group & Organization Management* 17 (1992), pp. 153–70, and C. Kirchmeyer, "Multicultural Task Groups: An Account of the Low Contribution Level of

Minorities," *Small Group Research* 24 (February 1993), pp. 127–48.

32. Hofstede, "Culture's Consequences."
33. Nina M. Reich and Julia T. Wood, "Sex, Gender and Communication in Small Groups," in *Small Group Communication: Theory and Practice,* 8th ed., eds. Randy Y. Hirokawa, Robert S. Cathcart, Larry A. Samovar, and Linda D. Henman (Los Angeles, CA: Roxbury, 2003), pp. 218–29.
34. Andrew J. Flanagin, Vanessa Tiyaamornwong, Joan O'Connor, and David R. Seibold, "Computer-Mediated Group Work: The Interaction of Member Sex and Anonymity," *Communication Research* 29 (February 2002), pp. 66–93.
35. Lindsey M. Grob, Renee A. Meyers, and Renee Schuh, "Powerful/Powerless Language Use in Group Interactions: Sex Differences or Similarities?" *Communication Quarterly* 45, no. 3 (Summer 1997), pp. 282–303.
36. Jeff Youngquist, "The Effect of Interruptions and Dyad Gender Combination on Perceptions of Interpersonal Dominance," *Communication Studies* 60 (2009), pp. 147–63.
37. Amy E. Randel and Kimberly S. Jaussi, "Gender Social and Personal Identity, Sex Dissimilarity, Relationship Conflict, and Assymetrical Effects," *Small Group Research* 39 (2008), pp. 468–91.
38. Priya Raghubir and Ana Valenzuela, "Male-Female Dynamics in Groups: A Field Study of The Weakest Link," *Small Group Research* 41 (2010), pp. 41–70.
39. Grob, Meyers, and Schuh, "Powerful/Powerless Language Use."
40. Scott A. Krebs, Elizabeth V. Hobman, and Prashant Bordia, "Virtual Teams and Group Member Diversity," *Small Group Research* 37, no. 6 (December 2006), pp. 721–41.
41. This information is taken primarily from Rick Hicks and Kathy Hicks, *Boomers, Xers, and Other Strangers: Understanding the Generational Differences That Divide Us* (Wheaton, IL: Tyndale House, 1999), especially pp. 229–353. Other sources of information include Jeff Feiertag and Zane L. Berge, "Training Generation N: How Educators Should Approach the Net Generation," *Education & Training,* 50 (2008), pp. 457–464; Therese Kattner, "Best Practices for Working with Millennial Students," *Student Affairs Leader,* 37 (2009), p. 5; Lynne C. Lancaster and David Stillman, *When Generations Collide: Who They Are, Why They Clash, and How to Solve the Generational Puzzle at Work* (New York: Collins Business, 2002); and Bruce Tulgan, *Not Everyone Gets a Trophy: How to Manage Generation Y.* (San Francisco, CA: Jossey-Bass, 2009).
42. Franklin B. Krohn, "A Generational Approach to Using Emoticons as Nonverbal Communication," *Journal of Technical Writing and Communication* 34, no. 4 (2004), pp. 321–28.
43. Stella Ting-Toomey, *Communicating Across Cultures* (New York: Guilford Press, 1999), pp. 45–54, 261–76.
44. Ernest G. Bormann, "Symbolic Convergence Theory and Communication in Group Decision Making," in *Communication and Group Decision Making,* 2nd ed., eds. Randy Y. Hirokawa and M. Scott Poole (Thousand Oaks, CA: Sage, 1996), pp. 81–113.
45. Catherine Cobb Morocco, "Development and Function of Group Metaphor," *Journal for the Theory of Social Behavior* 9 (1979), pp. 15–27.
46. Yuan Jiang, Susan E. Jackson, James B. Shaw, and Yunhyung Chung, "The Consequences of Educational Specialty and Nationality Faultlines for Project Teams," *Small Group Research* 43 (October 2012), pp. 613–44.
47. Jiang, Jackson, Shaw, and Chung, "The Consequences of Educational Specialty and Nationality Faultlines for Project Teams."
48. Warren E. Watson, Kamalesh Kumar, and Larry K. Michaelson, "Cultural Diversity's Impact on Interaction Process and Performance: Comparing Homogenous and Diverse Task Groups," *Academy of Management Journal* 36 (1993), pp. 590–602.
49. Jiang, Jackson, Shaw, and Chung, "The Consequences of Educational Specialty and Nationality Faultlines for Project Teams."
50. Watson, Kumar, and Michaelson, "Cultural Diversity."
51. Tessa V. West, Joe C. Magee, Sarah H. Gordon, and Lindy Gullett, "A Little Similarity Goes a Long Way: The Effects of Peripheral but Self-Revealing Similarities on Improving and Sustaining Interracial Relationships," *Journal of Personality and Social Psychology* 107 (2014), pp. 81–100.
52. Jiang, Jackson, Shaw, and Chung, "The Consequences of Educational Specialty and Nationality Faultlines for Project Teams."

53. Floor Rink and Naomi Ellemers, "Defining the Common Feature: Task-related Differences as the Basis for Dyadic Identity," *British Journal of Social Psychology* 46 (2007), pp. 499–515.

54. Tanja Hentschel, Meir Shemla, Jürgen Wegge, and Eric Kearney, "Perceived Diversity and Team Functioning: The Role of Diversity Beliefs and Affect," *Small Group Research* 44 (February 2013), pp. 33–61.

55. Jessica Leigh Thompson, "Building Collective Communication Competence in Interdisciplinary Research Teams," *Journal of Applied Communication Research* 37 (2009), pp. 278–97.

56. Ibid.

57. Bret H. Bradley, John E. Baur, Christopher G. Banford, and Bennet E. Postlethwaite, "Team Players and Collective Performance: How Agreeableness Affects Team Performance Over Time," *Small Group Research* 44 (December 2013), pp. 680–711.

58. Tarik Abdel-Monem, Shereen Bingham, Jamie Marincic, and Alan Tomkins, "Deliberation and Diversity: Perceptions of Small Group Discussions by Race and Ethnicity," *Small Group Research* 41 (2010), pp. 746–76.

**Chapter 7**

1. Sunwolf, "Getting to 'GroupAha!' Provoking Creative Processes in Task Groups," in *The Handbook of Group Communication Theory & Research,* ed. Lawrence R. Frey (Thousand Oaks, CA: Sage, 1999), p. 205.

2. Susan Jarboe, "Group Communication and Creativity Processes," in *The Handbook of Group Communication Theory & Research,* ed. Lawrence R. Frey (Thousand Oaks, CA: Sage, 1999), p. 336.

3. David F. Caldwell and Charles A. O'Reilly, III, "The Determinants of Team-Based Innovations in Organizations: The Role of Social Influence," *Small Group Research* 34 (August 2003), pp. 497–517.

4. Paul G. Bain, Leon Mann, and Andrew Pirola-Merlo, "The Innovation Imperative: The Relationship between Team Climate, Innovation, and Performance in Research and Development Teams," *Small Group Research* 32 (February 2001), pp. 55–73.

5. Bernard A. Nijstad and Paul B. Paulus, "Group Creativity: Common Themes and Future Directions," in *Group Creativity: Innovation through Collaboration,* eds. Paul B. Paulus and Bernard A. Nijstad (New York: Oxford University Press, 2003), pp. 326–39.

6. John J. Sosik, Bruce J. Avolio, and Surinder S. Kahai, "Inspiring Group Creativity: Comparing Anonymous and Identified Electronic Brainstorming," *Small Group Research* 29 (1998), pp. 3–31.

7. Nijstad and Paulus, "Group Creativity," p. 330.

8. Kenneth T. Goh, Paul S. Goodman, and Laurie R. Weingart, "Team Innovation Processes: Examination of Activity Cycles in Creative Teams," *Small Group Research* 44 (2013), pp. 159–94.

9. Jarboe, "Group Communication and Creativity Processes," pp. 336–41.

10. Marieke C. Schilpzand, David M. Herold, and Christina E. Shalley, "Member's Openness to Experience and Team's Creative Performance," *Small Group Research* 42 (2011), pp. 55–76.

11. Nijstad and Paulus, "Group Creativity," pp. 326–32.

12. Antonio Chirumbolo, Lucia Mannetti, Antonio Pierro, Alessandra Areni, and Arie W. Kruglanski, "Motivated Closed-Mindedness and Creativity in Small Groups," *Small Group Research* 36 (February 2005), pp. 59–82.

13. Asako Miura and Misao Hida, "Synergy Between Diversity and Similarity in Small Group Idea-Generation," *Small Group Research* 35 (October 2004), pp. 540–564.

14. Maritza R. Salazar, Theresa K. Lant, Stephen M. Fiore, and Eduardo Salas, "Facilitating Innovation in Diverse Science Teams Through Integrative Capacity," *Small Group Research* 43 (October 2012), pp. 527–58.

15. Alex Osborn, *Applied Imagination,* rev. ed. (New York: Scribner, 1957).

16. Vicky Putnam and Paul Paulus, "Brainstorming, Brainstorming Rules and Decision Making," *Journal of Creative Behavior* 43 (2009), pp. 23–39.

17. M. Basadur and R. Thompson, "Usefulness of the Ideation Principle of Extended Effort in Real World Professional and Managerial Problem Solving," *Journal of Creative Behavior* 20 (1982), pp. 23–34.

18. Putnam and Paulus, "Brainstorming," pp. 23–39.

19. Chirumbolo et al., "Motivated Closed-Mindedness."

20. J. H. Jung, Younghwa Lee, and Rex Karsten, "The Moderating Effect of Extraversion-Introversion Differences on Group Idea Generation Performance," *Small Group Research* 43 (2012), pp. 30–49.

21. Olga Goldenberg, James R. Larson, Jr., and Jennifer Wiley, "Goal Instructions, Response Format, and Idea Generation in Groups," *Small Group Research* 44 (April 2013), pp. 227–56.

22. Ross Tartell, "Power Up Your Brainstorming," *Training* (November-December, 2012), p. 14.

23. Hamit Coskun, "Cognitive Stimulation with Convergent and Divergent Thinking Exercises in Brainwriting: Incubation, Sequence Priming, and Group Context," *Small Group Research* 36 (August 2005), pp. 466–98.

24. Chirumbolo et al., "Motivated Closed-Mindedness."

25. R. Brent Gallupe, Alan R. Dennis, William H. Cooper, Joseph S. Valacich, Lame M. Bastianum, and Jay F. Nunamaker, Jr., "Electronic Brainstorming and Group Size," *Academy of Management Journal* 35 (June 1992), pp. 350–70. See also Joseph S. Valacich, Alan R. Dennis, and T. Connolly, "Idea Generation in Computer-Based Groups: A New Ending to an Old Story," *Organizational Behavior and Human Decision Processes* 57 (1994), pp. 448–68.

26. David Dryden Henningsen and Mary Lynn Miller Henningsen, "Generating Ideas About the Uses of Brainstorming: Reconsidering the Losses and Gains of Brainstorming Groups Relative to Nominal Groups." *Southern Communication Journal* 78 (January-March, 2013), pp. 42-55.

27. Russell L. Ackoff and Elsa Vergara, "Creativity in Problem Solving and Planning," in *Handbook for Creative and Innovative Managers,* ed. Robert L. Kuhn (New York: McGraw-Hill, 1988), pp. 77–90.

28. Accessed (again) on June 12, 2016, http://www.ideafinder.com/history/inventions/velcro.htm.

29. Del Jones, "GE Leader Recalls 'Eureka' Moment: Being No. 1 Was Limiting Opportunity," *The Cincinnati Enquirer,* April 8, 2001, pp. D1–2.

30. David L. Cooperrider and Suresh Srivastva, *Appreciative Management and Leadership: The Power of Positive Thought and Action in Organization.* rev. ed. (San Francisco, CA: Jossey-Bass, 1999); Gervase R. Bushe, "Appreciative Inquirey with Teams," *Organizational Development Journal* (Fall, 1998), pp. 41–50; Gervase R. Bushe and Neelima Paranjpey, "Comparing Generativity of Problem Solving and Appreciative Inquiry: A Field Experiment," *Journal of Applied Behavioral Science* 51 (September 2015), pp. 309–35.

31. Bushe and Paranjpey, "Comparing Generativity," p. 311.

32. Yuhhyng Shin, "Positive Group Affect and Team Creativity: Mediation of Team Reflexivity and Promotion Focus," Small Group Research (June 2014), pp. 337–64.

33. R. L. Firestein, "Effects of Creative Problem-Solving Training on Communication Behaviors in Small Groups," *Small Group Research* 21 (1990), pp. 507–21.

34. For a clear review of these issues, see Dale E. Brashers, Mark Adkins, and Renee A. Meyers, "Argumentation and Computer-Mediated Group Decision-Making," in *Group Communication in Context,* ed. Lawrence R. Frey (Hillsdale, NJ: Lawrence Erlbaum, 1994), pp. 263–82.

35. Columbia Accident Investigation website, "Columbia Accident Investigation Board Press Briefing," August 26, 2003, accessed (again) on February 7, 2011, http://caib.nasa.gov/events/press_briefings/20030826/default.html.

36. Marcia Dunn, "NASA Chiefs: Managers Must Embrace Change," Yahoo! News, accessed (again) on February 7, 2011, http://www.redorbit.com/news/space/54411/nasa_chiefs_managers_must_embrace_change/index.html.

37. D. Christopher Kayes, "From Climbing Stairs to Riding Waves," *Small Group Research* 37 (December 2006), pp. 612–30, and D. Christopher Kayes, "Dilemma at 29,000 feet: An Exercise in Ethical Decision Making Based on the 1996 Mt. Everest Disaster," *Journal of Management Education* 26 (2002), pp. 307–21.

38. Chirumbolo et al., "Motivated Closed-Mindedness."

39. Dennis S. Gouran, Randy Y. Hirokawa, and Amy E. Martz, "A Critical Analysis of Factors Related to Decisional Processes Involved in the *Challenger* Disaster," *Central States Speech Journal* 37 (1986), pp. 119–35.

40. Brashers et al., "Argumentation and Computer-Mediated Group Decision-Making."

41. Gouran et al., "A Critical Analysis of Factors Related to Decisional Processes Involved in the *Challenger* Disaster."

42. Sarah J. Tracy, "When Questioning Turns to Face Threat: An Interactional Sensitivity in 911 Call-Taking," *Western Journal of Communication* 66, pp. 129–57.
43. Richard Huseman, Glenn Ware, and Charles Gruner, "Critical Thinking, Reflective Thinking, and the Ability to Organize Ideas: A Multivariate Approach," *Journal of the American Forensic Association* 9 (1972), pp. 261–65.
44. Torsten Reimer, Sascha Kuendig, Ulrich Hoffrage, Ernest Park, and Verlin Hinz, "Effects of the Information Environment on Group Discussions and Decisions in the Hidden-Profile Paradigm," *Communication Monographs* 74, no. 1 (March 2007), pp. 1–28.
45. M. Neil Browne and Stuart M. Keeley, *Asking the Right Questions: A Guide to Critical Thinking,* 3rd ed. (Englewood Cliffs, NJ: Prentice-Hall, 1992), pp. 3–5.
46. Anne Clyde, "The Invisible Web," *Teacher Librarian* 29 (April 2009), p. 47.
47. W. L. Lym, "Tempting Students with Scholarly Research: Breaking the Fast-Food Research Diet," *College Teaching* 57 (Fall 2009), p. 237.
48. Tyrone Adams and Norman Clark, *The Internet: Effective Online Communication* (Fort Worth, TX: Harcourt, 2001), pp. 166–75.
49. Ibid., pp. 3–7.
50. Brashers et al., "Argumentation and Computer-Mediated Group Decision-Making," pp. 263–82.
51. Gouran et al., "A Critical Analysis of Factors Related to Decisional Processes Involved in the *Challenger* Disaster," p. 130.
52. Mark F. Stasson and Scott D. Bradshaw, "Explanations of Individual-Group Performance Differences: What Sort of 'Bonus' Can Be Gained through Group Interaction?" *Small Group Research* 26 (May 1995), pp. 296–308.
53. Richard Paul and Linda Elder, *The Thinker's Guide to Fallacies: The Art of Mental Trickery and Manipulation* (Dillon Beach, CA: Foundation for Critical Thinking, 2004).
54. Daniel C. Vock and Pauline Vu, "Va. Tech Tragedy Revives Gun Controversy," accessed (again) on December 22, 2010: http://www.stateline.org/live/details/story?contentId=199281; and Whitney Hodgin, "Concealed-Carry Controversy Ongoing After Va. Tech Shootings," accessed (again) on December 22, 2010: http://www.kstatecollegian.com/2.2506/concealed-carry-controversy-ongoing-after-va-tech-shootings-1.224273.
55. D. Cole, "Meetings That Make Sense," *Psychology Today* (May 1989), pp. 14–15.
56. David Henningsen, Mary Lynn Miller Henningsen, Jenifer Eden, and Michael Cruz, "Examining the Symptoms of Groupthink and Retrospective Sensemaking," *Small Group Research* 37 (2006), pp. 36–64.
57. Charles P. Koerber and Christopher P. Neck, "Groupthink and Sports: An Application of Whyte's Model," *International Journal of Hospitality Management* 15 (2003), pp. 20–28.
58. Brian Mullen, Tara Anthony, Eduardo Salas, and James E. Driskell, "Group Cohesiveness and Quality of Decision Making: An Integration of the Groupthink Hypothesis," *Small Group Research* 25 (May 1994), pp. 189–204.
59. Irving L. Janis and Leon Mann, *Decision Making: A Psychological Analysis of Conflict, Choice, and Commitment* (New York: Free Press, 1977).
60. Lucia Savadori, Lyn M. Van Swol, and Janet A. Sniezek, "Information Sampling and Confidence within Groups and Judge Advisor Systems," *Communication Research* 28 (December 2001), pp. 737–71; Michael G. Cruz and David D. Henningsen, "The Presence of Norms in the Absence of Groups?" *Human Communication Research* 26 (January 2000), pp. 104–24; Mark Schiettekatte and Alain Van Niel, "Effects of Partially Shared Information and Awareness of Unshared Information on Information Sampling," *Small Group Research* 25 (May 1994), pp. 189–204.
61. Janis and Mann, *Decision Making.*
62. Charles R. Franz and K. Gregory Jin, "The Structure of Group Conflict in a Collaborative Work Group During Information Systems Development," *Journal of Applied Communication Research* 23 (1995), pp. 108–27.
63. Markus Brauer, Charles M. Judd, and Vincent Jacquelin, "The Communication of Social Stereotypes: The Effects of Group Discussion and Information Distribution on Stereotypic Appraisals," *Journal of Personality and Social Psychology* 81, no. 3 (2001), pp. 463–75.
64. R. Spears and M. Leah, "Panacea or Panopticon? The Hidden Power in Computer-Mediated Communication," *Communication Research* 21 (1994), pp. 427–59.

**Chapter 8**

1. Jay Hall, "Decisions, Decisions, Decisions," *Psychology Today* (November 1971), pp. 51–54, 86–87; Jay Hall and W. H. Watson, "The Effects of a Normative Intervention on Decision-Making Performance," *Human Relations* 23 (1970), pp. 299–317; Irving L. Janis, *Groupthink: Psychological Studies of Policy Decisions and Fiascoes,* 2nd ed. (Boston, MA: Houghton Mifflin, 1982); Randy Y. Hirokawa, "Consensus Group Decision-Making, Quality of Decision and Group Satisfaction: An Attempt to Sort Fact from Fiction," *Central States Speech Journal* 33 (1982), pp. 407–15; Lester Coch and J. R. P. French, Jr., "Overcoming Resistance to Change," *Human Relations* 1 (1948), pp. 512–32; and Myron W. Block and L. R. Hoffman, "The Effects of Valence of Solutions and Group Cohesiveness on Members' Commitment to Group Decisions," in *The Group Problem-Solving Process,* ed. L. Richard Hoffman (New York: Praeger, 1979), p. 121.
2. Kathleen M. Propp, "In Search of the Assembly Bonus Effect: Continued Exploration of Communication's Role in Group Memory," *Human Communication Research* 29, no. 4 (2003), pp. 600–606.
3. Patrica Fandt, "The Relationship of Accountability and Interdependent Behavior to Enhancing Team Consequences," *Group and Organization Studies* 16 (1991), pp. 200–212.
4. Kyle J. Emich, "How Expectancy Motivation Influences Information Exchange in Small Groups," *Small Group Research* 43, (2012), pp. 275–94.
5. Charles Pavitt and Kelly Kline Johnson, "An Examination of the Coherence of Group Discussions," *Communication Research* 26 (June 1999), pp. 303–21.
6. Vicky Putnam and Paul Paulus, "Brainstorming, Brainstorming Rules and Decision Making," *Journal of Creative Behavior* 43 (2009), pp. 23–39.
7. Hirokawa, "Consensus Group Decision-Making," pp. 407–15; Hirokawa, "Why Informed Groups Make Faulty Decisions: An Investigation of Possible Interaction-Based Explanations," *Small Group Behavior* 18 (1987), pp. 3–29; and Hirokawa, "Discussion Procedures and Decision-Making Performance: A Test of the Functional Perspective," *Human Communication Research* 12 (1985), pp. 203–24.
8. Karen Tracy and Heidi Mueller, "Diagnosing a School Board's Interactional Trouble: Theorizing Problem Orientation," *Communication Theory* 11 (2001), pp. 84–104.
9. Carl E. Larson and Frank M. J. LaFasto, *TeamWork: What Must Go Right, What Can Go Wrong* (Newbury Park, CA: Sage, 1989), pp. 27–38.
10. Amanda Lee Myers, "Painsaking Care, Honor for 19 Fallen Firefighters," *AP The Big Story,* (July 7, 2013): Retrieved July 9, 2013: http://bigstory.ap.org/article/wildfire-cut-hotshots-access-safety-zone.
11. David Dryden Henningsen and Mary Lynn Miller Henningsen, "Examining Social Influence in Information-Sharing Contexts," *Small Group Research* 34 (August 2003), pp. 391–412.
12. Joan R. Rentsch, Lisa A. Delise, Eduardo Salas, and Michael P. Letsky, "Facilitating Knowledge Building in Teams: Can a New Team Training Strategy Help?", *Small Group Research* 41 (2010), pp. 505–523.
13. For example, see Randy Hirokawa, "Group Communication and Problem Solving Effectiveness: An Investigation of Group Phases," *Human Communication Research* 9 (1983), pp. 291–305.
14. John E. Dewey, *How We Think* (Boston, MA: D.C. Heath, 1910).
15. This research is synthesized in Dennis S. Gouran and Randy Y. Hirokawa, "Effective Decision Making and Problem Solving in Groups," in *Small Group Communication: Theory and Practice,* 8th ed., eds. Randy Y. Hirokawa, Robert S. Cathcart, Larry A. Samovar, and Linda D. Henman (Los Angeles, CA: Roxbury, 2003), pp. 27–38.
16. Lucia Savadori, Lun M. Van Swol, and Janet A. Sniezek, "Information Sampling and Confidence Within Groups and Judge Advisor Systems," *Communication Research* 28 (2001), pp. 737–71; Michael G. Cruz and David Dryden Henningsen, "The Presence of Norms in the Absence of Groups?" *Human Communication Research* 26 (2000), pp. 104–24.
17. Kyle J. Emich, "How Expectancy Motivation Influences Information Exchange in a Small Group."
18. Shirley Wang, "Emotional Intelligence, Information Elaboration, and Performance: The Moderating Role of Informational Diversity,"

*Small Group Research* 46 (June 2015), pp. 324–51.

19. Michaéla C. Schippers, Amy C. Edmondson, and Michael A. West. "Team Reflexivity as Antidote to Team Information-Processing Failures," *Small Group Research* 45 (December 2014), pp. 731–69.
20. Sandra E. Spataro, Nathan C. Pettit, Stephen J. Sauer, and Robert B. Lount, Jr. "Interactions Among Same-Status Peers: Effects of Behavioral Style and Status Level," *Small Group Research* 45 (June 2014), pp. 314–36.
21. Susan Jarboe, "Procedures for Enhancing Group Decision Making," in *Communication and Group Decision Making,* 2nd ed., eds. Randy Y. Hirokawa and Marshall Scott Poole (Thousand Oaks, CA: Sage, 1996), pp. 345–83.
22. Marshall S. Poole, "Decision Development in Small Groups II: A Study of Multiple Sequences in Decision Making," *Communication Monographs* 50 (1983), pp. 224–25, and "Decision Development in Small Groups III: A Multiple Sequence Model of Group Decision Development," *Communication Monographs* 50 (1983), pp. 321–41.
23. Randy Y. Hirokawa, "Group Communication and Decision-Making Performance: A Continued Test of the Functional Perspective," paper presented at the annual convention of the Speech Communication Association, Boston, MA, 1987; Randy Y. Hirokawa and Kathryn M. Rost, "Effective Group Decision Making in Organizations: Field Test of the Vigilant Interaction Theory," paper presented at the annual convention of the Speech Communication Association, Atlanta, 1991.
24. Elizabeth E. Graham, Michael J. Papa, and Mary B. McPherson, "An Applied Test of the Functional Communication Perspective of Small Group Decision Making," *Southern Communication Journal* 62 (Summer 1997), pp. 269–79.
25. Among these studies were John K. Brilhart and Lurene M. Jochem, "Effects of Different Patterns on Outcomes of Problem-Solving Discussion," *Journal of Applied Psychology* 48 (1964), pp. 175–79; Ovid L. Bayless, "An Alternative Model for Problem Solving Discussion," *Journal of Communication* 17 (1967), pp. 188–97; Carl E. Larson, "Forms of Analysis and Small Group Problem Solving," *Speech Monographs* 36 (1969), pp. 452–55; and Hirokawa, "Discussion Procedures and Decision-Making Performance."
26. Benjamin J. Broome and Luann Fulbright, "A Multistage Influence Model of Barriers to Group Problem Solving: A Participant-Generated Agenda for Small Group Research," *Small Group Research* 26 (February 1995), pp. 25–55.
27. Joseph A. Bonito, "An Information-Processing Approach to Participation in Small Groups," *Communication Research* 28 (June 2001), pp. 275–303; Michael G. Cruz, Franklin J. Boster, and Jose I. Rodriquez, "The Impact of Group Size and Proportion of Shared Information on the Exchange and Integration of Information in Groups," *Communication Research* 27 (June 1997), pp. 291–313.
28. Margaret Boos, Barbara Schauenburg, Micha Strack, and Michael Belz, "Social Validation of Shared and Nonvalidation of Unshared Information in Group Discussions," *Small Group Research* 44 (June 2013), pp. 257–71.
29. See Golnaz Tajeddin, Freank Safayeni, Catherine E. Connelly, and Kevin Tasa, "The Influence of Emergent Expertise on Group Decision Processes," *Small Group Research* 43 (2012), pp. 50–74; Emich, "How Expectancy Motivation Influences Information Exchange in Small Groups"; and Rentsch, Delise, Salas, and Letsky, "Facilitating Knowledge Building."
30. Charles Pavitt and Lindsey Aloia, "Factors Affecting the Relative Proportion of Reason and Preference Statements during Problem-Solving Group Discussion," *Communication Research Reports* 26 (November 2009), pp. 259–270.
31. Ibid.
32. Michael E. Mayer, Kevin T. Sonoda, and William B. Gudykunst, "The Effect of Time Pressures and Type of Information on Decision Quality," *Southern Communication Journal* 62 (Summer 1997), pp. 280–92.
33. For example, see Sidney J. Parnes, "Effects of Extended Effort in Creative Problem Solving," *Journal of Educational Psychology* 52 (1961), pp. 117–22.
34. Pavitt and Aloia, "Factors Affecting the Relative Proportion," pp. 259–270.
35. Renee Meyers, David Seibold, and Dale Brashers, "Argument in Initial Group Decision-Making Discussions: Refinement of a Coding Scheme and a Descriptive Quantitative Analysis," *Western Journal of Speech Communication* 55 (Winter 1991), pp. 47–68.

36. Graham, Papa, and McPherson, "An Applied Test of the Functional Communication Perspective of Small Group Decision Making."

37. Randy Y. Hirokawa, John G. Oetzel, Carlos G. Aleman, and Scott E. Elston, "The Effects of Evaluation Clarity and Bias on the Relationship Between Vigilant Interaction and Group Decision-Making Efficacy," paper presented at the Speech Communication Association convention, November, 1991.

38. Mary Ann Renz, "Paving Consensus: Enacting, Challenging, and Revising the Consensus Process in a Cohousing Community," *Journal of Applied Communication Research* 34 (May 2006), pp. 163–90.

39. Sue Barnes and Leonore M. Grueller, "Computer-Mediated Communication in the Organization," *Communication Education* 43 (April 1994), pp. 129–42.

40. Annette C. Easton, Nancy S. Eickelmann, and Marie E. Flately, "Effects of an Electronic Meeting System Group Writing Tool on the Quality of Written Documents," *Journal of Business Communication* 31 (1994), pp. 27–40.

41. Mathew Schwartz, "The Instant Messaging Debate," *Computerworld* 36 (January 2002), p. 40.

42. Judith Pena-Shaff, Wendy Martin, and Geraldine Gay, "An Epistemological Framework for Analyzing Student Interactions in Computer-Mediated Communication Environments," *Journal of Interactive Learning Research* 12 (Spring 2001), pp. 41–62.

43. John A. Short, Ederyn Williams, and Bruce Christie, *The Social Psychology of Telecommunications* (London: Wiley, 1976).

44. Laura Humbley, Thomas O'Neill, and Theresa Kline, "Virtual Team Leadership: Perspectives from the Field," *International Journal of e-Collaboration* 3 (January–March 2007), pp. 40–64.

45. Robert Johansen, Jacques Vallee, and Kathleen Spangler, *Electronic Meetings: Technical Alternatives and Social Choices* (Reading MA: Addison-Wesley, 1979).

46. Humbley, O'Neill, and Kline, "Virtual Team Leadership."

47. For a more detailed description of these support systems, see Joseph E. McGrath and Andrea B. Hollingshead, *Groups Interacting with Technology* (Thousand Oaks, CA: Sage, 1994).

48. Leonard M. Jessup and Joseph S. Valacich, eds., *Group Support Systems: New Perspectives* (New York: Macmillan, 1993).

49. Andrew Flanagin, Vanessa Tiyaamornwong, Joan O'Connor, and David Seibold, "Computer-Mediated Group Work: The Interaction of Member Sex and Anonymity," *Communication Research* 29 (February 2002), pp. 66–93.

50. S. Opper and H. Fresko-Weiss, *Technology for Teams: Enhancing Productivity in Networked Organizations* (New York: Van Nostrand Reinhold, 1992).

51. Andrea B. Hollingshead, Joseph E. McGrath, and Kathleen M. O'Connor, "Group Task Performance and Communication Technology: A Longitudinal Study of Computer-Mediated versus Face-to-Face Work Groups," *Small Group Research* 24 (August 1993), pp. 307–33.

52. Izak Benbasat and Lai-Huat Lim, "The Effects of Group, Task, Context, and Technology Variables on the Usefulness of Group Support Systems: A Meta-Analysis of Experimental Studies," *Small Group Research* 24 (November 1993), pp. 430–62.

53. Poppy Lauretta McLeod, "Distributed People and Distributed Information: Vigilant Decision-Making in Virtual Teams," *Small Group Research* 44 (December 2013), pp. 627–57.

54. Craig R. Scott, "The Impact of Physical and Discursive Anonymity on Group Members' Multiple Identifications during Computer-Supported Decision Making," *Western Journal of Communication* 63 (Fall 1999), pp. 456–87.

55. Poppy McLeod, "New Communication Technologies for Group Decision Making: Toward an Integrative Framework," in *Communication and Group Decision Making,* 2nd ed., eds. Randy Y. Hirokawa and Marshall Scott Poole (Thousand Oaks, CA: Sage, 1996), pp. 426–61.

56. Robert F. Bales, *Interaction Process Analysis* (Reading, MA: Addison-Wesley, 1950); Donald G. Ellis and B. Aubrey Fisher, *Small Group Decision Making: Communication and the Group Process,* 4th ed. (New York: McGraw-Hill, 1994); and Poole, "Decision Development in Small Groups II."

57. Ellis and Fisher, *Small Group Decision Making,* pp. 144–57.

58. Poole, "Decision Development in Small Groups II."

59. Renz, "Paving Consensus: Enacting, Challenging, and Revising the Consensus Process in a Cohousing Community."

60. Ibid.

61. SunWolf, "Counterfactual Thinking in the Jury Room," *Small Group Research* 41 (2010), pp. 474–94.

62. David R. Seibold, "Making Meetings More Successful: Plans, Formats, and Procedures for Group Problem Solving," in *Small Group Communication: A Reader,* 5th ed., eds. Robert S. Cathcart and Larry A. Samovar (Dubuque, IA: Wm. C. Brown, 1988), pp. 219–20.

**Chapter 9**

1. Joyce L. Hocker and William W. Wilmot, *Interpersonal Conflict,* 9th ed. (New York: McGraw-Hill, 2014), p. 13.

2. Ana Zornoza, Pilar Ripoll, and José M. Peiró, "Conflict Management in Groups That Work in Two Different Communication Contexts: Face-to-Face and Computer-Mediated Communication," *Small Group Research* 33 (October 2002), pp. 481–508.

3. Shannon Kerwin, Alison Doherty, and Alanna Harman, "It's Not Conflict, It's Differences of Opinion: An In-Depth Examination of Conflict in Nonprofit Boards," *Small Group Research* 42 (2011), pp. 562–94.

4. Karl Smith, David W. Johnson, and Roger T. Johnson, "Can Conflict Be Constructive? Controversy versus Concurrence Seeking in Learning Groups," *Journal of Educational Psychology* 73 (1981), pp. 654–63.

5. Charles R. Franz and K. Gregory Jin, "The Structure of Group Conflict in a Collaborate Work Group during Informational Systems Development," *Journal of Applied Communication* 23 (May 1995), pp. 108–27.

6. Charles Pavitt and Lindsey Aloia, "Factors Affecting the Relative Proportion of Reason and Preference Statements during Problem-Solving Group Discussion," *Communication Research Reports* 26 (November, 2009), pp. 259–270.

7. Ibid.

8. Ibid.

9. Mary Ann Renz, "Paving Consensus: Enacting, Challenging, and Revising the Consensus Process in a Cohousing Community," *Journal of Applied Communication Research* 34 (May 2006), pp. 163–90.

10. Rob Anderson and Veronica Ross, *Questions of Communication: A Practical Introduction to Theory,* 3rd ed. (Boston, MA: Bedford/ St. Martin's, 2002), p. 53.

11. Laura L. Myers and R. Sam Larson, "Preparing Students for Early Work Conflict," *Business Communication Quarterly* 68 (September 2005), pp. 306–17.

12. Kristin J. Behfar, Elizabeth A. Mannix, Randall S. Peterson, and William M Trochim, "Conflict in Small Groups: The Meaning and Consequences of Process Conflict," *Small Group Research,* 42 (2011), pp. 127–76; Kerwin, Doherty, and Harman, "It's Not Conflict, It's Differences of Opinion."

13. Harold Guetzkow and John Gyr, "An Analysis of Conflict in Decision-Making Groups," *Human Relations* 7 (1954), pp. 367–82; Behar, Mannix, Peterson, and Trochim, "Conflict in Small Groups: The Meaning and Consequences of Process Conflict."

14. Kerwin, Doherty, and Harman, "'It's Not Conflict, It's Differences of Opinion."

15. Behar, Mannix, Peterson, and Trochim, "Conflict in Small Groups: The Meaning and Consequences of Process Conflict"; Kerwin, Doherty, and Harman, "'It's Not Conflict, It's Differences of Opinion."

16. Luis L. Martins, Marieke C. Schilpzand, Bradley L. Kirkman, Silvester Ivanaj, and Vera Ivanaj, "A Contingency View of the Effects of Cognitive Diversity on Team Performance: The Moderating Roles of Team Psychological Safety and Relationship Conflict," *Small Group Research* 44 (2012), pp. 96–126.

17. Mahmut Bayazit and Elizabeth A. Mannix, "Should I Stay or Should I Go?: Predicting Team Members' Intent to Remain in the Team," *Small Group Research* 34 (2003), pp. 290–321.

18. Kerwin, Doherty, and Harman, "It's Not Conflict, It's Differences of Opinion."

19. Roger C. Pace, "Personalized and Depersonalized Conflict in Small Group Discussions," *Small Group Research* 21 (1990), pp. 79–96.

20. Jackie M. Wellen and Matthew Neale, "Deviance, Self-Typicality, and Group Cohesion: The Corrosive Effects of the Bad Apples on the Barrel," *Small Group Research* 37 (April 2006), pp. 165–86.

21. Behar, Mannix, Peterson, and Trochim, "Conflict in Small Groups: The Meaning and Consequences of Process Conflict."

22. Ibid.

23. Victor D. Wall, Jr., and Linda Nolan, "Small Group Conflict: A Look at Equity, Satisfaction, and Styles of Conflict Management," *Small Group Behavior* 18 (1987), pp. 188–211.

24. John G. Oetzel, "Explaining Individual Communication Processes in Homogenous and Heterogeneous Groups through Individualism-Collectivism and Self-Construal," *Human Communication Research* 25, no. 2 (December 1998), pp. 202–24.

25. Behar, Mannix, Peterson, and Trochim, "Conflict in Small Groups: The Meaning and Consequences of Process Conflict."

26. Linda L. Putnam, "Conflict in Group Decision Making," in *Communication and Group Decision Making,* eds. Randy Y. Hirokawa and Marshall Scott Poole (Beverly Hills, CA: Sage, 1986), pp. 16–23.

27. Lindred L. Geer, Karen A. Jehn, and Elizabeth A. Mannix, "Conflict Transformation: A Longitudinal Investigation of Intragroup Conflict and the Moderating Role of Conflict Resolution," *Small Group Research* 39 (2008), pp. 278–302. Chester S. Spell, Katerina Bezrukova, Jarod Haar, and Christopher Spell, "Faultlines, Fairness, and Fighting: A Justice Perspective on Conflict in Diverse Groups," *Small Group Research* 42 (2011), pp. 309–40; Helen Pluut and Petra L. Curseu, "Perception of Intragroup Conflict: The Effect of Coping Strategies on Conflict Transformation and Escalation," *Group Processes & Intergroup Relations*, 16 (2012), pp. 412–25.

28. Kerwin, Doherty, and Harman, "It's Not Conflict, It's Differences of Opinion."

29. Helen Pluut and Petra L. Curşeu, "Perception of Intragroup Conflict: The Effect of Coping Strategies on Conflict Transformation and Escalation," *Group Process and Intergroup Relations* 16 (2012), pp. 412–25.

30. Elizabeth Hobman, Prashant Bordia, Bernd Irmer, and Artemis Chang, "The Expression of Conflict in Computer-Mediated and Face-to-Face Groups," *Small Group Research* 33 (2002), pp. 439–65.

31. Ibid.

32. Laku Chidambaram, Robert P. Bostrom, and Bayard E. Wynne, "A Longitudinal Study of the Impact of Group Discussion Support Systems on Group Development," *Journal of Management Information Systems* 7 (Winter 1990/91), pp. 7–25.

33. Hobman et al., "The Expression of Conflict in Computer-Mediated and Face-to-Face Groups."

34. Ibid.

35. Myers and Larson, "Preparing Students for Early Work Conflict."

36. Karen Jehn, "A Qualitative Analysis of Conflict Types and Dimensions in Organizational Groups," *Administrative Science Quarterly* 42 (1997), pp. 530–57; Helen Pluut and Petra L. Curşeu, "Perception of Intragroup Conflict: The Effect of Coping Strategies on Conflict Transformation and Escalation."

37. Michael Song, Barbara Dyer, and R. Jeffrey Thieme, "Conflict Management and Innovation Performance: An Integrated Contingency Perspective," *Journal of the Academy of Marketing Science* 34 (2006), pp. 341–56.

38. Kenneth Thomas, "Conflict and Conflict Management," in *Handbook of Industrial and Organizational Psychology,* ed. Marvin Dunnette (Chicago, IL: Rand McNally, 1976), pp. 890–934.

39. Marshall Scott Poole and Melissa Dobosh, "Exploring Conflict Management Processes in Jury Deliberations Through Interaction Analysis," *Small Group Research* 41 (2010), pp. 408–26.

40. Hal Witteman, "Analyzing Interpersonal Conflict: Nature of Awareness, Type of Initiating Event, Situational Perceptions, and Management Styles," *Western Journal of Communication* 56 (Summer 1992), pp. 248–80.

41. Victor D. Wall and Linda L. Nolan, "Small Group Conflict: A Look at Equity, Satisfaction, and Styles of Conflict Management," *Small Group Behavior* 18 (1987), pp. 188–211.

42. Renee Meyers and Dale Brashers, "Influence Processes in Group Interaction," *The Handbook of Group Communication Theory and Research,* ed. Lawrence Frey (Thousand Oaks, CA: Sage, 1999), pp. 288–312.

43. Victor D. Wall, Gloria J. Galanes, and Susan B. Love, "Small Task-Oriented Groups: Conflict, Conflict Management, Satisfaction, and Decision Quality," *Small Group Behavior* 18 (1987), pp. 31–55.

44. Tim Kuhn and Marshall Scott Poole, "Do Conflict Management Styles Affect Group Decision Making?" *Human Communication Research* 26 (October 2000), pp. 558–90.

45. Renz, "Paving Consensus: Enacting, Challenging, and Revising the Consensus Process in a Cohousing Community."

46. Michael A. Gross, Laura K. Guerrero, and Jess K. Alberts, "Perceptions of Conflict Strategies and Communication Competence in Task-Oriented Dyads," *Journal of Applied Communication Research* 32 (August 2004), pp. 249–70.

47. Ibid.

48. Min-Sun Kim and Truman Leung, "A Multicultural View of Conflict Management Styles: Review and Critical Synthesis," *Communication Yearbook* 23, ed. Michael E. Roloff (Thousand Oaks, CA: Sage, 2000), pp. 227–69.

49. Judith Martin and Thomas K. Nakayama, *Experiencing Intercultural Communication: An Introduction* (Boston, MA: McGraw-Hill, 2001), pp. 173–74.

50. John G. Oetzel, "Explaining Individual Communication Processes in Homogenous and Heterogeneous Groups through Individualism-Collectivism and Self-Construal."

51. Gross et al., "Perceptions of Conflict Strategies and Communication Competence in Task-Oriented Dyads."

52. Leslie A. DeChurch, Jessica R. Mesmer-Magnus, and Dan Doty, "Moving Beyond Relationship and Task Conflict: Toward a Process—State Perspective," *Journal of Applied Psychology* 98 (2013), pp. 559–78.

53. Abby L. Mello and Lisa L. Delise, "Cognitive Diversity to Team Outcomes: The Roles of Cohesion and Conflict Management," *Small Group Research* 46 (2014), pp. 204–26.

54. Arie W. Kruglanski and Donna M. Webster, "Group Members' Reactions to Opinion Deviates and Conformists at Varying Degrees of Proximity to Decision Deadline and of Environmental Noise," *Journal of Personality and Social Psychology* 61 (1991), pp. 212–26.

55. Renz, "Paving Consensus: Enacting, Challenging, and Revising the Consensus Process in a Cohousing Community."

56. Stella Ting-Toomey, *Communication Across Cultures* (New York: Guilford Press, 1999).

57. Ibid.

58. Leslie A. DeChurch., Jessica R. Mesmer-Magnus, and Dan Doty, "Moving Beyond Relationship and Task Conflict: Toward a Process—State Perspective."

59. Steven M. Alderton and Lawrence Frey, "Argumentation in Small Group Decision Making," in *Communication and Group Decision Making,* eds. Randy Hirokawa and Marshall Scott Poole (Beverly Hills, CA: Sage, 1986), pp. 157–73.

60. Rick Garlick and Paul A. Mongeau, "Argument Quality and Group Member Status as Determinants of Attitudinal Minority Influence," *Western Journal of Communication* 57 (Summer 1993), pp. 289–308.

61. Lisa J. Gebhart and Renee A. Meyers, "Subgroup Influence in Decision-Making Groups: Examining Consistency from a Communication Perspective," *Small Group Research* 26 (May 1995), pp. 147–68.

62. Dale Brashers and Renee Meyers, "Tag-Team Argument and Group Decision Making: A Preliminary Investigation," *Spheres of Argument: Proceedings of the Sixth Speech Communication Association/ American Forensics Association Conference on Argumentation,* ed. Bruce Gronbeck (Annandale, VA: Speech Communication Association, 1989), pp. 542–50.

63. Gebhart and Meyers, "Subgroup Influence."

64. James B. Thomas, Reuben R. McDaniel, Jr., and Michael J. Dooris, "Strategic Issue Analysis: NGT and Decision Analysis for Resolving Strategic Issues," *Journal of Applied Behavioral Science* 25 (May 1989), pp. 189–201.

65. Roger Fisher and William Ury with Bruce Patton, *Getting to Yes: Negotiating Agreement without Giving In*, 2nd ed. (New York: Penguin Books, 1991).

**Chapter 10**

1. Michael Z. Hackman and Craig E. Johnson, *Leadership: A Communication Perspective,* 2nd ed. (Prospect Heights, IL: Waveland Press, 1996), p. 14.

2. Gary Yukl, *Leadership in Organizations,* 5th ed. (Upper Saddle River, NJ: Prentice-Hall, 2002).

3. John R. P. French and Bertram Raven, "The Bases of Social Power," in *Group Dynamics: Research and Theory,* 3rd ed., eds. Dorwin Cartwright and Alvin Zander (New York: Harper & Row, 1968), pp. 259–69.

4. Yukl, *Leadership in Organizations.*

5. Yukl, *Leadership in Organizations.*

6. W. Bennis. "The Challenge of Leadership in the Modern World," *American Psychologist*, 62 (2007), pp. 2–5.

7. S. A. Haslam, S. D. Reicher, and M. J. Platow, *The New Psychology of Leadership: Identity, Influence and Power* (New York: Psychology Press, 2011).

8. Michael W. Kramer, "Shared leadership in a Community Theater Group: Filling the Leadership Role," *Journal of Applied Communication Research* 34 (May 2006), pp. 141–62.

9. Ernest G. Bormann, *Discussion and Group Methods: Theory and Practice,* 2nd ed. (New York: Harper & Row, 1975), pp. 253–69; John C. Geier, "A Trait Approach to the Study of Leadership in Small Groups," *Journal of Communication* 17 (1967), pp. 316–23.

10. Katherine W. Hawkins, "Effects of Gender and Communication Content on Leadership Emergence in Small Task-Oriented Groups," *Small Group Research* 26 (May 1995), pp. 234–49.

11. Scott D. Johnson and Curt Bechler, "Examining the Relationship between Listening Effectiveness and Leadership Emergence," *Small Group Research* 29 (August 1998), pp. 452–71.

12. David A. Kenny and Steven J. Zaccaro, "An Estimate of Variance Due to Traits in Leadership," *Journal of Applied Psychology* 68 (1983), pp. 678–85; Robert J. Ellis and Steven F. Cronshaw, "Self-Monitoring and Leader Emergence: A Test of Moderator Effects," *Small Group Research* 23 (February 1992), pp. 113–29; and Steven F. Cronshaw and Robert J. Ellis, "A Process Investigation of Self-Monitoring and Leadership Emergence," *Small Group Research* 22 (September 1991), pp. 403–20.

13. Simon Taggar and Rick Hackett, "Leadership Emergence in Autonomous Work Teams: Antecedents and Outcomes," *Personnel Psychology* 52 (Winter 1999), pp. 899–926.

14. Robert S. Rubin, Lynn K. Bartels, and William H. Bommer, "Are Leaders Smarter or Do They Just Seem That Way? Exploring Perceived Intellectual Competence and Leadership Emergence," *Social Behavior & Personality* 30, no. 2 (2002), pp. 105–18; Simon Taggar and Rick Hackett, "Leadership Emergence in Autonomous Work Teams: Antecedents and Outcomes," *Personnel Psychology* 52 (Winter 1999), pp. 899–926; Robert G. Lord, Christy L. deVader, and George M. Alliger, "A Meta-analysis of the Relation Between Personality Traits and Leadership Perceptions: An Application of Validity Generalization Procedures," *Journal of Applied Psychology* 71 (August 1986), pp. 402–10.

15. Cecile Emery, Kim Daniloski, and Anne Hamby, "The Reciprocal Effects of Self-View as a Leader and Leadership Emergence," *Small Group Research* 42, (2011), pp. 199–224.

16. Amy B. Gershenoff and Roseanne J. Foti, "Leader Emergence and Gender Roles in All-Female Groups: A Critical Examination," *Small Group Research* 34 (April 2003), pp. 170–96.

17. Judith A. Kolb, "Are We Still Stereotyping Leadership? A Look at Gender and Other Predictors of Leader Emergence," *Small Group Research* 28 (August 1997), pp. 370–93.

18. J. Goktepe and C. Scneier, "Role of Sex and Gender Roles, and Attraction in Predicting Emergent Leaders," *Journal of Applied Psychology* 74 (1989), pp. 165–67.

19. Susan B. Shimanoff and Mercilee M. Jenkins, "Leadership and Gender: Challenging Assumptions and Recognizing Resources," in *Small Group Communication: Theory and Practice,* 8th ed., eds. Randy Y. Hirokawa, Robert S. Cathcart, Larry A. Samovar, and Linda Henman (Los Angeles, CA: Roxbury, 2003), pp. 184–98.

20. Kathryn Wickham and Joseph Walther, "Perceived Behaviors of Emergent and Designated Leaders in Virtual Groups," *International Journal of e-Collaboration* 3 (January–March 2007), pp. 1–17.

21. M. Sean Limon and Betty H. La France, "Communication Traits and Leadership Emergence: Examining the Impact of Argumentativeness, Communication Apprehension, and Verbal Aggressiveness in Work Groups," *Southern Communication Journal* 70 (Winter 2005), pp. 123–33.

22. Peter G. Northouse, *Leadership Theory and Practice*, 7th ed. (Los Angeles, CA: Sage, 2016).

23. Ralph M. Stogdill, Carrol L. Shartle, Willis L. Scott, Alvin E. Coons, and William E. Jaynes, *A Predictive Study of Administrative Work Patterns* (Columbus, OH: The Ohio State University, Bureau of Business Research, 1956); Ralph M. Stogdill and Alvin E. Coons, eds., *Leader Behavior: Its Description and Measurement* (Columbus, OH: The Ohio State University, Bureau of Business Research, 1957); and Robert Blake and Jane Mouton, *The Managerial Grid* (Houston, TX: Gulf, 1964).

24. Hackman and Johnson, *Leadership: A Communication Perspective*.

25. Kramer, "Shared Leadership."

26. John Gastil, "A Meta-analytic Review of the Productivity and Satisfaction of Democratic and Autocratic Leadership," *Small Group Research*

25 (August 1994), pp. 384–410; John Gastil, *Democracy in Small Groups* (Philadelphia, PA: New Society Publishers, 1993).

27. Yukl, *Leadership in Organizations.*
28. Ibid.
29. Susan A. Wheelan, *Creating Effective Teams: A Guide for Members and Leaders* (Los Angeles, CA: Sage, 2010).
30. Gloria J. Galanes, "In Their Own Words: An Exploratory Study of Bona Fide Group Leaders," *Small Group Research* 34 (December 2003), pp. 741–70.
31. William C. Schutz, "The Leader as Completer," in *Small Group Communication: A Reader,* 3rd ed., eds. Robert S. Cathcart and Larry A. Samovar (Dubuque, IA: Wm C. Brown, 1979), pp. 454–60.
32. Kramer, "Shared Leadership."
33. Fred Fiedler, *A Theory of Leadership Effectiveness* (New York: McGraw-Hill, 1967).
34. Paul Hershey, Kenneth H. Blanchard, and Dewey E. Johnson, *Management of Organizational Behavior: Leading Human Resources* (Upper Saddle River, NJ: Prentice Hall, 2001).
35. Robert P. Vecchio, R. Craig Bullis, and Donna M. Brazil, "The Utility of Situational Leadership Theory: A Replication in a Military Setting," *Small Group Research* 37 (October 2006), pp. 407–24.
36. Ibid.
37. Hershey, Blanchard, and Johnson, "Management of Organizational Behavior: Leading Human Resources."
38. Peter Gronn, "Distributed Leadership as a Unit of Analysis," *Leadership Quarterly* 13 (2002), pp. 423–52.
39. J. Kevin Barge, "Leadership as Medium: A Leaderless Group Discussion Model," *Communication Quarterly* 37 (Fall 1989), pp. 237–47.
40. David Collinson, "Dialectics of Leadership," *Human Relations* 58 (2005), pp. 1419–42; and Gloria J. Galanes, "Dialectical Tensions of Small Group Leadership," *Communication Studies* 60 (2009), pp. 409–425; and Kenwyn Smith and David Berg, "A Paradoxical Conceptualization of Group Life," *Human Relations* 40 (1987), pp. 633–58.
41. Galanes, "Dialectical Tensions of Small Group."
42. This information is synthesized from Frank LaFasto and Carl Larson, *When Teams Work Best: 6000 Team Members and Leaders Tell What It Takes to Succeed* (Thousand Oaks, CA: Sage, 2001); Gloria J. Galanes, "In Their Own Words: An Exploratory Study of Bona Fide Group Leaders," *Small Group Research* 34 (December 2003), pp. 741–70.
43. Wheelan, *Creating Effective Teams.*
44. Galanes, "Dialectical Tensions in Small Group."
45. Collinson, "Dialectics of Leadership."
46. Laura Hambley, Thomas O'Neill, and Theresa Kline, "Virtual Team Leadership: Perspectives from the Field," *International Journal of e-Collaboration* 3 (January-Marck 2007), pp. 40–64.
47. Much of the following information is discussed in detail in Gloria J. Galanes and Katherine Adams, *Effective Group Discussion,* 14th ed. (New York: McGraw-Hill, 2013), pp. 209–38.
48. Steven G. Rogelberg, Linda Rhoades Shanock, and Cliff W. Scott, "Wasted Time and Money in Meetings: Increasing Return on Investment," *Small Group Research* 43 (2012), pp. 236–245.
49. Oliver Burkeman, "Meetings: Even More of a Soul-Sucking Waste of Time Than You Thought," *The Guardian/Us Work and Careers* (May 1, 2014), retrieved July 28, 2016: https://www.theguardian.com/news/oliver-burkeman-s-blog/2014/may/01/meetings-soul-sucking-waste-time-you-thought.
50. Rogelberg, Shanock, and Scott, "Wasted Time and Money in Meetings: Increasing Return on Investment."
51. Chris Matyszczyk, "Here's Proof That Most of Your Meetings Are a Waste of Time," *INC.Com* (July 22, 2015), retrieved July 28, 2016: http://www.inc.com/chris-matyszczyk/here-s-proof-that-most-of-your-meetings-are-a-waste-of-time.html.
52. Galanes, "Dialectical Tensions of Small Group."
53. Hambley et al., "Virtual Team Leadership."
54. Carl Larson and Frank M. J. LaFasto, *Team Work: What Must Go Right/What Can Go Wrong* (Newbury Park, CA: Sage, 199), pp. 27–33.
55. Hambley et al., "Virtual Team Leadership."
56. Kramer, "Shared Leadership."
57. Dong L. Jung and John J. Sosik, "Transformational Leadership in Work Groups: The Role of Empowerment, Cohesiveness, and Collective-Efficacy on Perceived Group Performance," *Small Group Research* 33 (June 2002), pp. 313–36.

58. P. H. Andrews and R. T. Herschel, *Organizational Communication: Empowerment in a Technological Society* (Boston, MA: Houghton Mifflin, 1996).

59. Hackman and Johnson, *Leadership: A Communication Perspective.*

60. Astrid C. Homan and Lindred L. Greer, "Considering Diversity: The Positive Effects of Considerate Leadership in Diverse Teams," *Group Processes & Intergroup Relations* 16 (2013), pp. 105–25.

61. Robert J. House and Ram N. Aditya, "The Social Scientific Study of Leadership: Quo Vadis," *Journal of Management* 23 (1997), pp. 409–73.

62. Robert J. House, "Illustrative Examples of GLOBE Findings," in *Culture, Leadership, and Organizations: The GLOBE Study of 62 Societies,* eds. Robert J. House, Paul J. Hangers, Mansour Javidian, Peter W. Dorfman, and Vipin Gupta (Thousand Oaks, CA: Sage, 2004).

63. J. Dan Rothwell, *In Mixed Company*: Communicating in Small Groups and Teams, 9th ed. (Boston, MA: Cengage, 2016).

**Chapter 11**

1. Ann L. Darling and Deanna P. Daniels, "Practicing Engineers Talk About the Importance of Talk: A Report on the Role of Oral Communication in the Workplace," *Communication Education* 52 (January 2003), pp. 1–16.

2. Cindy Griffin, *Invitation to Public Speaking* (Belmont, CA: Thomson Wadsworth, 2004), chap. 5.

3. Dan O'Hair, Rob Stewart, and Hannah Rubenstein, *A Speaker's Guidebook: Text and Reference* (Boston, MA: Bedford/St. Martin's, 2004), chap. 6.

4. Darling and Daniels, "Practicing Engineers Talk," p. 13.

5. Ibid, p. 13.

6. Ibid., p. 88.

7. Ibid., pp. 96–99.

8. Cindy Griffin, *Invitation to Public Speaking* (Boston, MA: Wadsworth, 2009), pp. 103–5.

9. Ibid.

10. Stephenson J. Beck, Robert S. Littlefield, and Andrea J. Weber, "Public Meeting Facilitation: A Naïve Theory Analysis of Crisis Meeting Interaction," *Small Group Research* 43 (April 2012), pp. 211–35.

11. Ibid.

12. George Kennedy (trans.), *Aristotle, On Rhetoric* (New York: Oxford, 1991), p. 181.

13. Spectra IX (December 1973), n.p.

14. Jane Blankenship, *A Sense of Style* (Belmont, CA: Dickenson, 1968), p. 12.

15. Ibid., p. 41.

16. Karyn Rybacki and Donald Rybacki, *Communication Criticism: Approaches and Genres* (Belmont, CA: Wadsworth, 1991), p. 40.

**Appendix**

1. Stanley Seashore, *Group Cohesiveness in the Industrial Work Group* (Ann Arbor, MI: University of Michigan Institute for Social Research, 1954).

2. Complete information on constructing a SYMLOG diagram, along with an abbreviated explanation of SYMLOG theory, may be found in a workbook, R. F. Bales, *SYMLOG Case Study Kit* (New York: Free Press, 1980). An even more simplified explanation of SYMLOG theory and method for constructing a diagram may be found in Joann Keyton, "Coding Communication in Decision-Making Groups," in *Managing Group Life: Communicating in Decision-Making Groups* (Boston, MA: Houghton Mifflin, 1997), pp. 236–69. For readers who are interested in details of both the theory and methodology, we refer them to R. F. Bales and Stephen P. Cohen, *SYMLOG: A System for the Multiple-Level Observation of Groups* (New York: Free Press, 1979).

3. Dean C. Barnlund and Franklyn S. Haiman, *The Dynamics of Discussion* (Boston, MA: Houghton Mifflin, 1960), pp. 401–4.

INDEX